More
Boatkeeper

More Boatkeeper

An All-New Guide to Boat Maintenance, Repair, and Improvement

Advice on Keeping Your Boat Shipshape from the Columns of *Motor Boating & Sailing* Magazine

Edited by **Bernard Gladstone**

Illustrated by Fred Wolff

HEARST MARINE BOOKS/
New York

Library of Congress Cataloging-in-Publication Data

More Boatkeeper.
    Includes index.
    1. Boats and boating—Maintenance and repair—
Handbooks, manuals, etc. I. Gladstone, Bernard.
II. Motor boating & sailing.
VM322.M67   1988   623.8′223′0288   87-37924
ISBN 0-688-07645-9

Printed in the United States of America

First Edition

1   2   3   4   5   6   7   8   9   10

BOOK DESIGN BY ARLENE GOLDBERG

To all the crew I ever needed, my wife, Olga

ACKNOWLEDGMENTS

Through the years the ''Boatkeeper'' column in *Motor Boating & Sailing* magazine has greatly benefited from the tips, advice, and information supplied by boatowners throughout the country. Below is a list of the people who have contributed to the material in this book.

LIST OF CONTRIBUTORS

Armstrong, Thomas G.
Aronson, Carl E.
Baker, Don
Banse, Tim
Baxter, Terry I.
Beauchamp, Jim
Bock, Gordon H.
Boesser, George
Bond, David
Brown, Allen E., Jr.
Chey, Dr. Daniel S. I.
Conroy, Robert P.
Davidson, James H., Jr.
Davis, Ted
Dennis, Ed
De Pree, Ken
Deuble, Leonard
Dickey, William
Doyle, Jon R.
Firsty, Sherman
Frederickson, Peter J.
Gilbey, Michael
Gill, Dudley W.
Going, Jeffrey W.
Graffley, Joel W.
Hart, Jerrems C.
Healy, Will
Helster, Mort
Hendrickson, D. E.
Herbert, Dorothy L.
Hildre, Rolf
Huff, Dennis A.
Huffman, Robert E.
Jones, Edward D.

Lee, Arthur R.
Leicester, L. A.
Lipton, A. Allen
Lipton, Leonard P.
Marmer, Jerold
McCurdy, Lee
McRanie, Sandra
Melman, Joseph
Mierswa, Myles E.
Miller, William C.
Mitchell, Melissa
Monroe, Joe
Monsein, Sheldon
Munoz, William
Neville, Charles W.
O'Leary, Bob
Parris, Dody Welsh
Pektas, Jack
Prescott, Charles I.
Prucha, Larry
Rathbun, Ray
Riggs, Terry
Rusling, John A. III
Sheddan, Bill
Solystik, Linda
Solystik, Steve
Stephenson, Al B.
Strout, Stephen A.
Vasile, Kathy
Viney, H. F. ''Bert''
Voorheis, Frank
Wallace, William D.
Weiss, Herman J.
Wilkens, Richard W.

CONTENTS

x / Contents

SECTION 3: TOOLS, MAINTENANCE AND TECHNIQUES

INTRODUCTION

When the first edition of *Boatkeeper* was published in 1984 we all felt that it was (and still is) a truly complete volume—a compendium of the best material published up to that time in the popular "Boatkeeper" section that appears each month in *Motor Boating & Sailing* magazine.

However, just as that magazine's monthly "Boatkeeper" column is an ongoing feature that continues to publish new time- and money-saving ideas on how to maintain and improve your boat, so too have we discovered that it is time to add to the wealth of information already published in the first edition of *Boatkeeper* (accurately subtitled *The How-to Book of Modern Marine Maintenance for Sail and Power*).

This new volume, *More Boatkeeper*, is not in any sense a replacement for that first volume (which is still widely available and will remain in print for some time). It is a completely new collection of helpful and useful how-to material that will prove to be an invaluable addition to every boat owner's library. This edition includes an even more complete collection of articles describing working techniques, maintenance tips and boat improvement projects that will be of interest to every boat owner—from those who own only a small sailing dinghy to those who own a sixty-foot motor yacht.

Although a few of the articles included in this new volume may seem similar to some of the topics covered in the original *Boatkeeper* volume, there is actually no repetition of material. Some topics that seem similar are presented from a different viewpoint; others describe new or additional ways to solve problems that are constantly plaguing every boat owner. And still others may simply be updated material that has been published in *Motor Boating & Sailing*'s "Boatkeeper" section since 1984, the year the first edition of *Boatkeeper* was released.

By far the majority of *More Boatkeeper* is new and useful how-to material that has never before been published in book form, including innovative maintenance ideas, money-saving boat-improvement projects, time-saving and often unusual ways to handle troublesome boat-repair problems, and other material that was derived not only from my own experiences while owning and living aboard boats for almost thirty years but also from the experiences of dozens of other contributors to the "Boatkeeper" section of *Motor Boating & Sailing* (most of whom have been longtime loyal readers of that magazine).

The complete Contents at the front of the book not only illustrates the way in which this volume is organized, it also lists the individual articles that are contained in each section. In addition, there is also a detailed alphabetical index in the back of the book that will enable the reader to easily find the exact answer to his or her boat-maintenance problem or boat-improvement project.

—BERNARD GLADSTONE
"BOATKEEPER" EDITOR

MAINTENANCE AND REPAIR

Buying a Boat with Maintenance in Mind

Buying a new boat is, for most people, more of an emotional experience than it is a practical one. That's why so many buyers get carried away by something akin to love at first sight when a visit to the local boat show culminates in their signature on a dotted line. Blinded by her beauty and by glowing reports of how she will perform, you're convinced the boat was made just for you.

You've considered the price (it really is more than you wanted to spend—but what the heck, you only live once); you've considered the size and the power (not as big and as powerful as the one you really want—but it should be plenty for now; then maybe next year . . .). But the one thing that almost everyone overlooks is the maintenance factor.

There is obviously some maintenance required on any boat, but modern fiberglass boats require much less maintenance than wood boats. I can assure you, however (after owning about a dozen different boats in various sizes, both power and sail), that some new boats require a lot more maintenance than others—at least if you are an owner who prides himself on the appearance of your boat.

That's why, when shopping for a new boat, it is important to keep an eye out for potential maintenance problems. Look for materials and design features that will simplify maintenance—things that will make washing, waxing, and general upkeep no harder than necessary and will make it as easy as possible to keep the boat in Bristol fashion.

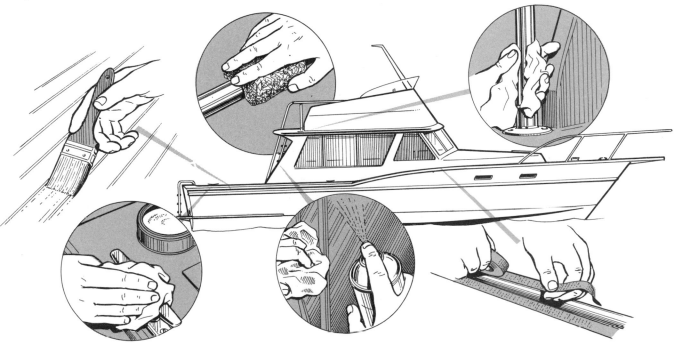

Some boats require more maintenance than others, so look for surfaces that will need extra care.

1

For example: Everyone admires the beautiful appearance of a real teak deck when it is clean and freshly oiled or sealed. But did you ever consider the amount of work required to take care of all that teak? Or how careful you must be to wipe up spills and pick up dropped food, oily rags, or anything else that can stain the teak? Obviously, some people feel that having a beautiful teak deck is worth the time and effort required to keep it looking that way—but for others the caretaking may be a drag and not worth the elbow grease and cost. The main thing is to know ahead of time how much work is involved and to be willing to accept that as part of the price of ownership, regardless of whether you will be doing the work yourself or paying someone else to do it.

If you are like most boat owners you probably enjoy spending time ''puttering around'' and doing miscellaneous maintenance chores on your boat. But weekend hours spent maintaining a boat are hours lost from using that boat. With this thought in mind, here are some helpful points to consider when shopping for a new boat:

Around the Outside

● Regardless of whether it is teak or mahogany, wood trim—cap rails, toe rails, hand rails, etc.—has to be maintained regularly. If you want it to look the way it was meant to, the trim will have to be regularly varnished, oiled, or treated with a sealer of some kind; so think carefully before you fall in love with all that beautiful

Nonskid decks are harder to keep clean than smooth ones, so don't opt for nonskid where it's not needed.

brightwork. It's true that without at least some brightwork most boats will tend to look too ''plastic'' or too bare, but the more wood there is, the more work you will have to put into upkeep.

● Even if you are willing to spend extra time or money maintaining brightwork, try to visualize any difficulty you will encounter in sanding and masking the wood when you have to strip it down. Are there nooks and crannies that you won't be able to reach? Don't forget, each piece of wood trim will require some masking—but can you reach into all the corners and tight spots that will need cleaning and varnishing?

● Beware of narrow strips of wood that are surrounded by fiberglass. Such trim is decorative and really dresses up a boat in most cases, but all the adjacent fiberglass will need protecting each time the wood has to be oiled or varnished. The process of carefully masking and sanding will take much longer than the actual application of varnish or sealer.

● Most fiberglass boats do not need painting (except for the bottoms), but many have built-in benches, deck boxes, and even wood-framed windshields or moldings that *do* need painting. This is not a serious problem as long as you realize that it will have to be done annually. Also, some regular caulking will be necessary around or next to this wood. And remember that wooden masts on sailboats, trawlers—or even on some motor yachts—will also require painting or varnishing at least once a year.

● Deck hardware such as stanchions, cleats, and chocks are usually stainless steel or chrome-plated. As a general rule, stainless (if of a good marine quality) will be easier to maintain than chrome plating over the long run. Chrome is more prone to eventual pitting or even wearing off in places. Stainless and chrome can be quickly brightened by polishing with a fleece-type metal cleaner, but when the metal ages or is neglected, chrome plating is much harder to restore—especially if exposed to salt water. And remember, cheap deck hardware that is made of die-cast pot metal, even if chrome-plated, is not only structurally weak, but also the plating tends to peel off after a while.

● Look at how hardware and other fixtures are positioned. For example: If stanchions, cleats, or chocks are located close against the cabin sides, or up against fiberglass or hardboard ''weather curtains,'' then you may have a devil of a time reaching around these pieces when polishing or cleaning, or when you want to tighten screws or bolts that hold them in place.

● If the boat has aluminum trim or moldings instead of stainless (for example, along rub rails), remember that aluminum is much more prone to pitting and staining if not frequently washed. It is also more difficult to polish when it oxidizes or starts to pit.

● Think twice before you fall in love with a lot of brass hardware and bronze trim. These metals are beautiful and very traditional-looking, but only when they are polished—a chore that will be required at frequent intervals. Protecting the metal with lacquer or similar clear metal coating can protect against oxidation for quite some time (if the metal is inside the boat), but eventually this coating will have to be renewed, which means you will then be faced with the time-consuming job of stripping and repolishing.

● Large glass sliding doors and big expanses of window glass help make the inside of a boat bright, but they also demand frequent washing or cleaning if you don't want to be looking through spots all the time. Also, they let lots of sun in, which not only makes the inside of the boat a lot hotter but also fades and prematurely ages interior furniture, carpets, curtains, etc.

● Many boat manufacturers use plastic laminates (Formica, Micarta, or a similar brand) to cover bulkheads or cabinets that are out in the cockpit or up on the flying bridge. Although this material is very durable and requires little or no maintenance other than periodic washing, remember that these materials will fade badly in the sun. If the plastic is white, or near-white, this is normally not a problem. But if you have a wood-grain pattern, fading will soon make it look like wood that needs refinishing.

● Nonskid surfaces on decks, steps, and ladders are essential for safety on most boats, but remember that heavily textured nonskid surfaces are a lot harder to clean than smooth surfaces. You want nonskid decking and treads where they are really needed, but having a large deck area coated with nonskid where it is not needed just means there will be a lot more scrubbing to do. The same holds true for grates—they are needed in cockpits and showers, but they should be easily removable for cleaning or for refinishing.

● Canvas and vinyl curtains can greatly increase the amount of usable space in a boat when it is raining or when you want protection from the sun, but remember that canvas and vinyl are relatively short-lived and will have to be replaced every few years. They also require a lot of scrubbing. Get the dealer to demonstrate how the canvas is actually put on and taken off. On some boats you may be unpleasantly surprised to discover what a chore this is, especially at the end of a long boating weekend or when you have to put the canvas up in a hurry because of a sudden shower. Some canvas enclosures may require an extra pair of hands to get the job done.

Around the Inside

● Bulkheads and cabinets made of teak or mahogany are beautiful to behold, but they require frequent cleaning

Laminates are easier to maintain than wood surfaces.

and periodic oiling or waxing to keep the finish from turning dull or oxidizing and cracking. Plastic laminates on cabinet doors and in galleys and heads will make maintenance a lot simpler—all you have to do is wash them regularly.

● When buying a cruising boat of any kind you probably will want one or two mirrors for practical reasons, but watch out for purely decorative mirrors. Not only are they a potential hazard inside a pitching, rolling boat, but they also are in constant need of cleaning and polishing and are subject to frequent fogging.

● Examine electrical panels, switches, and gauges with an eye to how hard it will be to repair or replace components when this becomes necessary. You want to be able to reach behind the panels easily when adding or replacing wires, or when trying to troubleshoot an electrical problem.

● Most boats nowadays come with carpeting in the main cabin areas, but make sure this carpet is the kind that can take moisture—preferably the kind that can be taken out and washed on the dock if necessary. It should be resistant to mildew and rot if it does get wet (don't forget the backing), since chances are that this will happen at one time or another. Carpet on bulkheads or hull sides should be easily removable, both for cleaning and for drying out.

● If there are built-in appliances in the boat—refrigerators, stoves, or washing machines, for example—see if you can get at them when and if service is required. Will you have to take the boat apart to remove one of the appliances if the unit has to be exchanged or removed for major repairs?

● Accessibility should also be considered when examining the head. Every marine toilet will need maintenance at one time or another—so how hard is it to get at the one you are considering? Are hose clamps accessible, and can you reach mounting bolts when necessary? The same holds true for the plumbing leading to both the head and galley sinks—can you get at the piping easily if a line breaks or becomes clogged, or if replacements are required?

● Since engine oil and other basic engine maintenance is required daily while cruising, note access to the engine room areas. If it means lifting hatches in the middle of the salon or cockpit, how much furniture or equipment will you have to move out of the way each time? Can you get at battery boxes, engine coolant fillers, oil dipsticks, and filters without tearing the boat completely apart and without becoming a contortionist? All too often, hard-to-reach places tend to discourage regular maintenance.

● Also, don't forget to note where seacocks and stuffing boxes are located. You not only want to be able to reach these in a hurry when an emergency occurs, but you also want to be able to get at them without too much difficulty for routine maintenance. For instance, if seacocks are not hard to reach you are more likely to shut them off each time you leave the boat for an extended period. And if stuffing boxes are easy to examine you are more likely to check regularly for leaks—and do any necessary tightening or repacking long before a serious leak can develop while you are at sea.

What to Do About Hull Blisters

In recent years the development of blisters in the gel coat on the bottom of fiberglass hulls has become an increasingly serious problem—on powerboats as well as sailboats, and on small runabouts as well as on luxury-class yachts. At first some people thought the problem was due to faulty manufacturing techniques during the layup process, while others believed the blisters resulted from improper gel coat application or formulation.

Experts still have differing opinions as to exactly *why* the problem occurs, but most of them do agree on *how* it happens. Basically it is because recent research has shown that fiberglass laminates—and the gel coats that are applied over them—are not completely waterproof, as

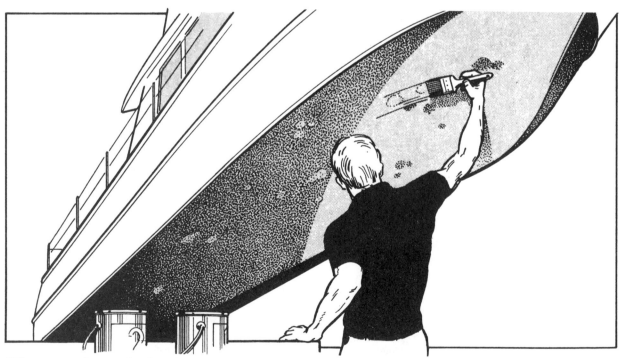

Blisters can be repaired and prevented by applying two or more coats of special epoxy resin.

originally believed. A good gel coat is a barrier to penetration by water, but it is not *completely* impervious to water passage or to moisture absorption. In time, depending on the thickness of the gel coat and how it was formulated and applied, if the gel coat is continuously submerged it will allow a limited amount of water to pass through it.

Contrary to popular opinion—and to what even the experts thought—fiberglass laminates will also absorb and hold sizable amounts of water when submerged. As a result, the water that comes through the gel coat eventually finds its way into the laminate by osmosis, working its way into the many little voids and pockets present in almost every laminate. Then, because of various environmental conditions and the buildup of vapor pressures inside the laminate, this moisture will in time try to force its way out through the surface—causing blistering of the gel coat and even the possibility of delamination of the fiberglass in some cases.

The water that remains in contact with the polyester resins inside the laminate also reacts chemically with those resins to form a sticky liquid that is usually brownish or amber in color and often smells like acetic acid. The buildup of this sticky liquid inside the laminate and under the gel coat further increases the pressure that causes blisters to form and swell, until they eventually burst and allow this liquid to ooze out.

Although blistering is mercifully a problem on only about 10 to 20 percent of all boats at this time, the problem is obviously serious enough to be of great concern to many boatowners, boatyards, and manufacturers. And the number of boats that are affected seems to be increasing from year to year—perhaps because there are just more boats around than ever before, or perhaps because the boats that are around are getting older and older (and thus have been in the water longer). Regardless of the reasons, the one question in almost everybody's mind is: What can be done about this problem?

Here again, all experts do not yet completely agree on a cure, but after talking to several manufacturers of paints and resins, and several builders of fiberglass boats, it appears there is at least a general consensus on the steps you should take if your boat has already been attacked by this "plague." If your boat does not yet have the problem, or if you are about to launch a new boat, this is the best time to prevent the problem (prevention is much easier, and more effective, than curing the problem after it develops).

Several of the larger paint companies, including International Paint, Pettit, and Woolsey, as well as several other companies who specialize in making resins and the materials that go with them, have introduced special epoxy resins and epoxy patching materials designed to

deal with blistering. Some resin manufacturers sell the components separately and supply application manuals or instruction sheets that tell you how to use their particular materials.

Although individual manufacturers' instructions will vary to some extent, here are the basic steps to follow to repair the bottom and protect it from future blister attacks:

1. After the boat is hauled, plan to leave it out of the water for some time. Puncture or open all of the blisters, then allow them to drain until nothing else oozes out. Wash the entire bottom with fresh water, scrubbing out the cavities or blistered areas with a stiff brush to get rid of all sticky residue.

2. Now take off all of the old bottom paint from the hull, leaving the bare gel coat exposed. This can be done by sanding, or by using one of the various paint removers that are made for application on fiberglass and get coat (ordinary paint removers may take off or damage the gel coat if you are not very careful). Do not remove the paint by sand-blasting, as this could seriously damage the gel coat and make it even more porous than it already is. However, in extreme cases where the gel coat is so badly blistered and damaged that it is no longer worth saving, it may be advisable to remove all of the old gel coat to get down to solid laminate. (In that case consult your boat yard or favorite manufacturer of marine paints to determine exactly what kind of protective coating you can apply to replace the original gel coat when you are finished.)

3. Allow the hull to dry thoroughly for at least three to four weeks (three to four months is even better). The boat should be stored indoors or at least out of the rain during this time. If the boat must be stored outdoors, keep it covered to keep rain off the hull. If the boat is on bare ground, it is a good idea to cover the earth under and around the boat with sheet plastic to keep moisture from attacking the laminate from beneath. Carry this plastic up against the sides to enclose the hull bottom, and if possible run a dehumidifier inside this "bag" for several days.

Because thorough drying is so important, it is wise to do all the preparatory work in the fall after the boat is hauled. Then you can allow the whole winter for the hull to dry before starting to repair and refinish it in the spring. It's important to understand that if any moisture is trapped inside the laminate when you start refinishing it, this moisture may lead to further blistering later on.

4. After the hull has dried, use an electric grinder or a small grinding wheel chucked in an electric drill to gouge out all the blistered and damaged spots. Clean out all softened laminate, loose material, and damaged gel coat until only solid material remains, then wash off the entire hull. Wipe the voids out with a solvent recommended by

A small grinding wheel in an electric drill can be used to clean out the blisters. Two-part epoxy putty is used to fill the cavities.

the manufacturer of the epoxy fairing compound you will be using (see below).

5. Using a two-part epoxy compound that is made for just this purpose, fill in all voids and cavities to restore the hull to a smooth, evenly faired surface again. Deep cavities are best filled in two layers to minimize shrinkage, but don't use just any two-part epoxy patching material. Buy one that is made for this purpose. When the patches have cured, sand smooth and then do more patching and filling if necessary. When patching is finished, sand the surface and wipe off all sanding dust. A final wet sanding is advisable to ensure smoothness.

6. Apply the first coat of one of the two-part epoxy resins that are made to seal fiberglass bottoms. Do not use an ordinary two-part epoxy paint if you want lasting results. You must use one of the specially formulated resins sold for just this purpose. These are pure epoxy resins (no solvent added) that form a much thicker film than ordinary paints. Most are harder to brush on than regular epoxy paint, and they cost more, but they are the only ones that will do the job well.

You have to apply enough coats to build up a thickness

of about ten mils (.010 inch). With some products only two coats will build to this thickness, but with others you will have to apply four or five coats. Check the manufacturer's specifications, and be sure you do not cheat—the full thickness is required to build up an effective and long-lasting barrier against water penetration in the future, so if you do cheat you will only be fooling yourself. Until recently this job used to take days or even weeks because of the number of coats of resin required to build up such a thickness and because of the amount of drying time required between coats. However, in the past year or two manufacturers have introduced quicker-drying resins that provide much faster buildup for each coat. They are a bit harder to apply and more difficult to sand smooth, but they do the job.

7. After the barrier coats of epoxy have cured for the recommended length of time, sand lightly and dust thoroughly. Then apply two coats of a good grade of antifouling paint. Be sure you allow adequate drying time between coats. This procedure should take care of the blistering problem for many years to come—at least that is what all current research by paint manufacturers and knowledgeable boatyards would seem to indicate.

As mentioned earlier, prevention is a lot easier than curing an outbreak of blisters after they have developed, so an increasing trend among boatyards and manufacturers is to advise putting on a barrier coat of epoxy resin as a

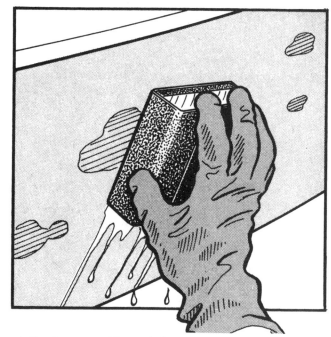

A final wet sanding of the patches will help get the surface smooth before applying two-part epoxy resin.

preventive measure—on new boats, as well as on older boats that do not yet have a blistering problem.

To be completely effective, the epoxy resin must be applied directly to the bare gel coat, before the first coat of bottom paint is spread. If there is already bottom paint on the hull, then it should all be removed as described above. Allow the hull to dry thoroughly before going ahead with the epoxy, and be sure you apply enough coats to build up the recommended film thickness. Then finish with two coats of the bottom paint of your choice.

How to Keep Props Free of Barnacles

Like most boatowners, I have found that no bottom paint seems to last long on props, shafts, and rudders. Even though the paint keeps the bottom clean, the underwater hardware seems to grow barnacles and grass in just a short time after launching, especially in Florida.

However, I have learned how to get around this problem: The last time my forty-two-foot powerboat was hauled I painted and cleaned the bottom in the usual manner, but I treated the underwater metal differently. Props, rudders, shafts, and trim tabs were cleaned thoroughly until the metal was bare and bright. Then all the

metal was painted with Interlux Prime Wash. After this had dried I applied two coats of Interlux Tri-Lux containing TBTF; then the boat was launched. At the end of that summer the props, rudders, shafts, and trim tabs were still clean, except for a little slime that washed off as soon as the boat was run. And I honestly believe that I will get another full year of boating before this coating has to be renewed.

How to Make an Old Boat Look New

Sooner or later there comes a time when you realize that your boat no longer shines like she once did. That original gleam is gone: The gel coat has a faded look; the brightwork is no longer bright; even the hardware and fittings are starting to look dull and corroded. But don't despair; it's not as hopeless as you think. There are a number of things you can do to rejuvenate these surfaces. The following steps can transform a forlorn-looking boat into a gleaming vessel you can be proud of. If it's time for a face-lift, here's how to do it.

A Face-lift for Fiberglass
Boat owners all learn that fiberglass is not maintenance-

Cleaning and polishing can often bring a dead-looking boat back to life.

free, as many first-time buyers think it will be. Sooner or later the gel coat will become drab-looking, which gives the whole boat a slightly shopworn look. This is when some people start to consider a paint job; but that is a time-consuming and expensive procedure that should be considered as a last resort only. Fortunately, there are quicker and easier measures you can take to bring back the original color and luster without going to the trouble and expense of painting.

If ordinary waxing will no longer bring up the shine or restore the original color, it means that the gel coat has begun to fade and/or oxidize, forming a film over the surface that dulls it. The usual method to remove this film is to use a polishing or rubbing compound before applying a paste wax.

Keep in mind, however, that these polishing compounds all have a mild abrasive in them and actually rub off a microscopically thin layer of gel coat whenever you use one. Therefore, they should not be used more frequently than necessary.

One thing a polishing compound *is* good for is removing stubborn scuff marks and stains that resist cleaning agents or solvents. Most surface stains can be rubbed off with a polishing compound and a piece of clean cloth. Wrap the cloth around one finger and dip it into the compound, then rub lightly until the stain disappears. It's a good idea before going ahead with the whole boat to try compounding and waxing only a small area first to see if this will actually do the job. If you decide to go ahead, schedule your work so you compound only those areas that you can also coat with wax on the same weekend. It is not a good idea to allow freshly compounded surfaces to weather for more than a day or two without applying a protective coat of wax.

You can apply the rubbing compound by hand, or you can rent an electric buffing machine to do the job. Before using a machine for the first time, practice on some scrap surfaces to get the feel of it. Don't try to use an electric drill equipped with a lamb's wool buffing attachment—you're better off doing the job by hand.

After using the polishing compound, wipe the surface clean, then start applying the paste wax. A hard paste wax will build up to a deeper and longer-lasting shine than a soft or creamy wax will, although paste waxes require more elbow grease. Always apply wax sparingly, in thin layers, and rub it out well. Remember that several thin coats will build up a harder and glossier finish than one heavy coat, but buff each coat before applying the next one. Buffing is what gives the wax its gloss hardness.

Another technique to brighten badly faded and oxidized fiberglass without all the work of a polishing compound is to use Marine Penetrol, a product made by the Flood Company, 1213 Barlow Road, Hudson, Ohio 44236 (this

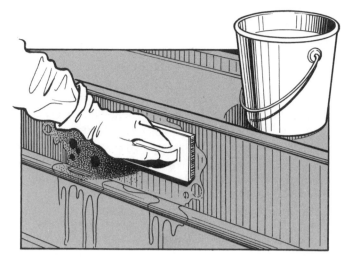

First scrub on Deks Rens with an abrasive nylon pad.

Then hose the Deks Rens off with plenty of water.

Finally, apply the Penetrol with a soft, clean cloth.

is the same company that makes Deks Olje). Most effective on dark or bright colors (because these fade more than light colors), Penetrol will even work on some boats where compounding and waxing fail to freshen up the original color (unless you put on about ten or fifteen coats of wax).

Have you ever noticed that faded fiberglass looks brighter when it's wet? Well, that is what Marine Penetrol does; it soaks into the gel coat and through the oxidized film at the surface to give the gel coat a permanently "wet look," thus restoring much of the original color.

When using Penetrol, here is the procedure to follow:

1. After washing the boat in the usual manner, give it a second scrubbing with Deks Rens, a product also made by the Flood Company. This is a strong grease solvent and cleaner (also excellent for use on teak) that contains a bleach. Mix it half and half with water and scrub it on with one of those abrasive nylon pads similar to the kind shown in the drawing. Wear rubber gloves to protect your hands, and don't stint on the elbow grease. Try to avoid working in direct sunlight and on very hot days because this will cause the cleaning solution to dry too fast.

2. Scrub a section at a time and let the cleaner soak into the surface for about ten minutes. Rinse off with a hose and lots of water, and if some stains still remain, repeat the scrubbing process. Dry with old bath towels to remove excess water and prevent streaking, then allow the surface to dry completely before applying the Penetrol.

3. Fold a soft, clean cloth into a pad and wet it with Penetrol. Wipe on over several square feet of the freshly cleaned fiberglass surface, then after a minute or two use a second, dry cloth to remove all excess Penetrol. Keep turning the cloth frequently. No rubbing or buffing is required; just wipe firmly enough to remove all excess from the surface. If you want a still higher gloss you can apply a hard paste wax after the oil has dried, but remember that this wax will have to be removed before more Penetrol can be applied in the future.

Gleaming Hardware

If hardware has not been badly neglected for too long, then you can usually restore the finish by using one of the excellent metal polishes available in all marine supply outlets. For mild oxidation and dulling I have found that an impregnated fleece product such as Nevr-Dull is one of the fastest and easiest cleaners to use. For more stubborn cases you will need a polish with a mild abrasive in it.

For severely oxidized or pitted chrome, rubbing with #00 bronze wool may be required. I find that dipping the bronze wool into Penetrol and then rubbing hard with this will really do a job on chrome or stainless steel that is showing signs of rusting or mild pitting (it also works on aluminum, brass, and bronze). After scrubbing, wait about five minutes, then rub off vigorously with a clean rag. After about five minutes, buff again with another dry cloth. If there is a buildup of the Penetrol in any place where you fail to wipe it off in time, you can use a small amount of acetone or paint remover to take off the excess.

Hardware that has been cleaned and polished can be kept up by wiping it down with a rag moistened with a moisture-displacing penetrating oil such as WD-40, LPS-1, or CRC. Wipe on sparingly and renew the coating at least once a month.

Wood and varnish cannot be neglected for long if you want to maintain it in bristol fashion; and nothing can make a boat look as worn and weathered as one that shows lots of dull or even cracked varnish.

Brighter Brightwork

There are really three secrets to a good-looking varnish finish: (1) Buy only a top grade of varnish and use it according to the instructions. (2) Start out by building up the finish with at least four to six coats of varnish, sanding lightly between coats. (3) Touch up scrapes, scratches, and worn spots as soon as they are noticed.

If you are boating in salt or brackish water, make sure you hose off all the varnish after each trip. If possible, dry with a chamois or with old towels. As you wipe the varnish dry, watch for abrasions or places where the varnish has been rubbed off. After you are sure the wood is dry, use a small cloth pad dipped into some of the same varnish and wipe this on over the worn spot.

Probably the most common mistake is allowing the varnish to weather too long before applying another coat. If you wait until the varnish starts to look worn all over, then you have probably waited too long. The idea is to apply another coat as soon as the finish shows signs of getting a *little* dull, or as soon as you notice a few worn spots. Usually this means applying another coat every four to six months, depending on exposure, although in some cases two coats may be needed to rebuild the original finish properly. Sand with #150 or #180 sandpaper, then dust thoroughly. Wipe off again with another rag that has been moistened with paint thinner just before you start applying the new varnish.

Flow the varnish on with a top-quality brush (badger hair is the best) and finish off with long strokes parallel to the grain. Keep sighting along the surface at a low angle to make sure there are no skips or drips, and smooth these off immediately before moving on to the next section. Don't try to go back over previously coated surfaces if the varnish has already started to get tacky. Wait till it dries, then sand out the blemishes and apply another coat.

Inside As Well As Out

Regardless of whether the wood (panels and trim) on the interior of your boat is teak, mahogany, or some other species of wood, after a couple of years the finish will start to get dull and dirty-looking. If ordinary cleaning and polishing won't remove the dark stains, your best bet is to wipe the wood down with a rag moistened with paint thinner. After you have wiped one section clean, wipe over that same area with another dry rag. Keep turning rags frequently as one side gets dirty, and change rags completely when there are no clean sides left.

If the finish on any of this interior wood looks dull, or is starting to show signs of wear, then it is usually not necessary to refinish it completely. You can restore the luster and brighten the finish by using a product called Minwax Antique Oil (found in many paint and hardware stores).

After cleaning with paint thinner as described above, pour a small amount of the Antique Oil onto a clean cloth pad, then wipe it on over the wood. Let this soak in for about five minutes, then buff off the excess with a dry cloth. Buff again with another clean cloth to bring up the shine and build a higher luster. If the finish starts to feel sticky when you try to wipe the excess off, then you have waited too long before wiping the excess off, or you have put on too much oil. To correct this, wet a cloth with more of the same oil and rub on over the surface again. Wait a minute or two, then buff again to remove excess.

If some of the plastic laminate on the inside is faded or dull-looking, you can often restore the luster by using one of the polishes sold for this purpose. Try a small section first to see how it works. Wipe it on as explained above, and be sure you carefully wipe off all excess before it can dry.

Miscellany

You can also brighten things up on the inside by cleaning or replacing the carpet or other floor coverings and by cleaning or replacing blinds, curtains, and other decorative accessories. Around the outside, cleaning those dirty yellow shore cords by wiping down one of the various products sold for this purpose will help a lot, as will replacing old dock lines with new ones. All these will go a long way toward making your boat look almost new.

How to Stop Those Pesky Leaks

Most boatowners expect to find some dampness and at least a little water in the bilge and in other places inside the

hull and below the waterline. But they do not feel the same way about leaks above the waterline—leaks inside a cabin or stateroom, or in any of the living and storage areas. Even a small leak that occurs only occasionally can be very annoying, in addition to being quite destructive. Leaks cause problems such as dampness and mildew in clothing inside hanging lockers or cabinets, water-staining of carpets and bulkhead panels, and even rotting of wood bulkheads or other structural members.

Sometimes leaks are easy to trace and correct—for example, when you find water coming in directly below or on the inside of a deck seam that needs caulking, or when water leaks in during a driving rain around a porthole that obviously doesn't close tightly enough. Unfortunately, such easy-to-locate leaks are usually the exception rather than the rule. More often than not the leak is maddeningly difficult to find; in fact, sometimes the task seems impossible.

But regardless of how elusive they may seem, all leaks *can* eventually be tracked down, and they *can* all be fixed, although there are times when you will have to do more than a little detective work to discover where the water is entering.

For example, everyone knows that water will not flow uphill—or will it? On a boat there may be times when that occurs. Water that normally flows down along a sloping deck or hatch cover may actually be forced *up* that same slope by the wind or by the boat's movement. Or the slope on a hatch cover or deck may change decidedly when the boat heels or lists, even momentarily. That's why you can't always be certain that the water is entering above where it shows up on the inside; under certain conditions it could be coming in at a point lower than where you find it on the inside.

Tracking down such leaks is seldom easy and almost always takes a considerable amount of time and patience. One of the best ways to find a really stubborn leak that only shows up during or right after a rainstorm is to track it down while the water is still coming in. You won't find much by crawling around on the outside while it is raining, but you may be able to spot the source if you start

Water can flow horizontally along cables until it finds a spot to drip down.

Every boat has spots where water tends to get in—arrows indicate the most common sources of trouble.

from the inside, at the point where the water is first visible.

Begin by using paper towels to dry off the wet inside surface. Then shine a bright light on the area while watching closely to see where water first appears. From that point on, keep following the stream or trickle of water backward to see if you can locate the point of entry. This may mean removing some moldings or panels, or even taking down part of the headliner, but in many cases it may be the only way to find the point of entry—or at least the path of entry (so you will know where the water is coming from).

I was once trying to find the source of a leak that allowed water to drip into a hanging locker and soak all our clothes whenever we had a heavy rainstorm. For months I had tried to caulk and seal every seam and joint around the outside that was anywhere near or above that hanging locker, but nothing seemed to help. Finally I decided to tackle the job from inside. I waited for the next heavy rain, and after about an hour I discovered that the water was dripping down through the holes in the perforated hardboard panel that served as a headliner for the closet.

After removing this panel I found a lot of wires bunched together, as well as a number of hoses that passed through this overhead space on their way to various parts of the boat. All the wires and hoses were wet, so I used paper towels to dry everything thoroughly. Then I shone a bright light into the area and waited. Soon I saw water creeping along the bunched wire harness from one side. This water flowed along the wires until it contacted one of the wood braces that went across to support the headliner; then it dripped down onto the headliner panel.

I still couldn't see where the water was entering, but I now could tell it was coming in from close to the port side of the boat, somewhere just at or below the deckline. Poking into that area with a stiff wire that had a piece of cloth bundled around one end helped me find how far under the deck (where I couldn't see) there was dampness. The next day, after the rain, I went outside and checked again. In the area where I had been poking there was a deck-mounted stanchion. I took out the fasteners that held the stanchion in place and squirted a little silicone caulking into each hole. Then I reinserted and tightened all the fasteners. Lo and behold—no more leak!

Wet Carpet Mystery

Another time there was a really maddening leak that kept wetting the carpet in our aft stateroom. I took up the carpet and could find nothing except damp decking (the plywood under the carpet). I dried off the plywood and decided to leave the carpet off during the next rain so I could watch where the water was coming from. But the next time it rained, nothing happened—the decking remained dry. Thinking that the problem probably was caused by condensation, I replaced the carpet. Two more rainy days passed with nothing happening, but the third time it rained, the carpet did get wet after about an hour or two.

I tried to figure out what was different this time. The only thing I could think of was that there was a lot of wind and the boat rocked quite a bit. That was the clue I needed to discover the cause of the trouble. A small amount of water was leaking in each time through some deck fittings above that stateroom. This water ran down along the inner side of the hull until it was stopped by a crosspiece on top of the plywood decking inside a hanging locker. A puddle would form there and remain until it got high enough to overflow the crosspiece and run out. The first two times the rain stopped before the puddle grew high enough to overflow. The third time it still didn't get high enough, but the boat's rocking caused it to overflow anyway—wetting both deck and carpet.

Of course, you can't always get away with tracking leaks from the inside this easily, or at least with this little damage. Sometimes it will be impossible without really ripping things apart. However, if you try to get some idea of the general direction that water emanates from, then carefully examine the boat exterior around that area. You may be able to find the source of trouble without going that far.

As the example illustrates, water can enter at one point and then travel a considerable distance sideways, running along wires, hoses, beams, or reinforcing struts before it trickles down into the cabin. It can also weep down along the inside of the cabin until it hits a crosspiece or other obstruction, then run sideways along this for some distance until it finally comes out through a crevice or seam of some type on the inside.

Solution for Window

This often happens when water seeps in around the top of a window frame or port light. It runs sideways along the top of that frame, then runs down around the rim until it gets to the bottom of the frame. There it finally comes out on the inside—several feet below where it actually entered and perhaps several feet off to one side.

Although you may be able to stop this type of leak temporarily by simply running a bead of sealant around the outside rim of the frame, this usually won't help for long—if it works at all. The only way to stop this kind of leak permanently is to remove the window frame or port frame, then rebed it with fresh compound before replacing it.

Keeping these points in mind, here are some other places that should be carefully examined when trying to track down a stubborn leak:

● Inspect window channels on sliding windows to see if they are clogged with debris that could be interfering with rapid drainage. These channels should have small drain holes or weep holes in the corners to help water drain out rapidly. If these holes get clogged—even partially—the window channels can fill up and overflow, allowing water to seep down behind the inside liner of the boat or behind the paneling used to line the inside.

● Inspect channels of sliding companionway doors in the same way—especially on powerboats with large sliding entrance doors that provide access from an open cockpit. If these channels do not drain properly they could allow water to seep in under the door or under the decking.

● Check the fasteners on all deck-mounted fittings, regardless of whether they are through-bolted or secured with screws. Water can seep in around these fasteners and work its way down through the holes into which they fit. If this is suspected, the only sure cure is to remove all the fasteners, then squirt a little silicone caulking into the holes before reinserting them. Don't tighten the fasteners all the way at first, just most of the way; then let the sealant cure for fifteen or twenty minutes before tightening the rest of the way. This keeps the compound from squeezing out before it has time to set up.

● On wooden boats a lack of bedding compound, or some that has become brittle, could be allowing water to puddle under the fitting and soak into and through the material underneath. Here again, you should remove the fitting completely, then rebed with fresh compound.

● Dig out old caulking around hatch frames that go through the deck if that caulking looks dried out or cracked. Dry the joint out thoroughly, then reapply fresh caulking compound, using either a silicone type or a polysulfide. Apply a liberal bead and try to avoid smoothing or pressing it down with your fingertip. The idea is to leave a convex surface on the bead of caulking, not a

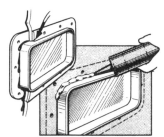

Effective caulking around ports and windows involves removing the frames.

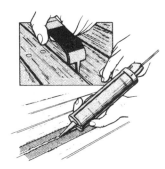

Old, cracked caulking must be dug out before recaulking planked decks.

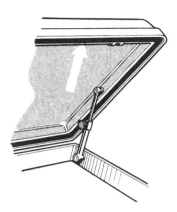

Rubber weather stripping can wear out and should be replaced.

concave one (the compound should bulge out slightly, not curve inward).

● Examine the joints where the vertical sides of the cabin or pilothouse meet the decks. If you suspect trouble here, don't just apply fresh caulking or sealant over the old material. Instead, scrape out all the old material, wipe the joint clean with paint thinner, then recaulk with fresh compound. If there is a quarter-round or cove molding covering this joint, look for slight gaps or for signs of the molding pulling away from either side. If anything looks suspicious, take the whole molding off, then apply caulking under it when you replace it. It seldom helps merely to apply fresh sealant along the edges of the molding; you must take it off to rebed it.

● If you have teak decks, check the sealant in the seams to see if any have loosened, or if there are sections where the sealant has cracked and pulled away from the teak plank at each side of the joint. Frequent scrubbing with harsh teak cleaners may have softened or eaten away some of the sealant, allowing water to seep in under the planks. While checking the sealant between the planks, also examine the plugs that cover the screws that hold the planks in place. If these plugs have cracked or fallen out, that, too, could serve as an entry point for water. Dig the old plugs out completely, make sure the screws are tight, then install new plugs that have been dipped into varnish or glue.

● Inspect joints where wood toe rails, cap rails, and covering boards or coamings sit on top of fiberglass or wood. The slightest gap or crack caused by loose fasteners or warping of these trim pieces can allow water to seep underneath and find its way into the boat through the fastener holes. If this is your problem, run a small bead of sealant along the joint, but put masking tape down on each side of the sealant first. When this tape is stripped off you'll have a neat-looking bead and little or no cleanup.

● Apply sealant or renew rubber gaskets behind electrical inlets, water inlet connections, or other fittings that go through the deck or cabin sides. All such fittings should have a gasket behind them, unless they are bedded in silicone or polysulfide caulking.

● Windshield gaskets made of foam rubber or plastic foam will in time dry out and crack, allowing moisture to enter during a driving rain or a pounding sea. All marine supply outlets carry replacement gasketing of this type, but if you cannot find what you need, try contacting the manufacturer of your boat or a dealer who handles that brand. There are times when no amount of inspection will help you to find the origin of a stubborn leak. But you can use a hose to locate the place where water enters. It's best not to spray water over a large area at one time—start with a slow but steady stream of water without using a nozzle.

Begin at the bottom or lowest point of the suspected area and let the water run for at least fifteen to twenty minutes while you keep an eye on the inside. If nothing happens, move the hose to a new location slightly higher up and repeat the process. Keep moving higher and higher. If this doesn't disclose the leak, start over at a different point a little more to one side or the other. Keep working from the bottom up, and from one side to the other, until you find a place where water starts to show up on the inside. Then—using all these hints—you'll know what you have to do.

Winning the Battle Against Rust and Corrosion

Rust and corrosion are major problems on every boat—not only on metal under the boat that is submerged, but also on metal and hardware inside the boat and out on the decks. Dampness, salt spray, and high humidity expose all metals to the constant threat of corrosion and oxidation, something that no boatowner can or should ignore for long.

Even stainless steel and aluminum—supposedly rust-resistant and impervious to oxidation when properly fabricated and installed—will corrode or oxidize under certain circumstances, depending on the type of alloy used in their manufacture, on the techniques used when the parts were fabricated, and on the amount of exposure the metal is subject to. Constant vigilance and regular attention to proper maintenance of all the metal in or on the boat is the only way to be sure that rust and corrosion will not eat away a good part of your expensive investment.

For rails and stanchions, marine paste wax is the best protection against corrosion.

Without getting involved in a lengthy, scientific discussion of how different metals and their alloys are affected, here briefly are the differences among the three basic types of corrosion most often encountered on a boat.

Galvanic Corrosion

Galvanic corrosion occurs whenever two dissimilar metals are submerged in or coated with an electrolyte (a liquid that conducts electricity). An actual battery is created that generates its own current. This current flows from one metal (which is called the anode and is the less noble of the two metals involved) to the other metal (the cathode, which is higher up on the scale of metals). In the process the anode slowly deteriorates or gets eaten away.

This is the same type of chemical action that takes place in a regular battery or "dry" cell (they are never really dry on the inside, since the electrolyte is a damp paste). In a battery the zinc outer shell is the anode, so it gets gradually eaten away as the flow of electric current carries particles of it over to the internal cathode (zinc is one of the least noble earthly metals).

Electrolytic Corrosion

This differs from galvanic corrosion in that the corrosion is caused by electric currents that come from an *outside* source, such as the ship's d.c. batteries or the a.c. current that comes in from the shore supply. The current usually comes from leakage due to an improper grounding system,

or from damp connections that allow current to leak into the bilge water (or into the water around the boat). There still has to be an electrolyte that carries current from anode to cathode, but the metals do not necessarily have to be dissimilar. However, erosion of the anode proves to be much faster if the two metals are different.

The amount of damage incurred and the speed with which the damage is done vary with the amount of "stray" current involved and with how far apart the two metals are on the scale of noble metals. The more different they are, and the farther apart (on the scale) they are, the more they will be affected by the stray currents.

Ordinary Corrosion

This includes rusting and pitting and is the type of corrosion most often associated with iron, steel, and other ferrous metals (other than stainless steel). For metals to rust, there must be oxygen present (in the water or in the air), and there must also be dampness present. Although aluminum, bronze, and most grades of stainless steel do not rust in the usual sense, they do corrode and form oxides on the surface when not protected against the elements. On iron and carbon steel, corrosion takes the form of commom brown rust—the type we all encounter daily on our automobile bodies, metal furniture, home appliances, toys, and yard equipment.

On aluminum, corrosion can form as a cloudy or dull

film that actually protects the metal against further corrosion and oxidation as long as the oxide film is not disturbed. Anodizing is a form of artificial corrosion. A coating of specially induced oxide protects the metal underneath against further corrosion—until it gets rubbed off by abrasion. In some cases aluminum can oxidize so heavily that it crumbles or decomposes into a white, powdery residue. This is particularly true of some aluminum alloys when brought into contact with salt water or salt spray.

On bronze and brass, oxidation takes the form of a greenish or brownish film that also protects the metal against further oxidation. And on stainless steel, corrosion can cause streaks of rust to form, especially around welded joints and crevices; it can also cause pitting on the surface.

Preventing Corrosion

To protect underwater and belowdecks metal components from galvanic corrosion, most boats use a system of sacrificial zinc anodes. These pieces of zinc are bolted to the rudders, shafts, trim tabs, and other underwater parts to serve as the anode for the inevitable "battery" that is formed between the different underwater metal parts on most boats. Instead of one of the parts being eaten away (a seacock, rudder, or strut, for example), the zinc anode will get eaten away.

Since salt water is a much better conductor than fresh water, galvanic corrosion is obviously a much more serious problem on boats that are used in sea water than on

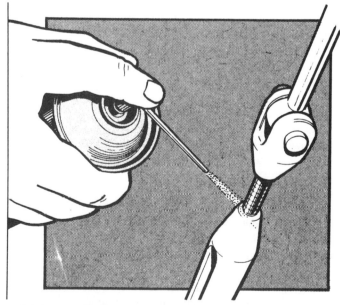

Moisture-displacing lubricant sprayed in crevices and on moving parts leaves a protective film to inhibit corrosion.

those used in fresh water. But even in fresh water galvanic corrosion can occur, because most large bodies of water have enough impurities in them that they still can serve as an electrolyte.

On many boats there is a central bonding system where all underwater metal parts are connected together with a heavy copper cable. This cable is electrically bonded to a large zinc anode under the boat or on the transom (where it will always be underwater, yet can be easily replaced when necessary). This system keeps all metal components at the same electrical potential—in other words, there is no difference in current potential, so no current can flow among the different parts to form a battery. Any galvanic or electrolytic corrosion that does take place eats away the zinc anode rather than the bronze or steel parts.

Boats that do not have a central bonding system use separate zinc anodes attached to rudders, shafts, struts, and trim tabs. Just make sure that all paint and foreign matter is removed under the zinc at the point where each zinc comes into contact with any metal, and make sure each zinc is firmly bolted in place to form a sound electrical connection.

Protecting against electrolytic corrosion is an entirely different matter. If a problem is suspected here, chances are that an experienced marine electrician will have to be called in to check for stray currents in the bilge or in the water around the boat.

The problem is usually more serious when there is a leakage from the a.c. shore power system (or onboard generator) because then you are dealing with higher voltages and often a larger flow of current. In some marinas where the electrical grounding system is poor, installing an isolation transformer on the boat is the only sure cure. These transformers eliminate any direct connection between the shore power system and the boat's system.

Ordinary Rust

To protect other metal parts that are not underwater against ordinary rust and corrosion—the kind that eats away at steel motor mounts, deck hardware, sailboat rigging, railings, cabinet hardware, door locks, and all the other metal parts found on a boat—remember that two elements must be present for rust to form on any metal: oxygen and moisture. Anything you can do to keep oxygen and moisture from coming in contact with the metal will help to protect it against corrosion.

One of the best ways to protect ferrous metals (iron and steel) is to paint them. As long as the paint film is not broken (not cracked or peeling) and is applied to all sides of the metal, the metal will not rust.

Galvanizing, a process in which the metal is coated with a zinc plating, also protects it against rust, but even this coating will wear away eventually. When this happens the metal should also be painted, but make sure you use a metal primer that will stick to galvanized metal.

Metal that has already started to rust cannot be just painted over to keep it from rusting further. Most paints will not stick well over rust, and even if the paint does last for a while the rust will probably continue to spread under the paint. There are some metal primers specifically designed to stick over solid rust (rust that is not flaking or loose), but in the severe conditions encountered in a marine environment even these paints don't always stand up the way you expect them to.

The traditional method recommended for painting rusty metal is first to use wire brushes, steel wool, or abrasive paper to scrape off all the rust, then apply a coat of metal primer before finishing with either one or two coats of marine enamel.

In recent years, however, several companies have introduced new chemical rust fighters that serve as "rust converters"—that is, they actually convert solid rust (rust that is not flaking or crumbling) into a stable, permanent film that then serves as an excellent base for painting over. They eliminate the need for using a special metal primer as a first coat, and the chemical reaction that occurs also protects the metal against further rusting.

Rust Converters

Since these "rust converters" are liquids that are easily applied by brush, they eliminate the need for most of the tedious scraping and sanding that would otherwise be required. They also make it a lot easier to treat all those small crevices and tight spaces where it would be almost impossible to reach with a scraper or wire brush.

Some of the most widely sold brands are Trustan 7 (made by the Trustan Co., 390 Tiffany Street, Bronx, N.Y. 10474), Extend (made by Loctite Corp., 4450 Cranston Court, Cleveland, Ohio 44128), and Neutra Rust (made by New York Bronze Powder Co., 201 Bay Avenue, Elizabeth, N.J. 07201). If you cannot find one of these products in your local marine supply store, try your local hardware store or home center.

For metal that you don't want to paint, other coatings can be applied to protect them against rust and corrosion. In engine rooms and similar places where appearance is only of secondary importance and where handling is seldom a problem, grease or oil have long been used. A layer of grease may not be neat-looking and will certainly make the surface hard to handle, but it is extremely effective in protecting metal parts such as propeller shafts, pump housing, and similar components. Keeping the surface coated with oil (by wiping with an oily rag periodically) will accomplish much the same thing, but it won't last as long.

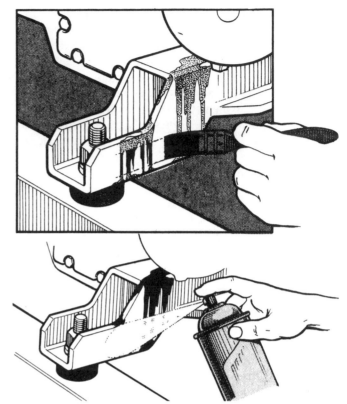

Liquid chemical rust converters can be brushed on to turn rust into a solid base that can then be painted.

However, oil and grease are messy and unsightly-looking, so most people obviously won't use them on exposed metal or on frequently handled pieces of hardware such as cleats, chocks, winches, railings, or other deck hardware. Fortunately, there are other preventive measures, and protective coatings, you can use on these surfaces.

Keep in mind that cleanliness is always a big help—all metals corrode faster when there are impurities and pollutants present. Always wash off salt spray at the end of each day's run and use a nonabrasive metal polish frequently on shiny chrome plate, stainless steel, and other polished metal. Even on supposedly rust-resistant stainless steel, rust streaks can form in crevices or wherever steel tools or abrasives were used in its manufacture (microscopic particles of the steel remain on the surface of the stainless and eventually rust).

After washing the metal, wipe dry and then wipe down with a rag moistened with one of the moisture-displacing penetrating lubricant sprays such as WD-40, LPS, or CRC. These do not leave an oily film on the surface if applied lightly, but they do displace moisture and leave a protective film that will help keep moisture from coming in contact with the metal. Most such sprays will have to be renewed fairly often, since they are thin coatings that will not withstand frequent washing with soap and water. Some of the newer formulations contain Teflon. They generally stick better and last longer when used to protect metals against unsightly corrosion.

Several companies also make heavier-duty clear coatings that will stand up much longer and won't wash off. These come packed in aerosol cans so they can be easily sprayed on metal hardware to protect it. They cannot be easily scrubbed off, but they can be washed off with a solvent (such as paint thinner) when you want to remove them.

Two products of this kind that I have successfully used on hardware around the outside of my boat are CRC Marine Heavy Duty Corrosion Inhibitor (made by CRC Chemicals, 885 Louis Drive, Warminster, Pa., 18974) and Rust Guardit (made by Schwab Industries, P.O. Box 1269, Sequim, Wash. 98382). For aluminum, a brush-on coating called MDR Aluma Coat (made by Marine Development & Research Corp., 116 Church Street, Freeport, N.Y. 11520) works particularly well.

The first two products leave a slightly sticky film (it won't rub off or cause stains but it does feel a bit tacky), so for handrails, stanchions, and grabrails I found that coating with a good-quality marine paste wax provides the best protection. Liquid waxes can also be used and are certainly quicker to apply, but they generally won't last as long.

Regardless of what type of coating you use to protect the metal—paint, wax, oil, or one of the clear protective sprays sold for just that purpose—remember that if you want full protection you must be careful to apply the coating inside all crevices, seams, or joints where water can collect.

Pay particular attention to crevices around screw heads, bolt heads, and nuts; water seeping in around them will often provide the ideal starting place for corrosion to form and then spread (that's one reason why bedding compound or some kind of flexible washer is important around most fasteners). Wherever possible, all sides of the metal should be coated, including the back and parts that are up against another surface or are normally not visible. Otherwise corrosion can start in these places, then gradually creep around to the front or face of the hardware.

Tools, fishing tackle, and other sporting equipment are also a problem when it comes to fighting rust and corrosion aboard a boat. Even when they are stored in a closed tool box or a tight drawer, dampness and moist air almost always cause some rusting of expensive equipment.

Keeping tools and tackle coated with a light film of oil (by wiping with an oily rag before putting it away) is the most common solution.

Painting Underwater Metal Parts to Prevent Fouling

While a good antifouling paint can be used to keep bottoms free of fuel-eating and speed-robbing underwater growths, most do not last long when applied to propellers, shafts, trim tabs, and other underwater metal. This is mainly due to the vibration involved, plus the friction created when paint is applied to rapidly rotating props and shafts.

However, a fair amount of antifouling protection can be provided by doing a really thorough job of cleaning the metal off first, washing with a strong solvent to remove all sanding residue, grease, and dirt, and then applying two or three coats of a top-quality organo-tin antifouling paint. Here is a technique that will help the paint stay on those metal parts longer, although it still may not last as long as it will on the rest of the bottom (this method should not be used on regular steel):

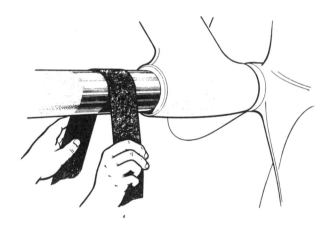

● Scrape the metal to remove all underwater growth, including old paint and oxidation. Then polish it by sandblasting or with a medium-grade emery cloth until the metal is bright and shiny.

● Wash clean with a strong solvent, such as the thinner used with vinyl bottom paint, a solvent-type surface cleaner, or a regular lacquer thinner.

● Apply one thin coat of a vinyl primer wash, such as the kind sold for dewaxing and preparing fiberglass, before putting on the first coat of vinyl bottom paint.

● Apply at least two coats of a good-quality, hard-drying, antifouling paint containing tributyl tin oxide (TBTO) or a similar organo-tin compound. (Do not use a bottom paint that contains copper or cuprous oxide.)

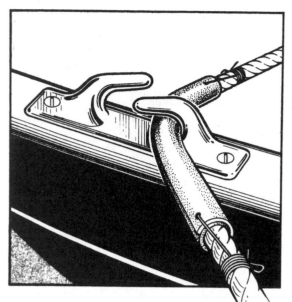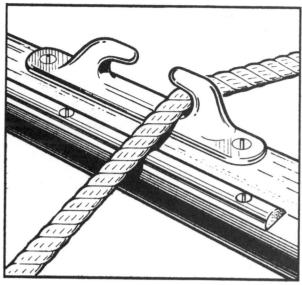

Rubber or plastic chafe guards (left) should be firmly secured to keep them in place. Strips of stainless steel molding (right) should be used to protect brightwork from abrasion from rubbing lines.

Winning the Battle Against Chafe and Abrasion

One maintenance problem that every boatowner is constantly faced with is battling chafe and abrasion. Not just the chafing that occurs on mooring, docking, or running lines, but also the chafing and abrasion of the boat when it rubs against docks or pilings, or when lines, hoses, and electric shore cords are dragged across it.

Chafing really causes two different kinds of problems: purely *cosmetic* damage that affects the appearance of the boat's brightwork, painted finishes, and gel-coat surfaces; and actual *structural* damage that can deform railings, trim, and pieces of deck hardware as well as seriously weakening ropes and lines so much that they have to be replaced entirely. A few commonsense precautions can protect your lines against these kinds of damage.

Chafing of lines is a potential danger whenever a rope runs across or rubs against wood, metal, fiberglass, or anything else that is solid, especially if that line is under tension and there is the likelihood of movement—a condition that is almost always present when a boat is in the water. Ropes and lines should be protected with some type of chafing guard at the point of contact, especially if there are sharp corners involved, or if the rope makes a sharp bend.

What can you use to provide this protection? Some type of sacrificial, cushioned padding that fits around the rope at the point of contact, or some type of wrapping that will take all the wear so the rope itself is protected. Although almost any type of canvas or rough fabric can be wrapped around the line to protect it, this is hard to keep in place and usually doesn't look very neat.

Most boatowners prefer ready-made rubber or plastic chafe guards that slip on over the line. Sold in all marine supply outlets, these come in various sizes to fit lines of different diameters, and they are split open along one side to make it easy to slip them on in the middle of the line. They usually come with short lengths of leather thong, or pieces of line, attached to each end so you can tie them on to keep them from slipping up or down along the line.

You can also make your own chafe guards by cutting pieces of ordinary garden hose to length and then slitting them lengthwise so you can slip them on. To hold them in place without sliding you can either wrap the ends with tape that overlaps onto the rope, or you can punch holes through each end and then slip short lengths of small-diameter nylon or Dacron line through these holes so you can tie the hose in place. To make it easier to slit the hose lengthwise, slide a large-diameter dowel (about equal to the diameter of the hose) inside the hose, then use a sharp knife or razor blade.

Two advantages to making your own chafe guards are (1) it's a lot cheaper than buying the ready-made ones, and (2) you can cut the hose to the length you want so you aren't limited to the comparatively short lengths of the ready-made units.

Instead of using regular colored garden hose, I prefer to use clear vinyl plastic hose, sold by the foot in most marine supply outlets. Clear hose enables you to see the condition of the rope *inside* the chafe guard—protection against unexpected failure of the line while in use.

Here are some suggestions for places to put a protective wrapping or chafe guard.

● Wherever a line goes through a chock, particularly if it turns at a sharp angle as it comes through, or if it is a dockline or mooring line that is likely to seesaw back and forth many times as the boat moves around. Just make sure the chafe guard is securely fastened to the line so it cannot shift or slide, and see that it is long enough so that extremes of movement (including tidal rise and fall) will not move it out of position.

● Wherever the rope passes through a hawsepipe or other opening and stays there while under tension. This is advisable even if the metal or plastic rim around an opening seems well rounded and fairly smooth.

● Any place a rope lies on top of, or rubs against, a railing, toe rail, cap rail, sail track, hatch cover, or other structural part of the boat.

● Any place two docklines cross while close together or in actual contact with each other; for example, where

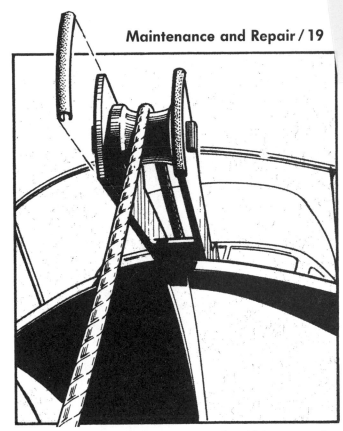

Forward edges of anchor davits should be covered with rubber guards to keep line from chafing on metal.

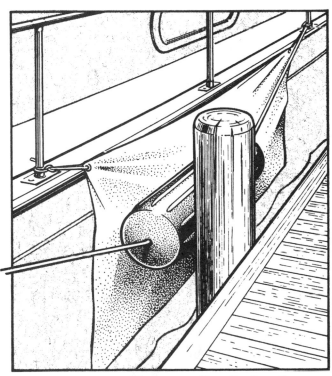

A canvas apron will prevent dirty fenders from marking your hull. Eyes on top edge are for ties.

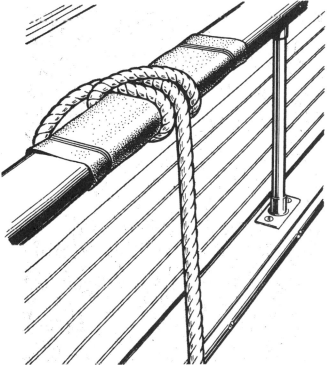

Wrapping canvas around handrails protects varnished wood against chafing from fender lines.

stern lines cross behind a boat when it is tied to a dock after backing in; or where spring lines cross and come close to each other while you are tied alongside. If the lines are rubbing against each other, even part of the time, then wrapping one or both with a protective guard is advisable.

● Where stern lines are wrapped around the corners of the hull after coming off a stern cleat or cleat located near the stern. This often happens when stern lines are crossed behind the boat. This will also protect the hull corners as well as the lines.

● Where long bowlines or spring lines come down at a sharp angle that causes them to rub against the hull or the toe rail at some point.

● On the anchor line where it passes through the bow chock. This should be applied after you have securely anchored so you know which part of the line will be rubbing. A long length of split hose probably will be preferable to a shorter ready-made type.

Although the first line of protection against chafe is some type of chafe guard, this is not always the answer. In some cases, applying chafe guards at every point of possible contact is impractical; in other cases, even with a chafe guard wrapped around the rope, some damage could still occur to smoothly varnished brightwork or to highly polished gel coat finishes. Remember that chafe guards are primarily designed to protect the lines, not necessarily to protect the surfaces against which they rub.

For example:

If your boat has wide toe rails with chocks mounted closer to the one edge than the other, chances are that when a line goes through that chock it will tend to rub on the other edge of the wood rail as the line slopes downward. To prevent this, install short strips of stainless rub molding as shown in the drawing (the kind that has a D-shaped cross section). These metal strips are smooth and curved on top, so they will hold the line up off the wood.

● On sailboats that have genoa tracks running along the rail it is often necessary to have lines crossing over the top of these from somewhere—for example, when a dockline is tied to a cleat or winch inside the rail. Chafe guards may help, but in places where the lines regularly have to lie on top of this track a wood block should be fastened to the deck alongside the track and a fair lead installed on top of this to guide the rope over. The block should raise the fair lead high enough to guide the rope over the railing without actually touching it.

● Where ropes, hoses, or electric cords normally come across the top of a varnished hatch, or one that has a plastic dome on top. And any place where ropes, hoses, or electric cords come around a varnished or painted corner. To protect these surfaces against abrasion you can glue

protective pads of teak or clear plastic to the surface, or you can screw strips of aluminum or stainless steel molding to the surface.

● If your boat has wood handrails around the sides and bow, you frequently have to tie fender lines to these rails to position them where you want them. To keep these lines from chafing the varnish, or even digging into and abrading the wood itself, wrap the rails with canvas or plastic before wrapping the fender lines around them. You can also buy ready-made vinyl straps with a metal eye on the bottom end that will do the job. These snap on over the handrail and can be easily moved to different locations.

Although the chafing caused by ropes and lines rubbing is undoubtedly the most common cause of abrasion damage around the outside of any boat, these are not the only culprits. Anchor chain, particularly where it goes across the deck or the surface of a bow pulpit on its way overboard, can bang up and down when the boat moves around, marking up fiberglass or teak on decks or bow pulpits.

To prevent this, place a heavy canvas pad on the deck under the chain while you are moored (the pad is removed when the anchor is stowed), or fasten a sheet of stainless steel to the surface under the chain, or install several rollers, mounted on top of blocks of teak glued to the deck, to guide the chain and keep it raised off the deck at all times.

Chafe damage to the hull or to parts of the brightwork can also result from the boat rubbing against docks and pilings. Many trawlers, as well as some powerboats and sailboats, come with solid rub rails of wood installed along the sides of the hull. These are designed to keep the hull itself from coming in direct contact with pilings, docks, and other structures while tied alongside. Naturally, these wood strips get banged up and definitely detract from the boat's appearance. That's why most boatowners will screw strips of stainless steel or plastic chafe molding along the face of these rails. (The plastic ones won't stand up as well as the stainless steel ones and may have to be replaced more often, but they will also cost a lot less.)

Another thing that often messes up the side of the hull on any boat is a dirty fender rolling up and down or moving from side to side while squeezed between the boat and a piling or dock. Keeping your fenders clean will minimize the amount of scrubbing you have to do on the boat itself and prolong the life of any gel coat or painted finish.

Of course, when you tie up alongside a creosote-coated piling, the fender won't stay clean very long—and when this creosote gets transferred to the side of your boat by the fender, you may never be able to get all of it off. A simple

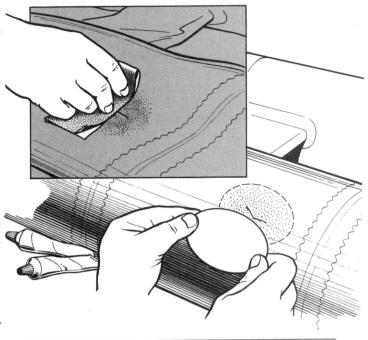

way to prevent this is to rig up a canvas "apron" with a few eyes along the top edge, then hang this over the side by tying it to a couple of stanchions. Position it so the fender will rub against this only, not against the paint or gel coat on the hull. The canvas will catch all the dirt and stains.

Keeping Antichafe Hose in Place

Most prudent boatowners use some type of antichafe guard on docking lines that pass over the edge of a dock or that rub against a post, a piece of hardware, or a corner of the boat. Some people use short lengths of garden hose to provide this protection, while others use slit rubber chafe guards sold in marine supply stores. Either type works fine—but only as long as the antichafe hose stays where it belongs. All too often, however, constant movement of the boat and the lines causes the antichafe hose to slide up or down the line, thus eliminating the protection it is supposed to offer.

A simple and inexpensive way to prevent this is to use a couple of nylon "wire ties" or "wire wraps"—the kind often used to bundle electrical wires inside the boat. After positioning the antichafe hose where I want it, I slip one of these tie wraps through the dockline just past the end of the hose, and then close the loop and pull it almost all the way closed. This effectively acts as a stop and keeps the hose from sliding past it on the line.

When the antichafe hose is next to an eye splice, only one tie wrap is needed. However, if the hose is in the middle of the line, then two tie wraps are needed, as shown here—one past each end of the hose.

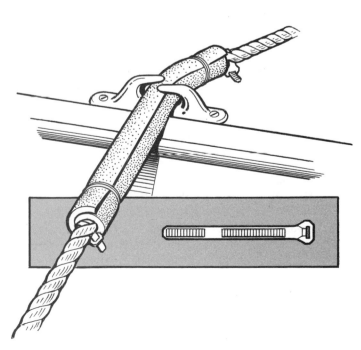

Caring for Inflatables

Keeping your inflatable boat fat and happy is simply a matter of following the manufacturer's operating instructions and providing basic, sensible care. Wood, aluminum, plastic, and other materials should be handled normally: varnish or paint wood, and use rubbing compound or wax on fiberglass.

Maintaining the boat skin itself will vary with the type of material and the construction techniques. To obtain parts and accessories or to repair your inflatable properly, you will need the brand, model, and year of your boat. If you're unsure of these particulars, the identification number from the plate in the boat will enable your dealer to pin them down.

Inflatables are most affected by operating pressure. Each manufacturer sets its own standard for pressure and offers gauges and pumps that will put the right pressure into its boats. An underpressure boat will bend and flex too much, allowing wear and abrasion to develop.

Basic detergents usually will suffice for cleaning an inflatable. More persistent stains can be removed with solvents such as acetone or MEK (Methyl Ethyl Ketone), keeping in mind that these chemicals can dissolve surface coatings or vinyl if applied too strongly. Silicone cleaners should not be used on inflatables, because continued use may allow the silicone to penetrate between the material and the glue and break down the adhesion. The result can be the lifting of seam tape, seams, and patches for items such as tow rings.

Whether you are covering a hole or providing some

abrasion protection, the key to successful patching is surface preparation. You must begin with the proper materials—fabric similar to that used in the construction of your boat and a compatible adhesive. (This is why the brand, model, and year of your boat are so important.) The patch should completely cover the area of damage and extend at least one inch around it. A one-inch hole would need at least a three-inch patch. The patch should be cut with rounded corners (an oval or circular patch works best) to keep the edges from peeling.

After cutting the patch to size, use a grease pencil or crayon to mark around the spot to be patched. Remove any paint, old glue, or other foreign substance from the area. Both the area to be patched and the patch itself will need to be roughed up with sandpaper or a pumice stone. Once roughed, the surfaces are ready to be cleaned. Acetone or alcohol applied lightly will remove sanding dust and surface oils and improve glue adhesion.

The actual application of the adhesive and the patch should be done in a dry place with the temperature ideally between 68 and 72 degrees F. After the patch has been applied, the boat should be left to cure for about seventy-two hours.

Which glue to use will depend on the construction. Vinyl boats can be patched with some quality one-part glues. In general, however, the supported material boats are better patched with two-part adhesives. (Manufacturers' repair kits usually are provided with a one-part adhesive for quick, temporary repairs.) Bostik two-part adhesive is one of the best-known glues used with the Hypalon-coated boats. However, this glue does not perform as well with plastomer boats, so take care to use the right adhesive.

Apply the adhesive according to the instructions for the number and thickness of coats (thin or "liberal"). For Bostik 2402 series, two coats are required, and they may be liberal. All of the adhesives have relatively short shelf lives and are dated; be sure your glue is current. Also, once the container is opened, the glue is usable for only a few weeks.

The boat should be deflated when applying the patch. When applying the adhesive (to both the skin and the patch), allow it to dry to a light tack. Test for tack with the back of your finger or hand. Then apply the next coat and again allow it to dry to a tack.

Placement must be done in one step, since the glue will not allow you to reposition the patch. Small circular patches can simply be set in place. Long or more complicated patches will require careful placement. Once the patch is in position, use a blunt instrument to push air pockets out of the glue. Work from the middle outward, smoothing bubbles and wrinkles. Use firmness and take time to work pockets out neatly.

Let the patch cure. If you can put some pressure on the patch, it will help create a stronger adhesion. This can be done by bringing the boat up to shape (but not full pressure) and placing a weighted object on the patch. When the patch has cured, clean off any excess glue from around the edges. If this is overlooked, the excess will discolor in sunlight and leave a messy spot.

The most frequent cause of pressure loss in an inflatable is a valve problem. Although manufacturers use different valves, the common traits are: tight closure, a good seat, and basic maintenance. In all cases, the final seal is the cap. Check your valve for sand or cross-threading; ensure that O rings are properly in place, and check diaphragms or spring-loaded flaps for tight closure.

Ten Tips for Trouble-Free Heads

All week long you've been looking forward to today's cruise—the engine is purring smoothly, the sun is shining, the wind is fair, and all seems well with the world. Then someone comes up from below and announces that the head is clogged or has broken down completely. At the time, of course, you have half a dozen guests on board.

Although most marine heads are surprisingly dependable pieces of equipment built by reliable marine manufacturers, they all require regular maintenance and more care than their shorebound cousins—and they all do break down occasionally. Sometimes it is simply because the head was not properly installed in the first place; sometimes it is because of carelessness (someone may have thrown something into the bowl they shouldn't have); and sometimes it is because of lack of proper maintenance. Only occasionally is a malfunction due to normal wear and tear.

In most cases an unexpected breakdown can be avoided if the skipper takes the time to maintain this essential piece of equipment properly and if he makes certain that all who use the head are familiar with its inherent limitations. This assumes, of course, that the head and its plumbing (inlet and outlet hoses and the seacocks or valves to which they are connected) were properly installed in the first place.

In a properly installed head it is essential that the two through-hull fittings or seacocks be located as far apart as possible—otherwise there is the unpleasant possibility that as the waste is discharged into the water through one seacock, some of it may get drawn back into the bowl through the other seacock. Even where there is a holding tank or an approved treatment device in the system, locating

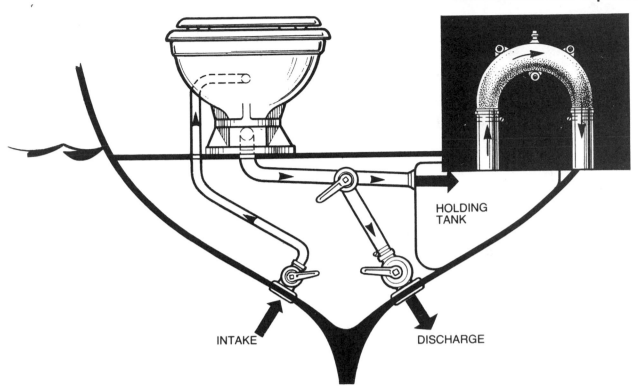

HOLDING
TANK

INTAKE

DISCHARGE

the two seacocks as far apart as possible is still quite necessary.

Probably the best setup is when the two through-hulls are located on opposite sides of the keel. That way there is practically no chance of waste being drawn back in through the inlet seacock. When this is impractical (or impossible), the discharge outlet should be located higher up on the hull than the intake and it should be well aft of it on the hull, so when the boat is under way the waste discharge will be carried behind the boat as it moves forward.

With toilets that are located below the waterline, it is also important that a vented loop be installed in the discharge line before it goes overboard (see opening drawing). If the discharge goes into a holding tank, then the holding tank should be lower than the toilet and the vented loop should be between the holding tank and the discharge or pump-out fitting (assuming the tank is below the waterline).

Another common installation mistake is having too many elbows and bends in the discharge line. A straight run between the head and the holding tank or treatment device, and then between the tank or treatment device and the overboard discharge fitting, is the ideal setup. Where curves are required, try to form gradual bends in the hose, rather than sharp bends or tight curves. And if possible avoid the use of ninety-degree elbows entirely (believe it or not, each elbow in the discharge line adds the equivalent of about another eighteen feet of straight hose to that line).

Since a marine toilet is essentially a mechanical device with a number of parts that are certain to wear out in time, one sure way to prevent being stuck with a nonworking head over a holiday weekend, or during a vacation cruise, is always keep a repair kit on hand. This kit should include all the replacement parts you are likely to need for normal maintenance—rubber O rings, flapper valves, and joker valves, plus miscellaneous gaskets, leather pistons, and any plastic components that the manual says will need replacing periodically.

The easiest way to make certain all these parts are on hand is to buy one of the repair kits sold by almost all manufacturers. These contain all the pieces you are likely to need so you can easily make repairs on the spot when problems develop. Even if you normally hire a mechanic to do the work, at least you know the parts will be there. But make certain you replace any kit parts you use immediately, instead of waiting for the next emergency to occur.

To decrease the possibility of such emergencies, here are ten important rules you should follow to help keep your marine head flushing smoothly all season, every season:

1. When you first come aboard, check to see that the seacocks for intake and discharge outlets are open—and make certain they are fully open, not just partway.

2. Make sure every time the head is flushed with paper or solid waste in the bowl that it is flushed long enough to

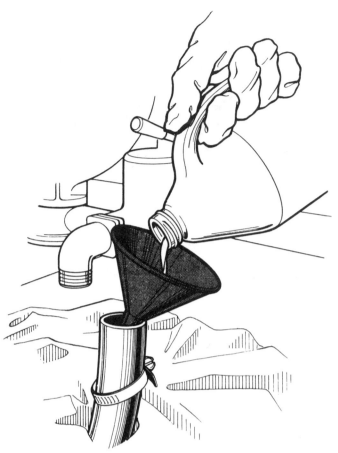

Hardened waste causes clogged lines; but a weak solution of muriatic acid removes buildup.

4. At the beginning of each season (or every two months if you boat year-round) inspect all the rubber parts in your toilet, such as joker valves, flapper valves, and so on. Replace any that look swollen, worn, or torn. At the same time, inspect the O rings and leather washers or pistons in the pump mechanism to see if any of these need replacing.

5. At least once during the season, as well as at the beginning and end of each season, lubricate leather pistons, O rings, and other parts that the manual says should be lubricated. If you're not sure what type of lubricant to use, Vaseline is always a safe bet.

6. If you boat where you occasionally encounter eel grass or lots of floating debris in the water, install a strainer in the intake line to keep this grass from being sucked into the line and then into the toilet itself. Grass or other debris not only clogs the line, it also clogs the small discharge holes around the inside rim of the toilet and is a frequent cause of odors when the toilet is not used for a while.

7. If your system has a Y-valve in it (for direct discharge overboard when you are beyond the three-mile limit), get in the habit of opening and closing this valve several times each year. Flush water through it in both directions (through each side of the Y) at the same time to help clean out waste trapped there. Otherwise solid material, such as the chemical buildup described above, will eventually cause the valve to "freeze" so you won't be able to move the handle.

8. Never use Pine Oil or similar deodorants and disinfectants that contain kerosene or other solvents; these can cause the rubber or leather parts to swell and to become inoperative. If a deodorant is needed to clean the toilet, use Clorox, but don't let it stand in the toilet for more than about one hour.

clear all waste out of the whole length of the discharge hose (the longer the hose, the longer the flush should be). Flushing only long enough to clear out the toilet bowl could still allow solid waste and salt to accumulate in the discharge hose and eventually harden there, partially clogging the hose.

3. To prevent this deposit from becoming thick, use a dilute solution of muriatic acid (one part acid and ten parts water) to clean out the toilet and the inside of the discharge hose. Disconnect the hose from the toilet and hold that end up as high as you can. Pour the acid solution slowly into the hose as shown at the left with the seacock closed, adding only a little at a time. Wait about half a minute to pour more in—just in case it foams over the top of the hose. Be prepared for a very smelly experience and be sure you wear rubber gloves to protect your hands. Also, line the floor of the head area with sheet plastic to catch spills. Let the acid work for about ten minutes, then reconnect the hose, open the seacock, and flush thoroughly.

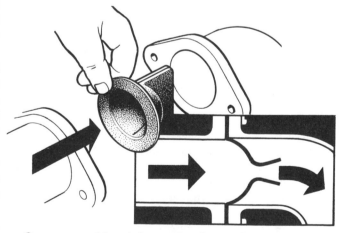

One-way rubber joker valve fits in flange in discharge line and keeps water from backing into bowl.

9. The biggest cause of marine head failure is improper use—especially by landlubber guests who do not realize the limitations of a marine toilet. Make sure all visitors know the rules about not throwing things like paper towels, sanitary napkins, and cigarettes with filter tips into the bowl. The best way to make sure they know the rules is to print up a large sign on cardboard or sheet plastic and hang it in a prominent place inside the head whenever guests are on board. Don't depend on the small plaques or tags that manufacturers supply—many are too small really to catch the eye and often are ignored by those using the head.

10. If you have an electric head, get in the habit of checking all terminals and electrical connections regularly to see if any wires or terminal screws have loosened, or if they are starting to corrode. Connections that do work loose, or those that start to corrode, can cause low voltage—and low voltage always leads to poor flushing action. Spraying at least once a month with a moisture-displacing spray such as WD-40, LPS-1, or CRC is a good way to prevent corrosion and a buildup of moisture that can lead to corrosion.

Maintaining Through-Hull Fittings and Seacocks

Both powerboats and sailboats have underwater openings fitted with valves used to admit cooling water for engines and air-conditioning systems as well as to discharge waste from sinks, heads, cockpit drains, etc. In most cases these hulls are largely ignored until something goes wrong—then the boatowner may find that the valve is stuck in the open position and cannot be closed, or worse yet, the fitting may crack or break while under way. That is why it is important that these fittings—and the hoses connected to them—be checked at least once a year, preferably before the boat is launched.

In a proper seacock, the position of the handle will tell you whether it is open or closed—when the handle is parallel to the hose and the center line of the valve, it is open; when it is at right angles to the center line of the valve, it is closed. Brass gate valves, which sometimes are used as through-hulls, have a round handle that gives no indication of whether it is open or closed. They also require many turns to go from fully open to fully closed, while a seacock opens or closes with a quick ninety-degree turn of the handle. This is one reason why brass gate valves should not be used for underwater through-hulls. Another reason is that the brass used in these valves tends to be very vulnerable to electrolysis and is more prone to "freezing" up or seizing up.

The accompanying drawing illustrates a popular version made by Wilcox and Crittendon and shows how the valve should be taken apart. You disassemble the valve by first removing the locknut and washer that are on the side opposite the handle; then use a wood or plastic mallet to tap the end of the shaft to force it out on the handle side. If it seems frozen and won't come out easily, try using a wrench on the nut that holds the handle in place to turn it and break it loose.

When the tapered plug is out, clean it thoroughly by soaking in vinegar and then rubbing hard with a coarse cloth. If there are scratches on this plug, use fine emery cloth to remove them, or apply valve grinding compound

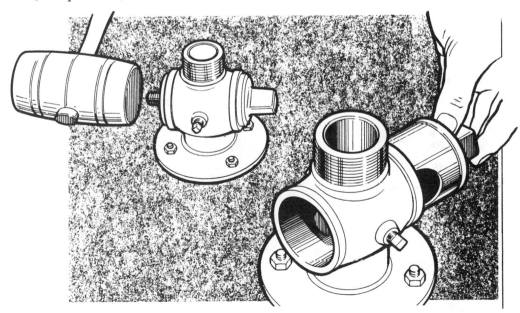

—use this to "lap" the plug inside the valve (by rotating it inside the body after you have smeared the compound around the outside of the plug) until it fits smoothly.

Finish by cleaning the tapered plug with a good solvent, then smearing waterproof grease over it before reinserting it inside its body. Replace the washer and locknut and tighten till the handle seems to have the right amount of tension (two wrenches will be needed for this—one to hold the nut and a socket to turn the locknut). When properly adjusted, the two nuts and the washer should turn together with the handle. Tension on the handle should be such that you can turn it without too much effort, yet it must be tight enough so it will not vibrate closed when under way.

Don't Forget the Hoses

While you are servicing the through-hulls, don't forget to check all the hoses connected to them. Most seacocks remain open all the time, so if a hose lets go, the boat could still be flooded.

Feel each hose to see if it is brittle, exceptionally soft, or exceptionally hard. Replace all those that look the least bit doubtful, especially if they are more than about five years old. When replacing hoses, make sure you get the right type for your particular application, and make sure it is the right size. Some can withstand heat and some cannot; some will not collapse under suction and some will; and some resist attack by oil or fuel, while others will not.

When replacing hoses it is sometimes just as hard to get the new one on as it was to get the old one off. Many times applying a little Vaseline will help. If that doesn't do the trick, try dipping the end of the hose in very hot water for a couple of minutes.

Don't forget to check the fittings on the other end of the hose—the end away from the through-hull. Where possible, use double clamps on all hoses that connect directly to a below-water-level fitting, and make sure the two clamp screws are on opposite sides of the hose (not on the same side). The clamps should be all stainless (not the less expensive automotive types that have nonstainless screws).

Stopping Leaks in Stuffing Boxes

Owners of boats with inboard engines expect to see some water in the bilge, but there is no need to tolerate any more than absolutely necessary—especially in a fiberglass boat.

In most cases the biggest single source of bilge water is a leaking stuffing box, yet many boatowners never pay any attention to these crucial fittings until they really start to pour water. They completely forget that stuffing boxes need routine maintenance just like other parts of the propulsion system, and they don't realize that a neglected stuffing box can cause damage to the propeller shaft and other components in the drive train.

Stuffing boxes are used to seal out water where propeller shafts come through the hull, while still allowing the shafts to rotate freely. They are also used where rudder posts pass through the hull, and for exactly the same reason—to seal out water while allowing the shaft to turn.

As can be seen in the accompanying drawings, a stuffing box (also called a packing gland) is actually a fairly simple device. Designs vary to some extent, but all

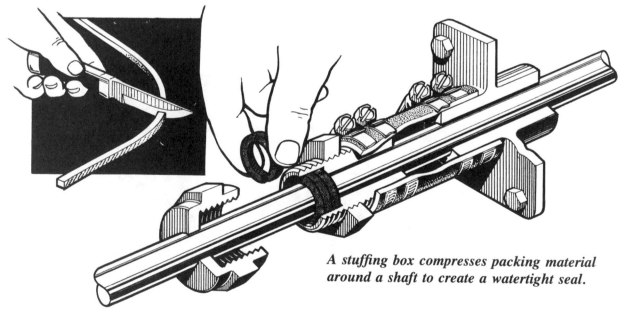

A stuffing box compresses packing material around a shaft to create a watertight seal.

stuffing boxes work on the same general principle: A large hollow packing nut screws on over the outside of a threaded sleeve through which the shaft (either propeller shaft or rudder shaft) passes. The hollow space inside the packing nut and inside the sleeve is filled with a packing material that consists of several rings of braided flax heavily impregnated with wax and lubricants. When the packing nut is tightened around this packing material it compresses it to create a watertight seal around the shaft.

Another variation on this type of stuffing box that is seen on some larger powerboats is the kind shown on page 28. Here the packing nut does not thread on or screw on over the outside of a threaded housing. Instead, one half of the stuffing box serves as a packing gland. It slides inside the other half and is kept in place by two threaded bolts or rods that go through the flanges of both the inner and outer halves of the stuffing box as shown.

Otherwise the principle is the same: Rings of the packing material fit around the shaft and inside the hollow core of the stuffing box sleeve. Tightening the nuts on the two threaded rods on each side squeezes the two halves of the stuffing box together and compresses the wax-impregnated flax on the inside to squeeze it tightly around the shaft.

Since a boat vibrates quite a bit when under way, all stuffing boxes have a locknut threaded onto the same housing as the packing nut. After the packing nut has been tightened, this locknut, which is much thinner than the packing nut, is tightened against it to keep the packing nut from loosening. It must be loosened before the packing can be loosened. (In the type of stuffing box or packing gland pictured on page 28, each threaded rod has two nuts on it—one to tighten the packing sleeve, the other to act as a locknut on each rod.)

Normally, when a stuffing box starts to leak, the first thing the boatowner will do is tighten up on the packing nut until the leak stops—and in many cases this is all that is required. However, it must be remembered that each time you tighten the packing nut you squeeze the packing on the inside a little more and force it tighter around the outside of the shaft.

This often stops the leak, but if you make the packing too tight it can result in damage to the shaft, because each time you tighten down on the packing it gets compressed more and gets packed harder. Finally, most of the wax that kept the flax soft is gone and the material is now hard enough to wear a slight groove in the shaft.

This groove causes the stuffing box to leak more, so you tighten it again—and the flax gets packed still harder. Friction between this now-hard packing and the rotating shaft makes the groove deeper and causes the packing to leak even more—so you tighten down harder and the damage gets still worse. (So does the leak in many cases.)

As with many other problems that crop up on boats, all of this trouble can be avoided by simply following a program of regular preventive maintenance. This means checking the condition of your stuffing box periodically throughout the season and repacking it at regular intervals. For weekend cruisers putting in new packing once every two years is probably adequate; but the job is simple enough (and inexpensive enough) to do every year for those who really want to avoid leaks and other stuffing box problems.

During the season the best way to check the stuffing box is to inspect it visually while the engine is running and the shaft is in gear (in other words, while the boat is underway). If you see a few drops—say, one or two a minute—then you are probably okay, though contrary to popular opinion it is not necessary to have water dripping at all. But if you see water dripping at a faster rate, or spraying out in a continuous mist or stream, then the stuffing box needs repacking, or the packing nut needs to be tightened.

While you are inspecting the stuffing box, carefully place your hand on the outside of it while the boat is running. The stuffing box should feel cool or just barely warm to the touch—indicating that the packing is not overheating. If it feels hot, then the packing nut is too tight or the packing on the inside has overheated because the packing nut has been tightened too many times or because the packing is worn out.

Since tightening a stuffing box is a lot quicker than repacking it (although repacking is not an especially difficult job), it obviously makes sense to try to tighten the packing nut first—unless you know the packing is several years old and has already been tightened several times, or unless the stuffing box felt hot when you touched it while the boat was running.

The first thing you will have to do before you can tighten the packing nut is loosen the locknut and back it off a couple of turns. Most open-end wrenches will not be large enough, so you will find a pipe wrench your best choice for this. If the locking nut is not too tight, you may even be able to use a large pair of water pump pliers or "channel lock" pliers to loosen it.

In many cases the locknut will be jammed on so tightly that you will need a really long-handled wrench to jar it loose—if you have room to swing a wrench that big. If you don't have a long enough wrench to break the locknut loose, or if there is no room to swing the handle of such a wrench, then there is another trick to break the locknut loose: Use a hammer and a punch or nailset as shown in the drawing.

Use the hammer and punch to tap sharply against one of the flats on the outside of the locknut, placing the punch near the end of one of the flats as illustrated so your blow results in a turning action on the nut. One or two taps from

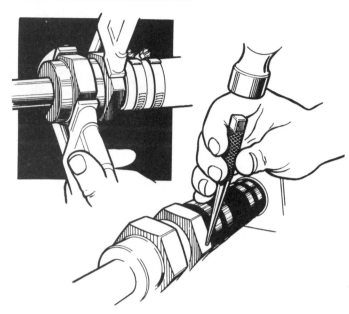

If wrenches don't loosen stubborn nuts, tap with a hammer and chisel, punch or nailset.

spirally wound around the shaft to build up the required numbers of layers. Instead, you should cut each ring as a separate piece that is wrapped around the shaft. Each should be just long enough so that when wrapped around the shaft the two ends will butt together without overlapping and without leaving a gap.

It's important that each piece fits this way—with no overlap and no gaps. Otherwise you are likely to have leaks. Measure the circumference of the shaft with a piece of string, then use this as a guide for cutting the first piece of flax to length. If in doubt, cut the piece a slight bit longer than necessary, then use a sharp knife to trim one end until it fits perfectly. After this first piece is right, use it as a pattern to cut the two or three more pieces you will need.

Loosen the locknut, then back the packing nut completely off its threads and slide it up on the shaft so you can get at the inside. Use a thin screwdriver or a bent piece of

a heavy hammer should do the trick. Once the nut is loosened even slightly, a large pair of pliers will turn it easily so you can back it off.

The packing nut can now be tightened until the leak stops, or slows to only about one drop per minute. Tighten it no more than necessary to stop the leak, then check this by running the engine with the shaft in gear. When you have it just right, use one wrench or pair of pliers to hold the packing nut in place, and use another wrench to tighten the locknut securely up against it.

To repack a stuffing box you will need some of the wax-impregnated flax that is sold for this purpose in marine supply outlets and boatyards. It is square in cross section and comes in various widths that range from ⅛-inch square to ½-inch square.

If you don't know what size packing you need (don't worry, most boatowners don't know until the first time they need it), then you will have to take the stuffing box apart by loosening the packing nut all the way so you can back it away from the shaft bearing. Then measure the space between the inside of the packing nut and outside of the shaft. If the old packing is not all burned and blackened, you may be able to remove it and use it as a guide. Otherwise, try to measure the clearance space closely to get the right size, since the better the packing fits, the easier the job will be and the longer it will last.

Flax packing is sold in rolls, by the foot or by the pound. You have to cut the pieces to length as needed. You will need three or four rings or layers of packing inside the packing nut, but the material should not be

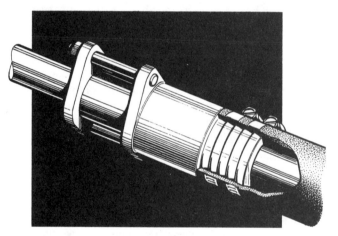

A variation on the double-nut gland is this bolt-tightened type; but the principle's the same.

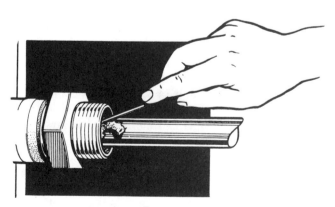

Completely remove the old packing before repacking. A thin screwdriver or bent piece of wire works well.

stiff wire to dig the old packing out of the inside of the packing nut. Work carefully to avoid scratching the shaft and be sure you get all of the old packing out. Remember it, too, was originally put in in layers, so make sure you don't leave any of the old layers still in place. If the packing has turned black, the old material may be easy to miss, as you can't easily distinguish it from the metal around it.

Now install the first ring of packing material, wrapping it snugly around the shaft and stuffing it neatly into its hollow recess. Push it in gently as far as you can with a screwdriver, but try not to cut or dig into the packing material. Now wrap a second ring of the packing material around the shaft and push it in on top of the first one. Make sure you stagger the joints in each layer and keep adding layers till no more will fit (you should get in at least three layers).

When you have inserted as many rings of packing as you can, screw the packing nut back into its threaded sleeve and tighten it as far as you can by hand. Back the nut all the way off again, then look inside to make sure the packing is still smoothly layered—and to see if there is now room for another layer of packing. If so, add it before retightening the packing nut.

Thread the packing nut back on and tighten as much as you can by hand, then use a wrench or pliers to give it an extra half turn. Start the engine and put the shaft in gear, then wait a minute or two and check to see if the stuffing box is leaking. If so, tighten it another half turn and check again. Tighten only till the leaking stops, then take the shaft out of gear and tighten down on the locknut to keep the packing nut from moving. As mentioned, you'll need two wrenches, or two pairs of large pliers to do this—one to hold the packing nut and one to tighten the locknut.

The next time you take the boat out, check the stuffing box again—to see if it leaks (which would mean it needs a little more tightening) or to see if it is getting hot while under way (which would mean the packing nut is too tight and should be loosened slightly).

Teak Maintenance—One Man's Experience

Everyone agrees that teak trim definitely adds a "touch of class" to any boat. Those who do have teak also agree that this is a true love/hate relationship, because in spite of its well-established reputation for being extremely durable and resistant to weather and rot, maintaining teak does take a lot of time and effort.

The first step in maintaining teak, no matter which type of finish you decide to use, is to clean and scrub the wood thoroughly before application of sealer, oil, or varnish.

Theoretically, you need do nothing to your teak except scrub it down occasionally, but as those who have tried going this route can attest (this includes myself), leaving teak untreated usually turns out to be a disaster. In spots it may actually weather to a pleasant silver gray, but it almost never weathers uniformly and usually takes on a mottled, dirty look that varies from light gray to muddy brown in different places.

On the other hand, when properly finished, teak is probably the most beautiful of all marine woods. It takes on a lustrous, rich glow that no other wood can match, and even when water works its way under the finish (as inevitably happens with all exterior wood finishes) the wood doesn't turn dark, as mahogany and many other woods do. Any worn or faded spots on finished teak are generally easier to touch up, so complete stripping and refinishing are not required as often.

Because teak is an oily wood it has a partly justified reputation for not taking well to varnish. Actually, if you take pains to clean the wood properly beforehand and do a good job of building up the required number of coats on the surface, teak can be beautifully varnished with a finish that will last just as well as on any other wood. It's also no more difficult to maintain.

Regardless of the finish you use—sealer, oil, or varnish—there are four rules you must follow:

1. Do your preparatory work thoroughly. Remember that dirt will be locked in for the duration after the finish is put on, so be sure the wood is clean before you start. Teak cleaners must be used with caution. Unless you keep them constantly wet they will discolor and leave streaky stains on paint and fiberglass. Read the directions carefully.

2. Make sure the wood is absolutely dry before you start applying any finish. Then try to get several coats on without long periods of weathering between coats.

3. Don't skimp. Never apply less than the minimum number of coats recommended by the manufacturer. Several thin coats are always better than one heavy coat.

4. Don't wait on maintenance. Apply one or two fresh coats as soon as you see signs of the original finish wearing thin or eroding.

Types of Finish

All teak finishing products can generally be classified in one of two ways: as penetrating finishes or surface coatings.

Penetrating finishes are formulated to soak deeply into the wood so there is very little or no surface film left. This includes all the various teak oils, teak sealers, and similar penetrating-type teak finishes.

Surface coatings are the varnish-type finishes designed for a clear coating on top of the wood. They do soak into the wood to some extent, but the bulk of the finish is on the surface. Most of these coatings build up a lustrous, mirrorlike finish, but some dry to semigloss or satin finish rather than a high gloss.

As the live-aboard owner of a forty-nine-foot trawler with plenty of teak trim around the outside as well as teak decks all the way around, I have had plenty of chances to try out all kinds of teak finishes. Naturally, my "tests" are not conducted in the way that a professional lab might do the job, but they do describe what I have discovered from using these products.

I tried two different brands of clear, two-part polyurethane varnish on various parts of the teak trim on my boat. Both come in new brushable formulations that a boat-owner can apply himself after mixing according to the directions furnished.

One brand recommended using a pigmented paste wood filler on the raw teak before applying the first coat, so I did. Then I brushed on three coats after mixing according to directions. I wound up with a mirrorlike, hard finish that looked beautiful and stayed that way for about a year. After that, however, the coating seemed to be evaporating or fading away in various spots. In many of these places the finish itself still seemed solid and I could see no peeling, but the wood underneath had turned white and looked faded. After a couple of more months exposed to the sun, the finish itself seemed to erode gradually until after eighteen months there were cracking and peeling in numerous places.

Recoating

I tried recoating some of these faded spots as soon as they were noticed—sanding lightly, wiping clean with solvent, then recoating with the same material. The finish on these spots seemed to hold up over the following year, but the spots themselves are still as white and faded-looking as ever. The spots I did not recoat began to crack and peel in numerous places after two years.

The second brand of clear, two-part urethane recommended applying several coats of either a regular marine varnish, or an epoxy varnish, as a base. If you use regular varnish as a base coat, you have to let it cure for at least a month or two before putting the urethane over it. If you use epoxy varnish as a base, you can put the urethane on within a couple of days. Over this the manufacturer recommended brushing on at least three coats of its clear, two-part urethane. I followed these directions exactly (using an epoxy varnish as a base) and ended up with a beautiful, hard finish that shone like a mirror. The finish stayed that way and retained its gloss even after fifteen to eighteen months of constant exposure to the weather.

A New Problem

However, after the first winter (my boat is uncovered all year) I noticed that wherever there was a seam through which water could penetrate and enter the wood under the finish—for example, where two pieces of teak trim were joined imperfectly, or where some caulking was cracked or missing—the urethane film had lifted or separated from the wood underneath so that you could easily pry it off and then peel it away in a solid sheet. The rest of the finish was still tough as nails and retained its full gloss.

Having tried several different sealers and oils on the teak trim as well as on the teak decks, I discovered that there are variations in how much they darken the wood and in how long they last before another coat or two is required. Generally speaking, the teak oils darken the wood less than the teak sealers do, but they also give the wood less of a finished appearance (the wood looks closer to bare wood). Also, the oils do not last as long as the heavier-bodied sealers do.

Advantages of Sealers

Teak sealers have more solids in them, so they stand up better under the damaging effects of sunlight. They tend to

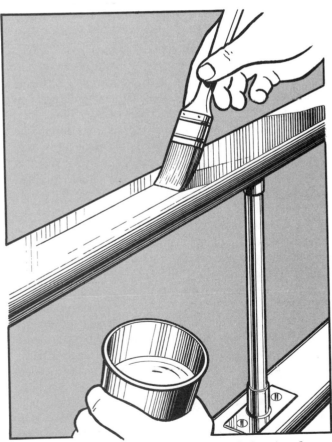

Teak can be successfully varnished, but it takes extra care in both preparation and application.

last a bit longer than the oils, and they build up more of a finish, so generally fewer coats are needed. Most brands will last at least five or six weeks before the finish shows signs of much weathering and another coat has to be applied. This will vary with exposure.

Teak oils and some teak sealers leave a dull finish that is not slippery, so most are excellent on teak decks. However, some sealers do build up enough of a finish to become a bit slippery when wet.

As for regular marine varnish, you should use one with an ultraviolet shield built in as part of its formulation, particularly where the wood is horizontal and will be exposed to lots of sunlight.

After cleaning and bleaching the wood (where necessary), allow the wood to dry thoroughly; then wipe down with a rag saturated with acetone before applying the first coat of varnish. Wear rubber gloves if your skin is sensitive, and remember that the acetone is highly flammable.

The acetone will not only help to dry out any remnants of moisture still in the wood, it will also remove any of the natural oils near the surface.

Thin the first coat of varnish with about 25 percent solvent to ensure thorough penetration, and thin the second coat with about 10 to 15 percent solvent. The third and subsequent coats should be thinned only enough to ensure free flowing and easy application. Avoid working in the direct sun or when the wood is very hot.

At least four to five coats should be applied initially. After this an additional coat should be applied about twice a year, once at the beginning and once toward the end of each season. A light sanding, followed by cleaning and dusting, will be required between coats.

Two Specialized Finishes

In addition to the finishes mentioned above, I have also been experimenting with two other finishes that do not fit into the "typical" categories already discussed.

The first is the popular Deks Olje system. The line consists of the No. 1 and No. 2 oil.

The No. 1 is something like a teak sealer, but with one important exception. The manufacturer recommends applying multiple coats on top of each other without waiting for the previous coat to dry. In fact, you are supposed to apply subsequent coats within about fifteen or twenty minutes of each other, while the previous coat is still wet. This wet-on-wet application method gives better penetration and ensures a full buildup of the finish. Five to six coats are recommended for normal teak, but porous spots may require up to ten or twelve coats if the oil keeps soaking in.

The No. 2 oil is more of a varnish than a sealer. It is

only used after the No. 1 oil has been applied on those surfaces where you want a high gloss finish. It should not be used on decks. Four to six coats are required to build up a lustrous gloss that is exceptionally easy to maintain. No sanding is required between coats, and when it starts to show signs of wear you merely scrub the surface clean, then brush on another coat.

I started out by using the No. 1 oil on the decks, and the No. 1 plus the No. 2 on all the trim or brightwork: caprails, handrails, window frames, etc. In each case I followed the manufacturer's directions.

I found that the No. 1 oil used alone on the decks stood up about the same as any of the other good teak sealers. Originally applied in multiple coats in the early spring, another two coats were needed after about eight or nine weeks (mid-August).

On the brightwork, however, the combination of the two products stood up exceptionally well. I did not have to recoat any of the brightwork that summer, but before winter set in I did apply one more coat of the No. 2 on everything. For almost four years an extra coat was put once a year on the vertical surfaces, twice a year on the horizontal surfaces, and always without sanding before application.

The finish remained glossy, with little or no signs of weathering. One drawback I did discover is that the finish is fairly soft and doesn't take abrasion very well.

However, after the fourth year the finish on all the horizontal surfaces started to break down completely—cracking, eroding, and wrinkling up in places.

In some places this deterioration was all the way down to the bare wood; in others only the last few coats seemed to be affected. I eventually had to sand all the finish down to the bare wood and start the process over.

One other product I have tried does not neatly fall into any of the broad categories described above. A varnish-type finish called Sunshield (Intertrade Corp., 36 Sir William Lane, Toronto Islington, M9A 1V1 Canada) has become quite popular with boatowners in Florida. It comes in both a high gloss and a satin finish, and it has a definite tint, an orange or rusty coloring, due to the heavily pigmented ultraviolet Sunshield.

Pros and Cons

Only two to three coats are required to build up a good finish, and no sanding is normally required between coats. I used the satin finish on the ladder going to the flying bridge, on the teak swim platform, and on some of the deck areas. All stood up very well after a full season of exposure.

The teak ladder was still in excellent shape after eighteen months and didn't look like it needed an additional coat, but I put one on anyway. The finish is still in excellent condition after almost twenty-four months of exposure.

Sunshield does have a couple of drawbacks. First, it is very slow-drying and may take days to lose its tacky feel completely. Second, when used on decks, even the satin finish can be quite slippery if you are barefoot (it's not too bad with most good boat shoe soles). Third, the finish is also very soft and easily scuffed by the slightest bit of abrasion.

Sprucing Up the Panels and Trim on the Inside of Your Boat

There are a great many owners of cruising boats who will spare no effort in maintaining the brightwork around the outside of the their boat yet will virtually ignore the wood panels and trim inside the boat. They will start sanding and varnishing the handrails, toe rails, etc., as soon as the weather breaks in the spring, but except for a casual wiping with a dust cloth, the interior panels and trim get little or no attention from one year to the next.

It's true that because the surfaces on the inside of your boat do not get the wear that outdoor brightwork does, years can go by before the wood and plastic surfaces on the inside will show any real signs of age. But a little attention paid to sprucing up the interior during the "off-season" (when you usually can't work on the outside anyway) will go a long way toward giving your boat that bright look it had when it was new—and will add considerably to the value of the boat when the day comes to sell it or trade it in for a bigger one.

The first step in rejuvenating wood panels or trim that is starting to look dull is to give the surface a thorough cleaning. As the years go by, a scarcely noticeable film of dirt will accumulate on all these surfaces, gradually darkening the color of the wood and creating a cloudy, dull look.

Sometimes washing carefully with a sponge dipped into a mild detergent is all that is required, but as a rule washing is generally not advisable on wood panels. Instead, try wiping down with one of the many cleaner/polishes sold for use on furniture and wood paneling. Experiment on a small area first to see how this comes out. Be sure you keep turning the rag to a clean surface as soon as it gets dirty; otherwise you will wind up just smearing the dirt around.

If this brightens and cleans the finish to your satisfac-

You can bring dull, drab interior paneling back to life if you know which products work best.

tion, then go ahead with the whole job. Finish up by applying a good coat of wax and buffing thoroughly.

If you find that just wiping with a cleaner/polish doesn't seem to help much, then you will have to give the panels a more thorough cleaning. Wipe the surface down with a rag that has been saturated with a nonflammable grease solvent, such as a dry cleaning fluid, or one of the solvents sold in hardware and marine supply stores as a replacement for carbon tetrachloride. Paint thinner also works well, but it is highly flammable, so don't use it unless the interior is well ventilated and there are no open flames (or lit cigarettes) inside the boat. Regardless of which solvent you decide to use, test it first on an inconspicuous corner of the paneling to see what effect it has on the finish.

Start the cleaning job by putting some of the solvent into a small pan or dish. Dip a folded rag into this and squeeze most of the liquid out; then rub on with a circular motion over a small section at a time. Wipe over this same section with a clean, dry cloth to pick up the excess liquid and loosened film of dirt; then move on to the next section. Refold each rag as soon as one side gets dirty, and change to a clean rag when there are no more clean sides left. Discard the solvent and replace it with clean liquid when it gets clouded with dirt.

After cleaning, the finish may look a bit dull and may have an uneven gloss in places. To restore the luster you

can use a wax or furniture polish, but I have discovered that for a more permanent and easier-to-maintain protective coating an excellent product to use is a hard-drying penetrating wood sealer—one that has either a tung oil or synthetic resin base (not linseed oil). Lemon oil and similar polishes will also work, but they need to be renewed more often, and if not thoroughly wiped off they tend to attract and hold dust and dirt.

A sealer that I have used for years with excellent results is a product called Minwax Antique Oil Finish. This is a wood sealer that is designed to give an ''oiled'' finish to previously unfinished wood, or to wood that already has this type of finish on it. However, I have found that it also works well over existing finishes—if you don't put too much on and if the surface is thoroughly cleaned first to remove all wax, polish, and dirt.

To apply, fold a clean piece of lintless cloth into a palm-size pad, then wet this cloth with the oil by holding it over the opening on the can and turning the can over quickly so liquid splashes onto the cloth. Wipe on over a few square feet at a time and wait about five minutes, then wipe down with a dry cloth to remove the excess—but don't rub hard. Wait another fifteen or twenty minutes, then wipe again with another dry cloth, only this time rub hard to buff the finish and bring up the gloss.

You'll wind up with a lustrous sheen that is tough yet

easy to maintain. Any time it gets dull, or gets lightly scratched, the finish can be easily restored by wiping more oil on in the same manner. I have used this same treatment to finish teak and mahogany accessories that were purchased "in the raw"—it's easier than trying to varnish these small pieces.

Touching Up Scratches and Nicks

Fine scratches and small nicks can be touched up so they will be almost invisible. Sometimes all you have to do is wipe on a little sealer as described above—the oil will darken the scratch enough to make it almost invisible.

Otherwise, you can touch the scratch up with a small amount of wood stain, applying it with a small artist's watercolor brush that comes to a fine point. Most paint and hardware stores sell a wide selection of different colors, or you can try one of the various furniture touchup products that are sold in paint and hardware stores. (These come in small bottles, often with little brushes attached to the cap.)

Determining the right color stain may take a bit of experimenting if you cannot find an exact match, so don't be afraid to try. If necessary, add two or more colors together till you achieve the tone or color you need. Test on the actual wood, but wipe off immediately if the color is wrong. Once you have mixed the right color, store in a tightly closed can or jar that is small enough so there is very little air on the inside—the stain will then last for years so you can use it for future touchups.

Remember that a stain will color or tint the scratch to make it less noticeable; it won't actually fill it in. If you want to fill in or smooth over the depression—desirable

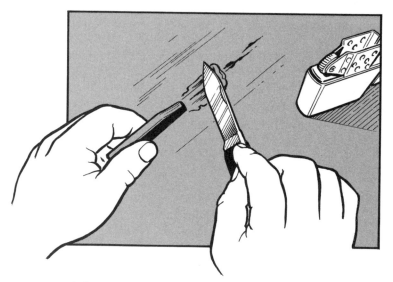

A hot knife works well with touchup sticks when it comes to filling in cracks, nicks, and screw holes.

with deeper scratches that go through the finish—or if there are nicks and screw holes to be filled in, then your best bet is to use one of the wax-base furniture touchup sticks or "pencils" (also called putty sticks) sold for the purpose. Available in almost every wood tone color to match all kinds of paneling, these sticks are designed to be used like a crayon—you rub them back and forth across the crack or hole to fill it in. Then you scrape off the excess with a stiff piece of plastic or the back of a knife blade.

A way to get better results with these touchup sticks is first to heat the blade of a knife in the flame of a cigarette lighter (don't use a candle; its flame is too smoky). Then scrape a little of the wax off the end of the touchup stick with this and use the heated blade to "butter" the wax into and over the depression. Build it up a little higher than necessary, then scrape off the excess with a razor blade or knife blade, but work carefully so you don't scratch the surface of the wood.

If the touchup stands out because it is duller than the surrounding wood, cover it with a little clear shellac, using a cloth wrapped around one finger. Wait about an hour for this to dry, then apply sealer as previously described.

Brightening Plastic Laminates

Panels of plastic laminate (such as Formica) get dull and drab-looking when exposed to the weather or to lots of sunshine—they inevitably bleach out and lose their color to a considerable degree.

Panels that have gotten dull-looking can often be restored by simply wiping on an oil-type polish that is made for use on plastic laminate; several brands are sold in many hardware stores and department stores. I have found that an even better way to rejuvenate these plastic panels when they get dull and faded-looking is to use Penetrol, an oil sold for use with paints and varnishes to make them brush easier.

After scrubbing the plastic clean, allow it to dry thoroughly (usually at least overnight), then pour some of the oil onto a cloth and wipe it on over the surface. Wait about five minutes, then wipe off with a dry cloth to remove all the excess and burnish the finish to build up the gloss. A second coat may be required if the surface is badly worn in places.

In extreme cases you can even apply a coat of clear polyurethane varnish over the laminate, but as a rule this is not a great idea. It's not that the varnish won't restore the luster and stand up well—it's just that eventually the varnish will start to wear off in places and then you will have a devil of a time sanding and removing the rest of it to achieve a uniform appearance before a new coat of varnish is applied over it.

Scratches, nicks, and similar blemishes in plastic laminate are almost impossible to touch up, so in most cases it doesn't even pay to try. Sometimes you can get by with covering them up to conceal the damage—for example, if the damage is on a bulkhead you may be able to hang a picture or lamp over it; if it is on a countertop, you may be able to fasten a cutting block or permanent "hot pad" over it.

If you wish, you can even paint over the plastic laminate to give it a solid color. Fill in any depressions or holes with epoxy putty, then sand these patches smooth. Scrub the surface clean, then sand with #100 sandpaper to knock off the gloss and give the finish some "tooth." Prime with an enamel undercoat, then apply two coats of marine enamel.

Holding That Patch in Place

The only chance most boatowners have to examine the bottom and make needed repairs to the underwater areas of their hulls is while their boats are laid up on land during the winter. Very often this inspection will reveal damage along the keel, or down near the bottom, caused by inadvertent groundings, striking submerged objects, etc. Applying a fiberglass patch to these damaged areas is fairly simple when you use fiberglass cloth and epoxy resin; but sometimes the patch sags—or even falls off entirely—before it cures.

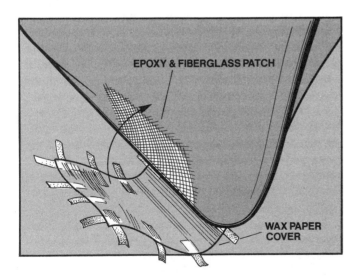

EPOXY & FIBERGLASS PATCH

WAX PAPER COVER

To prevent this, there is a simple trick that will also ensure a smoother patch: Use a piece of wax paper folded to a double thickness to hold the patch in place. After cleaning and roughing up the area, apply the

epoxy-saturated cloth (you should always use epoxy resin, rather than polyester, on underwater portions of the hull) and smooth it out with a brush, adding more epoxy as needed.

Now smooth the wax paper on over the patch and pull it tight, holding it in place with strips of tape (a second person is helpful when doing this). Remove the wax paper after the resin has set up and you will find a smooth, hard surface has formed over the patch. Then you only need to sand the area lightly and you are ready for the first coat of bottom paint.

Gripping a Washer

When assembling small parts you will often find yourself facing the job of putting a small lockwasher on a bolt that is pointing downward in an awkward corner or inaccessible spot. Every time you try to put the nut on, the lockwasher falls off. To solve this problem put a small dab of grease on the bolt or screw before slipping the washer on; the grease will keep it from falling off.

Give Your Boat an Electrical Checkup

For many boatowners the idle months of winter are an excellent opportunity to make repairs and improvements that usually are postponed during the boating season. Getting such work done now also eliminates that familiar midseason lament: "Should we stay tied to the docks today so I can get those chores done, or should we head out to see what the fishing is like?"

Although every conscientious owner remembers to give his engines a tune-up before the start of each season, few think about the need for scheduling a complete inspection of the boat's entire electrical system—including all 120-volt a.c. and twelve-volt d.c. circuits. During winter lay-up, however, you have an ideal opportunity to do just that—well before the spring rush begins and while there is still plenty of time to make needed improvements or repairs.

Most cruising boats have two separate current-carrying electrical systems: the twelve-volt d.c. system that comes from the ship's batteries (or alternators when the engines are running), and the 120-volt a.c. system that is supplied by dockside current when the shore cord is plugged in (or by an auxiliary generator while the boat is under way).

But there is also a third electrical system, the bonding

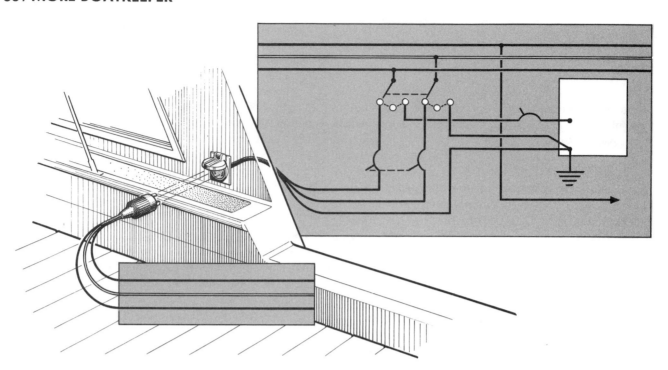

In typical dockside wiring installation three-conductor shore cord plugs into inlet on side of boat.

system, which is not really supposed to carry any current in the normal sense—at least when everything is working properly. Its function is to eliminate harmful stray currents, or electrical "leaks" that can cause electrolysis, by bringing all underwater metal parts to the same voltage potential. In the bonding system, which connects each metal underwater fitting to a common ground (usually the engine or the drive train), the main thing you should look for is a poor connection or a break in one of the grounding cables. Since many of these connections are underwater in the bilge, look for signs of corrosion, as well as loosening of nuts or bolts that connect the bonding wires to the main bonding conductor (usually a substantial copper wire).

Take extra care when inspecting the points where the main grounds are bolted to the engine. Make sure these bolts are right and are making good contact. Even a slight bit of corrosion here can affect the connection. If a connection looks doubtful, remove that bolt or nut and clean the metal with steel wool or an emery cloth. Then tighten firmly and spread a light film of waterproof grease over the connection to help protect against future corrosion.

When testing and inspecting the boat's electrical system, the old adage "If it ain't broke, don't fix it" really isn't a good one to follow, at least not if you want to prevent breakdowns and safety hazards *before* they can create a problem (usually when you are out on the water).

The best place to start is at the main electrical panel, where all the fuses or circuit breakers are located and where the main electrical bus bars are. If the boat has a 120-volt a.c. system in addition to the boat's internal twelve-volt d.c. system, then it is likely that both panels will be located here, although in some cases they may be separately mounted. Be sure you know which panel is which, and make certain each is clearly labeled so anyone can tell what circuit each breaker or fuse controls.

Make sure the a.c. shore cord is disconnected and the main battery switch is off; then, starting at the main panels, use a bright light to inspect each connection on each bus bar and terminal block as well as any other electrical connections you can see or reach. Even if they look fine, use a screwdriver, nut driver, or wrench to test and tighten each one. If the fitting or connection looks corroded, take it apart so you can thoroughly clean the wires and metal parts. After reassembling and tightening, spray all bus bars, terminal blocks, and other connecting points with a moisture-displacing rust-preventive such as WD-40, LPS-2, CRC, or a similar product.

If your electrical circuits are protected by fuses rather than circuit breakers, now is a good time to think about upgrading with new electrical panels that use circuit breakers instead. Circuit breakers make it easier to turn circuits or appliances on and off, and they eliminate the need for looking for spare fuses of the right size in an emergency. They also eliminate the possibility of someone replacing a fuse with a new one of the wrong size, and they make it easy to tell at a glance when a breaker is off. With fuses it is sometimes hard to tell if they are blown—especially when you are trying to inspect a twelve-volt fuse in really dim light.

Another safety improvement to consider is installing ground fault interrupters (GFI's) to a.c. outlets in the cockpit or on the outside of your boat, as well as to toilet or galley receptacles. The national electrical code requires these in all outdoor and damp locations in a house, but they are also just as valuable a safety precaution on most boats. The purpose of a GFI is to shut off the flow of current instantly when there is the slightest leakage of current to ground because of a short or defect in the wiring.

Contrary to what most people think, a fuse or circuit breaker won't save you from a dangerous shock if a short causes the housing on an appliance or tool to become "hot." That's because a fuse or circuit breaker doesn't react fast enough—but a GFI will. In other words, fuses are there to protect the wiring and the appliances from a dangerous overload; GFI's are designed to protect people who happen to touch them.

After inspecting the main panels and cleaning or tightening where necessary, start inspecting all wiring in the engine room and in the below-decks spaces. Check over all twelve-volt wiring leading to pumps, lights, and other current-using equipment inside and outside the boat.

Starting at the battery, take off the main cable connections and clean the terminal posts thoroughly. Then clean the cable ends with steel wool before replacing them. Tighten firmly, then coat the posts and the cable ends with a light film of Vaseline or a waterproof white grease. At the same time, check the cable connections to each of the main battery switches to make certain they are still tight, then spray each connection with a light film of rust-preventive oil to keep moisture out.

Use a bright light to follow the path of all wiring you can see in each compartment, regardless of whether it is a twelve-volt d.c. or 120-volt a.c. Take a close look at all connections that have been insulated by wrapping with plastic electrical tape; many times this tape will have to be replaced after a year or so because plastic tape doesn't hold up very well inside an engine compartment or where high heat is often encountered. If it has started to unravel or has become gummy and soft, remove it and replace with fresh tape.

A product that I have found works even better in damp locations, or in places where tape is difficult to apply neatly, is a brush-on coating called Liquid Lectric Tape. Sold in marine supply outlets and hardware stores, it is made by Marine Development & Research Corp., 116 Church Street, Freeport, N.Y. 11520. It's handy for sealing terminal connections as well as wire splices since

it dries to a thick vinyl coating that is just like a molded cover—making it ideal for electrical insulation as well as for protecting against loosening due to vibration.

Vibration is always a problem on boats, so make sure all cables and wiring harnesses are firmly supported with cable clamps or plastic tie wraps that are close enough together to keep the wires from swinging around and chafing. Cable clamps should be of plastic, or of metal that has been covered with rubber or plastic on the inside.

If you haven't already done so, hook up the battery cables and turn on the main switches. Now individually turn on each light, pump, and other piece of electrical or electronic equipment to make sure everything is working properly. If not, take steps now to pinpoint the source of the problem and to make any needed repairs.

If, for example, one of your cabin lights doesn't work, then the first thing you would check is the bulb. If the bulb is okay, use a voltmeter or test light to see if current is actually getting to that fixture. To do this, disconnect the wires leading to the fixture and touch the leads from the test light, or from the volt/ohm meter, to these wires to see if there is current flowing (make sure the circuit breaker is on).

If there is current coming to the fixture through those wires, then you know the fixture is at fault; if there is no current coming through the wires, then there is a break in one of the wires. To find out which wire is broken, use a continuity tester (this consists of a test lamp with its own battery to supply power for the lamp) or a volt/ohmmeter to check each wire for continuity. Shut off the d.c. Connect one lead from the test meter to one end of the wire and the other test lead to the other end of that same wire. Since the wire ends may be many feet away from each other, you may have to use an additional length of wire to connect one leg of the meter (or continuity tester) to the far end of that wire.

When trying to locate the actual break in the wire it is usually helpful to check the wire at various points. Note that if the test leads (from the test lamp or meter) are touched to any two places along an unbroken section of wire the test lamp will *not* light, even though the wire being tested is connected to a source of current. That's because current will flow through the wire (less resistance) rather than through the test lamp. However, when the test leads straddle a break, then the bulb *will* light because now the test lamp will complete the circuit (bridge the break) so current flows through the test light.

On some occasions a test light is more effective than a meter for determining where the problem lies. For example, if there is a switch in the circuit that is making poor contact yet is still allowing current to flow, then a meter would indicate continuity because it is so sensitive—even a very small part of the needed current will cause the

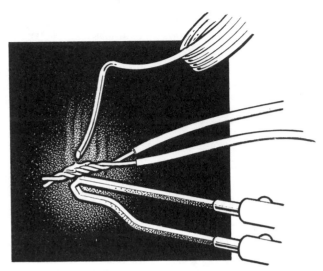

For a good connection, let the soldering iron heat the wires and then let the wires melt the solder.

needle to swing over. A test light, on the other hand, probably would not light up at all, or if it did light would be very dim, thus indicating that there is a problem, even without a complete break. This can be particularly important in circuits that supply power to electronic equipment; low power may cause erratic operation.

Here are some other points to keep in mind when making electrical repairs, or when wires have to be replaced or spliced:

● Never splice wires by simply twisting the ends together and then wrapping with tape. Instead, use crimp fittings or twist the ends into a pigtail and solder all the wires together, then wrap with electrical tape.

● To make a good soldered connection you should not melt the solder with your soldering iron or gun. Instead, use the iron to heat the metal wires (and the terminal to which they are being joined) until the wires are hot enough to melt the solder on contact. Hold the soldering iron or gun under or behind the wires, then apply the solder from the other side when you think the joint is hot enough. If it is, the solder will not only melt, it will also be drawn smoothly into the joint between and around the wires. If it lies over the surface only, then the joint is still too cold.

● When splicing wires, don't just spiral them around each other end to end, even if you plan to solder them. Instead, twist the ends together pigtail fashion, then solder. You can then wrap with tape or insulate the connection by twisting on a plastic "wire nut"—the kind normally used in house wiring inside a junction box.

● Never use these solderless "wire nut"-type connectors to splice wires inside a boat. Even though they are approved for use on land, they are *not* approved for use in

boats. Instead, join wires by soldering as described above, or use suitable-size crimp fittings (it's best to wrap these with tape, even if the fittings are insulated). Better yet, join 120-volt a.c. wires by splicing inside a regular junction box.

● Do not use solid-core metal wire and cables for 120-volt a.c. wiring inside a boat. All current-carrying a.c. cables should consist of *stranded* wire conductors, never solid-core wire. Solid wire will break when it is subject to constant vibration.

● While inspecting the 120-volt a.c. wiring, make sure the green ground wire is continuous and uninterrupted throughout the system. Also make sure it is solidly connected through the shore cord to the green wire on the dock. Don't make the mistake of disconnecting this wire to minimize electrolysis—in some cases it will help with this problem, but only with greatly increased risk of someone on or near the boat getting a dangerous shock.

Three Helpful Publications

For those who want more information, three helpful little books are:

● *Shore Power: Basic AC Electrical Systems on your Boat;* $3.75, from Marinco Electrical Products, 92 Hamilton Drive, Ignacio, Calif. 94947.

● *The 12 Volt Doctor's Practical Handbook;* $24.95, from Spa Creek Instruments Co., 616 Third Street, Annapolis, Md. 21403.

● *The 12 Volt Doctor's Alternator Book;* $17.75, also from Spa Creek (see above).

The Best Way to Paint Fiberglass Yourself

Everyone knows that fiberglass boats are virtually maintenance-free—that is, until the gel coat gets scratched and dull-looking and the whole boat begins to look faded.

Of course, regular washing and waxing will help keep the gel coat bright and shiny for years and can theoretically maintain its life almost indefinitely; but in the real world many boatowners find that there comes a time when the only way to restore the original brilliance to their boat is to give it a good paint job. The best way to do this is to have it painted professionally by an experienced shop with a good reputation. A professional painter will spray a boat with multiple coats of a two-part polyurethane such as Awlgrip or Imron and often make it look even better than new.

Finish coats are best applied by two people, using both a foam roller and high-quality brush.

Doing It Yourself

But what do you do if you can't afford the thousands of dollars it costs to have a professional shop do a job of this kind? Can a boatowner do it himself and get good results? The answer to these questions is a qualified yes: If you have the patience and if you take the time and trouble to follow directions and do all the preparatory work, and if you are realistic in your expectations, then you can get beautiful results that you will be proud of—maybe not as picture-perfect as a professional job, and maybe one that won't last quite as long, but a good-looking finish that you will have no reason to be ashamed of.

If you want to paint a typical fiberglass pleasure boat, here is how to go about tackling the job yourself. First, remember that it will take more than just a couple of days. If you were to have the boat done professionally, the shop would keep it for at least two weeks in most cases, so don't plan on rushing the job if you do it yourself. Since you will probably be working outside, plan for a period of mild, dry weather (fall is a good time), but also plan on being held up by bad weather.

One of the first decisions you will have to make is whether you want to use a regular alkyd marine enamel, or one of the new two-part polyurethane paints that now come in brushable formulations. I do not advise an amateur to spray any of these finishes, or to use the ''professional''-grade urethanes made for spraying. First of all, spraying requires good equipment and more than a little practical experience. Also, the solvents or reducers used for spraying are quite toxic, so you need plenty of good ventilation and special face masks to protect yourself

(but this is not a problem when the paint is applied by brush or roller).

Here are some other points to consider when trying to decide between using a regular alkyd marine enamel and a two-part brushable urethane:

● Alkyds are much easier for the average amateur to work with and to smooth off. They are not as sensitive to temperature and humidity when you are working with them.

● Properly applied, two-part urethanes will have a slightly higher gloss, but they can be the devil to smooth out when temperatures climb up into the nineties and humidity is high. You don't want to work with them when weather conditions are in that range. It's best to apply the two-part urethanes when temperatures are between 70° and 80° F. and when humidity is between 45 and 75 percent.

● Alkyds are more ''forgiving'' when you apply them. They tend to flow out smoother even if your workmanship is a little careless, or if you don't thin them properly. Two-part polyurethanes must be carefully thinned for each application—a little too much thinner and they will run and drip; not enough thinner and they will be ropey and hard to apply smoothly.

● Generally, the two-part urethanes will hold their gloss longer and last longer than the alkyds under similar exposures and conditions. You can expect an alkyd job to last about three years, but a good job done with two-part polyurethane will last from five to seven years in many cases.

● The two-part polyurethanes require more coats because they go on in thinner layers. Thus with urethane you need multiple thin coats (three to five coats); alkyds form a thicker coat so you can usually get by with fewer applications.

● The polyurethanes cost quite a bit more than the alkyds.

Preparation Is Crucial

Regardless of which one you select, remember that most of the work is done before you ever open the first can of finish paint. The success of every paint job depends to a great extent on how much care you take when you prepare the surface.

The first step is taking off as much of the deck and ornamental hardware as you can, and the more the better. Wherever possible remove cleats, moldings, ladders, lights, railings, etc. This will not only make sanding and preparation easier, it will also make it simpler to flow the paint on smoothly without creating lap marks or breaks in the finish. And it will give you a chance to have some hardware replated, or to replace it if pitting and corrosion have destroyed the appearance of the old pieces. Anything that cannot be removed, or that won't get painted, should be protected with masking tape—preferably the thin-line type that the pros use (it costs about three times as much and is harder to find in some areas, but it's worth it).

Next come sanding, filling, and smoothing—probably

Two-part epoxy surfacing compound is best for filling in scratches, gouges, and other defects.

the most tedious and time-consuming part of the job, but also the most important. Assuming that the fiberglass has never been painted before, the first step should be wiping the surfaces down with some type of solvent wash to remove all traces of wax, grease, and mold-release agent (this may have been left on since the boat was originally manufactured).

Filling the Holes

Grind or sand off any blisters that are evident in the gel coat, then fill the remaining recesses with a good-quality epoxy surfacing or fairing compound. Use this same material to fill in and smooth over all scratches, gouges, dents, and other defects. Don't stint on this part of the job, since defects will be much more noticeable when the new finish is applied. Use a plastic spreader or applicator rather than a metal putty knife to apply the filler, and apply several coats where needed to fill in completely. Sand carefully with #120 paper to remove rough spots, then with #220. Dust thoroughly, then wipe down the whole area to be painted with solvent or reducer. For this, use the thinner that you'll mix with the finish coats of paint.

The next step is applying a suitable coat of primer. It will serve as a base coat for your finish and also will fill in very small scratches and craze marks. If in doubt as to which primer to use, read the specifications or label of the paint you will be applying as a finish coat, then buy the one recommended by that manufacturer.

Brush the primer on carefully, with a brush at least three inches wide, or use a foam roller made for the purpose. Allow to cure for the time recommended on the label, then sand lightly with #120 or #150 sandpaper. Dust carefully,

Removing as much hardware as you can makes both sanding and painting easier.

wipe down with thinner, then apply a second coat if necessary (or recommended). A second coat is needed if the surface still has noticeable scratches or other dents that didn't get filled in by the first coat, or if the sanding cut through the primer in some places.

The Intermediate Coat

If the fiberglass has been painted before, then you may not need the same kind of primer. After patching and smoothing with filler you can use a regular undercoat if you will be painting with an alkyd enamel. If you will be painting with a two-part polyurethane, use an intermediate "tie coat" for the first coat as recommended by the manufacturer (some urethanes have solvents that will lift regular paints when applied directly over them). This intermediate coat will be a paint that will not "lift" the old paint yet will serve as a solid base for the new urethane.

The Finish Coats

The finish coats can be put on with brush or roller, but I have found that one of the best ways to get a really smooth finish is to use both—a foam roller to put the paint on, then a brush to tip it off and smooth it out. On most jobs this is best accomplished when two people work together—one putting the paint on with the roller, and one following right behind with the brush.

It is important that you use the right kind of roller and brush for this work if you want to get professional-looking results. The roller must be made of a plastic foam that will not soften or shred when attacked by the solvent in the paint; some cheap foam roller covers will literally fall apart when used with two-part polyurethane paints. Most marine supply stores now carry roller covers suitable for this kind of job. The brush should be of top-quality badger hair, or contain a high percentage of badger hair (the rest would be natural bristles). This type is not cheap—you can expect to spend from $20 to $40 for a three-inch-brush—but it is the only kind that will really do the job.

If possible, try to work in the shade, or on a day when there is very little sun. Avoid painting when temperatures are above 90° or below 60° F., and don't apply polyurethanes when the humidity is uncomfortably high. Make sure everything is ready and then start rolling the paint on a section at a time, working at a steady pace and not stopping till you come to a natural break in the surface.

The second person should follow behind with the brush. Do not dip this in the paint. Just use it lightly to smooth out air bubbles, ripples, and lap marks. Don't press hard, and use the flat side of the brush only; never use it edgewise. Only the tips of the bristles should come in contact with the paint while you are working.

Brush from the just-painted area back toward the previously painted area, and never lift the brush straight off the surface at the end of the stroke. Instead, arc it up and away from the surface gradually so there are no discernible brush marks or breaks left in the finish where the brush comes off the surface. Don't forget to get close to moldings and edges, and pick up more paint only when absolutely necessary to fill in a "holiday" or skip mark. Wipe excess off the brush if it accumulates enough to cause running or dripping.

If the boat has varnished brightwork on deck or as trim around the cabin sides and hull, then this, too, will have to be refinished. The wood should all be sanded down before the fiberglass is painted, then scrubbed clean if necessary with a teak cleaner or bleach. Allow to dry thoroughly, then cover with masking tape and paper before going ahead with the painting.

Finishing Woodwork

Wait for the paint to dry before you remove the masking tape, then wipe the wood down with thinner. Start applying the first coat of varnish or sealer, depending on the type of finish you are using. With sealers, follow directions on the package as to the number of coats required and how many coats should be applied. With most varnishes, at least three coats will be required to build up a decent finish—four to five will look better and will last longer.

Remember that if masking tape must be applied to the new paint during this varnishing operation, you must wait at least several days during nice weather for the paint to cure before pressing tape over it. Even after waiting for this period, test first in an inconspicuous spot by pressing the tape over the paint. Allow it to set for about an hour, then peel it off to see if it causes the paint to lift.

How to Prevent Mildew

It's one of the first nice weekend days in early spring so you've come down to the boat to start getting ready for the coming season. You step into the cabin and immediately shrink back. There is a terrible musty odor and, worse yet, when you look around you see signs of mildew everywhere. Ugly grayish stains and dark blotches are visible on many of the cushions, in the head, around the galley cabinets, and even on some of the bulkhead partitions. Many hours of work will be required to clean up this mess, and some of the mildewed fabrics may even have to be replaced.

Although this scenario is all too familiar to many boatowners, it is not necessarily something you have to expect or tolerate. Mildew *can* be prevented—or at least

Mildew-fighting measures include the installation of vents, electric heating cable, and proper cushion storage.

greatly minimized—if you are familiar with what it is and how it grows, and if you take a few commonsense precautions to keep it from ever getting started inside your boat.

Mildew is a growth produced by microscopic plants called molds, which are one of the many forms of fungus. The tiny spores that cause this growth are invisible and are present in the air almost everywhere. However, only when these spores settle on a surface where conditions are just right for further growth do they thrive and start causing problems.

They will thrive wherever they can find the conditions they need to grow: a relatively warm place where there is moisture present but no sunlight, little if any circulation of air, and of course something to feed on. They are particularly fond of paper, fabric, leather, wood, and other organic materials found in many paints and adhesives, but

they will also form on less porous materials such as plastic or fiberglass under certain circumstances—for example, if the surface is continually damp and is covered with a film of dust, dirt, grease, or other foreign matter.

Mildew needs warmth to grow, yet it often grows most rapidly when warm days are followed by chilly nights, because the warm and humid air trapped inside the boat during the day is chilled when it comes in contact with cold surfaces during the night and the moisture in the air condenses to form droplets of water (much like a cold can of beer ''sweats'' on a hot day). If there is no circulation of air to dry this moisture out, mold spores settle in and mildrew soon starts to grow rapidly.

As the mildew spreads, it often gives off a musty odor (most noticeable in confined or enclosed spaces) and starts to eat into and destroy the material it is attacking. Fabrics, papers, leathers, and similar materials are quickly discolored, and if the mildew is neglected long enough it will finally start to rot and disintegrate the material on which it is growing.

Preventing Mildew

Since mildew is a lot easier to prevent than it is to get rid of, your best defense is doing everything possible to eliminate the conditions it needs to grow and thrive. First you must minimize the amount of dampness in the air inside the boat—admittedly not a simple problem in a marine environment. The most important weapon in the battle against dampness is ventilation; the more you allow air to circulate, the better your chances of preventing mildew.

Dorade vents that allow air to flow through continually are essential. Some vents should be facing into the wind to catch prevailing breezes, while others should face in the opposite direction to allow air to flow out. It also helps if you can leave some hatches or ports open slightly, but this will obviously be limited by security considerations and by the need to keep rain out when you are not on board.

In addition to providing for air to circulate from outside, making sure that this outside air can circulate into the boat, it is also important to provide a way for air to circulate in all those closed-off spaces that are found in every interior. If locker doors and cabinet doors are solid, cut some openings in these doors or in the sides of the cabinets so you can install louvered vents or grilles that will allow air to flow through. In hanging locker doors it is best to install two vents in each door—one near the

bottom and one near the top—so dampness that does get trapped inside the locker will have a better chance of drying out before mildew can form.

As a live-aboard for many years, I have found that "sweating" or condensation inside large hanging lockers is often a problem that leads to mildew. Vents do help, but in cold weather they are often not enough. A trick that I found works particularly well is buying some of those electric "damp chasers" or "heating rods" sold in many marine outlets. These plug into ordinary a.c. outlets and subsequently give off mild heat that helps to dry out the inside of the space in which the rod is located.

Heating Cable

Even more effective than using these rods is using a length of electrical heating cable—the kind sold in hardware stores for protecting pipes against freezing. I use a brand called Frostex (made by Raychem Corp., 300 Constitution Drive, Menlo Park, Calif. 94025) because it does not require a separate thermostat and can be cut to any length needed (other heating cables cannot be cut to a designated length).

As shown in the drawing, this cable is curved back and forth across the cold outside bulkhead of the locker so its heat is uniformly spread throughout the locker to help keep the inside dry. The heating cable is held in place with short strips of duct tape, and the end of the heating cable is plugged into the nearest AC outlet. It needs no further attention, since it gives off heat only as needed; the colder it gets (and the more the chances of condensation forming), the more heat it gives off. When outside temperatures rise, the amount of heat given off is cut back proportionately.

Another thing that helps when you leave the boat, even for a few days, is to pull all the cushions away from their backrests so air can flow behind them. Also, prop up seat cushions and bunk cushions so air can circulate under and around them. Pay particular attention to where the ends or sides of a cushion or mattress butt up against a bulkhead or against the side of the boat. Mildew often forms at these sites because air cannot circulate and dry these areas out when condensation does form.

Of course, when you are cruising or staying on board, leaving cushions propped up or strewn about can be a mess. But make sure you check frequently under and around each cushion or mattress after a chilly night or morning. Dry off any dampness you do feel and then spray with a mildewcide or household disinfectant spray that will help discourage the growth of mildew.

A trick that often helps prevent condensation and mildew where the edge of a thick mattress or bunk cushion butts up against the side of the hull is to buy some porous air filters—the kind sold for use in home air conditioners.

To keep the head mildew-free, spray drains and other damp areas with household disinfectant.

Cut these filters in strips that are as wide as the cushion is thick, then wedge these strips between the edge of the cushion and the side of the boat, as shown in the drawing. The porous filter material will allow air to circulate and thus will minimize the chances of condensation forming between the cushion and the solid surface next to it.

Dry Everything Thoroughly

Since anything that adds to the humidity inside the boat increases the chances of mildew forming, it is foolhardy to bring wet clothes, wet lines, wet sails, or other wet gear inside the boat. These items should all be dried outside before bringing them below. If you can't hang them to dry outside, take them home with you and dry them out there before stowing them inside the boat. Also, remember that mildew thrives best on dirty surfaces and on materials that are soiled or sweaty—so don't pile up damp or sweat-stained and dirty clothes inside the boat. Have everything cleaned or washed before you put it away. Even sweaty sneakers or boat shoes should be dried outside and cleaned or sprayed with a disinfectant (sold in shoe stores) before storing. Make sure there is plenty of ventilation when you are cooking or washing up, and keep the bilge and the spaces under the floorboards as dry as you can at all times—especially when the boat is closed up and unventilated.

Chemical dehumidifiers like De-Moist (made by Coughlan Products, Inc., P.O. Box 409, Franklin, N.J. 07416) can also help a lot. It comes in bags of twelve ounces and

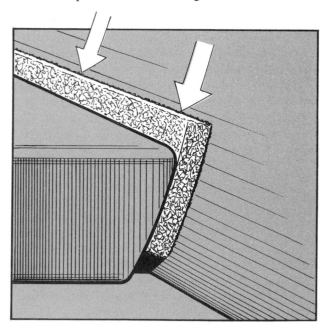

Porous air filters wedged behind cushions and mattresses allow air to circulate in these trouble spots.

fifty ounces, so you can hang it up inside lockers, heads, and staterooms. The granules inside the bag will absorb moisture until they are well saturated, but they will not drip. Then if you heat them in an oven for about an hour, the granules will dry out so you can use them again and again.

In drawers and wherever books are stored packed closely together, spread mothballs or moth flakes around. This is not a drying chemical, but it does give off vapors that help discourage the growth of mildew. The only disadvantage is that you will have to learn to live with the smell of the mothballs after the boat has been closed up for a while. And of course you will have to replace the mothballs as soon as they evaporate.

There are times when, in spite of all your precautions, mildew will show up anyway. So what do you do? Take action immediately. The quicker you get rid of the mildew the less it will spread and the less damage it can do.

Because mildew will not survive whenever there is plenty of sunlight and air, the first thing you should do is carry all removable items outside. Spread them out in the sun—away from the boat, if possible. Then use a vacuum or brush to get rid of as much of the mildew growth as you can. Do all this outside where possible, to avoid spreading the spores inside the boat. If you are using a vacuum, remember that the spores will be drawn into the bag, so empty it outside the boat as soon as possible.

To help ventilate objects that cannot be carried outside, and to do a thorough job of ventilating the inside of the boat itself, open all ports and windows and use fans where necessary to help circulate air and dry out all damp corners and crevices. It's also another good idea to use a portable heater to help dry everything thoroughly.

The Cleaner the Better

Anything that won't be harmed by washing should be scrubbed with soap and water, but be sure you rinse thoroughly to get rid of all soap residue. Baking soda and water work better than soap or detergent on some materials. Either way, after washing, rinse thoroughly, then allow to dry in the sun if feasible. Otherwise, use an electric dryer or blower to speed drying if you can. If mildew stains remain, try bleaching with a solution of lemon juice and salt. Let dry in the sun, then rinse with plain water.

If there is mildew on surfaces or materials that won't be harmed by a chlorine bleach, wash them down with a solution of liquid laundry bleach and water. Mix one part bleach with four parts water and wipe on liberally. Let this dry on the surface, then rinse off with lots of water and wipe dry. If the stains get lighter but still remain, then just repeat the washing process.

For cleaning mildew spots and stains on vinyl curtains,

shower enclosures, cockpit cushions, and deck furniture, I have found that the various mildew removers sold in marine stores work even better than bleach. MDR Mold Away (made by Marine Development & Research Corp., 116 Church Street, Freeport, N.Y. 11520) and Boaters Choice Mildew Remover (made by Boaters Choice, Inc., P.O. Box 700398, Miami, Fla. 33170) are two products of this kind that I have found work well on these surfaces. It also helps to spray damp places, like shower drains and behind toilets, with a household disinfectant such as Lysol Spray, as shown.

Mildew stains on leather and on fabrics that cannot be washed with water can often be removed by wiping with a cloth that has been dipped into a solution of half rubbing alcohol and half water. Dry with a fan or by hanging the objects outside in a breeze. On leather and some fabrics, thick soap suds (with little or no water) often work well. Scrub on with a sponge or soft brush, then wipe off with clean, damp cloths. Spraying with a mildew spray or a household disinfectant also helps remove the mildew and prevents it from returning.

Paper goods such as books, charts, etc., that show signs of mildew should be vacuumed to get rid of loose mold after taking them outside. If books are damp, fan the pages out in the sun to dry and sprinkle cornstarch or talcum powder between the pages, then shake this powder out after several hours. If the paper is washable or dampproof, wipe with a cloth wrung out in thick soap suds, then with another cloth dipped into plain water. Dry with paper towels. Before storing, sprinkle moth flakes between the pages or inside the folds of the charts.

Washing Sails the Easy Way

Owners of sailboats often neglect to clean their sails at the end of the season, or at the end of a long cruise, because professional cleaning is too expensive and they just don't have a tub or basin large enough to do the job at home. As a result, mildew is a fairly common problem on sails that have salt spray on them—especially when the sails are stored in dark, damp locations like the forepeak of the boat or a hanging locker or lazarette.

Fortunately there is a safe, simple method you can use to wash your sails yourself, right on the dock. Stuff the sail loosely into its regular sailbag, then use a hose to fill this bag with water and to flush away any salt crystals that may be embedded in the sail fabric. Adding a little lemon juice to the water also helps. If your sailbag has lots of leaky seams and won't hold water long enough to permit you to fill it, line it on the inside with a large plastic garbage bag before you start your task.

After the bag is full of water, slosh the sail around on the inside to wet all parts of the sail thoroughly. Dump out the water, then take the sail out and spread it on the grass in the sun until it dries completely. Don't hang it on a clothes line because it's harmful to allow sailcloth to flap around and snap in the wind. Fold the sail up and store after it is thoroughly dry.

Emergency Steering Cable Repair

One day I had my boat all loaded and ready to go when I discovered that there was something wrong with my steering—the wheel turned too easily and didn't seem to be moving the rudder. I started tracing the steering cable from the flying bridge down and soon found the problem. Where the cable passed near the engine the outer cable housing had chafed through and the inner cable was just pushing in and out of the broken housing as the wheel was

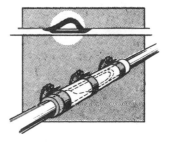

turned. The inner cable was not broken, but since it was not confined inside its housing it was not turning the rudder mechanism—it was just bulging out.

Rather than calling off the whole day's outing, I decided to try to make a temporary repair. I took a piece of half-inch PVC plastic pipe that was longer than the broken section of cable and used a hacksaw to slice this pipe in half lengthwise. I then oiled the cable where it was exposed and slipped the PVC pipe halves over the cable so the pipe would act as a temporary housing to confine the inner cable. Then I applied three stainless hose clamps around the outside to clamp the split pipe in place on the cable. This resulted in a steering cable that worked as good as new again. In fact, this "temporary" repair has lasted three years.

Give Your Boat a Midsummer Spruce-up

Although most boatowners traditionally think of spring as the time when they do what is necessary to maintain the bristol appearance of their boat—varnishing, painting, polishing, and so on—the experienced skipper soon learns

that there are never really enough spring weekends to tackle all these chores before the boating season gets under way. Even if he does manage to finish everything, maintaining a boat in shipshape condition is an ongoing process.

That is why it is a good idea to spend a few hours giving your boat a midsummer spruce-up. You can also catch up on repairs you may have been neglecting till now or that you didn't have time for earlier. (Remember, it is always easier to "touch up" a slightly damaged finish or brighten a partially dulled surface than it is to start from scratch.)

Varnish

Most professionally maintained yachts can keep that beautiful "showroom look" because the crew is constantly touching up the brightwork. All varnishes start to lose some of their luster after a few months. In addition, any injuries to the finish must be promptly repaired or water will get underneath·and do even more damage. That is why midseason attention to varnish is necessary.

The first and most important step is touching up nicks and small spots where the varnish has lifted or has been scraped off. First, sand each spot with a small piece of #220 sandpaper wrapped around your finger. If the wood has turned dark—often a problem with mahogany—you will have to go deep enough to remove the stain, which

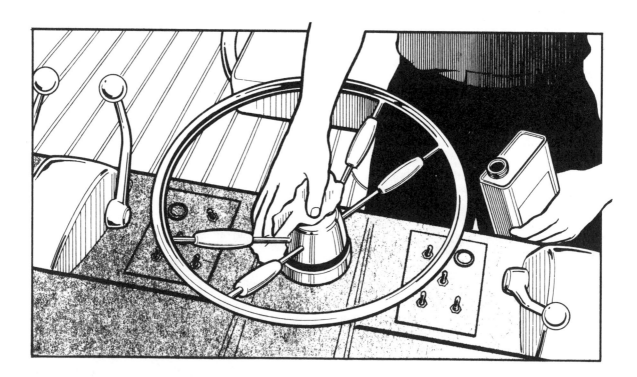

A midseason coat of liquid wax will help keep chrome and stainless hardware from oxidizing.

may mean sanding a larger area than you intended. If the stain is so deep that sanding won't remove it, you will have to try to bleach it.

Small spots may come out with ordinary liquid laundry bleach. Apply this to the darkened area with a cotton-tipped swab and allow the wood to dry. If the spot gets lighter, repeat the process two or three more times and then rinse the area with lots of water and allow it to dry completely before you go any farther. If the laundry bleach doesn't help much, or if the spot is too large for spot-treating in this way, you will have to strip the wood completely so you can use a regular two-part wood bleach, and then refinish it.

After the wood has been sanded and bleached (if necessary), apply a light coat of varnish to the damaged spot with a small artist's brush. Be sure you keep the varnish inside the damaged area, because any runover will cause a buildup that will show through when you apply a full coat of new varnish over the entire surface. If the excess gets smeared onto the surrounding surface, wrap a piece of cloth around one finger and wipe it off. Allow this touch-up to dry hard, then apply a second coat in the same way, again wiping off any excess that gets on the surrounding areas.

After you've finished, it's a good idea to give all your varnish a midseason recoating. Wash everything down, then rinse thoroughly with water to get rid of any soapy residue. After they're dry, sand the surfaces with fine (#220) abrasive paper, then remove the sanding dust by wiping it off with a dry cloth (shake out the cloth away from the boat at frequent intervals). Before varnishing each section, wipe it again with a cloth you've dipped in paint thinner. Then flow on a thin, smooth coat of varnish with a high-quality badger hair brush.

Fiberglass and Gel Coat

If the fiberglass is starting to look dull, it will probably need rewaxing. Paste wax is the most durable, but most boatowners don't want to take the time to apply it during the summer. Instead of doing nothing, however, you can protect your boat for the rest of the season by giving it a coat of good-quality liquid wax right after you wash it. These liquid waxes wipe on quickly and generally need no buffing. There are two basic types: cleaner/waxes that clean and wax at the same time, and liquid polymer or silicone waxes that do not have any cleaning action.

Use a cleaner/wax if the gel is getting dull or if it hasn't been waxed for some time. Use one of the other types if your fiberglass still has much of its original gloss, or if you have already given it a good coat of wax earlier in the year.

For fiberglass that is really dull and faded-looking, try applying a coat of Penetrol (an oil-type sealer sold in many

Penetrol will bring faded fiberglass back to life.

marine supply outlets)—directions are on the can. This treatment is a lot easier than waxing and buffing, and it really brightens up a dull gel coat finish—especially if the gel coat is a dark color.

Chrome and Stainless Steel

Nothing dresses up a boat more than bright, shiny metal hardware and fittings, but once the metal has been allowed to oxidize and get dull it requires long hours of tedious polishing—and even then you may never be able to recapture its original luster.

Chrome, aluminum, and stainless steel hardware must be kept clean, and this means washing it with soap and water, not just hosing it off. One way is to wipe the metal down with a cloth dipped in a moisture-displacing lubricant such as WD-40, LPS-1, CRC, or one of the brands that contain Teflon.

Another method that I have found works well on

Wipe moisture-displacing lubricant on electronic gear.

bowrails, fog bells, and other hardware that gets lots of spray—and is highly visible—is applying a liquid wax once or twice during the summer after washing. This is particularly important for the control handles, steering wheel, instrument gauge rims, and other metal trim on the console of an exposed helm. Besides normal dirt and salt spray, these metal pieces are attacked by perspiration from the helmsman's hands and by spilled drinks. Waxing them once or twice a season makes it easy to remove these pollutants and keeps the metal bright and shiny.

It is also a good idea to clean off the outside of your VHF radio, depth finder, radar, Loran, and other electronic equipment that is not built in. Dirty finger marks and streaks may not affect how this equipment operates, but they look messy. On the other hand, dirt or corrosion on plugs and connectors can interfere with efficient operation, so while you're at it, spray these plugs and fittings with a protective film of moisture-displacing lubricant or electronic cleaner.

Canvas and Plastic

Frequent washing with a mild solution of soap and water is essential for all canvas and fabric. Vinyl-covered cushions will stay cleaner and more supple if they are given a light coat of vinyl dressing about once a year, but make sure you clean the vinyl thoroughly first (otherwise stains will be locked in).

I find the best way to get cushions really clean is to take out the foam, then lay the vinyl covers out on a deck or dock for scrubbing. Most concentrated cleaners recommend that you dilute them with several parts of water, but I have found they work better if you use a much stronger solution that contains about one half or one third as much water as the label recommends.

After washing, spray all zippers with a silicone lubricant to keep them working smoothly, and do the same with zippers on drop curtains, Bimini tops, and sail covers. At the same time, spray all snaps, twist fasteners, and similar hardware to make them easier to open and close—and to minimize the chances of someone ripping the fabric by yanking too hard.

Clear vinyl should be washed with soap and water, dried with a soft cloth, and then given a light coat of a liquid spray wax to help it shed water and dirt and to help replace some of the plasticizers bleached out by exposure. I have used Pledge for years (not Lemon Pledge), and it has kept my plastic windows clear and supple much longer.

Dock Lines and Anchor Lines

Dock lines that are unraveling or that have frayed ends will detract from the shipshape appearance of any boat and reflect poorly on the seamanship of its skipper. That's why

Check all lines. Frayed ends should be whipped with twine or dipped into liquid plastic.

it pays to take time out during the summer to cut off or whip lines that have loose or ragged ends. Whipping can be done with waxed twine or with one of the various liquid plastic rope dips. If you whip in the traditional seamanlike manner—with twine—be sure you take enough wraps around the rope end to form a band at least as wide as the diameter of the rope and then end up with at least three or four tucks to keep the whipping twine from unraveling.

While checking each line, see if there are signs of chafe, particularly where the line regularly fits around a cleat or bitt or through a chock. Also check around each spliced eye to see if the part of the line that gets the most use is beginning to show signs of wear. If so, you may be able to cut the eye end off and then splice in a new eye. The line will be slightly shorter, but it will also be stronger.

For Smooth Patching

When working with patching compounds or fillers containing microballoons or Cabosil, getting a smooth finish on the patch can be a problem at times. One way to make the job easier and a lot less messy is with a sheet of waxed paper as shown here. Use a putty knife or spatula to spread on the amount of material required to fill in the defect, then smooth a sheet of wax paper over the surface. Press hard over the wax paper with a plastic or metal spatula,

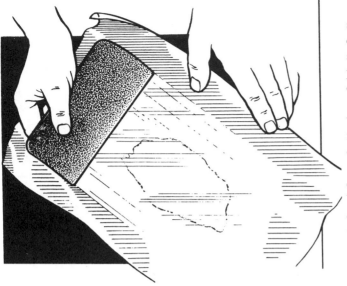

smoothing the material as much as possible and squeezing out any excess. Drag the excess material out to one side, then lift the wax paper and remove the unneeded compound. Replace the paper and give the patch a final smoothing, then let the compound set before removing the wax paper again.

Wax paper can also be used to get smooth patches on angular or curved surfaces. Spread the compound into the curve, then use the wax paper method to smooth it into a neatly curved or shaped contour, using a spoon for a tool or a specially rounded or shaped spatula.

Fiberglassing over Old Wood

Wood decks, wood cabins, and other wood structures on boats require a lot more maintenance than those that are made of all fiberglass. Fiberglassing over these surfaces not only cuts down tremendously on the amount of maintenance required, it also strengthens and waterproofs the original structure, which then needs little or no maintenance other than the occasional chore of painting.

Dry, sunny days when temperatures range between 70° and 80°F are best for this kind of work. Sections of wood that are rotted must be cut out and replaced since fiberglass resins will not bond over rotted wood. Neither will they bond over paint, varnish, or other finishes. This means all finishes must be scraped or sanded off before you start. You can use a chemical remover, but make sure you wash off all traces of the remover when you are finished (by wiping down with paint thinner or acetone).

Although fiberglass bonds to most woods when properly prepared, it bonds even better when applied over plywood because plywood is more dimensionally stable. If you have large flat areas to coat, consider covering these with

sheets of plywood first. The plywood must be screwed down with plenty of wood screws to provide a smooth, solid surface that also saves you the job of stripping and preparing the old surface—no need for sanding, patching, or smoothing over holes, cracks, and other defects.

Polyester resins are cheaper and easier to work with than epoxy resins, so this is your best choice. A wide nylon bristle brush makes the best applicator, but a roller or squeegee can also be used for applying the resin.

Woven fiberglass cloth is stronger than mat, so buy enough of this to apply two layers over the areas you will be covering. Buy at least 10 percent extra to allow for overlapping and waste. The cloth comes in various weights, but remember, the heavier the cloth is, the stronger the finished job (and the thicker and heavier it will be).

When preparing the wood, remove all hardware, then apply a coat of resin directly to the raw wood. Mix the hardener or catalyst with the resin according to the directions supplied, mixing only as much as you can use in about twenty minutes. Brush this on as quickly and as evenly as possible, then mix up another batch. When working with these resins—or when handling fiberglass fabrics—wear gloves to protect your hands and wear a long-sleeved shirt and full-length trousers to keep these materials away from your skin as much as possible. Also wear a respirator mask to protect against unhealthy fumes.

Most companies recommend rolling the first layer of fabric directly into the wet resin before it hardens, but I have found it better to let the resin harden first. Let it cure

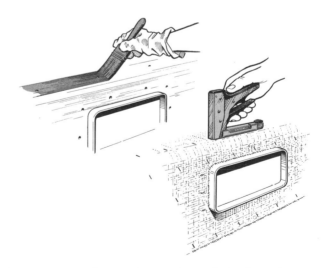

for seventy-two hours, then sand or grind off rough spots and bumps or bubbles. Then wipe clean with acetone. Cut pieces of the fabric to size as needed and use a staple gun loaded with stainless steel staples to fasten this cloth against the hardened resin. Stretch tight to eliminate wrinkles and to make sure the fabric is snug up against the dried resin at all points, and where pieces of fabric meet overlap them by about a half inch.

Now brush a second coat of resin on over the fabric, working it in to saturate the cloth. If you wish, you can add pigment to the resin this time to color it—but make sure you color all the resin (without hardener in it yet) at one time so the color will be uniform throughout. Allow this second coat of resin to cure again for seventy-two hours, then sand smooth. Wipe down with acetone and staple on a second coat of the fiberglass cloth. Make sure overlaps and seams do not fall directly over those in the first layer of cloth.

Now apply another coat of resin (with color added if you want color) and again allow seventy-two hours' curing time. Sand smooth when hard, then wet sand with No. 400 wet-and-dry paper. Finish by wet sanding again with No. 500 or 600 to get a fine polish.

Applying gel coat is a job for a professional, so your best bet if you want a really high gloss is to paint with a two-part polyurethane paint—the kind made for application by brush or roller.

When reinstalling all the hardware you will have to drill all new holes, so make sure you squirt a little silicone into each hole before driving in the screws or bolts to create a watertight seal.

Measuring Outboard Oil

Most of today's outboard motors require that you mix oil in with the gasoline, usually in a 50:1 ratio. The trouble is that when you have a small dinghy motor of only two to four horsepower it is impossible to buy oil in small enough quantities for accurate mixing—even if the motor has a separate 2½-gallon tank, like mine does. This means pouring a little out of the can to mix with a tank of gasoline, then having an open can of oil on board that is not easy to seal—and there is no simple way of measuring off a small amount of oil each time it is needed.

But I have found a solution to this: I measure and store the oil in those little plastic canisters that 35mm film is packed in. Each canister holds just about one ounce, so it is perfect for measuring. I pour the original pint can into a series of these small containers. Each has a tight-fitting cap that prevents spills.

For Bottom Cleaning

Here is another use for old athletic socks—particularly the long, heavy ones worn by joggers. They are great for wiping scum and new growth off the hull and its bottom, especially along the waterline. This is easiest when you can anchor the boat in about four or five feet of water so you can walk around it. Using a pair of these socks, slip

one over each hand, then wipe off the bottom and boottop stripe along the waterline. When it is not practical to anchor in shallow water, I sometimes don a life jacket with a line secured to it, then have a crew member tow me along the hull while we are anchored.

Cleaning Stern Drives

I have found a simple way to clean heavy growth off the bottom end of my stern-drive unit at any time during the season. I take a large, heavy-duty plastic bag, like a leafbag, and slide this under and around the bottom of the unit, including the submerged part. Work carefully to avoid snagging the bag on metal parts and possibly tearing it. Secure it the best way you can, and tie it at the top.

Now take a length of two-inch-diameter PVC plastic pipe about three feet long, and slip this inside the bag from the top so it reaches down to the bottom of the bag on the inside. Start pouring one gallon of liquid laundry bleach slowly down through the pipe so it runs down to the bottom of the bag. The bleach will reach the bottom, then slowly creep upward around the stern-drive unit until it is all covered with the bleach.

Leave the bag in place overnight, with the bleach on the inside. The next day all the growth will be gone, except for a cloudy white residue that can be brushed off easily.

Loosening Knots

Every once in a while even the most knowledgeable and experienced boatman will wind up with a knot in one of his lines that is almost impossible to loosen or untie—especially if it has been there for quite some time. One trick that often works is first to spray the knot liberally with one of the aerosol silicone lubricants that are widely sold in hardware stores and marine supply outlets. Apply it to all sides of the knot until saturated, then let it soak for a couple of minutes. Now when you tackle it again with a fid or screwdriver, or even with your fingers, the stubborn knot will be a lot easier to undo.

Stain Remover for Teak Decks

Anyone whose boat has teak decks knows how easy it is to create ugly stains when some mayonnaise or other greasy food falls from someone's overstuffed sandwich, or even

when someone steps on a peanut that has been dropped on the deck.

Fortunately, most of these stains can be quickly and easily removed with a simple remedy sold in all supermarkets and houseware stores—especially if you tackle the job promptly. Buy some spray-on carpet stain remover such as K2R, Carbona, or Blue Lustre #1. Use this to spray the stained area lightly. Watch as it turns to a white powder, then turns brown as it soaks the oil out of the wood. After several hours brush off the powder (or use a vacuum to pick it up), and presto—the stain will be gone.

This works even on sizable oil spills. Wipe up as much as you can with rags first, then use the spot remover as described. Don't be upset if it takes several applications.

Preventing Diesel Stains

When refueling a boat that is powered by a diesel engine, skippers are always careful to avoid overflowing or spilling the diesel fuel because diesel spills are hard to remove. However, when a spill does occur, quick action with a water hose is usually the immediate response. Although this usually helps, all too often the water doesn't always wash all the oily residue away, unless soap is also used—not always practical or even possible when tied to a fuel dock.

Long ago I discovered that it is much more effective to wet the hull and deck near and below the filler cap *before* removing the fuel tank cap and before starting to fill the tanks. Then any diesel fuel that is spilled will be much more likely to run off without soaking in because the surface is already wet, and there is also much less chance of an oily stain remaining. As a further precaution, it is a good idea to keep the area surrounding the fuel filler cap and that part of the hull that is just below it well coated with wax—to prevent the fuel from soaking in.

Organizing the Ice Chest

In many boats the ice box or chest is built against the outside of the hull so that its inside curves inward and the chest gets narrower near the bottom. The problem with this is that small bottles, jars, and other packages tend to get lost at the bottom and covered with layers of ice, which makes them hard to find.

We solved this problem very neatly on our boat by using a plastic waste container, such as the kind manufactured by Rubber Maid. After drilling a few holes in the bottom to let any trapped or spilled water run out, we place the container in the deepest part of the ice box and store most of our perishables in it. This keeps them out of the melted water and makes them easy to find.

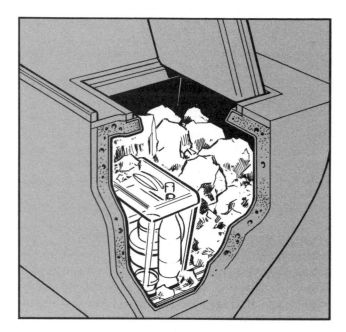

Ten Frequently Asked Maintenance Questions

1. Q: What is the best way to remove painted names, hailing ports, and registration numbers from a fiberglass hull without affecting the gel coat?

A: The method used by most professionals is to wipe the paint off with a strong solvent such as acetone. Actually, a fair amount of rubbing is required to do a thorough job, and since such solvents evaporate quickly, you will have to work fast. Wipe on with one rag, then immediately start rubbing with another rag and more acetone. Also, keep wiping and rubbing from the unpainted areas into the painted areas to prevent smearing the paint around. Change rags often—again to keep from smearing the paint around. Remember that acetone is highly flammable, so make sure there is plenty of ventilation and no open flames or smokers nearby.

Another method that many have found works even better is to use a spray-on-type oven cleaner. Spray the cleaner on liberally and let it soak into the surface for fifteen or twenty minutes. You should then be able to wipe off the paint and the oven cleaner with a rag. Either method will get the painted numbers and letters off the transom without harming the gel coat or the fiberglass.

2. Q: What is the best way to clean fenders that have stubborn, dark stains and streaks that won't come off with regular washing and scrubbing?

A: Over the years I have used several "nonmarine" products that work well on dirty fenders. One is a grease solvent such as regular dry cleaning fluid. Like acetone, it will take off most fender stains, but it won't attack the plastic the way acetone does. Another product that works well is a soap-impregnated steel wool pad—the kind used in kitchens for scrubbing pots. But in recent years several manufacturers have introduced special cleaners that work even better on fenders, shore cords, and similar items. Often labeled as either "fender cleaners" or "inflatable boat cleaners," these are solvents that eliminate the need for much of the rubbing that other products require, and they usually work better. Three brands I have used successfully are the ones made by MDR, Star Brite, and Seapower, but there are others on the market that I'm sure are also good.

3. Q: What is the best way to remove dark, oily-looking stains from the teak handrails, grabrails, and other teak trim around my boat?

A: The dark stains are usually caused by grime and greasy soil that has been rubbed in by handling, especially when palms are sweaty or dirty. Nine times out of ten this can be easily removed by wiping down with any of the household spray cleaners sold for use on kitchen cabinets and walls. An even quicker way to get the grime off is to wipe with a rag that has been moistened with paint thinner, which takes the soil off with very little rubbing; but be sure you change rags often, as they get very dirty. Test first to see if the thinner affects the finish on the wood, and remember that paint thinner is very flammable, so keep a fire extinguisher handy and make sure no one is smoking or has an open flame nearby.

4. Q: Although copolymer bottom paint lasts for several seasons, it doesn't last long on props, shafts, and other underwater metal parts. What can be done to keep this metal from fouling so rapidly?

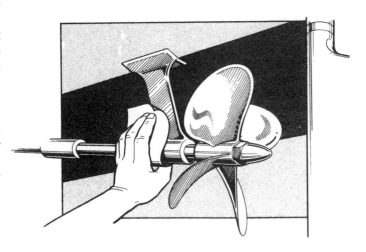

A: One of the main reasons that antifouling bottom paints do not stand up well on props and shafts is the much greater turbulence and underwater friction encountered by these high-speed rotating parts. Also, paints never adhere well to surfaces that are not thoroughly cleaned, and these metal parts are seldom cleaned properly before the paint is applied.

Several manufacturers of marine paint recommend a system for painting underwater metal, but in each case the most important point is to get the metal absolutely clean and bright before you start. Sandblasting is probably best, but you can also use abrasive paper or a power-driven wire brush (wear goggles when doing this). Just make sure all the metal is clean and bright when you are finished. Then wipe the metal clean with a solvent such as acetone, or the brand recommended by the manufacturer of the paint you will be using.

Follow this step immediately with a coat of the metal primer or wash-primer recommended by the paint manufacturer, then apply two coats of a vinyl-base or TBTF antifouling paint. For longest-lasting results, apply two coats of the copolymer over this. In all cases it is best to stick to the brand of one manufacturer, and follow the recommendations as to the solvent and primer coat. One final point: Don't expect the paint on the props and struts to last as long as on the rest of the boat. The high-speed spinning and the abrasive action of the moving water are just too much for most antifouling paints to withstand for very long.

5. Q: How do I remove the yellowish hull stains above the waterline on my fiberglass boat?

A: There are a number of specialty cream or gel-type cleaners that have been developed for just this purpose and are widely sold in marine supply stores. Some of these that I have used successfully are: Y-10, Star Brite Instant Hull Cleaner, and Boat Life's Fiberglass Kreme. All of these cleaners are effective without a lot of scrubbing. You simply wipe them on, allow them to soak in for a few minutes, and then rub lightly with a brush or sponge. Rinse off with either fresh or salt water.

6. Q: How do you paint metal parts in the engine room to keep rust from coming through so soon after painting?

A: The first step is to get *all* the rust off, but often this is impossible in an engine room because there are so many tight corners you cannot reach. A technique I have found that works well is to get off all the rust I can, then cover the metal and the rest of the rust with one of the various rust converters on the market. Three brands that I have had good luck with are Trustan 7, Neutra Rust, and Extend. If you cannot find them in your local marine supply store, try hardware stores and home centers in your area. When used according to directions, these solutions chemically convert the rust to a stable coating that inhibits further rusting and

provides an excellent foundation for painting. When this coating cures I then usually apply two coats of engine enamel.

7. Q: Is it safe to use a chemical paint remover to take off all the old bottom paint on a fiberglass hull, or is sandblasting a better idea?

A: Using a chemical paint remover is a perfectly safe and viable alternative—providing you use one of the specially formulated marine-type removers made for use over gel coat. Instructions furnished will tell you how to use them. Ordinary removers are stronger, but if you are not careful they could harm the gel coat, so stick with the marine type designated for this purpose.

Sandblasting can lead to trouble if it is not carefully done by an experienced operator who uses the right kind of fine sand and really knows what he is doing. Pitting of the gel coat can result, as well as an increase in the porosity of the fiberglass under it (which can lead to blistering). Some experts recommend using only ground corn husks, but others say that if a really fine grade of sand is properly used, no harm will result. But there is disagreement on this issue.

8. Q: Is there any way to restore the color and luster of faded wood-grain Formica cabinets and bulkheads?

A: Use a penetrating sealer such as Deks Olje #1 or Penetrol, both of which are sold in marine supply stores. Wash the surface down thoroughly first, then let it dry overnight. Wipe on one coat of the sealer with a rag or painting pad, then wipe off the excess after about ten or fifteen minutes. With Deks Olje wipe another coat on immediately. With Penetrol, wait for the first coat to dry, then wipe on a second coat. When this is dry, buff the surface with a clean cloth.

9. Q: When masking tape is left on too long, it is often very difficult to remove. What is the fastest and easiest way to get this tape off?

A: Ordinary masking tape should not be left on more than about twenty-four hours, especially when exposed to the sun. Next time use one of the special "thin line" tapes that automobile finishers use for striping and that some marine supply and hardware stores carry. It comes off much easier and it conforms to curves better because it is more elastic. Also, since it is thinner it leaves less of a ridge or thick edge when peeled off. However it does cost more—two or three times as much as ordinary masking tape.

As far as removing the tape that is already there, there are two methods that work. One is to use a solvent such as rubber cement thinner. Sold in art supply stores and in some stationery stores, this solvent is very flammable, so use proper precautions. It won't hurt paint, varnish, or gel coat and it will not actually dissolve or soften the tape, but it will dissolve the adhesive that holds it in place. The way

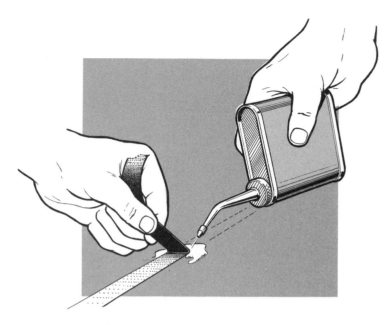

to use it is to peel back a corner or edge of the tape, then use a hypodermic-type oiler or glue applicator to squeeze a little of the solvent down in back of the tape, as shown in the drawing. As this starts to soften the adhesive, peel more off and apply additional solvent to soften the next section, and so on. Where you can't peel the tape off at all you will have to scrape or abrade it enough so that the solvent can get at the adhesive on the back side.

Another method that works is to use mild heat to soften the tape and adhesive. This will allow you to peel it off more easily; then you can wipe off the residue with rubber cement thinner. For heat you can use a hair dryer or a heat gun. Just don't hold the heat gun in one place too long or you may scorch the finish.

10. Q: What is the best way to take care of clear vinyl panels and roll-up curtains to keep them from turning white and cloudy and deteriorating so fast?

A: Probably the most important maintenance step is keeping the vinyl clean and washing salt off at the end of each day. If possible, after washing, dry with a chamois or soft towel. Never roll the curtains up while they are wet, and always unroll them to allow water to run off when it is raining or when hosing the boat down. Allowing water to remain inside the rolled-up vinyl is one common cause of cloudiness, although the sun is also a strong contributing factor. When you have to clean side curtains, wipe them with a wet cloth, never a dry one, and don't use soap any more often than necessary (soap takes out some of the plasticizers). Every four to six weeks spray on a light coat of spray wax such as Pledge, then wipe clean (don't use Lemon Pledge; only regular Pledge). The wax helps replace some of the plasticizers that washing and leaching remove.

Repairing Holes and Dents in Fiberglass

All too often it is not until your boat is hauled out of the water that you really notice the damage that may have been done to the hull during the past season. (That sizable "ding" near the port quarter is a painful reminder of the time you were a bit careless backing into your slip last month . . . and that dent—or is it a hole?—on the foredeck is an equally unpleasant souvenir of the time a "helpful" guest dropped the anchor one morning.)

Fortunately, fiberglass hulls can be repaired fairly easily. The repair should be just as strong as the original laminate, but this depends on achieving a good bond between the new patch and the existing laminate. The trickiest part is getting the repair to blend in neatly so it won't be noticeable. For those with no experience in working with fiberglass and resins, some practice on a scrap surface—or starting with a small job where appearance really doesn't matter—is advisable before tackling anything important.

We all know that fiberglass is made up of multiple layers of fiberglass fabric that has been saturated with resin. The combination creates a laminate that is tougher than any of the ingredients it is made of, and when the fiberglass materials are wet with resin they can be molded or shaped to match almost any contour.

There are two types of resin used for repairing or laminating fiberglass: polyester resin and epoxy resin. For most jobs, polyester is your better choice; it costs less than epoxy and is much easier to work with. However, epoxy is stronger for laminates where great stress is involved, and under certain conditions is also preferred for some underwater repairs.

Resins Vary

Polyester resins vary in two respects—in their consistency and in how they cure. The most widely sold consistency is what is normally referred to as "regular" or "standard," but for application on vertical or overhead surfaces you can buy a "thixotropic" type that has an additive that makes it more resistant to sagging and running (it's also harder to spread and requires more effort to "wet" the fabric).

In addition to varying in consistency, polyester resins also vary as to how they cure. All require some heat to set, so they are best used at temperatures between 60° and 80° F., and all set faster at higher temperatures—which is why it is best not to use them in direct sunlight or on very hot days. However, there is one type known as *air-inhibited*

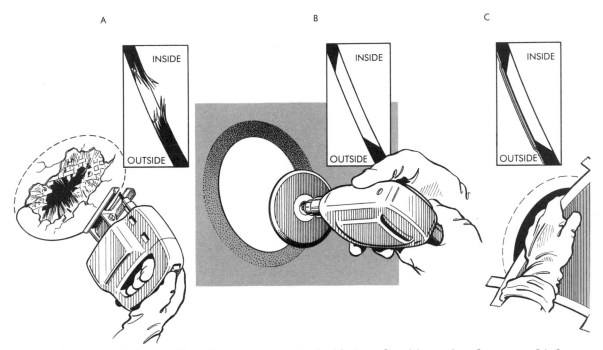

Patching holes in fiberglass may seem intimidating, but it's easier than you think.

and another type known as *nonair-inhibited*. Here's what all this means:

Air-inhibited resins never really harden fully in the presence of air, so the surface remains tacky after it cures. This is desirable on sizable jobs when you have to cover large areas with several layers of glass and resin, because each layer will bond better to the one underneath if it is still tacky. However, to get the *final* layer to harden you have to seal the surface to keep all air away during the process.

This is accomplished by either spraying the last coat of resin with a "mold release" such as PVA (polyvinyl alcohol), which seals out air, or by taping a layer of cellophane or Saran Wrap over the surface of the final coat of resin. After the final coat hardens, this cellophane can be peeled off (or the PVA washed off with water). These air-inhibited polyester resins are not easy to find, so you may have to shop around a bit or order them from a mail order house.

Most of the polyester resins that are sold over the counter to boatowners are nonair-inhibited. These contain wax or a similar ingredient that floats to the surface after the resin is applied to create a film that keeps air away so the resin can dry hard at the surface. Thus they are simpler and more "foolproof" for amateurs to use and are ideal for such jobs as laminating fiberglass over wood where you want to end up with a smooth, hard finish on the surface.

All resins come with a separate catalyst that must be added before use. Only a very small amount is needed for each batch, and the directions supplied will give you the specifics. Just remember that the more catalyst you add the quicker the resin will start to gel or harden, and the less working time you will have. Also, the higher the temperature, the quicker it will start to gel, so the less catalyst you need. Usually it is safest to err on the low side when adding catalyst (you can always speed up drying by using a heat lamp, or by adding a little more catalyst to the next batch).

Cloth, Mat, and Roving

The fiberglass fabrics used for laminating come in three basic types: cloth, mat, and woven roving. Cloth is the most expensive and requires the most layers to build up a given thickness, but it does help add strength on large patches. Fiberglass mat consists of short lengths of fiber put down in a random pattern to form a nonwoven, felt-like pad. Woven roving is a thick, woven material with a basket weave pattern. Like mat, it adds thickness, but it also adds more strength. However, used alone it creates a laminate that is not as waterproof as mat or cloth, so it is almost always used in combination with mat. In fact, most boats are built of alternate layers of roving and mat, so these are the materials suggested for most boat repairs.

For most small to medium-size repairs you may find it easier to use alternate layers of mat and cloth instead of roving. You will have to apply more layers to build up the thickness required, but cloth is not as hard to wet with resin as roving is and you will usually end up with a stronger and more waterproof repair.

Filling Small Holes

If you are just filling a small hole (up to about a half inch in diameter)—like a bolt or screw hole—chances are you won't need any fiberglass fabric. Such holes can be filled with a putty made by mixing some catalyzed resin with a filler, such as cut-up strands of fiberglass mat. Use a round file or small hand grinding tool to bevel the edges of the hole first on the outside and then on the inside so the edges of the laminate are V-shaped on both sides, as in the drawing. If you can't get at the inside, bevel the outside and then use a rattail file to taper the inside edges by pushing it through at an angle from the outside. The tapered edges on each side should be at least half as wide as the diameter of the hole.

The hole will be filled from the back side (if you can reach it), so cover the front side with a wide strip of tape that will act as a backing. This tape should be wide enough to cover the tapered edges, too. Now fill the hole from the back, packing the putty in firmly so it comes flush up against the tape on the outside, then spread it a little on each side of the inside of the hole.

If you cannot get to the inside, here's how you can do

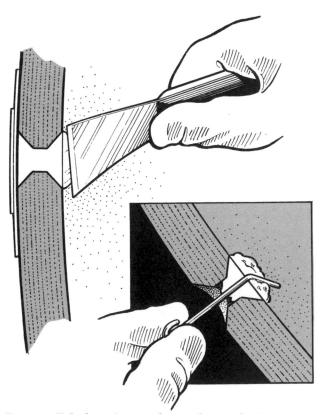

For small holes, the patch can be made from either the inside or the outside.

the job from the outside: Jam some thickened resin putty into the hole and use a small piece of wire with a right-angle bend on the end to pull this wad of putty tight up against the back side of the hole as shown. Pack in enough putty to fill the hole about halfway to the surface, then allow this to harden before filling the hole the rest of the way.

In either case, after the hole has been filled and the putty has hardened (and the tape backing, if used, has been removed), the outside will have to be wet-sanded, first with No. 220, then with No. 400 paper. After this it can be touched up with a little matching gel coat to match the rest of the laminate. The gel coat can then be given its final wet sanding with No. 600 paper.

Patching Larger Holes

Larger holes, deep dents, and cracked sections are repaired by filling with fiberglass and resin after first cutting or grinding away all damaged or partially delaminated material. It's usually quickest to use a saber saw for cutting back to solid material and to eliminate sharp corners or edges (step 1 in the opening drawing).

The best repairs are made if you can work from the back side (the technique to use when only one side is accessible will be described later). After cutting away all the damaged material, use an electric disc sander or grinder to taper the inside edges of the hole (step 2), grinding back at least two or three inches on all sides. Wipe off all grinding dust and clean the area on both sides by wiping down with a rag saturated with acetone.

You have to create a backing surface on the outside so the finished laminate will conform to the existing contour. Use a sheet of cardboard covered with Saran Wrap, or a thin sheet of plastic laminate (such as Formica). Press this tightly against the outside of the hole and secure it with tape, clamps, or a temporary adhesive (step 3).

Now you can start building up the patch from the inside. Cut a piece of fiberglass cloth slightly larger than the hole, then cut a series of additional pieces of cloth and mat, each slightly larger than the previous one so they will overlap when applied. Lay the first piece of cloth on a scrap piece of plywood or cardboard, then mix as much resin and catalyst as you think you can use up in twenty minutes (it starts to set up after that).

Brush this resin liberally onto the tapered edges of the hole, then over the first piece of cloth you have waiting. Saturate it thoroughly, then pick it off the cardboard and press it into place over the hole—against the plastic-covered cardboard you have secured to the outside (step 4). The cloth should slightly overlap onto the tapered edges of the hole. Smooth this out with your brush, then spread on another layer of resin and press the next piece of fabric (mat) on top so it overlaps the first piece of cloth.

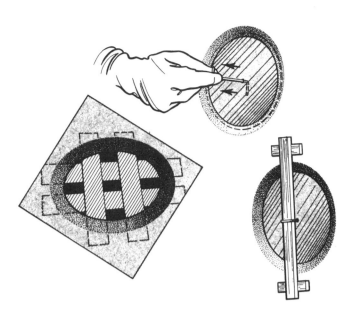

Here are two methods of patching a larger hole from the outside when inside access is impossible.

Wet this thoroughly with resin and jab vigorously to help it penetrate and to work all air bubbles out to the edges. Continue laying on alternate layers of mat and cloth, wetting each one thoroughly with resin.

If you have to build up a total thickness of more than three-eighths inch, apply the laminate in two stages to keep it from overheating (thick layers of resin heat up faster than thin layers). Lay up about half the layers and wait for this to cure, then proceed with the second stage. Ideally, the last layer should overlap the existing laminate so the repair is slightly thicker than the original material.

When you cannot get at the back of the repair you will have to do your tapering of the hole from the outside. After cutting away all the damaged or delaminated material, grind the edges to a taper as previously described, making certain the taper extends back at least two to three inches from the opening on all sides. Dust thoroughly, and clean the surface with acetone.

Even though you are working from the outside, some kind of temporary backing is needed on the back (inside) to provide a form for the first layers of cloth and resin. One way to do this is to cut a piece of stiff cardboard a little larger than the hole, then poke a piece of wire through the center of it. Fold or bend the cardboard enough to push it through the hole, then pull it tight against the back side with the wire (step 1 above).

To hold it there you can wrap the wire around a stick long enough to reach across the front of the hole, pulling the wire tight enough to hold the cardboard in place (step 2). This can be left in place until after the first coat of cloth starts to set, after which the wire can be cut off.

Another way to create a backing is to use several strips of fiberglass cloth that are slightly longer than the hole is wide. Each strip is saturated with resin, then you reach through the hole with your fingers and press this resin-saturated strip against the back side of the hole (step 3). Apply several strips, crisscrossing them to close the opening gradually.

Wait until the strips harden so they create a "grid" that will serve as a backing for the actual laminate. You can then lay up the alternate layers as described above, wetting each one with the catalyzed resin as it is applied. Again, make sure you brush out or squeeze out all air bubbles by working them out toward the edges with a jabbing motion. Fill the hole slightly above the surface, leaving room to sand the surface flush.

If you have been using a nonair-inhibited resin (one that contains no wax), the last layer will not harden properly unless you spray it with PVA or cover with Saran Wrap as soon as the last coat is applied. Leave this on until the last coat is fully cured, then wash off the PVA with water (or peel off the plastic wrap). You can now sand the surface smooth, using No. 180 or No. 220 to level it off flush with the surrounding surface, but use masking tape to protect the existing gel coat. For a final smoothing you will have to wet-sand, first with No. 220, then with No. 400. Touch up with a little gel coat to match the color, then polish to a high gloss by wet-sanding with No. 600. Wait a couple of days before polishing with wax to restore the original luster.

2 PROJECTS AND IMPROVEMENTS

One Dozen Winter Boat-Improvement Projects

Most owners can't use their boat during the winter, but you can use those off-season months to improve and add to your boat—projects that you never seem to have enough time for during the regular season. Here are twelve winter projects you can tackle that will enhance your boating pleasure and comfort next year.

1. Add Line Cutters to Your Propeller Shafts

If your boat has a propeller, there is always a danger of fouling when the prop (or props) gets tangled in an underwater line. This is particularly true in areas where there are lobster pots, crab pots, fishing nets, or trap lines. Regular fishing lines and heavy growths of weeds also can foul propellers.

A new line and weed cutter (above) that fits over the propeller shaft completely eliminates this problem. Made of extra-hard, rust-resistant stainless steel and called Spurs, this is a rotating cutter that mounts on the shaft directly in front of the propeller—between the prop and the strut. It includes a second stationary cutter that does not rotate and that rides in a groove around the outside of the rotating cutter. A wedge-shaped holding block mounted on the side of the shaft strut keeps this stationary cutter from turning when the shaft and rotating cutter are turning. When a line gets wrapped around the shaft or caught in the propeller it will get sliced off neatly by the powerful viselike cutting action of two cutters—the rotating one that spins with the shaft and the stationary one that is almost touching it. The cutting action is much like that of a large paper cutter, except that it is rotary.

Available direct from the manufacturer—Spurs Marine Mfg., P.O. Box 3118, Bahia Mar Station, Fort Lauderdale, Fla. 33316—as well as from boatyards and marinas, these line and weed cutters come in sizes to fit all propeller

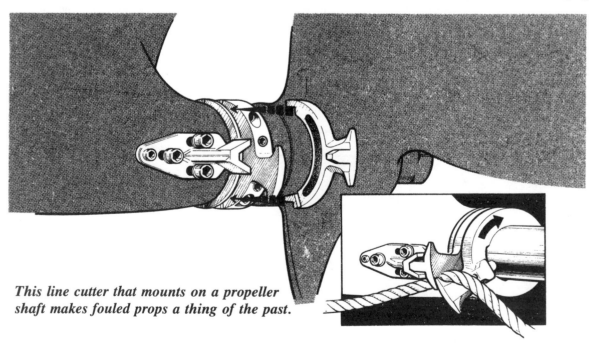

This line cutter that mounts on a propeller shaft makes fouled props a thing of the past.

shaft diameters, from 7/8″ to 5½″. Prices vary with the size, starting at $180 for a set that will fit shaft sizes from 7/8″ to 1½″ in diameter (you need one set for each shaft). The cutter mounts between the strut or stern bearing housing and the propeller, so there must be enough space between them to provide the amount of clearance needed (at least 13/8″ for most popular-size shafts).

Detailed installation instructions are furnished with each set of Spurs, but it is a good idea to do a dry run first—that is, put everything in place and see that it is working properly before tightening it down. There are two set screws that lock the assembled unit to the shaft, but before inserting and tightening them, dimple the shaft slightly with a drill bit of the same diameter as the hole. Then when the screws go in they will lock firmly in place to keep the cutters from slipping when a really heavy line is encountered. Also, check alignment of the cutters to make sure they are square to the shaft before tightening all screws securely.

If you want to test the cutters before the boat is launched, spray a little penetrating oil on the bearings to lubricate them, then spin the prop by hand and slide a length of line between the cutters—it will get chopped off neatly! If you do not get a clean cut, however, don't worry. When the shaft is driven by the engine while the boat is under way, the line will get chopped off neatly.

2. Storage Space Improvement

Many boats have lockers, lazarettes, and hatches that have considerable capacity for storing lines, fenders, extra hoses, etc., but that also make it almost impossible to find small items that tend to get buried near the bottom under a pile of bulky equipment. In addition, the cover or hatch that provides access to this locker or lazarette usually is not as large as it could be, so often there is space at either side of the hatch opening or lazarette cover that is hard to reach.

A neat way to solve both of these problems is shown in the first drawing. Mount an ordinary plastic dishpan—a stainless steel pan could also be used if you don't mind the expense—on wood rails so that it slides out of the way to one side as shown. This enables you to keep small items—paint brushes, shock cords, spray cans of lubricant, etc.—out of the way yet instantly accessible in the pan.

Normally, the whole pan is pushed to the side—much like a drawer—so it is hidden under the top at one side of the opening. That way it doesn't interfere with the storage of bulky items underneath it or in the rest of the locker. But when you want some of the small items that are in the pan you just pull it out to expose the contents so you can reach in easily.

The wood rails consist of lengths of two-by-two lumber fastened in place with epoxy or self-taping screws, spaced

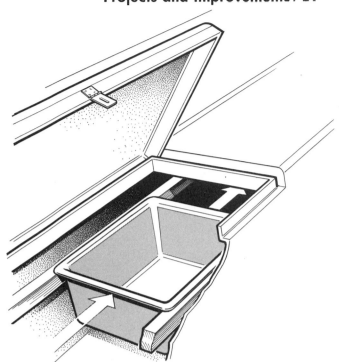

about half an inch down from the top with spacer blocks and just far enough apart to catch the rim of the dishpan you will be using. Sand the top of each strip smooth before installing it, then give it several coats of sealer and wax the top edges to help the pan slide easier. Add a small block of wood to act as a stop at the far end of each wood strip (on the inside) to keep the pan from sliding off the end if you push it too far, or when the boat is pitching while under way.

3. Let There Be Light

Most stock sailboats have two- or three-piece drop boards that slide in from above to close off the companionway entrance when the cabin has to be closed off. Unfortunately, sliding these boards into place while you are aboard—to keep out the rain, or to keep the inside warmer on a chilly day—also closes off a good deal of the natural light that normally comes pouring in through that large opening.

A simple way to keep the inside warm and dry while still letting in light is to replace one or more of the drop boards with transparent material. The new boards actually consist of wood frames with a sheet of clear plastic (Plexiglas or Lexan) fastened over the outside. You can make one such drop board to replace only the top one, or you can make a complete set of two or three to replace all the original boards when you are on board (when leaving the boat you will still want to install the original solid wood ones). Or you can make a single panel to fill the whole opening, as shown in the second drawing.

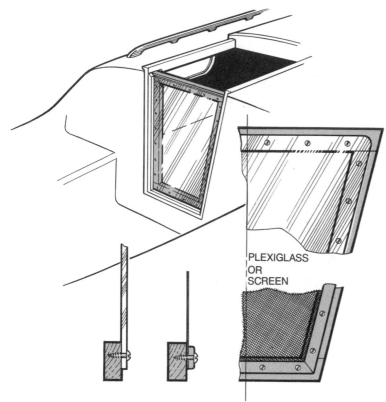

PLEXIGLASS
OR
SCREEN

Though the most handsome-looking block will be one made of teak, mahogany or some other wood can also be used. The wood should be coated with a couple of coats of penetrating sealer to help preserve it, then either varnished or painted to blend in with the rest of the boat.

As can be seen in the drawing, two boards at least ten to twelve inches wide and approximately twelve to fifteen inches high are used for each side. The horizontal spacer blocks along the top and bottom should be the same thickness as the stanchions and railings (usually seven-eighths inch or one inch in diameter). Buy wood that is slightly thicker, then plane or sand these pieces to the thickness needed. Use stainless steel bolts and nuts to assemble the whole thing as shown in the accompanying drawing.

The best location for this motor block is on a section of rail where there is a vertical stanchion. That way the block will not rotate over the horizontal rail when the motor is fastened to it. If you cannot find such a spot and must mount the block where there is no vertical stanchion, then you will have to mount a second block of wood on the deck directly in front of the bottom end of the outboard motor when it is in place. You can then lash its lower end

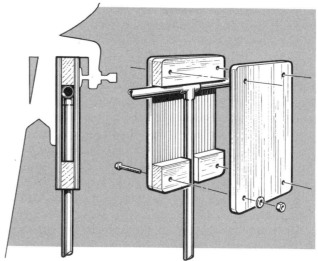

To make each frame, use two-inch-wide strips of lumber equal in thickness to that of your original drop boards so they will fit neatly into the same grooves as the original boards. Use the original boards as templates to cut a cardboard pattern, then use this as a guide in assembling each frame. Corners are formed with half-lap joints and assembled with screws and waterproof glue.

After each frame is assembled, try it in place of the drop board it is supposed to replace to make sure it fits, then install the clear plastic on the outside by drilling holes at 6″ intervals and then fastening it in place with round-head screws (brass or stainless steel).

This same technique can be used to build a removable screen for the companionway that is neater and stronger than the usual fabric screen secured with zippers or Velcro strips. Build the frame as described above, then cover the whole thing with insect screening instead of clear plastic. Attach the screening with a staple gun, then cover the edges with half-round molding for a neat finish.

4. Outboard Motor Bracket

Many cruising boats carry a dinghy powered by a small outboard motor, but finding a place to stow that auxiliary motor is often a problem. It is best to stow the motor vertically, yet keep it where it will be easy to get at when needed. One of the best ways to do this is to mount the motor on the yacht's stern rail or side rail, using a wood mounting block similar to the one shown here.

to this block of wood with shock cord or a piece of line to keep it from rotating or swinging in and out.

5. Improving the Fresh Water System

If your boat has a pressurized fresh water system, there are two improvements you can make that will be greatly appreciated by everyone who cruises with you next summer: You can add an accumulator tank and a water filter to the system.

The accumulator tank will do four things: (1) It will reduce the noise made by the pump when running by minimizing "water hammer." (2) It will lengthen the life of the pump by not making it cycle off and on as often. (3)

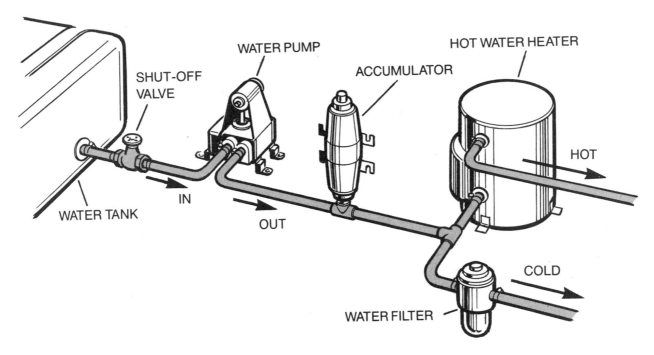

It will provide a reservoir of pressurized water so the pump won't have to come on when only a small amount of water is needed (a great advantage at night). (4) It will provide a more even flow of water at the faucets without annoying pulsing or surging as the pump cycles off and on.

Installing a water filter will help to ensure cleaner and better-tasting water wherever you cruise. A good filter will take out rust, dirt, and sediment as well as objectionable odors and tastes that are sometimes present in your water tank—or that get picked up when away from your home dock.

Accumulator tanks, which are made by Jabsco (Model 12573-0000 or 18818-0000), are installed by simply cutting into the water line on the discharge side of the water pump, as shown in the drawing. It should be installed as close to the water pump as practical, using an ordinary tee cut into the line. If your system has a dockside water connection (for keeping the system pressurized without using the pump when at dockside), then install the accumulator tank between the dockside connection and the pump.

Water filters sell for from twenty-five to fifty dollars in most plumbing supply houses and hardware stores; they are also available from some marine supply outlets. The ones made for household use generally use one of two types of replaceable filter cartridges—one that filters out dirt, rust, and sediment, and another that filters out objectionable tastes and odors. If you have both problems you may need two separate filters installed in series (one right after the other). However, some "heavy duty"

cartridges contain a finer filtering medium that is supposed to take care of both problems at once.

In my own boats I usually install two filters: a large one near the water pump with a dirt and sediment cartridge to take care of all the water coming into the boat system (from the tank or from the dockside connection), and then a second, smaller one with a taste and odor cartridge that is installed in the water line leading to the galley sink. In that way the water used for drinking and cooking gets an extra treatment to filter out unwanted tastes and odors before you use it.

Again, installation is fairly simple. You cut into the water line at some point after the accumulator tank and after the hot water heater (unless you want the hot water also filtered); then use the necessary fittings to install the filter in the line. Most come with an assortment of adapters to fit all types of metal or plastic pipe, but if your boat uses plastic tubing for the water lines you will have to buy a couple of nipples of the proper diameter to accept the tubing.

One word of warning: These household water filters are NOT designed to remove harmful bacteria from polluted water. They are only designed to improve the quality of regular municipal water supplies—supposedly already treated for harmful bacteria that can cause illness. If you will be traveling to foreign ports where you suspect the water may not be potable, there are special water treatment and filtration devices you can buy (these cost much more than the home water filters described above—usually several hundred dollars for a model that will treat only a limited amount of drinking water).

6. Track for Sliding Fender Hooks

Many motor yachts and cruising sedans have splash curtains or enclosures under the handrails around their raised aft decks for privacy, as well as to keep the deck dry. But this also makes it very difficult to tie fenders to any of these railings. The hardboard or sheet plastic used for these splash curtains fits right up against the bottom of the railings, so you cannot tie a rope around and you can't reach the stanchions on the inside.

The same problem also occurs where there is a section along the side or back of a boat without convenient railings for tying a fender, and no cleats located where you need them. Even where there are one or two cleats mounted along that area, all too often they're not located just where you need them for fenders.

I've found that a convenient way to solve this problem is to mount a length of regular sail track along the area where you need to hang fenders. On this sail track you can then mount one or two slides or "cars" with big metal loops or eyes in them (spinnaker pole slides have the biggest eyes). You can slide one of these eyes along the track to wherever you need to hang a fender, then tie the end of the fender line to the loop on the slide.

When mounting the track it's best to secure it with small bolts that go clear through the hardboard or plastic that is used as a splash curtain. If the material is flimsy, use a strip of half-inch plywood at least two inches wide on the inside of the thin material as a backing plate for mounting the track. This plywood backing plate should be at least as long as the sail track and should be attached with bolts

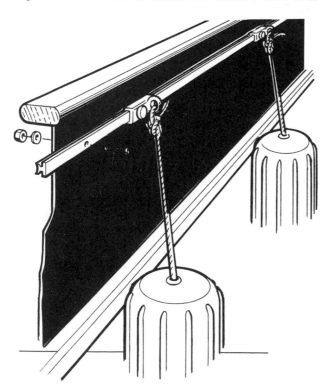

long enough to go through the track, the splash curtain material, and the plywood strip behind it. Most such sail tracks have mounting holes spaced either three or four inches apart, and you should use a bolt in each hole to ensure a really secure mounting.

In some cases it may be necessary to mount the track on the side of the cabin, or even along a caprail or toerail. In these installations you may not be able to use bolts because you cannot get at the back side, so you will have to use stainless steel self-tapping screws instead. If so, get the longest strip of sail track there is room for, as this will allow for more mounting screws—and therefore for stronger anchoring—than would be possible with fewer screws.

7. Installing a Stereo System

A number of stereo systems sold through marine outlets are specifically designed for use afloat, but the vast majority of stereos installed on boats are designed for automobiles. Generally these are twelve-volt systems that work out well on the water—if you select good components and weatherproof speakers.

Speakers for automobile systems are often installed in the doors of the car, so these speakers must be reasonably resistant to moisture to withstand the drips and leaks that inevitably develop there. Some have cones made from a special waterproof fiber; others use plastic speaker cones. Just make sure that the cones in the speakers you select are waterproof before you buy them and that the metal trim and hardware are also rustproof. If you plan to install speakers in an open cockpit, it's best to buy those that are designed for marine use and really waterproof. Don't use horns (like you'd use with a loud hailer); they won't give very good sound reproduction.

Good-quality automobile stereos are also built to withstand some fairly extreme changes in temperature without lowered performance. However, remember that auto systems are designed to provide adequate sound in relatively small areas (the inside of a car), so if you have a large boat and really want good reproduction, you may be better off with a good-quality home system—provided all components will be inside and protected from the weather, and provided there are 110 volts a.c. aboard all the time. Or you may want to buy one of the marine systems designed for large boats.

The first thing to decide when installing a stereo system is where to put the speakers. Installing them to achieve good acoustics is seldom easy. Boats are not roomy enough in most cases, and there aren't that many good locations for each speaker. Try to locate them as far apart as possible, and try to avoid mounting them where they will be facing each other. With the typical four-speaker set you will want at least two inside the cabin and perhaps two others out in the cockpit or aft deck. Remember that if you

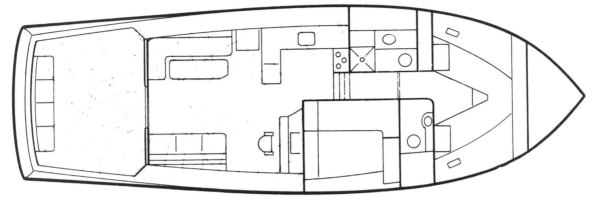

A typical four-speaker stereo installation covering cabin and cockpit.

hope to be able to hear music out in an open cockpit when you are under way with engines running, chances are you will need bigger speakers and possibly a separate, more powerful amplifier.

If you want speakers out on the back deck or in a cockpit, try to locate them where they will be partially sheltered from the weather—under the coaming, for example, or inside a seat locker. Or you can cut an opening in the cabin bulkhead, then install the speakers in an enclosure on the inside with the cone pointing out toward the transom. In center console boats or where the helm is exposed, at least one of the speakers can be installed under the helm in most cases.

Inside, the boat speakers can often be installed in the headliner, but this will usually involve some tricky refitting, so look for a simpler location. If your boat is built with an inner lining or shell, then the space left between the inside cabin lining and the outer hull is often more than adequate for this purpose. Also, think about installing speakers inside strategically located lockers or cabinets. Then you can cut an opening so the speaker will face out where you want the sound to go.

For best fidelity, speakers should be placed in a baffle box or enclosure. This also protects the back of the speaker against damage when it is installed in a cabinet or hanging locker where other items are stored. The speaker box can be built of marine-grade plywood and should be at least a couple of inches larger than the speaker on all sides. It should also be deep enough to leave at least one or two inches behind the speaker, and it should be firmly fastened to the bulkhead or cabin liner so it won't rattle or vibrate.

Instead of building a speaker enclosure of wood, you can also make one from an oversize plastic kitchen bowl. Many of these have rims that make it easy to fasten them in place over the back of the speaker by driving screws through the rim as shown.

When selecting locations for speakers you will also have to consider the difficulty of snaking wires to them. And if you are installing a system sold for use in cars, remember that the speaker wires supplied probably won't be long enough. To avoid electrical losses be sure to use wire a bit heavier than what is supplied—usually no. 16 wire will be adequate, but for really long runs in a large boat use no. 14. Secure or bundle wires at frequent intervals (fifteen to eighteen inches) to minimize damage from chafing.

The tape deck, radio, amplifier, and other components should be mounted inside or under the console where they will be completely protected from the weather and moisture. And make sure all pieces are firmly strapped down or bolted in place—don't trust the front mounting plates supplied with some sets. Install the radio antenna anywhere that is convenient, but the higher the better (it does not have to be outside; it can go under the helm on a flying bridge or inside the console on a fishing boat). With most sets the instructions also advise establishing a good ground connection. This can be done by running a heavy wire directly to the battery or to a sizable underwater ground.

8. Umbrella Holder

There are many times when donning foul-weather gear is inconvenient. In such cases keeping a large umbrella handy is easier and quicker.

One problem with keeping an umbrella on a boat is where to store it so it will be quickly accessible yet won't get damaged by having equipment thrown on it. I found that a simple length of plastic pipe makes an excellent holder that can be easily mounted alongside a companionway door.

For most large umbrellas (like those used by golfers) a piece of plastic pipe with a 1½-inch inside diameter and 9- to 10-inch length works well. Two ⅛-inch-diameter holes for mounting screws are drilled through one side of the pipe as shown, so that self-taping screws about ¾-inch

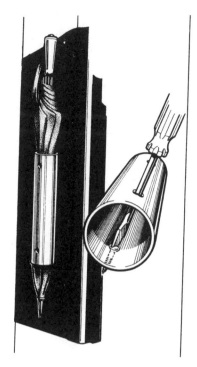

long can be used for mounting the holder on a bulkhead or companionway frame.

To enable you to reach the screw heads from the other side when mounting the holder, two additional holes, each ¼-inch in diameter, are drilled directly opposite the first two (smaller) holes. These larger holes will allow you to insert a screwdriver through the pipe wall so you can reach the screw heads on the other side and drive them home after drilling suitable pilot holes in the mounting surface.

9. Folding Cockpit Table

This is a clever yet simple woodworking project that will serve two handy functions in cruising powerboats that have an open cockpit. In most boats of this type— sportfishermen, sedans, or classic-style lobster boats— there is a goodly amount of potential storage space that is mostly wasted around the inside of the cockpit, just under the coaming. In most cases this space is used only to push things out of the way when the cockpit gets too cluttered. At best there may be a few hooks or simple racks installed to hold fishing poles, boat hooks, and so on.

By adding plywood bulkheads under the coaming to enclose this space across the stern (and possibly along the sides) you can create a series of cabinets for neatly storing extra lines, paint supplies, extra hoses, or any of the myriad other maintenance products and tools often needed on a boat.

Not only will you be building useful storage cabinets, but by adding a drop-down cover or door for the center cabinet as illustrated here you can also create a handy cockpit table that is instantly available when needed. Unlike the usual portable folding tables, this one is permanently mounted so it cannot fall over, and since it folds down out of the way to form a door for the cabinet, it takes up no storage space when not in use.

The material used for enclosing the cabinet and for building the fold-down table, was ¾-inch-thick marine plywood, although ½-inch plywood would probably work almost as well. Fasten 1-inch-square wood cleats to the deck and to the underside of the cockpit coaming with screws to form a backing or frame for supporting the plywood. Instead of trying to cut the plywood to fit, cut pieces of cardboard to the right shape first and use these as a pattern for cutting the actual pieces of plywood to size and shape.

Trim the cardboard pattern to fit with a pair of scissors or a razor so you can get as accurate a guide as possible, and if necessary use several overlapping pieces joined with masking tape to make fitting easier. When this cardboard fits perfectly, use it as a pattern to copy its outline onto the marine plywood. Cut the plywood to shape and size with a saber saw, then fasten it in place with waterproof glue and rustproof screws of stainless steel or brass.

The opening for the dropleaf table should be cut out and finished with molding around the edges before installing the sheet of plywood in its place. Dimensions can, of course, be varied to suit, but the table shown here measures 29 inches long and 21 inches wide (front to back), so you will have to cut an opening in the plywood that is about ⅝ inch wider and ⅝ inch higher than the size of the door/table that will fit into it (the extra half inch is to allow clearance for the moldings that will be added around the edges of the table, and around the opening in which the table fits when it is folded down).

To finish off the plywood edges around the opening in which the drop-leaf table fits, strips of ¾-inch by ¾-inch corner molding or corner guard are installed as shown in the drawing. This will give the opening a finished look and cover up any irregularities in the plywood edges. Then, to act as a stop for the drop-leaf table when folded down and to help keep water out of the cabinet, wood strips 1½ inches wide and ⅜-inch-thick are fastened against the back side of the plywood as illustrated. Use waterproof glue and small screws to fasten these strips of molding in place so that about ½ inch sticks up into the opening to act as a door stop molding when the cabinet is closed.

The edges of the plywood table are covered with 1-inch-wide batten strips glued and nailed flat against each edge, with corners mitered. This gives the tabletop the appearance of being made of solid wood and also makes it look a little thicker than it actually is when in raised position.

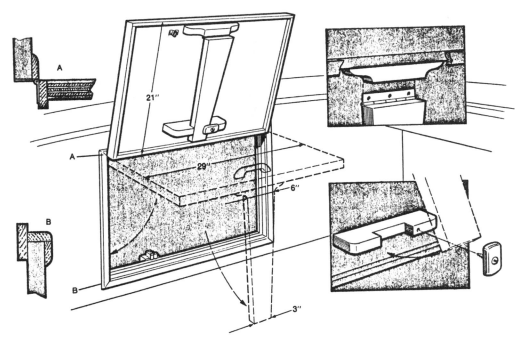

This folding cockpit table also provides a transom storage area.

The folding gate leg that supports the table when it is set up is hinged to a block of wood screwed and glued to the underside of the top as shown in the drawing. A second block of wood, cut out as shown, is fastened to the bottom of the table at the other end to hold this leg in place when it is folded, or when you just want to raise the table to get into the cabinet behind it. A small pivot block holds the end of the leg inside the recess cut in this block, as shown in the drawing. The table/door unit is then attached to the top of the plywood opening with standard butt hinges. The project is finished by attaching a handle to raise the table/door and then installing a couple of friction catches to hold the table/door closed after it is folded down.

Paint the whole thing with a good grade of marine primer, then finish with two coats of marine enamel to match the rest of the boat. To minimize the likelihood of warping, make sure you paint the table and folding leg on all sides and edges, not just on the parts you can see. A coat of wax lessens chances of scratches.

10. Private Entrance for Cat

Many boatowners who take their cats along when cruising find that the best location for a litter box is inside the enclosed head, where it's out of the way most of the time and where any mess is easy to clean up. Others who do not have a separate enclosed head may put the litter box in a forward stateroom or locker—wherever it will be out of sight behind a door.

However, in each case this means that the door leading to the head (or forward stateroom) has to be left open all the time—a nuisance at best and a potential hazard when you are under way. To solve this problem, one clever owner installed a small, free-swinging "private cat door" through which his cat can enter or leave at any time, whether the door to the head is open or not.

To fashion such an entrance for your pet, start by

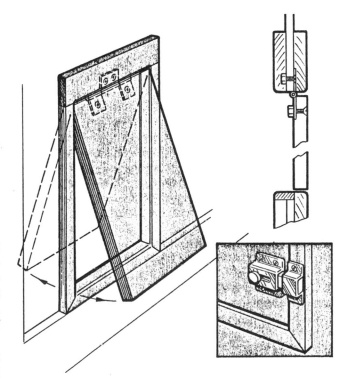

cutting an opening large enough for the cat to walk through easily in the door near the bottom of the central panel. Then cut a piece of ½-inch plywood to serve as a swinging door for this opening. A single, nonmortised-type butt hinge, similar to the one shown here, is then used to hang this plywood door in its opening so that the panel can swing freely in either direction when the cats wants to go in or out. The center leaf of the hinge is attached to the large door at the top of the opening by fastening it to the face of the door panel with short bolts and nuts, or with rivets. A strip of wood ¾ inch by 2 inches is then fastened across the top of the opening to cover this hinge leaf. But cut a recess on the back of this wood strip with a chisel to accept the hinge leaf. That allows the strip of wood to fit flat against the face of the door panel when it is screwed into place.

The other two hinge leaves are attached to the back side of the swinging panel, again by using short bolts and nuts or rivets. This allows the door to swing easily in either direction when the cat pushes it. To finish off the opening, glue wood batten strips (¼ by 1 inch) around the opening as shown. To ensure privacy when someone is using the head—and doesn't want a cat barging in—a small catch was installed on the inside of the swinging door so the cat door could be locked.

Although most cats will be wary of pushing their way through at first, a little patience on your part in demonstrating how the door works will soon get your pet over its fears. Walk the cat slowly back and forth through it a few times while you hold the door open, then let the door drag over its back as it goes through. It won't take long until the cat learns how easy it is to push the door open without help from a person on board.

11. Deck Storage Box

Most boats need more storage space for extra lines, cleaning materials, etc., and one of the handiest containers for such items is a deck box that can sit on the bow or in the cockpit. Buying a fiberglass box is quite expensive, and for those of us who do not have a woodworking shop, building one at home can be difficult.

However, here is a way that even an unskilled woodworker can make a deck box for his boat. It involves buying a ready-made wood storage box from a store that sells unfinished furniture. You then modify this box to make it suitable for use on a boat (or on a dock). Most unfinished-furniture stores sell such boxes for storing blankets, linens, etc. They come unfinished but are complete with a hinged lid. The one I bought measures thirty inches long by fifteen inches wide by fifteen inches high, just about right for my boat's requirements.

Like most such boxes, mine came with cut-out hand holes for carrying at each end. I cut these openings larger

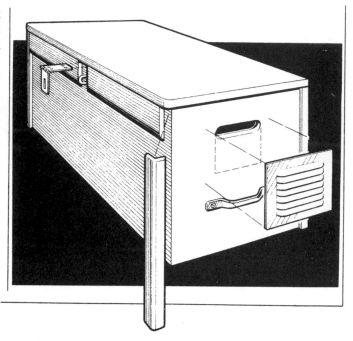

and used them as ventilation openings, then covered them with five- by six-inch stainless steel louvered vents (sold in most marine supply outlets). In addition to adding the vents, I also added two chrome-plated lifting handles on each side below the vents, not only to simplify moving the box around but also to permit lashing the storage box to stanchions when necessary.

The only other modifications needed were to add moldings on each outside corner to cover end grain and to give the box a more finished appearance, plus adding a strip of wood along the top front edge to strengthen it. I also added a chrome-plated hasp to the front so the box could be locked and had a local canvas man fashion a Dacron cover for the box to help protect the contents against the weather. This cover has grommets along the bottom so it can be lashed down if need be. The finished box is painted (it could also be varnished) to match the rest of the boat.

12. Storage Bench for Aft Deck or Flying Bridge

Two things most boats can use more of is storage space and seating capacity. The easily built plywood bench shown here helps meet both these needs. In addition to providing comfortable seating for three or four adults (or a place to stetch out when you are alone), it also creates a lot of additional storage space that can be used for lines, fenders, electric power cords, or cleaning supplies. When it's the right size, the under-seat storage space is also a perfect place to keep a large cooler for storing cold beer, soda, and other beverages.

Depending on what length you make it and on the

amount of space available, a bench of this kind can be mounted on an aft deck, in a cockpit, or on a flying bridge. It is built of marine-grade plywood, except for the wood cleats used on the inside and the pieces of ¾-inch-thick mahogany used for the trim—the top cap and the arms (teak can be used if you don't mind the extra expense). The cap piece across the top of the bench back is a length of ¾-inch by 6-inch mahogany (actually 5½ inches wide), and the arms and arm supports are cut out of ¾- by 3-inch lumber. If the upright backrest is left off, the unit could easily serve as a combination dock box and bench, or as a deck box/bench for use on the bow or on the flying bridge.

The bench is assembled with wood screws and glue; there are simple butt joints at each corner. To reinforce these corners, 1-inch-square wooden cleats are screwed and glued to the inside of each corner as shown.

Dimensions can, of course, be varied to suit individual needs and requirements, but it is generally best to stick with the dimensions shown for the height of the seat off the floor and for the minimum seat depth (front to back) needed for sitting comfort. The overall length of the bench can be varied easily, but to minimize waste, try to sketch out how the pieces of plywood you'll need will be cut out of standard 4- by 8-foot panels.

When the bench is completed, the plywood parts can be finished on the outside with one coat of marine underbody followed by two coats of high-gloss marine paint—or the whole unit can be covered with plastic laminate (such as Formica, Micarta, or Wilsonart). The mahogany trim is finished with three to four coats of marine varnish. The hinged seat lids that swing up to provide access to the storage space underneath should be given at least two coats of a penetrating wood sealer or marine varnish on both sides as well as around the edges. This will seal the wood against moisture absorption and thus keep the plywood lids from warping later on.

The final touch is to have cushions made for the seat and

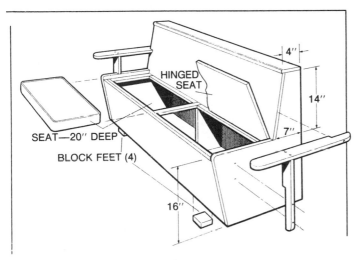

the back section to provide more comfortable seating. If the bench will be out in the weather it is also a good idea to have a waterproof cover made that will slip on over the whole unit—to keep water out of the storage space under the seats as well as to protect the cushions and the finish.

How to Soundproof Your Boat

A day out on the water is supposed to be a pleasant, relaxing time—but it's hard to relax when you have to shout to be heard over the din of a noisy engine (or engines). And it's hard to enjoy a quiet afternoon at anchor when your generator makes such a racket that you're constantly aware of it.

Ideally, acoustical materials that will minimize engine noise should be installed when a boat is built, but as we all know, this isn't always the case. There are, however, a number of things you can do to diminish or muffle the sound of noisy engines, generators, and other mechanical equipment.

Engine noises and other belowdecks mechanical noises are transmitted in one of two ways—by sound waves traveling through the air or by vibrations that travel through stringers, planking, and other solid parts of the hull.

To minimize noise from vibration, resilient pads or spring-mounts can be installed under your engines to keep them from transmitting vibrations to the structural parts of the hull. To fight airborne noises you can install acoustical materials that will enclose the source of the noise and help to absorb it while also acting as a barrier to its passage.

Because banging, knocking, shuddering, and other forms of noise-making vibrations are often due to a poorly tuned engine, the first logical step to take in eliminating vibration is to have a mechanic do a proper tune-up. Sometimes it's simply a matter of adjusting timing or changing spark plugs, but in other cases mounting bolts and set screws may have to be tightened or fan belts replaced. It's amazing how much noise these simple procedures can eliminate sometimes.

The next step is to minimize vibration by making sure there are good vibration pads under each engine or piece of machinery. Bolting directly to a stringer or to the hull means that all vibration generated by the machinery is transmitted to the hull and carried throughout the boat in much the same way that a drum transmits noise throughout a room. That is why all good engine installations include pads, springs, or other vibration absorbers under the legs.

A layer of acoustical insulation under the hatch cover effectively reduces engine compartment noise.

However, remember that even when such mounts were properly installed by the builder, many times they are only marginally efficient, so it may pay to replace them with new ones. Also, after a number of years they will lose their resiliency, and then they must be replaced or added to. The same holds true for auxiliary generators, water pumps, and other noise-making pieces of machinery; all should be mounted on vibration-absorbing neoprene or plastic pads, or on special spring-mounted platforms that keep vibration from being transmitted to the hull. If the engine is on a platform, then the platform should also be secured to the hull (or to stringers tied to the hull) with spring-mounts or flexible mounts that will further help to absorb vibration.

Once you have done all you can to cut down on vibration and thus eliminate much of the noise at its source, the next step is to confine and absorb the noise by installing acoustical (sound-absorbing) materials around the engine or engines. This entails lining the engine compartments with a material that will absorb and deaden sound and cut down on its transmission to the rest of the boat.

There are basically three kinds of insulation used in boats for absorbing or deadening noise: acoustic tile and panels made of wood fiber or compressed pulp (similar to the kind used in homes); fiberglass batts or blankets with a facing of plastic, foil, or other nonpermeable material; and plastic foams of various types, including laminated foams (made of plastic or fiberglass) that are combined with lead, either as a facing or as a layer between the foam.

Some boatbuilders don't put in any sound-deadening materials at all. Many others use the fibrous acoutical panels or tiles because they are the least expensive. Some use fiberglass blankets. Only a few use the more expen-

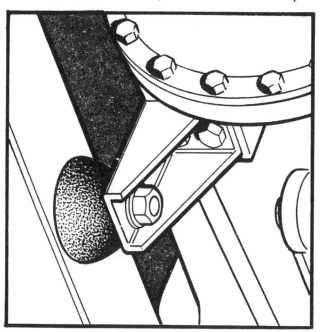

Resilient mounting pads reduce engine vibration noise.

sive—and most effective—laminated lead-and-foam insulating materials to line engine boxes and engine rooms.

Fortunately, boatowners who are plagued with noise and not satisfied with the insulation they now have can add their own lead-and-foil insulating foam to the engine compartments and underdeck spaces. This will help tremendously in reducing the amount of noise heard in the cockpit, saloon, and other areas when under way. The only trouble is that this material is not easy to find in local marine supply outlets, nor can it be easily ordered from every boatyard.

However, at least three producers cater to do-it-yourself boatowners and will sell to consumers in any quantity they need (including cut sheets). One is Noise Reduction Enterprises, 6 Dodge Street, P.O. Box 907, Essex, Mass. 01929; another is American Acoustical Products, 5 Cochituate Street, Natick, Mass. 01760; and the third is The Soundcoat Company, #1 Burt Drive, Deer Park, N.Y. 11729. All three sell a wide range of acoustical materials—foam and fiberglass sheets with and without a lead laminate in the center (or on the face) in different thicknesses and with either a single or a double layer of lead embedded in the foam.

Noise Reduction Enterprises makes a very wide selection of materials. They sell fiberglass (with or without a lead sheet in the center) from 1 inch to 4 inches in thickness. They also sell lead/foam composites from ½ inch to 3 inches in thickness, including a lead/foam material that has a double layer of lead between three layers of foam for maximum sound-deadening qualities. This material costs almost twice as much as the lead/foam that has only a single layer of lead.

American Acoustical Products makes a fiberglass/lead composite and a foam-and-PVC composite that they claim are almost as efficient as the lead/foam composites (but cost considerably less).

None of these products is cheap, but they all help make boating a lot more enjoyable. You can expect to spend from about three to eight dollars per square foot for these soundproofing materials, depending on the type of material you choose and on the thickness you select. Just remember that as a rule fiberglass costs less and is completely noncombustible. Foam will burn if a fire starts, but it will not support flames by itself. However, foams are acoustically more effective for the same thickness and will cost more. Practically all of these materials come with some type of plastic or foil facing on one side to protect the foam against absorption of water, oil, or fuel when installed in the bilge areas or in an engine room.

Lead-foam composites are generally recognized as the most effective sound deadeners for a given thickness, and those having a double layer of lead are obviously a lot more effective than those that have only a single layer.

Several types of acoustical insulation are available.

With any of these products, the thicker the material, the better soundproofing it will provide. On a boat, space restrictions often keep an owner from installing the thickness he would like, so you may have to compromise by installing only as much as there is room for. But remember, foam with a lead laminate on the inside is almost twice as effective as the foam alone, so you need only half as much. Even if you cannot put in enough soundproofing to eliminate the noise completely, in most cases you can put in enough to reduce the noise to an acceptable level.

Engines enclosed by an engine box or compartment are obviously the easiest to soundproof. Line the sides and top of the compartment or box with the thickest material that you have room for—preferably one of the foam-lead composites (you get more soundproofing per inch of thickness that way).

In larger boats where engines are belowdecks, the solution lies in covering the underside of the deck and the hatch covers with soundproofing. Also cover the sides of the hull (or engine compartment) with the same material. Here again, the thicker the better, and use the lead-foam composite for best results. While you want to use the thickest material you can afford—and have room for—be careful not to "smother" the engine by blocking off any required air flow. Also do not jam insulation in so snugly that the engine will overheat. Most sheets are four by eight feet in size, but the companies that cater to consumers will usually be glad to cut half sheets, or even smaller, when needed. A lot depends on what you need and on what they have on hand at the time.

To hold the insulation in place, one of the most popular methods is to use contact cement, applied to the back of the foam and onto the surface against which it must fit. The cement can be applied with a brush or a foam paint roller, but a roller is much faster and easier to use. It is best to apply two coats of the cement to each surface, spacing the coats about ten minutes apart.

The soundproofing materials can all be cut when necessary with a sharp knife or pair of large scissors, and exposed edges should be sealed with duct tape, or by folding an excess flap of the vapor barrier around the edge before pressing it into position.

Mechanical fastening is often used instead of, or in combination with, contact cement. This means fastening the material in place with nails or screws, and using strips of wood over the face to hold it. Obviously, the fasteners have to be long enough to go through these strips and through the insulation without crushing it.

Of course, in fiberglass boats you cannot usually use nails or screws. An alternative is to use cemented-on fasteners that consist of a perforated metal plate with a long, nail-like spike protruding from the center (see the accompanying drawing). Available from Noise Reduction Enterprises (NRE) as well as in many building supply centers, these fasteners are first cemented in place against the fiberglass with epoxy adhesive. Then the insulation is simply pushed on over the spike and held there by means of a push-on capnut and large washer. Once on, the cap cannot be pulled or vibrated off. As a rule, the fasteners should be spaced no more than about twenty-four inches apart on overhead installations.

Mechanical fastening is not always required on vertical or sloping sides because contact cement usually will be enough if you have cut the foam or fiberglass for a snug press fit. But it is needed when fastening to an overhead

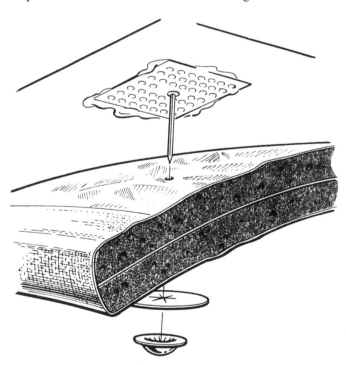

Special fasteners are available to hold insulation on hatch covers and overhead surfaces.

surface such as a hatch cover or decking over the engine. You can use contact cement to hold the foam or fiberglass when you first push the sheet of soundproofing into place, but in overhead installations vibration will cause this to loosen in time, so some type of mechanical fastening is essential.

With any of these materials, it is advisable to plan carefully to avoid waste. The companies mentioned above will help you figure out how much you need—and what would be the best thickness—if you send them a sketch with dimensions of the area to be soundproofed. The head of NRE says the company will put together a kit for you containing everything you need for your job, usually for less than it would cost to buy the components separately.

Storage Space Improvements

When I bought my trawler it had sliding doors that provided access to the space under the dinette seats. The trouble with this arrangement is that any items stored behind these doors tend to get pushed around and jumbled up on the inside, making it hard to keep things neat or to find what you want in a hurry—especially small items. That's why I decided to take the doors off and then build in drawers under these benches instead.

At the same time I solved another problem of how to add additional storage space for the canned goods and other staples we needed on longer cruises. I had discovered that the bulkhead that formed the back of the dinette bench went all the way down to cabin floor level, where it joined the edges of the cabin floor. As in most trawlers and many cruising sailboats, there was a good deal of additional space along the outboard side of this bulkhead—space under the walk-around decks against the outside of the hull—that was inaccessible and therefore wasted (see drawing).

To make use of all this potential storage space and to make more efficient use of the space under the dinette, I began by removing the sliding doors and building a solid front with cutouts for two large drawers as shown in the drawing. Then before installing the home-built drawers I used a saw to cut through the bulkhead in back, thus opening up the "hidden" space behind the dinette so I could use it for additional storage for seldom-needed items during the season, or for storing extra supplies and parts during longer cruises.

Since the original plywood floor ended at the bulkhead that formed the back of the dinette, it was necessary to extend this floor by adding a piece of new plywood to the outboard area. A cardboard template was cut first to

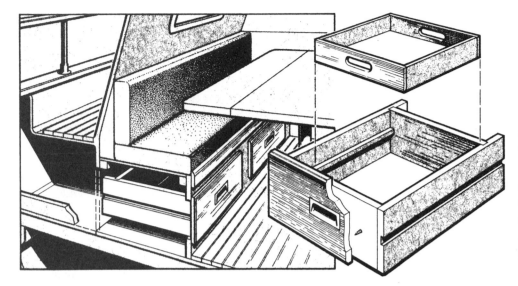

Drawers provide efficient storage space under seats; "waste space" below the side deck is also utilized by cutting through the bulkhead behind the drawers.

ensure a snug fit, then this was used as a pattern for cutting the plywood floor to fit. In most cases the slope of the hull will enable you merely to wedge this piece of plywood in place against the hull while fastening it down along the inboard edges with nails or screws. A three-inch-high wood rail was added along each side of this new floor to keep canned goods and other small items from rolling off the ends and down into the bilge area.

I built the drawers ten inches deep, since these fit best in the space I had, but then I built additional sliding trays that fit inside each drawer and slid along small cleats fastened to the sides as shown. In that way I can more easily sort out or stack the items kept in these drawers without piling things too keep.

The drawer sides are made of ¾-inch-thick lumber, with a dado (groove) cut along the length of each side. When the drawer is in place, this groove fits over a wood rail or strip that is fastened to the inside of the bench frame on each side of the drawer. Lubricating this rail with paraffin or silicone will make the drawers slide easily, yet if the rail is a reasonably snug fit inside the groove along the drawer side, it will enable you to pull the drawer almost all the way out without tipping or falling.

Note that the front of the drawer consists of two pieces of wood, one fastened to the front of the other. The facing or front piece should be wide enough to overlap and cover up the edges of the drawer frame. The back and front pieces that fit between the sides of the drawer frame can be of ½-inch or ¾-inch-thick lumber, and the bottom of the drawer can be made of ¼-inch plywood or hardboard screwed to the bottom edges of the drawer sides, as well as to the bottom edges of the front and back pieces.

To secure the drawers closed when under way, a small hook-and-eye or a barrel bolt can be installed on each drawer, though I have never found this necessary on my

boat. To reach the newly floored storage space behind the drawers, I slide the drawers all the way out, then lift off the seat cushion and the seat bottom panel. I can then reach into this extra storage space quite easily.

Spice Storage

Never wanting to let anything go to waste, I've finally found a use for all those plastic containers that hold 35mm film. Instead of throwing them out, rinse them thoroughly in detergent and fill with the spices you use most in the galley. The containers are waterproof and airtight and will hold enough fresh oregano, paprika, thyme, or basil for a weekend sail's menu.

Reinforcing Weak Chainplates

Like many other stock sailboats, mine had the chainplates through-bolted to one of the wooden bulkheads inside the boat. Unfortunately, sooner or later enough fresh water leaked in to cause some dry rot in that bulkhead, thus weakening the chainplate mounting. Here is how I repaired this damage on my boat while also creating a stronger and safer mounting than I had originally.

Each chainplate is a piece of ¼-inch-thick stainless steel about 2 inches wide and with four holes running in a vertical line down the center. Four ⅜-inch bolts go through this and through the wooden bulkhead behind it. I discovered that the wood around the top bolt had started

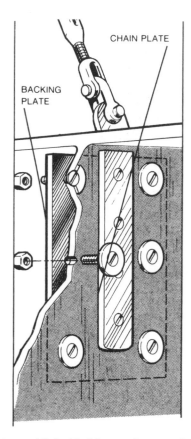

CHAIN PLATE

BACKING PLATE

to deteriorate, and I decided it was time to take corrective action.

First I had a local machine shop make up a stainless steel backing plate that would fit on the opposite side of the bulkhead, directly behind the existing chainplate. I supplied the shop with a cardboard template with holes marked in it to match the original four holes in the chainplate exactly. The new plate was made about 6 or 7 inches wide so there would be room for an additional row of bolts on each side of the chainplate. Thus the original four bolts would go through the chainplate, then the bulkhead, then the backing plate. But in addition there would be six more bolts to take the load—three on each side of the chainplate. These would go through the bulkhead and the backing plate and would serve to spread the tension or load over a much wider area, thus making it stronger than before.

Before the new backing plate was installed, however, I first had to repair the dry rot. This was accomplished by digging out the rotted wood, then mixing an epoxy liquid (I used Git Rot) with sawdust and packing this into the cavities. I allowed this to cure completely before reassembling everything. I did not consider this patching job would be supporting the load—it was just to make sure all the rot was gone and the cavities were filled enough to create a solid surface. The six new bolts, coupled with the

original four, are enough to make the boat safe and solid again.

Engine Smoke Alarm

When we moved out of our apartment we took our smoke alarm along, intending to use it in the cabin or galley area of our boat. But after trying it in various locations, we found it much too sensitive—it would go off every time we used the toaster or had a fire going in our wood-burning stove.

However, we have now found a useful place for it—in our engine room. It is mounted above the engine within easy arm's reach after we remove the companionway steps. When everything down below is functioning properly, the alarm is completely silent. But the least bit of overheating of a pump, fan belt, or piece of electrical equipment sets the alarm off—usually a little too easily, admittedly.

Since a smoke alarm has no on/off switch, when it does go off there is no easy way to shut off the howl it makes while we are checking into the problem, if any. So we modified the alarm by adding an on/off switch as shown here. The idea is that if the alarm goes off you immediately want to investigate—but you don't want the alarm screaming in your ear while you look. The switch enables me to turn it off quickly while I check. If there is something smoldering, I can quickly attack the problem with my Halon fire extinguisher.

The switch is a simple toggle type mounted on the cover as shown. One wire from this switch is soldered to the line going to the positive terminal on the alarm's circuit board, while the other line goes to the clip that snaps on over the

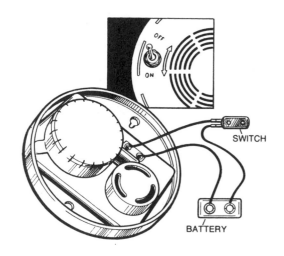

SWITCH

BATTERY

nine-volt battery terminal (you can buy these clips at a Radio Shack store). The negative terminal is then joined to the negative battery terminal clip and the battery is mounted in a new position (to leave room for the switch) by securing it inside the cover with a piece of duct tape.

When buying a smoke alarm for this purpose, the less expensive models (usually costing about fifteen dollars) work best. The more expensive ones have a temperature sensing device that will activate the alarm at about 135° F, but this temperature can be reached in an engine room when motoring on hot days. The cheaper models do not have these sensing alarms, so they are activated by smoke or fumes only.

Sunshade for Sailboats

On a hot, sunny day the open cockpit of a sailboat can be quite uncomfortable at times, regardless of whether you

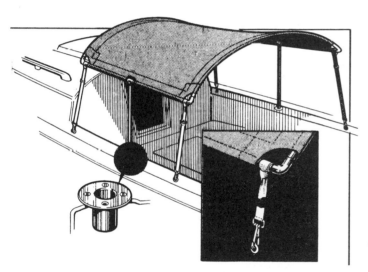

This sunshade relies on just two gunwale-mounted flagpole sockets for support; straps do the rest.

are under power or sail. Time aboard can be a lot more pleasant if you have a sunshade that does not interfere with the movement of the boom or the mainsail.

Many sailboat owners solve the sunshade problem by installing a folding canvas Bimini top. However, this kind of sunshade consists of three separate pipes bent into a U-shape, and the configuration usually makes it difficult to climb into or out of the cockpit on any sailboat less than thirty feet long.

A friend of mine neatly overcame this obstacle by

building a rigid canvas top supported by a stainless tubing frame, as shown in the accompanying drawing. The canvas top was formed by bending tubing to fit, allowing plenty of camber so it will shed rain easily. Then the canvas cover was sewn together with wide hems or pockets along the sides, into which the tubing fits. Stainless steel, flush-mounted flagpole sockets were inserted on each side of the cockpit, aft of the winches, to act as supports for the sunshade. Then small, adjustable straps were installed fore and aft to keep the top rigid when it was set up. The stainless steel elbows in each corner can be unscrewed to allow the entire top to be rolled up for easy stowage when not in use.

During a period of heavy rain the boat's regular canvas dodger is put up, then connected to the sunshade with a twelve-inch-wide strip of canvas. This gives the skipper excellent protection against the weather in a downpour.

Filler Cap Tool

Removing the filler cap from the water storage tank of an engine that has a fresh-water cooling system can sometimes be difficult with only your bare hands, especially since the cap often is located in an out-of-the-way spot where you can't really press down hard enough while turning.

The simple plywood tool illustrated here eliminates most of this struggle. It consists of two pieces of quarter-inch plywood, one cut out to fit neatly over the contour of

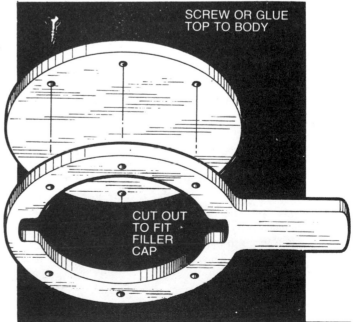

the filler cap, the other a round disk that acts as a cover and serves to stiffen the cutout piece when attached to the top of it with glue and short screws as shown.

Dinghy Gunwale Fender

The accompanying drawings show the method I used to create a shock-absorbing fender along the length of my dinghy—to protect it from damaging the side of my yacht when it comes alongside, as well as to protect the dinghy. The only materials required are two long lengths of ⅛-inch nylon cord (solid core) and a series of short lengths of ½-inch inside-diameter clear plastic tubing. Total cost in my case was under ten dollars.

My dinghy is made of fiberglass, and the fiberglass is sandwiched between two teak strips that serve as gunwale guards along the top. To install the full-length fender I drilled a series of ⅛-inch holes through the fiberglass just below the two strips of teak. These holes are spaced 4 inches apart immediately below the gunwale, along the full length of the sheer.

After the holes are drilled, the next step is threading the nylon cord through the holes by looping it diagonally over the top of the gunwale as shown. The cord comes out one hole on the outside of the fiberglass, then goes in through the next hole from the inside. Thread the cord through two or three holes, then use the cord as a guide to measure how long the pieces of plastic tubing must be to go over the cord from one hole to the next (the cord will be threaded through the center of each short length of tubing).

It's best to cut the first piece of tubing a little longer than you think it should be, then gradually trim it shorter until it fits snugly over the gunwale when the cord goes through it and over the gunwale on its way into the next hole. Remember, the tubing does *not* go through the holes in the fiberglass—each piece is threaded over the cord and is just long enough to go from one hole to the next. After you have experimented to determine the correct length for these pieces of tubing, cut as many lengths as you will need to do the job (one to fit between each pair of holes).

Now use a flame to melt the end of the nylon cord so you can shape it into a point (this will make it easier to thread the cord through the holes). Rolling it rapidly between two smooth, hard surfaces while it is still soft is the easiest way to do this. Cut a piece of the cord long enough to go through all the holes along one side of the dinghy—plus a generous allowance for the spiral path it will follow, and a little extra for pulling tight at the end.

Then tie a knot in the opposite end. Starting at the transom, thread the cord through the first hole from inside the dinghy. Push the cord end through the first short length

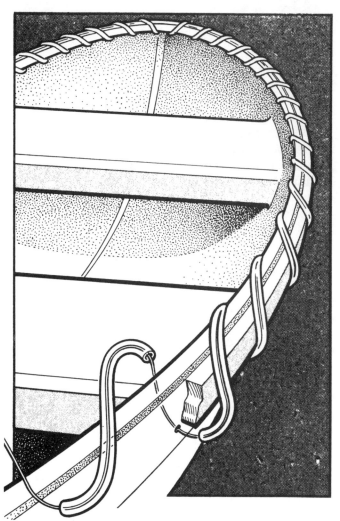

A combination of nylon cord and plastic tubing makes a great small-boat rubrail.

of plastic tubing, then cross the cord and tubing diagonally over the top of the gunwale so you can thread the cord through the second hole from the inside again. Now slide another piece of the tubing on over the cord, then lay this diagonally over the gunwale and thread the cord through the next hole.

Continue in this manner until you have threaded the nylon cord through the last hole next to the bow. There should be a short length of plastic tubing covering all the exposed cord (between holes). Don't try to pull the cord up just yet. Tie it off loosely at the bow temporarily, then start back at the transom and pull the cord tight, one hole at a time. Work your way back to the bow again and this time tie the cord off permanently. If you have pulled each loop tight the cord will be tightly encircling the gunwale with diagonal loops from transom to bow, and the short lengths of tubing will arch up to create an effective fender that will protect both the dinghy and the yacht. After you've done one side, repeat the process on the opposite side to finish the job.

Stowing Dinghy Oars

Stowing the oars and the oarlocks for the average fiberglass or wood dinghy is always a problem, especially on a sailboat, where more often than not the dinghy is kept upside down on a cabintop. Oars always fall out if stored inside the dingy, as do the oarlocks. Yet if you don't store oars and oarlocks inside the dinghy, chances are that sooner or later you will lose one, or will launch the dinghy without them.

Like many other sailboat owners, we used to keep our oars in a lazarette, but we got tired of finding them covered with cushions, swim ladders, fenders, and other paraphernalia—and the oarlocks always seemed to disappear into the bottom of the locker where they couldn't be reached. So we did a little alteration to the inside of our dinghy that created neat storage spaces for oarlocks and oars.

The oarlocks nest in a specially fitted drawer that slides out from under the midship seat in the dinghy, and the oars fit along the bottom of the dinghy under the seats. They are held in place by a wood retaining strip that holds the blade tips at one end and a plastic collar that fits over the handles at the other end—and they stay in place even when the dinghy is turned over.

As shown in the drawing, the oarlock drawer is routed or carved out to match the shape of the oarlocks so they won't rattle around. This drawer is designed to open aft so anyone in the back or middle of the dinghy can get at them. The drawer cannot come completely out of its tracks because of a stop screw that hits a strip that goes across between the drawer guides. A metal line cleat is fastened to the front of the drawer so it can be used as a drawer pull, as well as to secure a small line that holds the oars in place. Hooks set on each side of the drawer keep it closed, but we reversed one of these hooks so gravity will keep it closed even when the dinghy is upside down.

To hold the oars in place I first installed a piece of 1-inch-by-2-inch mahogany against the small bulkhead under the stern seat, positioning it about 1 inch off the bottom of the dinghy. The tips of the oar blades fit under this when they are in place. Next, I cut a 3-by-6-inch retainer collar out of ⅛-inch-thick rigid plastic, as shown in the drawing. Two holes 1½ inches in diameter were bored through this as shown, centering them 3 inches apart. These slip on over the two oar handles when they are laid side by side in the bottom of the dinghy. Two additional small holes ¼ inch in diameter were drilled between the larger holes so that the end of a 4-foot length of ⅛-inch line could be tied through them as shown.

When storing the oars we slide them in under the seats

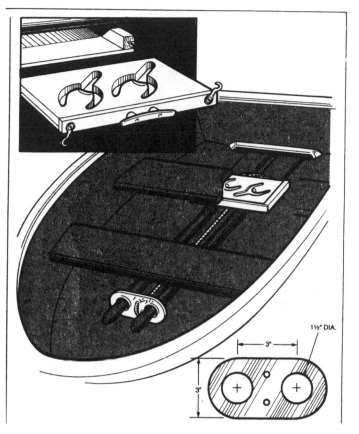

so the blade tips go under the wood strip beneath the stern seat. Then the plastic collar is slipped over the handle ends and the line is run aft, pulled tight, then tied to the cleat, which also acts as the drawer handle. Keeping the line taut serves to hold the oars firmly in place and also keeps the oarlock drawer closed (the hooks serve merely as backups for this). This setup keeps the oars and oarlocks always in place, even when the boat is turned upside down, yet they are instantly available inside the boat when needed.

Outboard Motor Cover

A sturdy canvas cover for a small outboard dinghy motor is always a good idea because it will serve at least two useful purposes: (1) It helps protect the finish on the motor from the elements and helps to ward off corrosion, and (2) it makes the outboard motor less conspicuous and thus less of a temptation to thieves when the motor is left exposed in the cockpit or clamped to a stern rail or bracket.

An excellent and durable cover can be improvised from an old canvas boat bag (also called an ice bag). These convenient carry-all bags have two strong canvas handles and are widely used by boatowners (who often tend to throw them out when they get really grubby-looking).

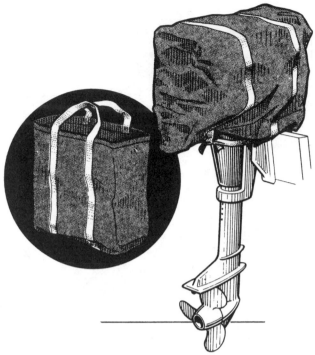

Instead of discarding the bag, use it as shown to form a cover for your small outboard. The bag will cover the powerhead of most four- to six-horsepower motors when turned upside down. The two handles can be pulled together underneath the powerhead, then lashed together with a small piece of light line tied with a slipknot. And it doesn't look too inviting to thieves.

Shoreside Storage: Dock Box or Steps

Every boatowner who keeps his boat in a marina or dockside berth of any kind soon learns that setting up a dock box reasonably close to his boat can make life a lot easier. A well-found dock box can hold many items that you really don't have room for on the boat, as well as supplies and materials you would rather not store on board even if you do have room for them—such as flammable solvents, paints, and similar products that produce odors and are dangerous to store below.

A roomy dock box can also be used to store portable power tools, vacuum cleaners, and other household appliances that you bring from home during the boating season. Leaving them safely locked in a dock box not only solves the problem of where to store them on an already crowded boat, but it also means you don't have to lug them back and forth every time you need them.

A list of items that are likely candidates for dock box storage includes the following:

● Paints, varnishes, and thinners. These are not only messy and take up a lot of space on the boat, but they also are a fire hazard. You may want to take some of these items along for touch-ups when you go off on a long cruise, but otherwise there is no need to carry them on the boat all the time.

● Mops with long handles, scrub brushes, and other hard-to-store cleaning supplies that would otherwise be left lying around in the cockpit or would get jammed into a lazarette or a cockpit hatch next to the engines. This includes reserve stocks of rags and paper towels.

● Extra hoses and long shore cord extensions. You may want to take these with you when you go off on a vacation cruise of several weeks, but when you are going out for just the day, or overnight, why carry all this along?

● Scuba diving gear and water skis (unless you use these every time your boat goes out). Many cruising boats carry gear of this kind for occasional use but rarely have enough extra storage space available for it, so the equipment winds up cluttering the cockpit or engine room. Leaving it in the dock box and putting the equipment on board only when you are planning to use it enables you to keep things a lot neater and save valuable onboard storage space for other items.

● Soda and other drinks. Many boatowners buy soda and beer by the case. Instead of storing the full cases on board the boat, store only a few six-packs at a time and keep the reserves in your dock box.

● Bulky appliances and portable power tools are not needed on a day-to-day basis when cruising, so leave them all in the dock box and take them aboard for the day only when needed.

● It's always handy to have scrap pieces of teak or mahogany on hand, as well as leftover lengths of aluminum or stainless steel molding, pieces of tubing, etc. Keep these in the dock box instead of throwing them out—then you won't have to go hunting for them when a piece is needed.

● Store extra fishing reels, rods, spools of line, and similar gear that you aren't likely to need each day. That way you can grab your tackle when you feel like a day of fishing without having onboard storage space taken up.

Organization

By now you should have some idea of how useful a dock box or set of storage steps can be. Of course, the box should be equipped with a sturdy hasp and a padlock to keep your gear reasonably secure; and you shouldn't leave things in the box that you're likely to need when away from your home dock—items like fenders and extra lines.

To keep the inside of your dock box from becoming a hopeless mess, organize the contents in a sensible manner. One of the best ways I have found to keep things neat is to store most of the smaller items in plastic containers that can be stacked or lined up next to each other. I use plastic wastepaper baskets or plastic kitchen garbage cans to store items such as cleaning supplies, paints, etc. Try to buy rectangular baskets or containers rather than round ones, since they waste less space inside the box. For example, you can use one basket or container for paints, another for cans of polish, boat soap, and other cleaning supplies, and a third for rags, brushes, etc.

Another handy way to keep things neat is to use rectangular plastic dishpans as storage containers. These can be filled with groups of allied items, then stacked one on top of the other, with the least-used group of items on the bottom and the most frequently used ones on top.

To simplify finding things when you need them, make a list of where things are inside the box along with a little sketch showing how the pans or baskets are arranged. Tape this list and the sketch to the inside of the dock box lid so that when you open the box all you have to do is look at the list and glance at the sketch to see exactly where different groups of items are stored. But remember:

To keep things neat you'll have to resist the temptation to throw items in without putting them in their proper place—take a minute to put them back where they came from and you will always be able to find them.

Once you've decided that you need a dockside storage box, your next decision is whether to buy one or build your own. Actually, you have three choices, depending on the type of boat you own: (1) You can buy a prefabricated fiberglass dock box or deck box from a marine supply store or marina. (2) You can build your own dock box of plywood in the size you want. (3) If you own a boat that has a relatively high freeboard for boarding, so that steps would facilitate getting on and off, then you can build a set of wooden steps with a storage area underneath.

Molded fiberglass dock boxes come in many different sizes and styles. They are generally attractive-looking, extremely durable, and completely maintenance-free. Unfortunately, they all have one other thing in common—They're expensive. Prices for most models start at close to two hundred dollars, and go up to six hundred or seven hundred dollars if you want one long enough to accommodate fishing rods. But you can build a homemade box out of exterior grade plywood in the size you want for just a fraction of this amount.

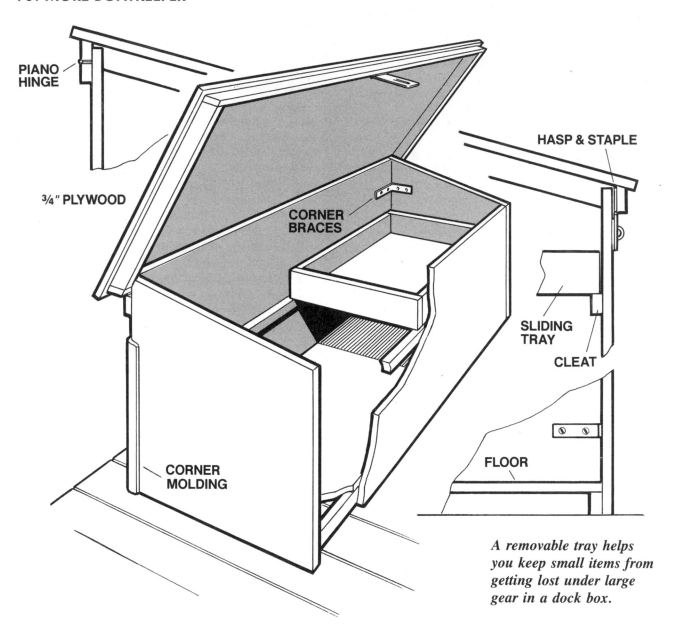

PIANO HINGE

¾" PLYWOOD

CORNER BRACES

CORNER MOLDING

HASP & STAPLE

SLIDING TRAY

CLEAT

FLOOR

A removable tray helps you keep small items from getting lost under large gear in a dock box.

Building Your Own

The above drawing shows one way to build a box of this kind out of ¾-inch exterior grade A/C (one good side) plywood, using simple butt joints reinforced with metal corner braces on the inside. Or you can use marine grade plywood that is good on both sides—if you can find it in your local lumberyard—but it will cost about two and a half to three times as much and is not necessary. Properly painted exterior-grade plywood will last for years and the interior defects won't be noticeable (as long as you make sure to assemble the box with the good side out).

As shown in the drawing, the lid is attached along the back with continuous-type piano hinges. The box is higher at the back than at the front so that the lid slopes forward

when closed to help ensure better runoff of water, and there is a rim of one-by-two lumber fastened around the edges of the top to form an overlapping "lip" that also serves to keep water out. In addition, these strips also cover up the raw edges of the plywood lid on all four sides. They are attached to the edges of the plywood with glue and serrated nails (bronze or stainless), with corners mitered and rounded off for a neat appearance.

The floor of the box rests on one-by-one-inch strips or cleats screwed along the bottom of each side and the front and back pieces, as shown in the drawing. This allows for an air and drainage space under the floor to help keep dampness out of the wood.

One useful feature included in this box is a sliding tray

on the inside that rides on one-by-one-inch strips fastened to the inside of the front and back pieces. Similar to the kind of tray found inside trunks and old army footlockers, this tray can be used to hold many small items that would otherwise get lost in the jumble. It can be slid back and forth or lifted completely out when you have to hunt for items in the bottom of the box.

Storage Steps

Building a set of wooden steps with storage underneath is similar to building a simple dock box. The difference is that instead of a lid on top, you have a door in the back to provide access to the storage space underneath. The door could be built in the side instead, but then the door would have to be shorter or lower and it would be harder to reach the contents on the inside. In addition, if you ever had to turn the steps around to board on the other side, the door would be inaccessible (facing the boat).

Made of the same kind of exterior grade plywood described above, the steps are assembled in much the same way—with glue and serrated nails. The door is hung with a piano-type hinge, and it closes against one-inch-

wide strips of wood screwed to the inside of the plywood around all four sides of the opening. In other words, the strips act as a combination door frame and stop molding, and help keep water out of the inside when it rains. Foam weatherstripping fastened to the face of these strips will also help provide a watertight seal.

Treads and risers can be cut out of the same plywood as the sides, but solid lumber will make a neater job since there will be no porous plywood edges showing. The size of the steps will, of course, have to vary to suit the overall height needed, but as a rule you should try to make treads at least nine to ten inches wide (front to back) and risers no more than eight to nine inches in height. These are fastened in place with waterproof glue and serrated nails driven into the edges of the plywood sides after the plywood has been cut out to provide a support for the treads and risers.

Handrails

To make the handrails for these stairs—which is advisable if the steps are more than two treads high—ordinary two-by-three-inch lumber can be used. But make sure you

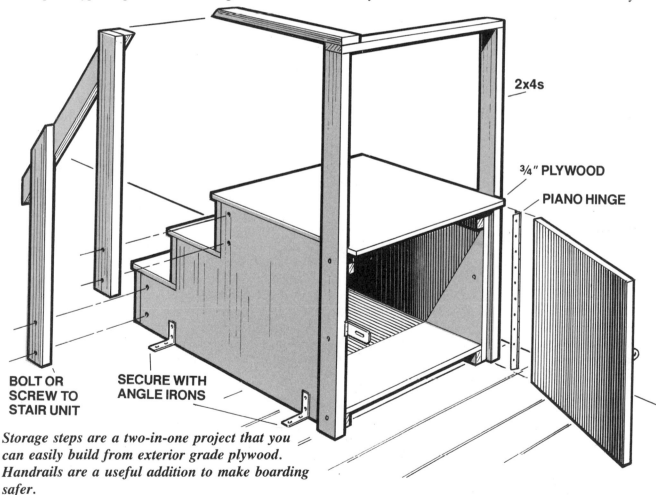

2x4s

¾″ PLYWOOD

PIANO HINGE

BOLT OR SCREW TO STAIR UNIT

SECURE WITH ANGLE IRONS

Storage steps are a two-in-one project that you can easily build from exterior grade plywood. Handrails are a useful addition to make boarding safer.

buy pieces that are straight and relatively free of knots and other serious defects. The vertical pieces that serve as posts are fastened to the sides of the steps with bolts, and the horizontal pieces that serve as the actual rail are then nailed to the tops of these pieces. Sand all edges, and round off all corners.

To simplify painting the steps or dock box, apply a prime coat to the raw wood after pieces are cut to size but before they are assembled. In that way you can prime both sides more easily and thus help minimize the chance of water absorption. Plywood manufacturers recommend using latex exterior house paint and a latex primer for best results. These paints are softer and more flexible than many oil paints—and all marine paints—so they are not as likely to check or peel after a couple of years have gone by.

Adding a Dorade Box Ventilator

Needing more ventilation in my boat, especially in the dinette area, I decided that the best way to get this was to build a dorade vent—a box-like cover that fits over an opening cut in the cabintop. It has a scoop-type cowl vent that can be turned to face the breeze; but the box on which this cowl vent is mounted traps and drains water without allowing any to enter.

Although the box can be built of any wood, I built mine of three-quarter-inch teak since I felt this would help dress the boat up a bit. Dimensions are not critical—the box can be long and thin, or short and wide, and even the height can be varied to suit—but generally it should not be less than the six inches indicated in the drawing.

Plastic cowl vents are made by several different manufacturers and can be purchased from most marine supply outlets. I used three-inch Nicro/Fico vents, but the four-inch vents will admit 70 percent more air, so if space allows, you may prefer to use these larger vents.

The dorade box was assembled with screws and glue, with all screws countersunk and the holes filled with wood plugs. The box is fastened to the top of the cabin by means of wood cleats along each side. These are bedded with sealer, then screwed to the cabintop so they will be just inside the sides of the box when it is placed over them. The box is screwed to the cleats along each side.

Before fastening the box in place, several small notches or weep holes are cut along the bottom edge so water that gets in through the cowl vent can escape out the bottom of the box. Also, a three-inch hole (the size of the cowl vent) is drilled through the cabintop to let the air in.

On the outside of this hole fasten a bulkhead flange that

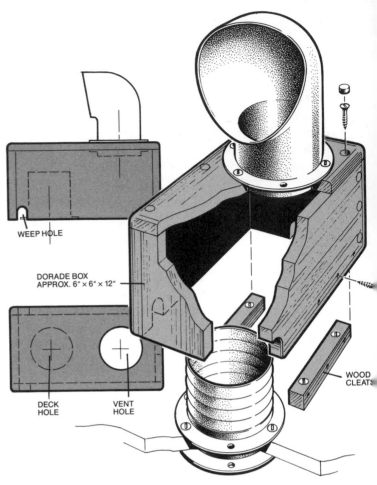

This dorade box ventilator will allow fresh air to enter the cabin but will keep water out.

is used for bilge blower tubing, bedding it with plenty of sealer to make the joint weathertight; then attach a short piece of three-inch-diameter blower tubing to this flange so it sticks up about two or three inches above the cabintop. This will let air in over the top but will keep any water that might enter the box through the cowl vent from entering the interior of the boat (unless the water should rise up that high inside the dorade box).

Opposite the hole in the cabin top, drill another three-inch-diameter hole in the top of the dorade box. Install the deck plate for the cowl vent over this. Finally, a second deck plate is installed on the inside over the hole cut through the cabintop. This also makes it possible for you to close off the air intake from inside—simply by screwing the deck plate cover on from below.

Track for Folding Canvas Top

On many boats that have folding canvas tops over the exposed bridge there is a problem stowing this top when it is not in use because when you fold it forward to get it out of the way the framework is not long enough to allow it to fall far enough forward. Instead of folding down in front of the windshield when the frame is folded forward, it stops when it is only about halfway down on the windshield, so it forces the skipper to stand in order to see clearly over and beyond the folded canvas.

I solved this problem on my boat by installing a sliding track along each side of the bridge. I then attached the bottom of the canvas frame to a slide that moves back and forth inside this track, as shown in the accompanying drawing. When the canvas top is up and stretched tight this slide is moved all the way back as far as it will go toward the rear (aft) end of the track as shown.

When the frame is folded forward the slide also is pushed forward to the other end of the track so the folded frame can fit easily past the front of the windshield and fold down out of the way, as shown by the dotted lines in the drawing. The dimensions can, of course, be varied to provide a longer track if necessary to fit your boat.

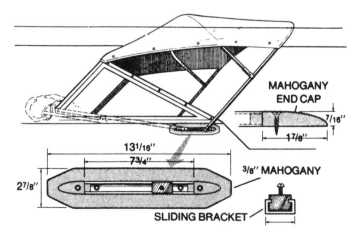

The sliding track and the bracket that slides inside it can be purchased at many hardware stores and home centers, as well as from marine canvas shops. The track is mounted on a piece of mahogany or teak that is attached to each side of the bridge with screws, and additional blocks of wood are shaped to serve as stops that will prevent the sliding brackets from coming out of the tracks at either end.

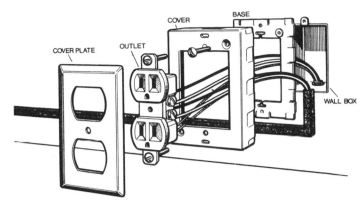

One convenient way to add extra electrical outlets to your boat is to use a surface wiring system.

Adding Extra 110-Volt Outlets to Your Boat

Nowadays most cruising boats, including those of comparatively modest size, have 110-volt shore cords and appropriate wiring inside the boat so that those aboard can enjoy the luxury of watching television, or using an electric toaster, hair dryer, or microwave oven, as well as being able to use portable power tools that run off household current. Even those boats that do not have an auxiliary generator to provide this AC current while under way will still have the convenience of plugging in when dockside.

However, although most new boats come with a shore cord and circuit breaker panel in addition to dockside wiring, they usually include only a minimum number of 110-volt outlets throughout the interior—perhaps one in the galley area and one in the salon area. Seldom if ever are there enough outlets conveniently located where they are really needed.

Many boatowners get around this shortage by using an assortment of extension cords and multiple outlet taps, but even at best this is a makeshift arrangement that is not only inconvenient but also can be quite unsafe. For example, if there is only one outlet in the galley and you want to use a toaster having a cord that won't reach that outlet, then using an extension cord could be a real hazard because of the load that a toaster draws; it's even worse if the cord has to be draped across the stove or sink area.

Fortunately, adding some extra outlets is really not all that difficult if you are careful to follow all recommended wiring practices and if you remember that adding outlets *does not increase the capacity* of that circuit; it only adds

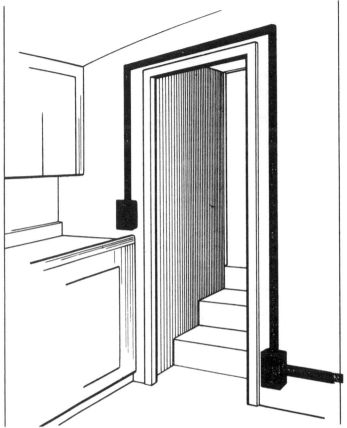

Elbows make it possible to run raceways around obstacles. First push wires through, then cover elbows.

house, a boat requires wiring that is resistant to moisture, and only *stranded* wire or cable is acceptable—never use cable that has solid wires or conductors in it; the vibration encountered on a boat when under way could cause problems because solid wire is more brittle and thus more likely to break. Approved types will be labeled type SO, ST, or STO.

In addition to using the right type of cable or wire, make sure you also use wire of adequate size. Use No. 14 wire for most standard fifteen-amp circuits, and use No. 12 wire for twenty-amp circuits or those that you think will be carrying heavier loads (like a toaster or heater). The wire should be supported at intervals of no more than eighteen inches with plastic cable straps, and it should be installed so it will be out of the bilge water. All such wiring should be three-conductor cable that has two current-carrying wires—one white and one black—and one grounding wire that never carries current (a green wire).

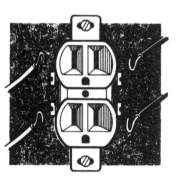

For receptacles, keep both black wires on one side, whites on the other.

convenience. In other words, a circuit with a 15-amp breaker can only carry a maximum load of about 1,500 to 1,750 watts, no matter how many additional outlets you add. The benefit gained is that you can place the outlets where they will be more accessible, or more convenient, and thus will eliminate the need for extension cords.

In almost every case, adding an outlet to an existing circuit is done by tapping into one of the existing outlets or receptacles and then extending new wires to where you want the new outlet. The walls in a house are hollow, so running wires from one room to another—or from one part of a room to another—is done by snaking the wires through the walls. In a boat this can sometimes be done, but in many cases it is not practical because the "walls" in a boat are not usually hollow—they may be made of solid plywood or may consist of a plywood skin over a fiberglass liner. So you can't simply snake your new wires through from one place to another in many areas.

An alternate method that is often used is to run wires straight down into the engine room or bilge area and then run them along under the cabin sole until you can bring them up to where the new outlet will be located. Unlike a

All wiring should run in one continuous length from one outlet box or receptacle to the next one. Never splice 110-volt AC wires by simply joining them together and then wrapping with tape. If a splice becomes necessary, it should be made inside a regular junction box with all unused openings sealed off. To connect the wires together, use crimp-type connectors—not the regular twist-on solderless connectors (often referred to as a Wire Nut, although that is actually one company's brand name) that are used in household wiring.

Although there will be many instances when you can run the new wires through hollow spaces such as cabinets and enclosures, or when you can run wires down into the engine room and then up to the location where the new outlet will be, there are situations where this won't work, or when it will involve a great deal of unnecessary labor. In these cases running wires along the surface is often the most practical (and sometimes the only) solution. This

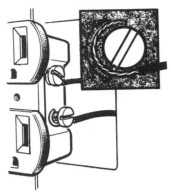

Loop wires in clockwise direction around terminals before tightening.

doesn't mean you should just tack extension cords up with staples or plastic cable clamps. This is not only unsightly, it also can be unsafe because the wires are exposed and thus easily damaged. Also, sunlight and exposure will dry out the plastic insulation in time and it will start to crack, thus increasing the possibility of an accidental short—or even a dangerous shock.

The best way to handle this is to use a surface wiring system that runs the wires through a metal raceway that can be fastened against the surface. Long used by electricians to add outlets, switches, and fixtures in commercial and industrial installations, these metal raceways or channels are now being sold in home centers and hardware stores for use by do-it-yourselfers. Though they are designed for use in the home, there is no reason why they could not be used inside a boat (not outside, or where they would be exposed to the weather or to water splashing on them). The only limitation is that they should only be used on a boat (or homes) where the original a.c. wiring is a properly grounded three-wire system—that is, with two hot wires (one white, one black) and a separate ground wire (green).

The green wire should be unbroken as it goes from one receptacle or fixture to another, and it should be connected

Crimp-on fittings can be used instead of wire loops.

directly to the green grounding wire coming in from the dock, as well as to the boat's main ground. It should never be connected to any of the "common" (white) wires on the boat, or to any terminal point that will permit it to carry current.

Called On-Wall Wiring and manufactured by the Wiremold Company of West Hartford, Conn., these raceway channels are a half-inch in width and are attached to the surface with special clips that you install first—the channel simply snaps into place. For rough or irregular surfaces where the clips cannot be used, special mounting straps can be used instead.

Each raceway can hold up to three No. 12 wires or five No. 14 wires, and the system includes a variety of elbows and tees so that raceways can be routed around obstructions or joined where necessary. There are also special surface-mounted outlet boxes available that will accept standard, UL-listed outlets and switches. The raceways come in five-foot lengths and can be easily cut with a hacksaw when shorter lengths are needed.

Generally speaking, you install the raceways against the bulkhead first, then push the wires through. Where there are right-angle elbows in the raceway it is easier to leave the cover off the elbow and then push the wires through from the elbow, working in each direction, rather than trying to push the wires around the bend when working from one end.

To hook up to an existing receptacle, remove the cover plate from the existing outlet box first, then attach a special base plate that enables you to add the new surface-mounted extension box on top of the existing one. The same receptacle can then be remounted in the new extended box, after which the original cover plate can be replaced. The base plate of this surface-mounted box has an adapter that makes it possible to slip the tongue end of the raceway into the box when you are ready to install the first length of raceway. After the first piece is in place and mounted in its clips, keep cutting new pieces and adding them on until you have run channels all the way to where the new outlet is to go. Then start pushing wires through (three conductors) so you can complete the job.

Regardless of whether you are using this type of raceway system or simply running plastic-covered cable through bilge areas and enclosed compartments, it is important that you follow good wiring practices to ensure a safe installation. Here are the important points that should be kept in mind when you start with the actual wiring:

1. Before taking off any cover plates or making any connections, make sure the power has been shut off—either by throwing the appropriate circuit breaker on the main panel, or by pulling out the dockside shore connection.

2. When connecting up to an existing receptacle, start by removing the cover plate first. Then take out the two screws that hold the receptacle in place against the front of the box (one at the top and one at the bottom) and pull the receptacle out carefully without disconnecting any wires at first—so you can see how the wires are connected to the various screw terminals before you start removing them.

3. If there are other wires joined together inside the outlet box but not connected to the receptacle, leave them alone.

4. After noting which wire goes to which terminal, you are ready to hook up your new wires. Remember: Always hook white wires to the same terminal screws that the old white wires were hooked up to (usually a lighter-colored screw) and black wires to the same screw terminals that the old black wires were attached to. In other words, join white to white and black to black when attaching to wiring, or when adding new wires.

5. When joining wires to the screw terminals on the side of the receptacle, there are two methods you can use: You can wrap the bare ends of the twisted wire ends directly around the terminal screw before tightening it, or you can add a spade-type crimp-on fitting to the end of the wire first, then slip this under the terminal screw before tightening. If you elect to wrap the bare wires around the terminal, make sure you wrap them clockwise around the screw. This will tend to tighten them further as the screw is tightened. Before doing this, make sure you have twisted the wires tight so no loose strands end up sticking from under the screw head.

6. If there is no room for additional wires on the same terminal screw, or on the screw next to it (on the same side), you will have to join the wires together separately and then add a short "pigtail" length of wire to this junction to connect both wires to the terminal. For making a pigtail connection of this kind use crimp-type connectors—DO NOT use twist-on-type solderless connectors on a boat.

7. Outlet boxes and junction boxes can be either metal or plastic, but unused openings should be sealed off. If the box will be used where the weather can get at it (like out in the cockpit) or where there is a chance of exposure to moisture, then make certain you use a weatherproof outlet box in conjunction with a rubber-gasketed weatherproof cover.

8. If you are installing an outlet in the galley area, in a shower, or out in the cockpit, then use a Ground Fault Circuit Interrupter (GFCI) receptacle. This is a special type that protects against lethal shock in damp locations (it is required by the building code in homes and is recommended by the ABYC for boats in these locations). It fits into a standard outlet box and is installed in much the same way as a regular receptacle, except that most do not have terminal screws; they have short lengths of wire that are attached directly to the circuit wiring with crimp fittings.

Improved Bilge Pump Circuit

Automatic bilge pumps are a great idea for most boats, but they do have one drawback—especially if your boat is left on a mooring for days on end. Very often the float switch will kick the pump on repeatedly without doing any real work, thus running the battery down needlessly and greatly shortening the life of the pump and the float valve.

For example, the pump often kicks on to discharge a small amount of water in the bilge but kicks off in a minute or two. Then the water in the hose runs back into the bilge, raising the level enough to kick the pump on again—and accomplishing nothing except adding extra wear to the float switch and pump and creating a drain on the battery. Sometimes the boat gets rocked or heeled over enough to slosh water up against the float switch and activate the pump, but again, nothing much is accomplished.

To solve all these problems I rewired my automatic pump as shown so that it now has *two* float switches, one a few inches higher than the other. Nothing happens until the water gets high enough to close the upper float switch. When the water closes only the lower switch, the pump

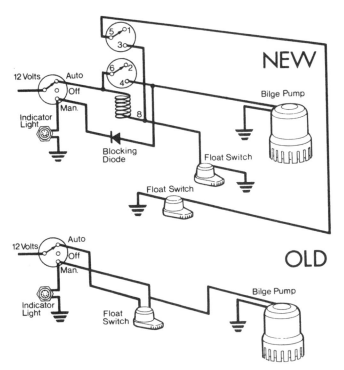

Two float switches replace one in this bilge pump plan.

does not go on—it must get high enough to close the upper switch momentarily as well. Once the upper switch closes, current flows through the relay coil to energize it (I used Radio Shack's part No. 275-218B, a 12-volt d.c. plug-in relay).

This closes the contacts that send current to the pump through the upper float switch and closes another set of contacts (on the same relay) to activate the lower float switch. The pump then comes on and stays on until the water drops low enough to release or open the lower float switch. The upper float switch may make and break contact several times, but it will draw an arc only once per pumping sequence, so the switch will have a much longer life.

Both float switches will have a longer life because the amount of current flowing through them (when closed) will only be about half an ampere—the amount needed to activate the relay—instead of the five amps needed to power most pump motors. And when the pump runs it will move more water—from four to eight inches, depending on the distance between float switches. In sailboats with a deep narrow bilge, spacing one switch about eight inches higher than the other would be about right. But in powerboats with wide, shallow bilges, I would space the switches no more than about three to four inches apart vertically.

The main switch used is an SPDT, center ''off'' switch that is usually standard on most boats. It has a manual position that bypasses everything and sends power directly to the pump. The five-amp blocking diode (two three-amp diodes can be used in parallel if you can't find a five-amp one) in the circuit allows the twelve-volt indicator light to come on only when the pump is working in the manual mode; it warns you not to leave the boat with the switch in the manual position.

Automatic Locker Light

Most lockers on a boat do not have lights inside, so it is often necessary to use a flashlight to find things on the inside, especially at night. I solved this annoying problem by installing an automatic twelve-volt light in each of my lockers. The circuit is set up (as shown in the accompanying diagram) so that each time the door is opened the light on the inside comes on. To activate or turn on each light I used a two-piece magnetic switch like the ones normally used on doors and windows when installing a burglar alarm system. The sealed switch is inside one of these pieces; the second piece is a magnet that, when held close to the switch piece, will either open or close that switch, depending on the type of magnetic switch it is.

You have to use the type called ''normally open'' (NO).

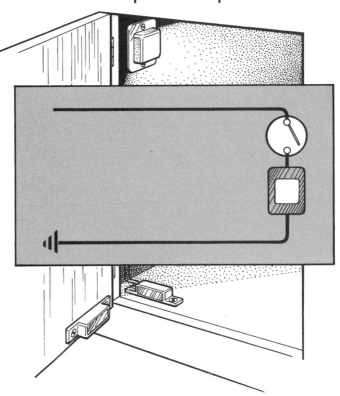

What this means is that in its normal position, with the magnetic half close to the switch half, the circuit is open. When the magnet is pulled away from the switch the switch closes and thus completes the circuit to turn the light on. The piece with the switch on the inside   that is, the piece wired into the circuit—is mounted on the doorjamb or frame. The magnet half is mounted on the door so that it is right next to the switch when the door is closed. Opening the door separates the two, causing the switch to close and turn on the light.

The twelve-volt lights used are surface-mounted, dome-type utility lights that can be purchased in most auto supply stores. The magnetic switches are available in all electronic supply stores as well as in many hardware stores. I used Radio Shack switches (Part #49-512). These switches are suitable for low voltages only, so use them with twelve-volt lights only. You could install a small battery for power, but I found it simpler to wire the lights to the ship's twelve-volt supply, using the wiring diagram shown here as a guide. **One word of warning:** Make sure these switches are not within five feet of the ship's compass because they could cause magnetic interference.

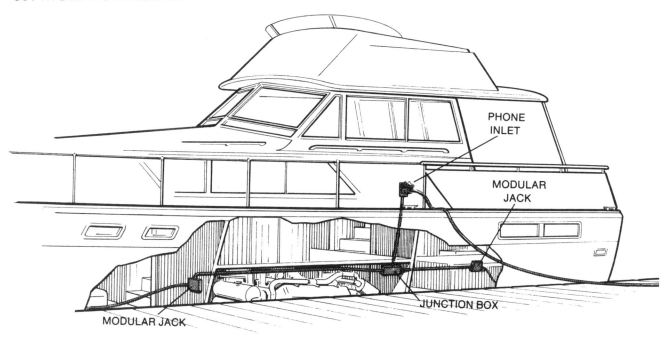

Wiring your boat for a phone is safe and easy, with components available at your local phone store.

A Phone for Every Boat

Although most boats nowadays are wired for dockside 110-volt electrical power, it is only in the past few years that more and more boats are also being wired for dockside telephone service. It's true that not everyone wants a telephone on board—some owners are glad to get away from it—but many people find that in spite of the drawbacks it is a great convenience to receive phone calls onboard or merely to pick up a telephone on the boat and make a call in complete privacy, without trying to get through to the busy marine operator or having to hike up the dock to the nearest phone booth.

The necessary jacks, plugs, and other components needed to install your own telephone lines have been widely available in local hardware stores, home centers, electronic supply stores, and phone centers ever since the big split-up of AT&T and the lifting of restrictions on installing your own phones and wiring. And since the whole project involves working with small-gauge wires that carry very little current (although voltage can run as high as eighty to ninety volts when the phone is ringing), there is little or no shock or fire hazard even if you do something wrong. The worst that can happen is that the phone won't work.

When wiring a boat for telephone service, light-duty two-conductor cable that contains a pair of No. 22 or No. 24 wires is all you really need, but you are better off using a light-gauge four-conductor phone cable that is standard for phone hookups (it's sold in all phone centers and most stores having the usual telephone equipment).

First of all, the four-conductor cable is color-coded to conform with industry standards and will match all standard telephone wiring accessories and junction boxes (this makes it much easier when wiring, since you don't have to guess which wire goes where). Second, this cable meets industry standards for insulation, and it really doesn't cost much more than most two-conductor cables. Third, by running the four-conductor cable you will always have an extra pair of wires in place—just in case you run into trouble with the original pair or want to add more phones.

All telephone jacks, junction boxes, and other equipment used have four terminals that are color-coded to match the four-conductor cable. The extra terminals are there to accommodate such refinements as a second line, a lighted phone, or in some cases a hold button, etc. The four wires in a standard telephone cable are colored red, green, black, and yellow. In almost every case the two wires used to give you a dial tone—and to connect you to the system—are the red and green wires. (The black and

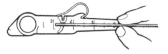

A special telephone wire stripper comes in handy.

yellow wires are used for phones with dial lights, or for other refinements.)

When you want to install telephone wiring in a house the phone company will bring its wiring into your home and end it in a junction box that is officially called a Network Interface. This fancy name indicates that this is the point where the company's wiring (its network) ends and connects up with (interfaces with) the homeowner's wiring. When you are installing a telephone on a boat, however, there's a slight difference. A boat obviously has to be able to unplug when it leaves the dock, so the phone company ends its wiring at an outlet box or plug-in type receptacle on the dock. This outlet serves as the network interface—in other words, it is the junction point where the company's wiring, and its responsibility for the maintenance of that wiring, ends. From that point on, all wiring and the maintenance of it is up to you.

This dockside telephone outlet has a receptacle on the front with a waterproof cover that snaps closed when the outlet is not in use. When your boat is at the dock you simply plug one end of your telephone power cord into the outlet on the dock and then plug the other end into the telephone inlet jack on your boat—the same way you plug your electric cord in for shoreside power.

The cord used (in most areas the phone company will supply it—at a price, of course—or you can buy one from many marine supply outlets) has a special plug at each end to fit into the three-prong receptacle on the dock jack and the boat jack (inlet). Only two of these prongs are actually used by the telephone wiring in the boat; the third prong, which is just a round pin in the center, is a ground. It is flat on one side so you can insert the plug only one way and thus are always assured of maintaining polarity. (Actually, polarity is important only if your phone system uses push-button tone dialing; with rotary dialing or pulse dialing, polarity is immaterial as long as you have the right pair of wires hooked up.)

As with any wiring job on the inside of a boat, the most difficult—and most time-consuming—part of the installation is running the wires from one place to another. You can run wires on the surface along the base of the bulkhead

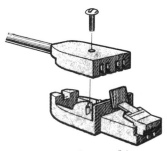

Modular plug adapter for making up your own cords.

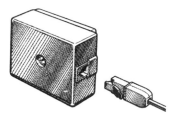

Modular jacks mount on walls to accept plugs.

if you wish, but it's neater to conceal the wires as much as possible; so you'll probably want to run them through the engine room or through lockers when practical. Just be sure that if you do run wires through the engine room or bilge areas that they are located where they will not get wet. Also, keep wires away from engines and other sources of heat, and where possible try not to run wires less than six inches away from antenna wires or 110-volt a.c. wiring. Wrap with tape wherever there is a chance of abrasion of where the wire will come in contact with sharp edges as the boat moves.

Where to Start

Start the job by installing the inlet into which you will plug the telephone cord coming from the dock receptacle. These inlets are standard fixtures (usually made by Hubbell) that look much like an electrical shore power inlet. Furnished directions will tell you the size hole needed, so make sure you have (or can borrow) a hole saw of the proper size to cut through the wood or fiberglass side of your boat. Before drilling the hole, give some thought to where you want to locate it. Choose a spot that will be convenient to get at when you want to plug in, and one that is close to the electrical inlet for the shore power cord. In that way all shore cords will come aboard in the same general area and you can keep them neatly together.

Inlets usually are located on the side of the cabin or helm console, or inside a cockpit bulwark where you can reach it easily when plugging in. Just be sure the spot you select will also enable you to reach the back side (the inside) of the fixture so you can connect the wires on the inside without too much difficulty.

After installing the inlet, the next step is installing one or more modular jacks inside the boat where you will want the phones located. If you plan on more than one phone or extension, you will need a separate modular jack at each location. As shown in the drawing, these modular jacks are small, square boxes with a receptacle for a telephone wire's plug on one side. When the cover of this jack box is removed (by loosening the screw in the center) you will see four color-sided terminals on the inside—one for each of the four colors in the cable. The four-conductor cable from the inlet on the outside of the boat is connected to this jack, so color coding of wires and terminals match; then the cover is replaced.

If you are installing more than one such modular jack because you want more than one phone—one in the salon and one in the stateroom, for instance—then the wire coming from the main inlet should go to a centrally located junction box first. Wires can then lead from this junction box to each of the modular jacks because the junction box has color-coded terminals on the inside that allow you to connect as many as four different cables. A junction box (or a modular jack box) should always be used when joining or splicing cables. It is *never* a good idea to splice cables or wires directly to each other, and most telephone companies strongly advise against the practice.

Jack As Junction Box

Where the wiring layout is such that one modular jack is "downstream" or in line with the others, then the first modular jack on the line can be used as a junction box. In other words, you can run your cable from the inlet directly to the first jack, then connect the wires for the second modular jack to the same terminals inside the jack box before continuing on to the next one. Just remember that all wires must be connected in parallel—in other words, always connect the green to green, the red to red, etc.

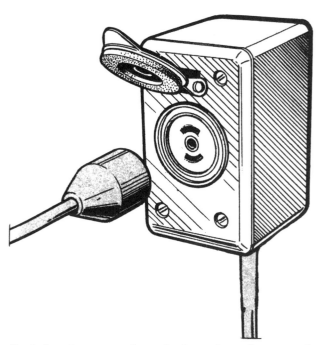

Jack box is mounted on dock so that phone cord from boat can be quickly plugged in.

When connecting wires you will obviously have to strip the insulation off first. Ordinary stripping tools don't work too well with these wires because of their small gauge. The same holds true for using a pocket knife or pair of diagonal wire cutting pliers—unless you are *very* careful you are likely to nick or break the fine wires. That's why it is best to buy one of the special telephone wire strippers sold for this purpose. They make the job of stripping these fine wires almost foolproof.

The cord supplied with your phone will have a small modular plug on its end that is shaped to fit the opening on the side of the modular jack box. You can buy phone cords and extension cords with these plugs already attached in various lengths, so you will seldom have to make your own. But if you do have to make one up in a special length, then you can buy a telephone wire plug that comes with a modular end plug or fitting that will snap into a modular jack opening. These telephone wire plugs usually come with clear instructions for attaching them to a standard phone cord.

After all the wiring has been completed you are ready to plug your telephone into the modular jack inside the boat. Plug the dock phone cord into the inlet on the outside of the boat and plug the other end of the cord into the dock receptacle. You should hear a dial tone and be able to make or receive calls, assuming, of course, that the phone line has already been hooked up and duly tested by your local phone company.

If you don't get a dial tone inside the boat, take your phone and cord over to someone else's boat where you know a phone is working and try it there. If it works, you know the problem is with the wiring on your boat and you will have to go over your wiring again. If your phone doesn't work on that boat (but theirs does), then the problem evidently lies in your phone or phone cord.

The New Cellular Phones

Instead of going to the trouble of wiring for a standard telephone, many boatowners are thinking about installing a cellular phone on their boat. It sounds like a great idea for a number of reasons: It eliminates the need for another "umbilical cord" going to the dock; it assures you of a private telephone line while you are out on the water, as well as when you are tied up to the dock; and you can use the phone at *any* dock while on a cruise. But before plunging ahead there are some drawbacks you should consider.

The first obstacle for most people is price. Cellular phones are expensive. Although there are signs that cellular phones will be coming down in price in the future, as of now you still have to pay from about a thousand to two thousand dollars for one of these phones. This is for the kind that is permanently wired into the boat's power supply. If you want one of the fully portable jobs that has its own built-in battery power pack and can be carried around like an attaché case (so you can use it in your car as well as on the boat), then the price will go as high as three thousand dollars or more for one unit.

Consider the Costs

Buying the equipment is only one part of the cost of operation, however. Monthly fees vary with different mobile communications companies (these are the companies that set up and operate the "cells" or networks you will use), but generally you can count on a charge of from thirty to forty dollars a month for the service. But this doesn't include the actual toll charge for each call *plus* about thirty to forty cents per minute for airtime. Airtime charges mean that you pay for every minute you are on the air—while receiving calls as well as making them, even if there is no answer. Obviously, the bills mount up.

Since cellular phones are primarily designed for use in cars, trucks, and other land vehicles, some problems have been encountered with corrosion or vibration when they are used in a marine environment. Because of this, AT&T has just introduced a cellular yacht telephone specially designed for use on recreation boats.

"The cellular yacht phone is designed with parts and materials that are much more resistant to corrosion on the inside," explains Burke Stimson, an AT&T district manager in the Northeast, "and it also has its components specially seated or mounted so they will be less susceptible to damage from vibration—another problem on most boats." The new yacht phone sells for about $2,900, complete with a special marine-type whip antenna that is externally mounted for greater sound range.

Check the Map

If you decide to install a cellular phone on your boat, investigate the cellular companies in your area first (the FCC requires that there be at least two companies servicing each city or community). Bear in mind that cellular phone service is not available everywhere yet (Stimson says that by the end of this year three quarters of the nation will have cellular service available). Even where there is cellular service in a metropolitan area, however, cells may overlap to leave "blank spots" where your phone will be inoperative in some places, especially out on the water. So when choosing a company, ask to see a map of the areas covered, and try to pick the company that has the most antennas near the water. If antennas are located farther inland, coverage over the water will be more limited.

Versatile Swim Ladder

When I started shopping around for a swim ladder for my thirty-five-foot sloop I found that none of the commercially available models would meet my needs. I wanted one that would collapse and stow easily and one that could be placed at various locations around the deck on either side. That is why I decided to build one using pieces of one-inch-thick teak for the steps, and four lengths of three-eighths-inch nylon rope for the supports on each side.

The steps each measure fourteen inches long by four inches wide, and each has four holes drilled near each of the corners so the nylon line can be strung through. The steps were correctly spaced—about twelve inches apart—along this line by tying a figure eight knot in the line directly above and below each step, as shown.

To make the ladder hang straight down into the water I weighted the two bottom steps with lead. A five-eighths-inch-diameter hole was bored into the edge of each step, then molten lead was poured in to fill each of these holes to within half an inch from the surface. When the lead cooled, teak plugs were then inserted in the steps' edges to cap the holes and cover the lead.

The last step was fastening one-inch-diameter rubber

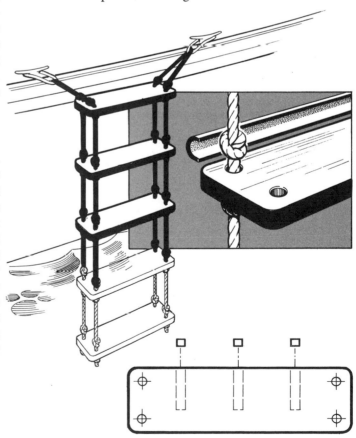

bumpers to the edges of the top two steps where they came in contact with the hullsides when the ladder was hung in position. These prevented marring of the fiberglass as the ladder swung back and forth when in use.

Gas Tank Rack

Portable metal gasoline tanks tend to slide around and leave scratch marks and red paint streaks. You can put the tank on a piece of carpet, but if the carpet is continually wet the dampness will tend to discolor the fiberglass finish on the boat and may hasten rusting of the metal tank.

I found that the neatest way to get around these problems is to build a small rack of teak strips similar to

the one shown here. Short angled pieces of teak across each of the corners will keep the tank from slipping off the top of the rack, and white rubber pads under each corner of the rack keeps the rack from moving around when the boat rocks or is under way. This arrangement keeps the tank high and dry above water in the bottom and also helps to protect the tank against rusting.

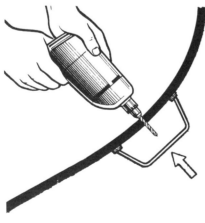

Installing a Through Hull Without Hauling

There are many occasions when a boatowner wants to install a depth finder, sumlog, or other instrument that requires a new through-hull fitting but is reluctant to pay for an extra haul-out in the middle of the season. To avoid that extra expense, here is a proven method I have used several times that makes it possible to complete an installation of this kind while the boat is still in the water—and without taking on much more than about one gallon of water in the process.

It doesn't require special equipment, but it does require the help of someone who can dive under the boat and, equipped with mask and snorkel or with an air tank, do some simple manipulation of a special cup on the first dive, then push the new fitting in from underneath during the second dive. Here are the steps to follow:

1. Drill a quarter-inch pilot in the spot where the fitting is to go, *using a battery-operated drill or a double-insulated drill plugged into a Ground Fault Circuit Interrupter (GFCI) to protect against any possibility of shock.*

2. When the bit comes through, leave it in place to keep excessive amounts of sea water from entering, then have the diver go under and place a cup, bowl, or small pail over the hole, centering it over the drill bit. This container, whether cup, bowl, or pail, should have a rim of soft foam rubber cemented around the edge so when it is pressed against the bottom it will form a fairly watertight seal.

3. When the diver has this in place, he taps on the hull to let you know so you can then safely withdraw the drill bit. The pressure of the water will hold the cup or bowl in place against the outside, so the diver can come up.

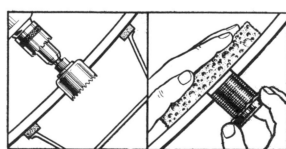

The drill bit is kept in place until the diver—preferably equipped with tanks—places the container securely over the hole. Note soft, foam rubber rim on container.

4. Working from the inside, you can now use a hole saw to cut the size hole needed. When this is done, apply a suitable bedding compound around the rim of the through-hull fitting and hand it to the diver, who will carry it underwater to be pushed in from the outside.

5. After removing the hole saw, press a large sponge tightly over the hole from the inside and hold it there to keep water from entering. Signal the diver to remove the cup or bowl, and shove the precaulked fitting in from the outside. As you feel the fitting come in, pull the sponge away to allow the fitting to come all the way through.

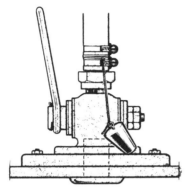

Handy wood plug is a good idea.

6. When it is all the way through, fit the wood spacer on from the inside (if needed), then put the nut on and tighten the fitting in place. If the fitting has a sleeve that has to be installed first, then before the job is started make sure you fashion a tapered wood plug that you can push in temporarily. This can be easily removed afterward to allow the rest of the fitting to be inserted.

Securing Small Appliances

Toaster ovens, countertop microwave ovens, TV sets, and similar appliances can be secured on a countertop or cabinettop by using two or three blocks of wood as shown here. Screw one wood block to the countertop so its edge presses snugly against the front face of the appliance, then

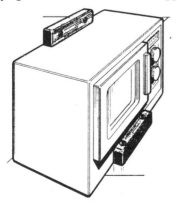

screw a second block to the backing surface as illustrated so its bottom edge presses down against the top of the appliance. If you use cup washers or finishing washers under the screws they will be easy to remove without damaging the surface and can be replaced without leaving an unsightly hole.

Save Ice by Plugging Drain

The common method of draining an ice box is to allow water from the melted ice to drain directly into the bilge through a length of hose attached to a hole in the bottom of the box. But this also allows the cold air inside the box to escape in the same manner, greatly shortening the life of the ice inside the box—especially on hot days.

We developed a very simple solution to this problem that anyone can use to help prolong the life of the ice inside the box. Insert a snug-fitting cork in the end of the hose to keep the cold air from ''falling'' out. In warm weather this cork must be removed at least once a day to let the water drain out, but at the same time you can drain the water directly into a bucket and thus eliminate the need for pumping out the bilge as often. This is a real bonus for those who don't have electric bilge pumps.

Diver's Trick Helps Find Overboard Items

When something is accidentally dropped overboard, even a trained diver often can have trouble finding it because the exact spot where the item went over is not always known—especially if several hours go by before the diver goes down to look. This is particularly true if the bottom is muddy or if the water is murky so that vision is limited. Nothing is more frustrating than knowing where something went over but not being able to find it.

A friend and former Navy diver helped me solve this problem once when I accidentally dropped something overboard. The item dropped was a spring for which I had no replacement, yet without it the jam cleat for my main sheet was virtually useless—and I was leaving on a trip across open water with high winds expected. I definitely would need that jam cleat.

My friend told me to drop a weight of some kind overboard immediately in the exact same spot, but to tie a length of heavy white nylon cord to the weight. Allow the weight to fall freely, and then take the slack out of the line and hold on to it.

When the diver went overboard to look for it, all he had to do was follow the white line down to the bottom, then search the area around it. The spring I was looking for was within about a foot of where the weight was resting on the bottom, so it was quickly found. It's best to use a fairly heavy weight so it will stay put when it falls. In most cases the weight will be within a foot or two of the object you are looking for.

Hidden Lock for Hatches

Many boats have large hatches or lazarettes in the cockpit sole—sometimes these are merely engine hatches, but sometimes they are storage compartments for fishing gear, fenders, extra lines, boarding ladders, scuba diving gear, etc. Yet in a surprisingly large number of boats there is no easy way to lock these hatches for security when you are not aboard. Some people install hasps and padlocks, but these leave a lot to be desired in appearance, and they are easy to trip over.

An ideal solution is to install a hidden sliding bolt that locks the hatch from underneath, as shown in the accompanying illustration. Inexpensive to make and install, this sliding-bolt ''lock'' is invisible from the outside and virtually trouble-free. It consists of a broomstick or similar pole that slides through two guides that are permanently fastened under the deck as shown. One is secured to the bottom of the hatch cover, and the other is fastened to the

Keep your extra gear and valuables out of the reach of intruders by installing this ingenious, hidden latch lock made out of a broomstick.

deck so it is exactly in line with the first one. When the pole projects through the two, it keeps the hatch from being opened.

To slide the broomstick back and forth to lock or unlock the hatch, attach a bolt at right angles to form a handle. This ''handle'' projects up through a slot cut in the cabin sole, inside a space that is normally concealed. In our boat the slot is in the sole under a dinette seat, but it could be in almost any convenient location inside the boat where the projecting ''handle'' will be out of the way yet easy to reach.

For accurate alignment of the two hardwood guides, install the one under the deck first, after boring the hole through the bulkhead that will serve as a guide for the broomstick. Then, while inside the hatch, with the cover in place, position the second guide to make sure the pole will slide back and forth easily.

Making Your Own Porthole Screens

Although many of the newer stock boats come equipped with plastic portholes that contain removable insect screens, many older boats, including most of those with bronze opening ports, do not have any insect screens. Making screens to fit these can be a problem because the screen has to fit inside the opening when it's closed, yet be able to withstand wind, rain, and salt water.

Using the method shown here, you can make inexpensive port screens that will not detract from the appearance of your boat and do an excellent job of keeping insects out while resisting attack by the elements. The ''frame'' for each screen is made of quarter-inch-diameter plastic fuel hose.

Using a length of string, measure the inside circumference of the port to be fitted, then cut a length of hose one inch longer than this measurement. Cut a wedge out of one end of the hose as shown in the drawing, then soak the other end in hot water for a minute or two to soften it. Now compress the end where the wedge has been cut out and force this compressed end into the other end (the one that just came out of the hot water) to form a closed loop of hose. This will be the frame for your screen.

As soon as you have done this, fit the loop of hose into the porthole frame (from the outside) to ensure a snug fit— at this point you can still pull the end out slightly or push it in a little more to get the right fit. Now wrap some Scotch tape around the joint to keep the ends from slipping in or out.

Remove the loop of hose from the port and use this to make a cardboard pattern the size and shape of the port (trace around the outside of the hose to make this pattern).

Using this pattern as a guide, cut a piece of nylon tent screen material to match, then use a piece of #100 grit sandpaper to roughen lightly one side of the hose "frame" (the side against which the screening will fit).

Coat this abraded side with contact cement, then apply a coat of contact cement around the perimeter of the piece of screening you have just cut out, applying it heavily enough to fill in all the holes in the mesh. Wait till the cement on both surfaces has dried to the touch (ten to twenty minutes with most brands), then push the loop of hose back into place inside the porthole. Now carefully press the screen into place over the hose, working from the top down and pressing outward to the rim in all directions to ensure a wrinkle-free screen.

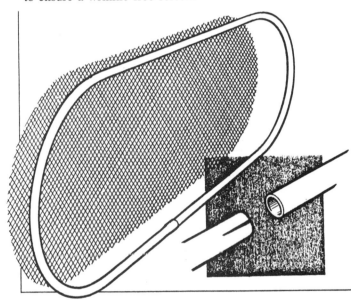

If the ports on your boat do not have pegs to keep the screen from falling out or blowing away, cut some small blocks of wood no higher than the thickness of the hose, and epoxy these in place against the port frame. Position them carefully so the port will press against the screen to hold it in place when it is dogged down.

If your boat has extra-large ports that create a problem with the hose sagging or deforming when you fit it in place, use metal screening instead of nylon mesh; the metal will help the loop of hose hold its shape.

Sailboat Compass Mount

On a small sailboat there is not always a convenient place to mount a compass where it can be easily seen from the cockpit, and where it can be quickly removed for safe stowage. The unit shown here solves both those problems. The compass is mounted on a removable bracket at the

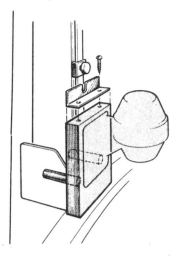

foot of the mast, just above the companionway steps leading into the cabin. It consists of a 4″ × 6″ piece of mahogany, ¾″ thick, and a short piece of 1″ aluminum angle that goes across the top as illustrated.

The piece of aluminum angle is notched at the center so that it can slip under a sail track top, then is screwed to the top edge of the vertical wood block. The compass is secured to the front of this same block with brass screws. The whole assembly is then set up against the foot of the mast and is locked in place by the sail track stop. The two dowels (one on each side of the mast) are attached to the wood block by boring a hole in the wood, then coating the end of the dowel with glue and pushing that end into the hole. These dowels give the mount stability and keep it from swinging around.

Mounting Transducers in Smaller Boats

Depth-sounders are one of the least expensive electronic aids to safe navigation—and to finding where the fish are. Yet many smaller boats still do not have them. One reason involves the problems often associated with installing a through-hull transducer.

The traditional (and still most popular) way to install a transducer is to drill a hole through the bottom of the boat and then mount the transducer so that its bottom face is directly in the water. However, owners of runabouts and outboards are often reluctant to drill through the bottom; they worry about problems that can occur with a hull made of two layers of fiberglass with an air space between, or of sandwich construction (two layers of fiberglass with wood or foam in the center).

Because of this valid concern and because of problems often encountered with water turbulence under high-speed

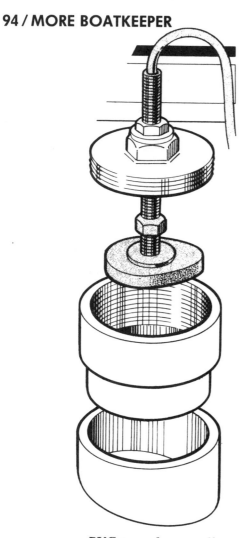

PVC transducer well.

hulls and smaller fishing boats, many owners use other methods of mounting a transducer. One is to mount the transducer on the outside of the transom so it sticks down into the water. The other is to mount it inside the hull, which does not have to be drilled because the transducer sits in the bilge and sends its rays down *through* the fiberglass.

As a rule, transom-mounted transducers are more popular on outboards, inboard/outboards, and similar vessels. This positioning eliminates the need for drilling holes in the bottom and makes it easy to clean off the face of the transducer at regular intervals. The transducer should be mounted snug against the transom and should be placed where it points straight down and will always be underwater. There should be a relatively smooth flow of water past and under the face of the transducer at all speeds.

Mounting a transducer inside the hull is another practical method because of the acoustical characteristics of fiberglass (this method works only in fiberglass hulls). Many experts feel it is preferred over a standard through-

hull fitting for high-speed boats because there is less chance that turbulence will interfere with an accurate reading, and that the transducer will be damaged by striking a partially submerged object.

Most manufacturers make special mounts and specially shaped, puck-type transducers for mounting inside a hull. As a rule, the transducer is permanently attached to the inside with a two-part epoxy or with a fiberglass resin, but this works only on hulls made of a single thickness of fiberglass—it won't work with aluminum or any type of sandwich construction.

If possible, install the transducer as near the center line as practical, and in a part of the hull that always is solidly in the water while under way. When cementing the transducer in place it is important that the surface be thoroughly cleaned off first and that enough epoxy or resin is used so there are no air pockets or bubbles left between the face of the transducer and the hull.

To get around the problems of such a permanent mounting and to make it impossible for air bubbles to interfere with accurate soundings, some prefer to mount the transducer so it sits in a pool of liquid. Various methods for accomplishing this have been worked out by different boatowners, and special housings can be purchased from marine supply stores for mounting a transducer in this manner.

One *Boatkeeper* reader—Charles B. Husick of Great Falls, Va.—has submitted the following idea, which he says has been working fine in his boat. He built a "well" in which the transducer floats, just above the inside surface of the hull. This well is filled with mineral oil, which does not evaporate and which will not interfere with the transducer's transmission or reception. As shown in the accompanying drawing, the well is made from a short length of PVC pipe (sold in plumbing supply outlets) large enough to accept the transducer body on the inside. A short-threaded coupling or adapter is attached to the upper end of this pipe with PVC cement, and a matching threaded plug that can be screwed into the coupling serves as a cap or cover for the finished well.

The first step is to trim the bottom end of the PVC pipe so it will fit snugly against the contours of the hull when mounted vertically against the inside (it's best to mount the transducer vertically so it will point straight down). The trimmed pipe is then cemented in place with an epoxy putty or cement applied liberally around the bottom rim. After this dries, check for leaks by temporarily filling with water. If there are leaks, fill or patch these with more epoxy before proceeding.

Next, use the PVC cement to "weld" the threaded female coupling in place at the top of the pipe; then drill a hole through the matching threaded plug to accept the stem of the transducer. Fasten this in place with the nuts and washers provided, then fill the well about half full with mineral oil (sold in drugstores) and screw the plug into place at the top to complete the installation.

Drop-Leaf Serving Table

One thing every galley is always short of is adequate counter space and serving space when meals are being prepared. To solve this problem on our boat—and to keep the navigation table (which is close by the galley) from becoming loaded with pots, pans, and dishes—I built the drop-leaf serving table shown here. I built mine of teak, to match the interior of my boat, but the same kind of table could just as well be built of mahogany, maple, or any other hardwood.

Start by measuring the space where the table will go to determine the largest table that will fit comfortably when in the raised or working position. Then check to see that this size will also fit when the leaf is dropped (make sure it won't cover some drawers or cabinet doors that you have to get at frequently).

Now cut the top to the size you want and round off all the outside corners. Sand smooth and attach two brass hinges as shown to fasten it against the bulkhead. To hold the table up use a removable length of 1-inch hardwood dowel, beveled at each end. Two "retainers" for this dowel, one fastened to the bottom of the table and the other to the bulkhead against which the table is mounted,

A dowel makes a simple support for this collapsible serving table and can be stored in a nearby drawer.

are fashioned out of pieces of scrap wood, then fastened in place with screws.

To hold the table in the open position, the dowel is inserted in these "retainers" to serve as a prop. To close the table you simply lift the dowel out and lay it aside.

If you cannot get a single piece of ¾-inch-thick solid wood that will be wide enough to make the table in one piece, then your best bet is to use a piece of hardwood-faced plywood for the top. The exposed edges of the plywood can be covered or finished off by using wood veneer "tape" that comes in ¾-inch or 1½-inch-wide rolls. Sold in most lumber yards, this wood veneer tape comes in colors to match most hardwoods and is attached to the edges with glue or contact cement.

Safety Shutoff for Dockside Water

When I started living aboard my boat at the dock each weekend, I decided to hook up to dockside water in order to be able to use all the water I wanted. However, it is important when using dockside water that the water supply be turned off when leaving the boat unattended—otherwise, if a hose or line breaks, the boat can take on water and can sink.

I worked out a solution that minimizes the possibility of forgetting to do this. I use a water-actuated timer that limits the amount of water that can come into the boat at any one time—regardless of whether I am on board or not. These timers, sold in hardware stores and garden supply outlets, are attached to the spigot before the water hose is connected.

The timer runs only when a faucet inside the boat is opened and the water is actually running. You set a dial on the timer indicating how long you want the timer to run, or how much water you want it to deliver; the timer will shut itself off when that period has expired. In other words, after a predetermined amount of water has run through it, the timer will automatically shut off the supply of water—whether due to a break in the hose or to your using that much water.

Built-in Wastebasket

If you want to keep the inside of your boat clean you must have a trash basket or waste receptacle, preferably one that is built in and is out of sight. Many boats have a lazarette or similar storage space next to the cabin. If your boat is set up this way, all you have to do is locate a bulkhead common to the two spaces and accessible from both sides.

Then make a cutout to provide an opening into the lazarette from the cabin.

A wastebasket can then be placed inside the lazarette so it can be reached from the cabin to throw something into it. We cut an opening about 4½ inches square, just high enough so that when the basket was placed inside the lazarette the opening is about even with the top of the basket.

To make the cutout, four holes were drilled for the jigsaw blade first, one in each corner of the outlined cutout. A keyhole saw or a hacksaw can also be used. Smooth off the edges of the opening and secure the wastebasket in the lazarette (under the opening) with shock cord. Now make a door for the opening out of a

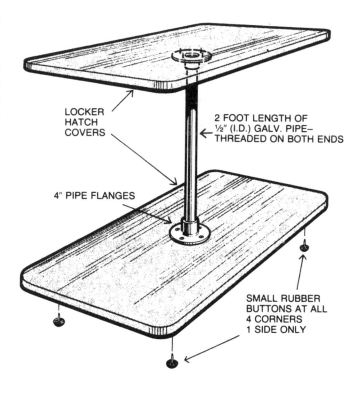

LOCKER HATCH COVERS

2 FOOT LENGTH OF ½" (I.D.) GALV. PIPE— THREADED ON BOTH ENDS

4" PIPE FLANGES

SMALL RUBBER BUTTONS AT ALL 4 CORNERS 1 SIDE ONLY

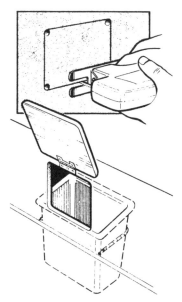

piece of teak. The door should be about one inch bigger than the opening in length and width. Mount this over the opening with a self-closing cabinet hinge (it should be brass to ensure against rusting), and attach a rubber bumper to the edge of the door to minimize slamming.

Self-Stowing Cockpit Table

Eating out in the cockpit on a warm summer evening is much pleasanter when there is some kind of table in front of you, rather than having to balance things on your lap or putting everything on the seat next to you. However, finding room for the storage of such a table when it is not in use can be quite a problem on a twenty-six-foot sailboat.

We solved this problem by creating a table out of material that was already on board so there would be no additional storage problem. Like many stock sailboats of

this type, the lockers under my settee berth are accessible through two removable ¾-inch-thick plywood boards that measure about 16 by 32 inches. We decided to use these hatch cover boards for our table when one is needed. One hatch board serves as the top for the table, and the other serves as the base.

As shown in the drawing, we attached a ½-inch pipe flange (which is about 4 inches in diameter) to the underside of each hatch cover. When we want to use the hatch covers as a table we simply take them out from under the settee cushion and connect the two with a 2-foot length of ½-inch pipe that is threaded at both ends. Four rubber buttons were fastened to the surface of one hatch cover (the one that serves as a base) so that the plywood would not scratch the fiberglass cockpit sole and to help it sit evenly without rocking.

When we are finished using the table, we simply unscrew the pipe from each flange, then replace the hatch covers in their normal position under the settee cushion— the rubber buttons on the one hatch cover do not get in the way of the cushion at all. That way the only extra piece we have to stow is the 2-foot length of ½-inch pipe. Total cost for everything: about five or six dollars.

Bilge Pump Indicator Light

An automatic bilge pump that turns itself on when bilge water rises above a preset level is a great safety feature and adds to the peace of mind of most boatowners. However, it's difficult to know when a problem is developing, or already exists, since it's hard to tell when—or how often—the pump kicks on. Also, some pumps are not wired with a manual "On" switch, so you have to go down to the bilge and manually lift the float to make sure the pump is in working order.

To solve these problems I replaced the original On-Off switch on the master panel of my bilge pump with a

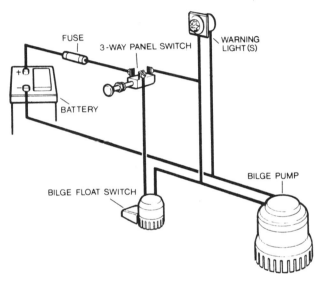

three-way pull switch that provides for "Off," "Auto," and "On" positions. I also wired an indicator warning light into the circuit that will go on every time the pump is operating. The simple wiring circuit and hardware required to do this are shown in the accompanying drawing.

Now before starting the engine all I have to do to make certain the bilge pump is operational is pull the switch out to its manual "On" position. The indicator light comes on, and I can hear the gurgling noise the pump makes as further confirmation that it is working. Then I simply reset the switch to its "Auto" position and relax.

Improving the Boat Trailer

A major problem with boat trailers is getting the boat centered on the trailer when it is being hauled out of the water. Some of the newer trailers come with centering guides or retrieval devices, but many older ones do not. If your trailer is not one of these newer models, you don't

have to rush out and spend a lot of money for a new trailer or for new attachments to have the same convenience.

For about fifteen dollars worth of materials you can build a simple, fender-mounted centering guide similar to the one shown here. The only requirement is that your trailer have strong metal fenders securely fastened to the trailer frame. A good test of the fender's strength is to stand on it; if it supports your weight it is strong enough to do the job.

As shown in the drawing, each guide unit consists mainly of two wood blocks: a mounting board made from a piece of 2 × 4 about ten inches long, and a guide board of 2 × 6 lumber that is about 12 inches long. The 2 × 4 mounting board will be bolted edgewise to the top of the fender as shown, with its longest dimension directly above and in line with the trailer's axle.

Before cutting one end of this mounting board off at the required angle, you will first have to make sure the boat is properly centered on the trailer. Hold the mounting block in position on top of the fender so the end is against the side of the hull. Now scribe the end of the board so it approximately matches the hull's angle at this point. Cut off the end of the board to match this angle, making a straight cut even if the hull is curved. The idea is to achieve the best possible angle so that when the guide block is attached to the mounting block it will make contact with the largest amount of hull surface. After doing this on one side of the boat, repeat the procedure on the other side, using the second block.

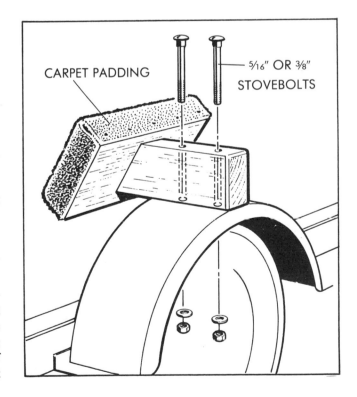

After cutting the mounting blocks off at the proper angle, attach the guide blocks to each mounting block with 3¼-inch-long flathead wood screws with the screw heads countersunk. Cover the face of each guide block with pieces of carpet to provide padding for the hull, then drill two vertical ⁵⁄₁₆-inch holes through the mounting blocks as shown so that the blocks can be attached to the top of each fender.

Before drilling matching holes in the fenders, hold the blocks in place so the carpet facing just barely touches the hull on each side. A slight amount of clearance is advisable. The guides are meant to assist in centering the boat, not to hold the boat in place when on land. If they are too tight against the boat, the hull will be ''pinched'' between them when you haul the boat out of the water.

After establishing the correct position for each one, mark the fenders and drill the appropriate holes. Round off all sharp corners on the wood pieces and paint them if desired, then mount the assembled guide units with ⁵⁄₁₆-inch bolts about 4½-inches long. Use lock washers under each nut and be sure the bolts do not stick down so much that they will damage the tires when you hit a bump. Better yet, install the bolts with the heads on the bottom (under the fenders) and the nuts on top. In that way you can be sure the bolt ends won't stick down where they can accidentally damage the tires.

Extension Cord Holder

This dolly for holding a shore power cord or long extension cord neatly coiled up and out of the way can be quickly and easily fabricated from pieces of hardwood. It is designed so that when you need the cord you only have to uncoil or unwrap as much as you need, and it has hooks at the top (easily bent out of aluminum or stainless steel strips) that enable you to hang it out of the way on one of the lifelines or handrails where it will always be quickly available. When not needed it can also be neatly stowed in

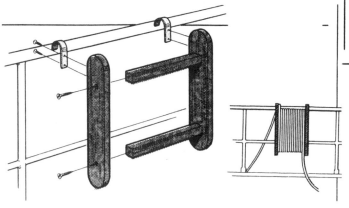

a locker without having the cord get tangled up or fouled around other objects in the same storage bin.

After cutting all pieces to size, sand them smooth and lightly round off all the sharp edges, then assemble the unit with screws and waterproof glue as shown. Paint or varnish as desired, then attach the hooks at the top (for hanging it up). Buy these hooks in marine supply stores, or you can bend your own out of aluminum or stainless steel.

Custom Patterns the Easy Way

Building things for the inside of a boat is never as simple as building things for the inside of a house—nothing is ever square, and sides or bulkheads are never exactly parallel. In addition, there are always curves and notches that make fitting pieces a tedious, time-consuming, and often frustrating job.

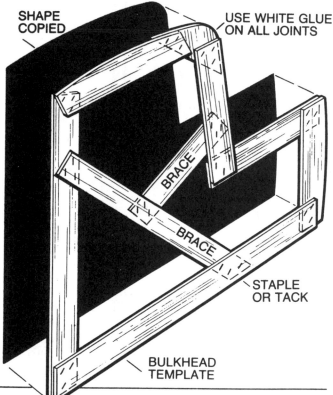

SHAPE COPIED

USE WHITE GLUE ON ALL JOINTS

BRACE

BRACE

STAPLE OR TACK

BULKHEAD TEMPLATE

There is a method that can make things a lot easier and save your time and your temper—as well as cut down on the amount of wasted material. You simply make a rigid pattern first. The pattern is then used as a guide to cut out the piece needed. A rigid pattern is a lot more accurate, and a lot easier to work with, than a paper or cardboard pattern.

Let's say you are going to replace a bulkhead that is badly worn, or you want to dress the bulkhead up by covering it with a piece of plastic laminate. That piece of laminate must be cut to an exact fit ahead of time if you want the job to look right. A rigid pattern is the key.

For making a pattern of the kind shown here, I like to use pieces of inexpensive ⅛-inch-thick "door skin" plywood, or if that is not available, ¼-inch gum plywood. I get the lumberyard to rip the sheet up into strips 2 to 3 inches wide, providing enough material to last through dozens of projects. Strips are then joined together as shown, using staples and glue.

When making a pattern start with a straight, long piece if possible. Cut it about ½-inch shorter than you need it and lay it along the edge you are trying to copy. At this point don't worry about the ends; you just want a clean fit along the length of the pattern. Attach this piece temporarily to the bulkhead, using clamps if practical. If the piece is to be covered, you can also use small screws or staples, but make sure they don't go through to the other side.

Now cut the next piece that will join it, but make it slightly longer than needed so it will overlap at the end. This time trim the end to fit exactly, using a saw, knife, or rasp. When it fits, use white glue and staples to join it to the first piece at the proper angle. Continue adding strips around the perimeter in the same way, allowing each to overlap the end of the last one and trimming the ends to fit before joining it to the first piece with staples and glue. When the outline is finished, staple on some crosspieces or corner braces for extra support for the pattern.

Wait overnight for the glue to set, then take off the clamps (or screws) that held the pattern in place. Remove the pattern and take it carefully out of the boat so you can carry it to your shop, or to wherever you will be working on the project. Be careful not to bang it or bend it accidentally. Of course, you have to make certain that the pattern is not too large and unwieldy to get it off the boat.

Mooring Chain Backup

Most permanent mooring systems use galvanized chain to secure the mooring buoy. Sooner or later this chain corrodes and wears out so it must be replaced periodically. That is why prudent owners will lift out and inspect their mooring chains at the beginning of each season. But what happens if the chain parts or breaks in the middle of the season, or if you neglect these annual inspections? The boat may break away and drift off on its own—sometimes with calamitous results.

To prevent this we use a ¾-inch nylon mooring line in parallel with the chain to serve as a backup. The line runs from the eye of our mushroom anchor to the pennant on our float and is installed when the mushroom is lifted out of the water to inspect (or replace) the chain. After the eye

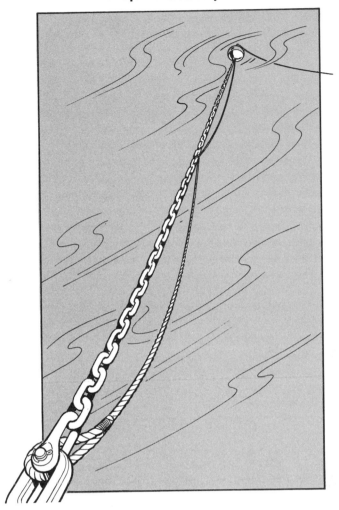

splicing thimbles are installed at each end of the line, the line should be six to twelve inches longer than the chain so it will always be slack. In that way it will take no strain until and unless the chain breaks; then the line serves to keep the boat from drifting away. We tie the nylon line loosely to the mooring chain at five- or six-foot intervals with small pieces of light line. This nylon line does not deteriorate quickly and will outlast several replacements of galvanized chain.

Stowing Hoses and Shore Cords

On most sailboats dockside water hoses, electrical shore cords, and telephone cords are left lying along the deck. This is not only unsightly, it also tends to collect dirt and stains. And it can also be a hazard underfoot at times. I have found a neat solution to this problem: Suspend all the cords and hoses from the lifelines with shock cord, using the simple system illustrated here. This keeps the water hose and shore cords neatly off the deck, and it allows me to undo them quickly when I am ready to get under way.

Start by temporarily tying the power cord and water hose to the lifelines, using short pieces of light line at each stanchion. Then mark the cord and hose to indicate each point where it is tied and to tell you where to attach the short pieces of elastic shock cord later on. Now untie the cord/hose combination, then wrap a piece of shock cord tightly around them at each of the pencil marks.

To secure this shock cord permanently to the hose and shore cords, clamp the shock cord in place by crimping it on with hog clamps as shown (you can use a pair of pliers to crimp the clamps if you don't have the special tool normally used). Now attach an S-hook to the other end of each piece of shock cord by crimping one side of the

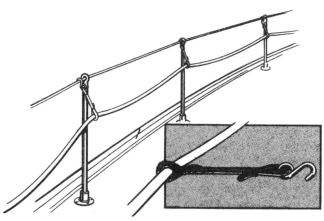

S-hook tightly to make it stay attached to the shock cord. Leave the other end of the S-hook open so you can attach it to the shock cord after you wrap it around the lifeline. Wrap the pieces of shock cord around the lifeline near each stanchion (where you originally had it tied), then hook the open end of the S-hook over it to hold the hose and shore cord up out of the way. When ready to leave the dock, just unhook all the S-hooks and you can coil up the hose and shore cord as usual.

Shading Out the Light

The transparent open hatch usually found in the forward V-bunk area of most boats is great for letting in light and air during the day, but it leaves something to be desired at night when you want more privacy or when you want to block out some of the light during the early-morning hours when you sleep. Like most boatowners I used to cover this hatch each night by draping a tarp over the outside, but the tarp had to be unrigged each day as we got under way, and I had to go outside to put it on or take it off.

Then I decided to use an ordinary roll-up window shade

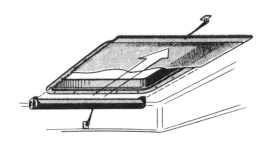

made for home windows, except that my shade would be mounted so it rolled horizontally across under the hatch (as seen in the drawing). The shade brackets were fastened to the overhead with self-tapping screws on one side of the hatch frame. Then a hook was attached to the hatch frame on the opposite side. This enables me to tie the pull cord—normally used to pull the shade down but used here to pull the shade across the hatch opening—to an adhesive-backed hook to hold the shade in place when it was unrolled. The shade itself is an inexpensive plastic one that blocks out the light and is not affected by moisture. Such shades are sold in many hardware stores and home centers for about five or six dollars, and dealers will usually cut them to size.

Improving the Float Switch

Many of us have had the experience of looking into the bilge and finding the bilge pump submerged while the float switch is pointing upward (in the "On" position)—yet the pump is not running. In most cases flicking the float arm a couple of times, or rapping the switch once or twice will turn it on and activate the pump so that all seems well—until it happens again.

The reason for this problem is that even the best switches work best and last longest when there is a snappy on/off action that ensures positive contact. However, the typical float switch closes gradually as the water rises, so there is always some arcing as heavy loads of current start to flow through the switch when the contacts are barely touching. Pitting and oxidation are common results, until the switch doesn't turn on the pump even when mechanical closure is complete.

The accompanying wiring diagram shows how I worked out an easy fix for this problem of arcing and intermittent operation. This simple modification also helps prolong the life of the switch and the pump. All you need are a relay (available from any Radio Shack or similar store), plus a one-ampere diode and some hookup wire. The relay should be the kind that has a normally open double pole double throw (DPDT) switch that has each set of contacts rated at ten or fifteen amps at twelve volts.

The relay is wired into the existing float switch and pump circuit as shown in the diagram. Even though only one set of connects is needed, a piece of jumper wire is connected across the parallel set of contacts (as shown) to provide added insurance or "redundancy" to the relay. With this setup there will always be two sets of contacts closing each time the switch comes on, not just one. If one pair of contacts oxidizes, the other set will still make full contact—giving you thousands of on/off cycles before wear becomes a problem.

Since these relays (at least the one from Radio Shack) come in a clear plastic case, you will be able to see when the contacts are wearing, so you can replace them at your leisure. Mount the relay in a dry location where it will not

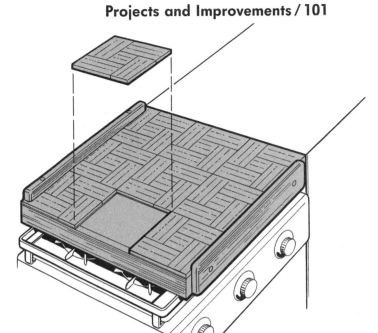

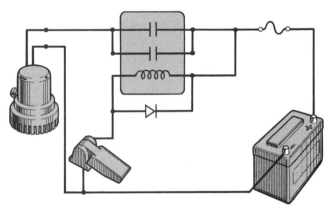

get splashed or sprayed. Now when the float switch calls for current it will activate the relay, and the heavy current needed by the bilge pump will flow through the relay contacts instead of through the float switch—so the switch will live a lot longer.

The diode (see diagram) extends the life of the switch even further by allowing current to flow in only one direction. Just connect it as shown; hooking it up backward will cause the diode or the fuse (or both) to blow.

More Counter Space in the Galley

Although my boat came with a large, three-burner alcohol stove, I found that when we used a stove we were usually tied to the dock and were plugged into shore power. Under those conditions we rarely needed more than an electric hot plate.

Because the alcohol stove left us with very little counter space in our galley—and because there is always a need for more counter space in boat galleys—I decided to double the amount of counter space by covering the stove with a piece of three-quarter-inch-thick plywood that

could be removed when the stove was needed. The plywood panel was cut large enough to extend over the stove's safety rails. Two strips of wood were fastened to the underside so they would just fit inside the stove's side and front rails and thus lock it securely in place once it was positioned. The back edge fits snug up against the bulkhead behind the stove.

To improve the appearance of the plywood and to give it a good-looking finish, I covered it with self-adhesive teak parquet floor tiles. I also added safety rails of half-inch teak around the edges to keep things from sliding off when the boat rocks. This entire panel lifts off easily on those rare occasions when we do want to use the alcohol stove.

Test Circuit for Filter Alarm

I thought I would have complete peace of mind about the fuel for my diesel engine when I finished installing one of those fuel filters that have a circuit that senses the presence of water in the fuel and then sounds a buzzer and activates a red warning light. Each time I came aboard and started the engine I glanced over to see if the red warning light came on—but even though it didn't, I always wondered if the system was really in working order.

To test the system (to make sure the light was still good and all wiring was intact) I had to lift the engine hatch and use a short piece of wire to short out the two terminals on

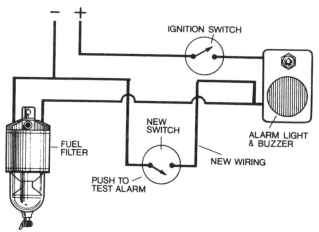

the filter (if there was water present on the inside, these terminals would get shorted out and thus send current to the alarm system). I did this occasionally, but not often enough to prove anything because it was a burdensome task that I often skipped. I decided that the way to restore confidence in my system without having to climb down and test it each time was to wire a small "push to test" switch or button into the circuit, as shown in the accompanying wiring diagram. It is conveniently located near the helm, so that before starting the engine I can activate the switch momentarily (it can be either a push-button or a spring toggle). If all is in working order, this will cause the buzzer to sound and the warning light to come on—without shorting out the filter terminals manually. If the test indicates everything is working, I can start the engine and know that my warning system will tell me if the fuel filter gets contaminated with water.

Custom-made Warm Wheel Cover

Like many other sailboats, ours has a stainless steel steering wheel that can get quite cold when sailing in chilly weather. We tried wearing leather gloves to keep our fingers warm, but the gloves were always getting misplaced and mismatched. However, we have now figured out a way to cover the wheel inexpensively with a nonslip grip that also provides a warm surface to hold on to.

The solution lies in using a "sport grip" steering wheel cover, the kind widely sold in automobile parts stores and variety stores. The only problem is that these synthetic covers are made to fit over wheels with a maximum diameter of about eighteen inches, so for the twenty-eight-inch wheel aboard our boat we used two covers and glued them together end to end with contact cement. This gave us one long piece that fit our wheel without any waste. A

thirty-inch wheel would have posed no additional problem.

If your wheel is over thirty-two inches in diameter, however, you would need to buy three wheel covers of this type. Divide the wheel on your boat into three sections, then cut each wheel cover to the length needed to provide three equal sections. When cutting them, remember to leave the laces attached to each end, and allow about one extra inch for overlapping and gluing. Also, make the combined length of all pieces just a few inches less than the total circumference of the wheel, so you can stretch the covers neatly for a proper fit. To figure out the circumference of your wheel multiply the diameter by 3.14, then allow for the overlaps and for the fact that the covers should be stretched slightly to fit snugly over the rim of the wheel.

When joining covers together, we found contact cement worked well. We clamped the overlap with pieces of scrap wood and C-clamps, which we left in place overnight.

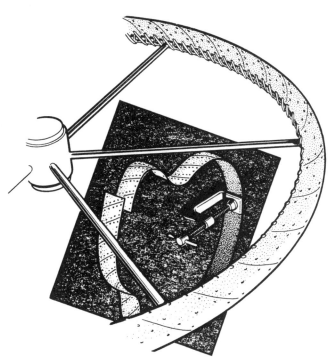

When you glue the pieces end to end, arrange them so the laces are 180 degrees apart from each other to form the circular cover desired. Stretch the assembled unit over the rim of your steering wheel and lace it on according to the directions on the package.

Our wheel cover has been exposed to the elements for over two years and is still in excellent shape, but a canvas cover could be added to prolong its life even more.

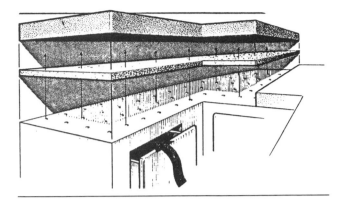

Solving a Condensation Problem

When living aboard any kind of cruiser during periods of damp, chilly weather, many boatmen find that condensation forms under the mattresses, especially in forward staterooms. We had a lot of trouble with this when cruising in southern Alaska one year, but we finally solved the problem.

We took the mattresses off and then drilled a series of half-inch-diameter holes through the plywood bunktops as shown. (There is a set of drawers underneath, so we took the drawers out first to avoid getting sawdust in them.) The holes were spaced over the whole area covered by the mattresses, and located so they were about five inches apart, center to center.

Next we took the mattress dimensions, or a paper pattern of each mattress, to a local commercial air conditioner filter supply house that stocked a material called Hog Hair, which is approximately half an inch thick and is used to custom-cut filters for large air-conditioning units. We had them cut a piece the size and shape of each mattress (they have equipment that can do this a lot easier and faster than you can). This filter material was placed on top of the plywood; then the mattresses were put back on. The holes in the plywood, combined with the Hog Hair underneath, allow air to circulate under the mattresses so that condensation is no longer a problem. It helps if you also leave one or more drawers under the bunk open about an inch so that air can enter from below.

Stowing Cockpit Cushions

Most cruising sailboats have cockpit cushions that make sitting and relaxing in the cockpit a lot more comfortable, but stowing them out of the way when you don't need them can be a problem. They are also awkward to hang up when you want to dry them out after they have gotten wet.

We solved both these problems with the system illustrated here.

Using short pieces of shock cord and some strips of webbing or vinyl, I attached two plastic snap hooks (the kind sold in marine stores for use with shock cord) to the edge of each cushion. I sewed them onto the back edge near the bottom so that when the cushions are in use the hooks won't be noticeable. When the cushions are to be stowed, or hung up to dry, we use the snap hooks to hang

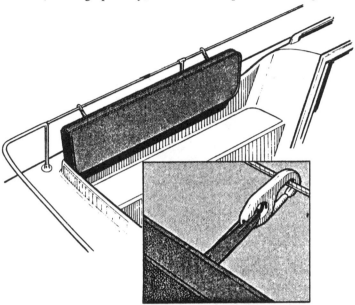

them from the lifeline across the sides of the cockpit. The cushions can also provide some privacy to the cockpit in a crowded anchorage—for example, when taking cockpit baths in hot weather.

Floating Switch Protector

Electric bilge pumps often have separate float switches with a hinged arm that floats upward to turn the pump on as the water rises above a certain point. The problem is that all too often a piece of drifting wood, a piece of foam, or some other debris in the bilge gets wedged under the floating arm while it is in its raised position. As a result the arm cannot drop to shut the pump off when the water level drops. The pump just keeps on running while you are not on board until eventually the battery goes dead.

I built a protective cage out of galvanized steel mesh that would keep floating debris from coming close enough to clog the float switch.

I cut a piece six-inches wide and sixteen-inches long and bent the sixteen-inch length to form a round tube of wire six-inches high. The ends were overlapped and stitched together with fishing line, after which I cut away

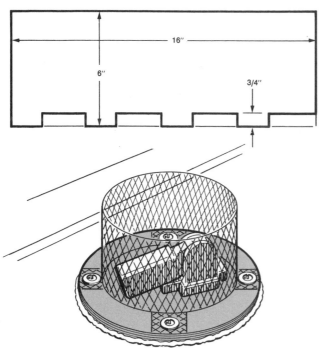

sections from the bottom edge to leave three-quarter-inch tabs that could be folded out at right angles. These tabs are used to fasten the finished cage down against the bottom of the boat.

In a wooden boat you can fasten the cage directly to the bottom with stainless screws. In a fiberglass boat first epoxy a piece of waterproof plywood to the bottom, then screw the cage down and sit the float switch on the inside.

Good Terminal Block

Most boat wiring harnesses connect the dashboard instruments to the battery and provide power for accessories with a hot lead on the ignition switch. But after a few pieces of electronic equipment have been added, the current draw through the relatively low-gauge wire can cause current levels to drop down below an acceptable level.

The solution to this problem is to run *a pair* of heavy wires directly from the battery or battery switch—one from the positive post and one from the negative post (you could also use the engine block if that serves as the ship's negative or ground). You need two wires, because there is no sense in having a good hot lead if the ground wire is not large enough to carry the load, and both must be equally heavy. Ordinary wire such as that sold in marine supply outlets is not heavy enough.

I found that the best kind of wire to use (and the cheapest for the purpose) is standard four-gauge welding wire. It's built to take lots of abuse and will carry a heavy

load. It is available from all welding supply houses, as are the crimp connectors you will need for the ends. I crimped these on, but also soldered them in place just to play safe.

To provide a junction point for these wires I made up a connection block out of a six-inch-square piece of quarter-inch Plexiglas. I used two strips of brass with brass screws and nuts as shown in the drawing to create a line of terminals for hooking up all the wires needed for the various electrical accessories. In-line fuse holders are needed for each piece of equipment, and labels can be added to indicate positive and negative strips as well as to label wires going to each piece of equipment. After all wiring is done, spraying with a moisture-displacing lubri-

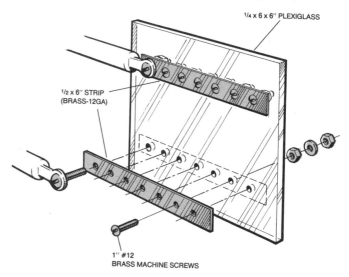

cant such as WD-40, LPS, or CRC will help to prevent corrosion and oxidation. A light coat of Vaseline smeared over all the various connections will accomplish much the same thing.

Battery Terminal Connector

Like most boatowners, I have found that in recent years I was continually adding new electrical equipment to my boat—communication and navigation gear—that required running a wire from the battery for a source of power. After a while I had so many splices and wires that the terminal connections around the battery were getting quite sloppy and hard to maintain.

I solved this with the inexpensive but effective terminal strip shown in the accompanying drawing. It is both neat and easy to maintain.

I cut the terminal strip out of a piece of twenty-two-gauge sheet copper. It can be cut to any convenient shape and size as long as it will fit the space available next to or

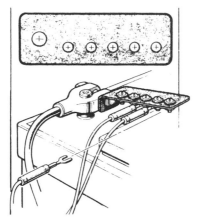

above the battery post. The next step is to drill a hole in one end of this strip through which the battery terminal screw will fit. Then drill a series of quarter-inch holes to accommodate as many other connections as you think you are likely to make at this point.

To play safe, allow for a few holes more than you now need, so future equipment can be easily added. Through each of these holes you can then insert a very short quarter-inch bolt with washer and locknut (or lockwasher). This will be used to secure the crimp-on spade connectors for each equipment wire.

Now you can slip this strip on over the battery terminal screw and then tighten it securely in place, after which all other wires can be connected to this same strip.

Just remember to install an in-line fuse holder for all wires attached to the positive battery post in this manner, and remember that any equipment connected directly to the battery in this manner will remain operable even when the battery switch is off. The added safety and neatness are well worth the few minutes this strip takes to make.

Adding a Fresh Water or Salt Water Washdown

Cleaning up a cockpit—anything from mopping up a spilled beer to washing away the mess that remains after cleaning a bunch of freshly caught fish—is not a major chore when you are dockside and can use a water hose to do the job, but it *can* be a problem when you are out at sea or at anchor. Your only options then are to trundle out containers full of water from the galley or try to maintain your balance while dipping buckets over the side.

The same holds true when trying to clean mud and seaweed off the bow after the anchor has been hauled on board—again not difficult when you can use a water hose at the dock, but quite a chore when you're anchored in some distant cove.

Such cleanup problems can be easily solved, however,

by the simple addition of a cockpit (or anchor) washdown to your boat's plumbing system. Usually offered as an option by boat manufacturers and sometimes included as standard equipment by quality-conscious builders, a cockpit or anchor washdown is simply an onboard, outside water spigot that permits you to hook up a regular garden hose even when you are nowhere near a dock—a great convenience that is not difficult to add to almost any small or medium-size cruising boat that already has a pressurized water system.

Two kinds of washdowns are normally installed for the purposes described above: One is a fresh water washdown that uses water from the boat's existing fresh water tanks; the other is a salt water washdown that draws sea water in from under the boat. A fresh water washdown in the cockpit, or near the swim platform, is also useful for taking a quick shower after a swim or a grueling fight with a big fish, but it is obviously practical only when there is enough fresh water on board.

In most boats equipped with a pressurized fresh water system, a fresh water washdown is easier to install than a salt water washdown because you don't need an extra pump and you don't have to worry about installing an additional through-hull fitting. All you have to do is tap into the existing fresh water system by cutting into the fresh water supply line after it comes out of the pump. After cutting the water line, install a tee and reconnect the original water line to the other end of the tee. Then use the extra opening in the tee fitting to connect up the new length of water line that will run up to the cockpit (or up to the bow if that is where you want the washdown). There the end of the new water line will be connected to a regular garden faucet or spigot. You should use a bronze or chrome-plated spigot for this if you want it to withstand the marine environment for long.

There is one danger you should be aware of when installing any kind of outside washdown: If the spigot or faucet develops a leak, or if someone forgets to turn it all the way off after it is used, then it could completely empty the boat's water tank before you discover the problem. If the spigot is in the cockpit, this can happen even when you're not on board due to strangers (or pranksters) coming aboard to get water.

To prevent this it is important that you remember to turn off the fresh water pump when you leave the boat at a dock for any length of time (you should do this anyway, just in case one of the water lines should break or a fitting should spring a leak). In addition, you should install a second shut-off valve somewhere inside the boat—preferably close to the water pump if that's not too inconvenient. This valve is left in the off position normally, and it is turned on only when you anticipate the outside washdown will be needed.

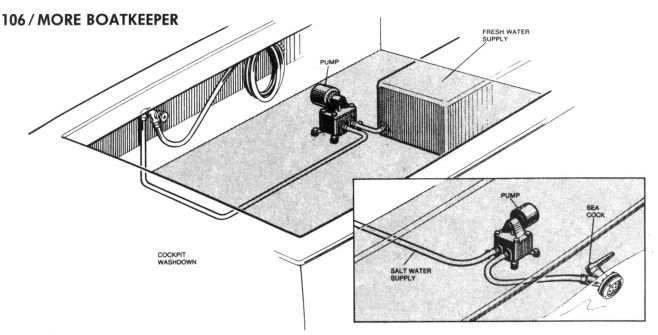

For fresh water, use existing system. For salt water (insert), pump and through hull are needed.

For a salt water washdown you will normally need a separate pump belowdecks that is attached to a through-hull fitting so it can draw water from under the hull as shown in the opening drawing. Installing an extra seacock is the best way to handle this (normally a very difficult job to accomplish during winter lay-up), or you can decide to use an existing seacock.

If you decide to use an existing inlet, make sure this will have no detrimental effect on the seacock's original function. For example, you could remove the existing raw water line and install a tee fitting that will allow you to hook up an extra water line for a cockpit washdown, but never do this with one of the seacocks that supply cooling water to the engines or to an auxiliary generator—you could be cutting down enough on cooling water to harm your engines.

On the other hand, you could tap into a seacock that supplies water to one of the toilets. Just remember that when the cockpit washdown is in use it will greatly cut down on the flow of water to that toilet; so if you are hooking both a cockpit washdown and a toilet to a single seacock, make sure that everyone aboard understands not to use one while the other is in use.

For the salt water pump you can use any conventional twelve-volt bilge pump or fresh water pump. Since most water pumps will *push* water better than they will *pull* it, you will get your strongest stream if you install the pump as close to the seacock as possible. Mount the pump up out of the bilge water by screwing a piece of three-quarter-inch waterproof plywood to one of the stringers to form a plat-form, or fiberglass a piece of wood in place. You can also

fiberglass a couple of wood or metal brackets to the side of the hull, then mount the plywood base on top of these.

After the pump is mounted, run suitable-size wire (check the specifications that came with the pump) to the battery or to a main bus bar for the hot lead, and run another wire to the negative bus bar. Splice in a switch by cutting into the hot line and running a two-conductor cable (of the same size) up to a switch located in a convenient place—usually in or near the cockpit. If possible, have this switch inside a locked cabinet where strangers cannot reach it when you are not on board.

Probably the hardest part of hooking up a washdown is running the water line from belowdecks up to the cockpit (or out to the bow in the case of an anchor washdown). Snaking a water line through the confined spaces behind a locker or cabinet, or through passageways that are already jammed full of cables, wires, and tubing can be a chore; but it can be greatly simplified if you use plastic pipe rather than the traditional copper tubing.

Widely available in most home centers and plumbing supply outlets as well as in some marine supply outlets, plastic pipe and fittings are much lighter and easier to work with than copper, and it eliminates the need for using a torch (always a potential hazard on a boat) for soldering. Cutting, fitting, and joining plastic pipe calls for only ordinary hand tools that most boatowners have on board, and plastic pipe will never rust, rot, or corrode. In addition, its much smoother inside finish means less friction and better water flow, with much less likelihood of clogging due to chemical buildups.

This combination of advantages not only explains why

more and more do-it-yourself homeowners are using this type of plumbing (except for some communities where antiquated plumbing codes still forbid it), it also explains why they are ideal for use on boats. In fact, plastic plumbing is being used as original equipment by an increasingly large number of boat builders:

Two different types of plastic plumbing on the market are approved for use with potable water. One is polybutylene (PB) pipe; the other is chlorinated polyvinylchloride (CPVC) pipe.

In general, you will find that PB pipe is easier to install because it is flexible, making it simpler to snake the pipe around obstructions and through narrow or crowded spaces. In addition, the ability to bend the pipe makes it easy to go around obstructions without need for a lot of extra fittings.

CPVC pipe is fine for some installations, but it is rigid. This makes it tougher to install inside a boat where straight paths are seldom if ever found. However, where the pipe will be visible, rigid CPVC pipe makes a much neater-looking installation.

The fittings used with CPVC are permanently cemented in place, so you cannot twist the fittings or make adjustments to improve alignment after the fitting is in place. Also, once assembled, you can't take a joint apart without cutting the pipe. The special/solvent literally "welds" the fitting to the pipe (it chemically reacts to join the two pieces together).

As shown in the drawing, there are three steps to assembling CPVC joints: (1) Clean the end of the pipe with a small piece of fine abrasive paper. (2) Coat the outside of the pipe end with a small amount of cement,

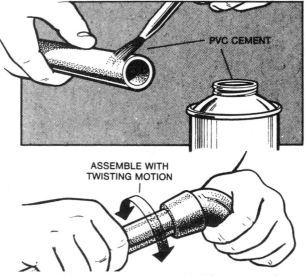

To join plastic pipe, coat end with cement, insert into fitting, then twist back and forth to spread the glue evenly.

brushing it evenly over the area that will fit inside the fitting. (3) Slide the end of the pipe into the fitting, then immediately twist back and forth a quarter turn to spread the cement around evenly. Remember that you have only a few seconds to line things up properly. Once the cement starts to set, the pieces cannot be moved.

The fittings used with PB pipe are compression-type fittings that require no cement. You slide a threaded collar onto the end of the pipe first, then slip a plastic or metal compression seal over the end of the pipe (some have a thin metal notched "lock washer" or ring that fits on over the end of the pipe to help to hold it firmly in place after the outside collar is tightened). Push the pipe into the body of the fitting, then slide the collar down and tighten it. No cement, pipe dope, or Teflon tape is needed—just screw hand tight, then give it an extra half turn with a wrench or a pair of water pump pliers.

As a further bonus, most plastic fittings of this type can also be used with copper tubing or copper pipe as well as with most plastic pipes. Thus it becomes a simple matter to hook up to existing water lines, or to replace damaged metal plumbing with new plastic pipe. All kinds of transition fittings or adapters are available to simplify this—enabling you to go from threaded to plastic pipe or vice versa, as well as to go from copper to plastic and back.

Regardless of the brand or style used, all PB fittings are designed so you can take them apart at any time and reassemble without damaging the pipe or the fitting. In addition, PB pipe offers another bonus: It is not normally damaged by freezing the way metal pipe is. PB pipe is flexible, so it can expand enough to keep the pipe from splitting or cracking if ice forms on the inside of it.

Because of this and because plastic pipe is a lot stronger and more permanent than plastic or vinyl tubing, many boatowners are gradually replacing the clear vinyl or plastic tubing that many builders originally installed for the fresh water system inside their boats.

Replacing the clear vinyl tubing with PB pipe eliminates problems such as tubing cracking or splitting, or hose clamps working loose in various places.

Safety Rail for Galley Stove

It seems that the moment the cook steps away from the galley stove some wise guy goes whizzing through the anchorage, or some boat throws up a massive wake that causes you to go dashing back to the stove to try to avert a disastrous spill from one or more hot pots on the burners.

An inexpensive and simple solution to this problem aboard our boat was to build an aluminum guard rail around the top of the range, using half-inch-wide aluminum stock that you can buy in any local hardware store.

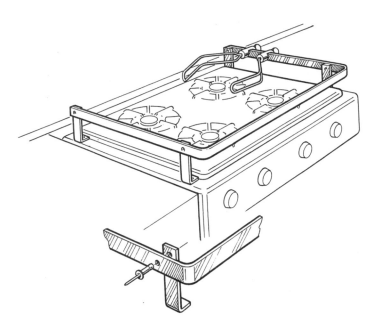

Measure the length of each side, plus the front and back of the stove, to determine how many feet of the aluminum you will need. Add at least eighteen-inches extra to allow for angled support pieces that you will have to make for each side of the rail.

Before bending the aluminum to shape, cut off four short pieces about three inches long to form the supporting "legs" or brackets that will hold the railing in place. Bend the last half inch of each of these short pieces to form a lip that will act as a base for the legs that will support the rail on top of the stove. Form the aluminum railing by bending the rest of the aluminum to fit the outside edges of the rangetop. Bend the corners carefully to a smooth curve, rather than trying to form a sharp corner.

Next, drill eighth-inch holes along each side of the rail near the front and back corners for the Pop rivets that will be used to attach the support brackets. Drill corresponding holes near the top end of each of those brackets and drill the same holes in the bent end that will rest on top of the stove so that you rivet the brackets to the stovetop. Attach the brackets to the rail with aluminum rivets, leaving the bent end at the bottom. Then set the railing, with brackets attached, on top of the stove. Position it where desired, then mark locations for the rivet holes that must be drilled in the rangetop. Drill those holes and attach the assembled rail to the top of the stove with aluminum rivets.

As an added refinement you can buy sliding pot retainers or holders that will clamp onto the aluminum rail. These can be adjusted to fit around individual pots to keep them from sliding around inside the railing.

Improving Alcohol Stove

When an alcohol stove is used to prepare a full meal, it often means that the pressure in the tank must be renewed several times while cooking. Since our alcohol tank is in a locker under the settee, this means getting down on hands and knees to do the pumping.

To eliminate this nuisance, I bought a small twelve-volt compressor designed to pump air into flat tires on a car (you can get such a compressor for about twenty dollars). I hooked this up to the tank in place of the hand pump (the

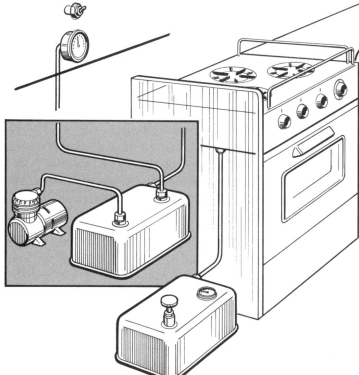

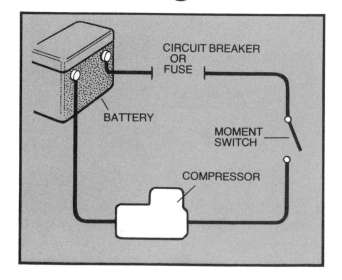

shaded inset in the drawing shows the new setup). Then I supplied power to the pump by connecting it to the battery through a momentary switch (press to turn the compressor on; release to shut it off) and circuit breaker as shown. The switch is located in a convenient locker where it can be easily reached, and pushing it builds up the needed ten pounds of pressure in just a few seconds.

But I still had to get down to look into the locker to read the pressure gauge on the tank while holding the switch down. To eliminate this, I took the gauge off the tank and mounted it in the locker next to the switch that controls the compressor. To connect the gauge to the tank, I ran a length of fuel hose from it to the tank. Hose clamps are used to ensure airtight joints.

Now pressure can be maintained while cooking by glancing at the gauge occasionally, then pressing the switch when more pressure is needed.

For More Ventilation Below

Since my thirty-three-foot sailboat did not have a forward hatch, I decided to install one. I was limited in the amount of deck space available where the opening would have to be cut, so I purchased a twelve-inch-square Bomar hatch that would fit. The hatch has a heavy aluminum frame with a one-inch flange that not only makes for a neater installation (it covers up ragged edges where the hole was cut), but also helps hold the sealant used to waterproof the opening after the hatch is in place.

When selecting a spot for the deck opening, I found that I would have to move the mainsheet. After centering the hatch in the right position, I penciled in the outline, then cut a hole through the deck with a saber saw, cutting just inside the outline to make the hole slightly smaller than actually needed. This enabled me to use sandpaper and a file to trim the hole to the exact size needed so the hatch frame would fit snugly in the opening. I found it best to sand a little at a time, then see where the hatch was binding each time by looking up while I was still below.

When it finally fit in easily without binding, I coated the exposed edges of the plywood deck core with an epoxy sealer to make sure water could not soak into the wood. When this was dry, I used a two-part Thiokol sealant to bed the hatch as I pressed it into place from above.

Since my deck has a slight curve to it, I used enough Thiokol to fill the slight gap that remained under the flange on each side. Then I drove screws into the deck through the holes in the hatch frame to secure it but was careful not to overtighten them and thus distort the frame. A thick rubber gasket comes with the hatch to ensure a good seal, but there is no sense tempting fate by exerting too much force with the screws.

Homemade Cockpit Awning

Sailing in the hot sun, especially when there is little or no wind, has given me painful sunburns, so last summer I did some serious thinking about a suitable cockpit awning I could put up myself. Standard commercial dodgers only shaded the forward part of the cockpit, and most commercially available awnings would not permit sailing when the awning was up because they all seemed to fit over the

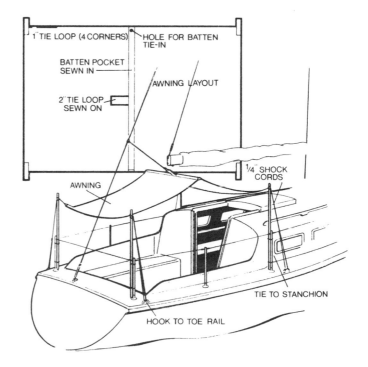

boom. As a result, we designed and made our own awning out of waterproof coated nylon available from most outdoor equipment supply houses.

The awning shown here is about eight inches narrower than the boat and extends from the stern pulpit to just aft of the mainsheet. And since it fits under the boom, we can use it while sailing in light to moderate winds. A wood batten that fits into a pocket we sewed across the awning about midway between the fore and aft ends helps to support it.

The corners of the awning are suspended on adjustable tent poles or boat hooks with shock cords tied to grommets in each corner of the awning, then looped over the top of each pole and pulled down for proper tension. We tie the bottom end to hooks or eye straps on the deck after the poles are set up and lashed to lifeline stanchions. In the center, the awning is supported by a short piece of line that runs from a loop sewn onto the midpoint of the center batten to a ring tied to the backstay overhead.

Our awning has two advantages over others we have seen: The waterproof fabric protects the helmsman in a light rain, and by removing the aft poles we can tie down the awning to the stern pulpit or rail to keep the late-afternoon sun out of the cockpit.

Coffee Maker Holder

The possibility of encountering rough seas and wakes from passing boats always made it necessary to stow our electric coffee maker before we left the dock. To eliminate the need for this, my husband rigged up an inexpensive yet

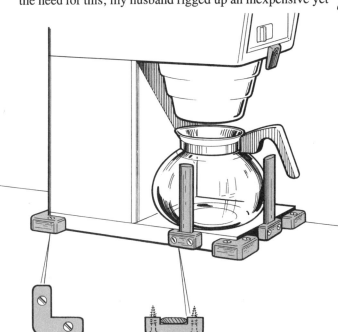

attractive method to hold our coffee maker securely in place. It required only a few small pieces of teak, as shown here.

First cut L-shaped pieces of teak to fit each corner of the coffee maker when it is standing on the counter. These pieces are pushed against the base for a snug fit; then holes are drilled through each piece so that each one can be screwed down. To secure the glass carafe or pot, and the filtering mechanism at the top, cut U-shaped pieces of wood and attach these to the base of the coffee maker with screws. A removable strip of teak is then slipped into the slot formed by the U-shaped pieces to secure the glass pot when under way. When this strip is removed, the pot can be pulled out as needed. All the wood pieces were then stained and varnished.

Extension Handle for Dinghy Motor

When one person runs a small skiff or dinghy with an outboard motor, he or she must sit near the stern to reach the motor's tiller. As a result, the dinghy runs bow high, with the stern end squatting low in the water. Sitting farther forward would solve this problem, but then you cannot reach the handle on the outboard.

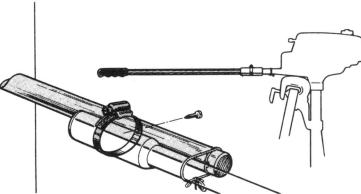

An easy solution to this problem is to make an extension handle for the outboard motor as shown here. For the handle itself you will need an old mop handle or broom handle cut to the length desired. The new handle should allow you to sit in the middle seat for the best balance. You will also need a stainless steel hose clamp large enough to go around both the wood handle and the tiller handle (about two inches in diameter).

After positioning this clamp where needed, a small hole is drilled through it so a wood screw can be driven through the clamp and into the wood pole to keep the clamp from getting lost when it is loosened or when the extension handle is not needed. Another, slightly larger hole is also drilled through the wood pole near its end so that a piece of nylon twine can be threaded through for lashing the end of the pole to the motor handle.

Paint the pole to match your motor, then slide a rubber bicycle handlebar grip over the end to finish the job.

Tool Storage

Like many other boatowners, I found that storing the tools I needed on my thirty-two-foot sailboat was a bit of a problem, especially if I wanted to have them dry and easily reachable when needed. However, I found some unused space under the companionway steps leading down

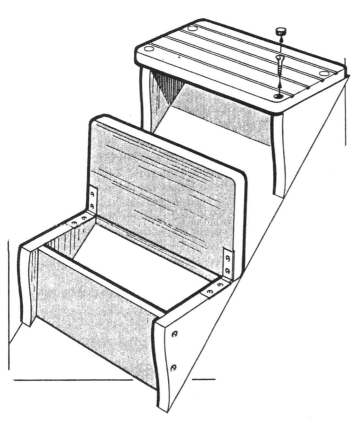

to my main cabin. As indicated in the drawing, I removed the existing teak tread by chipping the wood plug and backing out the screws that held it in place. Then I installed a fill-in board along the front between the brackets the tread rests on. The original tread was then reinstalled on top of the original brackets with hinges so that the space underneath would be easily accessible.

This little storage space is large enough for most of the screwdrivers, pliers, tape, and similar supplies that I seem to need on almost every outing. It even has room for an extra ignition key and a spare pair of eyeglasses.

Dinghy Storage

Most dinghies do not have any storage space at all, so there is never anyplace to keep a flashlight, a couple of tools, spare oar locks, parts for the motor, and perhaps a couple of Band-Aids. I solved this problem simply by attaching a small plastic tool box to the bottom of one of the dinghy's seats, as shown here.

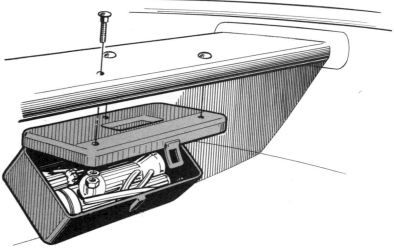

Buy an inexpensive tool box of the size desired (don't forget you will need room for the box to drop down when you want to open it). If it has a handle on top, remove it. My box had a handle that folds flat inside a recess so it didn't get in the way, but if your box has one that sticks up it will get in the way when you try to attach the lid to the bottom of the seat as shown. Also, if there are any other projections that stick up on top and will prevent the lid from going flat against the bottom of the seat, these, too, will have to be trimmed off.

I attached the lid to the seat bottom by using quarter-inch stainless steel bolts and nuts as shown. It's best to drill the holes in the box lid first, then make a template with a piece of paper and transfer this layout to the seat. Then you can drill the matching holes through it. I found it best to make the holes in the seat slightly oversize by reaming them out with a rat tail file or similar tool; this made it easier to line them up evenly with those in the box lid when the bolts were inserted.

Anchor Line Reel

Those of us who own small cruisers with cuddy cabins have at least one problem in common—what to do with a hundred or two hundred feet of wet anchor line after we

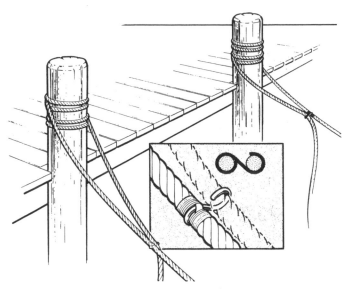

take it in. My twenty-one-foot cruiser, for instance, is equipped with a bow pulpit, but there is no rope locker underneath because the V-berth forward takes up all the space under the deck in the bow area.

Here is how I solved this problem: I first mounted a hardwood panel about twelve inches by twenty inches on the bow rail, securing it near the bow pulpit with five one-inch U-bolts. I then purchased an ordinary garden hose reel at a local hardware store and bolted this to the board in about the center so the anchor line can be wound up on the reel as I pull it in. The reel has a rotating handle that I can turn with one hand while I pull in the line with the other hand. The board was stained and varnished to match the wood trim on the rest of the boat, and the reel was painted to blend in.

Easy-to-Reach Stern Lines

When boats are docked in a slip where they have to back in between pilings so that the stern of the boat is near the dock behind them, a problem often encountered is how to handle the permanent stern dock lines. Most boatowners prefer to leave these permanent lines behind, still attached to cleats or pilings on the dock, so they can just be picked up again when they come back in. Most people simply throw the ends off the boat onto the dock when they leave, but they are then hard to reach when you back in (without hitting the dock) unless someone is standing there to hand them to you.

The drawing shows a simple solution that I worked out. First I rigged guidelines from the dock pilings to the pilings out near the bow of the boat when it is in its slip.

These help guide me when I'm backing in, and they keep me from drifting over into the next slip if there is a wind blowing or a current running. Then I permanently attached two S-hooks to each of these guidelines by crimping or bending one half of the "S" tight around the guideline on each side and then wrapping them with sail twine. Finally I attached these hooks to each line about five feet out from the dock piling, as shown.

Alcohol Stove Repair

Like most alcohol stoves, ours has a tank with a built-in pump that can be used to keep the tank pressurized. However, after a while our tank would not maintain its pressure because an inner check valve had developed a slow leak—a problem that also contributed to the corrosion and disintegration of some of the pump plunger parts. After purchasing a special wrench and replacement parts from the manufacturer we still were unable to remove the check valve to replace it.

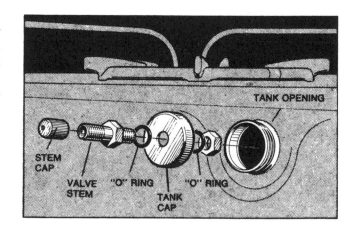

To salvage the stove I decided to modify the cap through which the pump shaft previously had protruded. I drilled and tapped it to receive a tire-valve-type air fitting similar to the kind used on automobile tires. As shown in the drawing, O-rings and Teflon tape were used to achieve an air-tight seal after the cap was replaced. Then I purchased a small, hand-type bicycle pump, and I now use this to pressurize the tank.

The one-way valve inside the new fitting now serves as a backup for the internal valve. The bicycle pump is attached only when pressure in the tank needs to be built up again. The rest of the time the pump is stored in a galley drawer. The amount of pressure inside the tank at any time can be measured by using an inexpensive tire gauge that has low-pressure readings.

Longer-Lasting Rubber Caps

Boatowners who have chairs, tables, stools, or other pieces of furniture with tubular metal legs normally fit rubber caps (often referred to as rubber crutch tips) over the bottom end of each leg to protect floors and decks from scratching. The trouble is that in the kind of salty, sunny conditions in which most deck furniture is used, the metal legs soon start wearing through the soft rubber caps and the leg ends start cutting into or scratching your decks or cabin soles and the furniture loses its grip.

To prevent this there is a simple protective measure you can take. Place a metal washer in the bottom of each rubber cap before sliding it on over the end of the metal leg. The washers will keep the sharp metal ends on the legs from cutting through the soft rubber of the caps so that they will last almost indefinitely. For best results, use a washer with an outside diameter that is approximately the same as the inside diameter of the rubber cap. Then say good-bye to scratched decks and floors for good.

All-Weather Radar Viewer

A lot of sportfishing boats, as well as many cruising boats with flying bridges, have their radar units mounted up on the bridge. This is because when the weather turns bad and radar is needed, skippers prefer to be up on the bridge and out in the open where they can hear horns, bells, sirens, and other aids to navigation—as well as other boats or breaking surf.

One popular way to mount the radarscope on the bridge is with a tilt-out "laundry hamper"-type bin that you simply pull out to view the radar when needed. When the radar is not in use the bin tilts back under the helm to keep the radar out of the weather. The only trouble with this

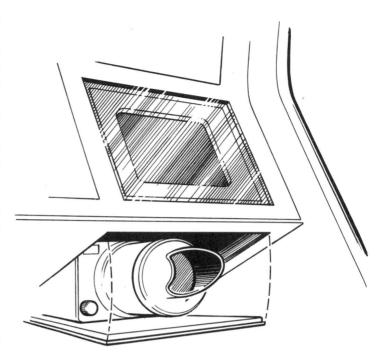

setup is that when it is raining and you want the radar unit out where you can see it, you are also exposing it to the damaging effects of the weather—water can quickly ruin an expensive radar viewing unit.

To get around this on my boat I cut an opening in the top of the console and then covered this with a small piece of automobile safety glass. This is firmly bedded with compound and is held down with strips of molding or clips around the edges. If your console is curved at the top, you will first have to shape an adapter block of mahogany or teak to fit the console; then cut your opening in this and mount the glass on top. I painted the area around the glass with flat black paint to minimize reflections.

Now when it is raining I need only swing out the radar long enough to adjust it, then close the "hamper" and watch the scope through the weatherproof window on top. You may not be able to use the magnifier when it is in this closed position, but you should still be able to see enough to make things out.

Securing Anchor and Chain

With thieves operating so freely around marinas, docks, and mooring areas, one popular target is an expensive anchor sitting up on the bow. Usually it is attached to a short length of chain that goes down into the rope locker, where the chain is attached to the anchor rope. All the thief has to do is pick the anchor up, pull the chain out until the rope is exposed, then simply cut the line with a

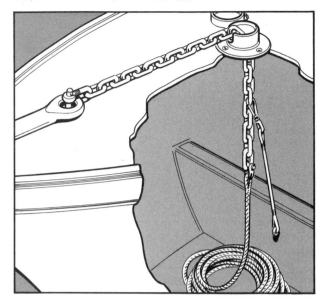

sharp knife—and he walks off with both anchor and chain.

One easy way to frustrate this type of burglar is to secure the end of the chain inside the rope locker as shown here. Install a galvanized eye-bolt through the forward bulkhead, then attach a short piece of line to this with a snap hook at the end. When you leave the boat, pull the chain down tight from inside, then snap the hook into the chain. This will prevent the anchor chain from being pulled out from above. To frustrate those who might try to unshackle the anchor from the chain by unscrewing the shackle pin on the bow, make sure the shackle that holds the anchor to the chain is screwed in as tightly as possible; then secure the pin with several turns of stainless wire threaded through the hole in the end and wrapped around the shackle.

A final word of caution: Always make sure you unsnap the belowdecks piece of line from the anchor chain before leaving the dock, so that the anchor will be ready to drop in a hurry if need be.

Storing Small Parts in a Dock Box

I have worked out a very neat way to add small-parts storage to a large dock box without taking up any extra space on the inside and without having these small items get lost in the bottom. Our dock box is a large fiberglass model with a cavernous interior that just seemed to eat up small items, which disappeared once inside—until I installed two long storage "shelves" along the inside of the back wall as shown here.

These shelves actually consist of two lengths of U-shaped household plastic roof gutter, which I bought from a local home center. These gutters come in ten-foot lengths, so I was able to cut two shelves from one length. Each gutter section is about four inches square in cross section, which is just right for holding cans of oil, extra filters, cans of cleaner, etc. Special mounting brackets are available for fastening these gutters to the house, so these were used to fasten them to the back wall of the box.

End caps are also available, so I used one of these at the end of each shelf. In my case I decided to install the gutter lengths so that one end is butted tight against the end of the

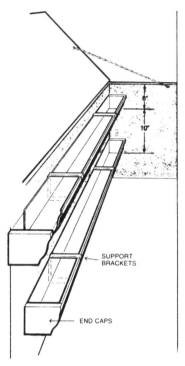

SUPPORT BRACKETS

END CAPS

box. The other end was then closed off with an end cap. I used two brackets to mount each shelf, and I ended them about eighteen inches from the left end of the box to provide room for very bulky items in that area. Total cost for everything was about ten dollars.

Nonslip Hangers

Regardless of whether they are made of wood, metal, or plastic, most clothes hangers allow pants or slacks that are folded over the bar of the hanger to slide off when boats are under way due to the constant vibration and shaking motion. As a result, neatly pressed trousers or slacks often wind up in a heap on the bottom of the locker, where they can get dirty as well as getting creased.

A trick I use to prevent this is to coat the bar on each hanger with a light film of silicone rubber adhesive (the kind made by GE and Dow). After this silicone has dried

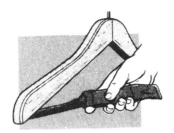

(it takes about an hour), it leaves a nonskid surface on the bar that will completely eliminate the problem of pants or slacks dropping off in the future.

Removable Dinghy Motor Pad

I have a small outboard motor for my dinghy, and when I use the motor, I like to keep the dinghy's transom from being crushed by the motor's clamping screws—but I don't like having a protective pad there all the time. So I made a removable mounting pad that can simply be dropped in place when the motor is to be used, yet can be removed instantly when it is no longer needed. I have been using the pad shown here on my dinghy for over six years, and the transom still looks as good as it did when we bought it.

To make this motor pad you will need two pieces of ½-inch-thick plywood that are about 14 inches long. One piece is 5 inches wide and the other is 6½ inches wide. The wider piece fits on the outside of the transom, and the narrower piece fits on the inside. After cutting them to size, clamp these two pieces temporarily in place against the inside and outside of the transom. Then join them at the top with two strips of flat aluminum bent over the tops as shown. Next attach the aluminum strips to each piece of plywood with wood screws, then tack pieces of thick leather or rubber across the top directly beneath where the motor clamp will go to protect the exposed top edge of the transom when the motor is in place. The completed motor pad can be lifted off easily when it is not needed, and quickly dropped back into place when the motor is to be mounted.

3 TOOLS, MAINTENANCE AND TECHNIQUES

The Boatkeeper's Basic Tool Kit

I was relaxing on my aft deck waiting for guests to arrive when a boating neighbor from a few slips away came dashing over. His boat, which was powered by twin outboards, was fully loaded and ready to go, but just as he was set to start the engines he noticed fuel squirting out from a fuel line connection. He had been unable to stop the leak. Could I help him out?

Always a good neighbor, I walked over and had a look. A threaded fuel line fitting had vibrated loose, and apparently all it needed was tightening. However, when I looked closer I saw that the hex head fitting had been badly rounded off so it was no longer possible to tighten it with a wrench. The only wrench he had on board was an adjustable wrench that was too bulky to fit in the narrow

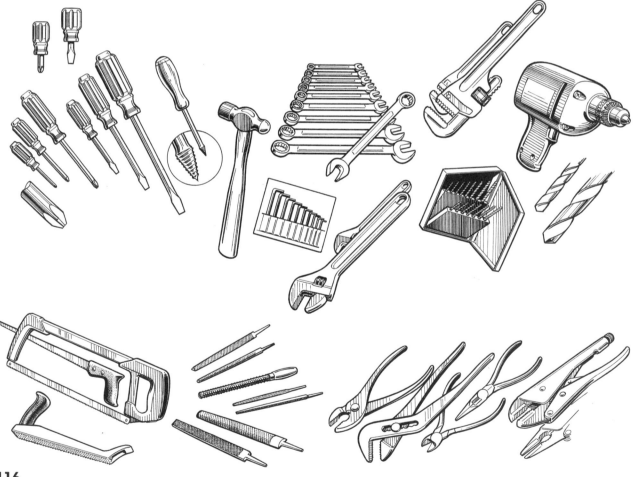

space where the fitting was located. So he had tried to tighten the brass fitting with a pair of pliers. Not only couldn't he get a tight enough grip to stop the leak, but also in the process he had ruined the fitting.

Fortunately, he was still at the dock and the proper tools could be located. But what would have happened to that poor soul had he been out on the water? For lack of a few wrenches—tools that every boatowner should have in his tool kit—he might have drifted for hours until help arrived, or he might have had to call for a tow.

The moral of the story is simple: Every boat larger than a dinghy should have at least a basic kit of tools on board at all times. Of course, the size of this kit and the variety of tools required will vary with the size and complexity of the boat and with the amount of cruising one does. The skipper of a fifty-foot motoryacht will obviously need a much more complete set of tools than the owner of an eighteen-foot outboard; but there are still certain tools that will be common to both and that should be part of every onboard tool kit.

Screwdrivers: You need at least three. One medium and one large-size screwdriver with a flat blade to fit conventional slotted screws, and one medium-size screwdriver with a Phillips blade to fit screws with a cross slot or Phillips head. A few additional sizes are not a bad idea—a couple of stubby or "shortie" screwdrivers (one flat-blade and one Phillips) to get into tight places; and an extra-long screwdriver with a wider blade.

Pliers: Two pairs are the absolute minimum—one needle-nose pliers with built-in wire cutters on the side; and one slip-joint or adjustable water pump pliers, the kind that has angled jaws and can be set for various-size jaw openings (these are also called channel-type pliers because Channel-lock is one of the original brand names). If there is a likelihood you will be doing much electrical work, then a pair of diagonal cutting pliers will also come in handy, as will wire strippers.

Locking Pliers: One of these versatile tools, which are actually a cross between a pair of pliers and a wrench, should be in every tool kit (Vise Grips are probably the best-known brand name, but there are others). They can be used to grip tightly where no other tool will hold—for example, when the head has broken off a screw or bolt, or, as in the example at the beginning of this article, when a nut has been rounded off or a screw head will no longer accept a screwdriver blade or wrench. They can be used instead of a wrench when the right size is not available, and they can be locked onto the work so that you can turn or twist without losing your grip. They also make great clamps for holding pieces in place while drilling, filling, or soldering. Models are available with straight or curved jaws, and with powerful wire cutters or bolt cutters built right in.

Fixed Wrenches: A set of open-end wrenches ranging from about ¼ inch to ¾ inch is a must, but most owners of medium to large-size cruising boats will probably need wrenches going up to ¹⁵⁄₁₆ inch in size. Since there are places where a conventional open-end wrench will not fit, a wiser choice is to buy a set of combination wrenches that are open-end at one end but that have a box wrench of the same size at the other end. Box wrenches wrap completely around a nut or bolt head to ensure a stronger grip that won't slip, and they can fit in places where there is not enough clearance for the jaws of an open-end wrench.

If you like to do your own maintenance work, then a compact socket wrench set with a ratcheting handle is something you will want to add. Socket wrenches are faster and grip stronger than open-end wrenches when you can fit them over the top of the fastener, and the ratcheting handle, combined with the various extensions available, will enable you to reach into places where there is no room to swing a conventional wrench.

Adjustable Wrenches: You should have two adjustable wrenches—say, a six-inch and a ten-inch—for those jobs where you don't have a wrench of the right size, or where you need two wrenches of the same size (you can use one adjustable and one fixed wrench). You will also want at least one pipe wrench for gripping rods or pipes as well as for working on shafts and stuffing boxes. In larger boats two pipe wrenches will be needed: one medium-size (about eight inches) and one large size (about ten or twelve inches).

Allen Wrenches: Sometimes referred to as Allen keys, hex keys, or setscrew keys, these are not really wrenches at all. Consisting of an L-shaped steel rod with a hexagonal cross section, they are primarily needed for setscrews that have a recessed opening into which the Allen wrench fits. Either end of the key or wrench can be used, depending on which is easier to reach and on the amount of leverage required (inserting the shorter end of the L gives you greater leverage).

Hammer: If you carry only one hammer, your best bet is a medium-weight ball-peen hammer (also called an engineer's or machinist's hammer). That's because you seldom do much nailing or much nail-pulling on a boat, but you are likely to use your hammer for pounding on metal or hitting a cold chisel, and a regular carpenter's hammer should not be used for this kind of work. The polished head of a nail hammer is not made to withstand blows of this kind.

Saws: A hacksaw, or some type of utility handsaw with a metal cutting blade, is not a tool you will use every day, but it is a tool that is periodically needed—for example, to cut off a bolt that you can't get out any other way; to cut through some cables that must be removed; to cut through a pipe or exhaust line that is "frozen" in place; or even to cut through a padlock when you have lost the key. A hacksaw will also cut through fiberglass and it will cut wood—but very slowly. If you anticipate having to cut wood very often, include a small carpenter's saw as well.

Chisels: A cold chisel is another one of those seldom-needed tools that should still be included in every boat-owner's tool kit because it could be just the thing needed to chop off a stubborn bolt or rivet, or split a cable that must be cut in a hurry. It is also a good idea to carry two or three wood chisels of varying sizes—say, ¼ inch, ½ inch, and ¾ inch. You will find need for these when it is necessary to notch into a wood stringer, bulkhead, or cabinet frame while installing new hardware, or when making up fairing blocks for mounting equipment above- or belowdecks.

Electric Drill and Drill Bits: Although you can prob-ably get by with a hand drill for most jobs, the low cost and compactness of modern electric drills make it unnec-essary to go through the tedium of drilling holes by hand. For boats that are berthed at a dock where electricity is available, or those that have their own auxiliary genera-tors, choose one of the variable-speed, reversible 110-volt electric drills that are double-insulated. Ideal for use as an electric screwdriver as well as a drill, these "shockproof" models do not require a three-conductor (grounded) outlet. For those who do not have 110-volt power available, and for maximum convenience even if you do have power on board, the best choice would be a cordless drill with a rechargeable battery pack.

You will obviously need a set of twist drill bits that can be used for drilling in metal as well as wood. These come in sets that go from ¹⁄₁₆ inch up to ¼ inch or ⅜ inch, depending on the size drill you have. For boring larger holes through wood or fiberglass, a set of spade bits that will bore holes up to about 1½ inches will come in handy when installing new equipment or when making alterations on the inside.

Files and Rasps: You should include at least one flat mill file for general deburring and smoothing of rough metal edges, as well as one round file for reaming out or enlarging holes in metal or fiberglass. A half-round wood rasp will also come in handy for smoothing or shaping wood and fiberglass, or you can use one of the Surform-type rasps that are sold for this purpose (Surform is the brand name for Stanley's version of this tool).

Miscellaneous Tools: One little tool that can be espe-cially handy is a screw starter. Resembling an awl with a threaded point that is tapered, this tool is ideal for making pilot holes or starting holes for wood screws—for exam-ple, when screwing cable clamps to bulkheads or when mounting galley fixtures.

Another "tool" that every boatowner should have on board is a small, inexpensive voltmeter or multimeter. These are invaluable when trying to track down electrical shorts or other problems. They can be used for measuring voltage and amperes, and to check for continuity where you suspect a bad connection or broken wire.

If you regularly have to do some wood finishing, you will also want a couple of wood scrapers for removing old paint or varnish, and either a hand-sanding block or an electric sander (the high-speed compact finishing sanders often referred to as "Palm sanders" are probably the most useful for this).

Other tools that will prove useful are:

● Two flexible putty knives in different sizes for patching and filling wood surfaces and also fiberglass.
● A sharp stainless steel utility knife or rigger's knife.
● A retractable steel tape measure that will extend to at least twelve feet, preferably one with a rust-resistant coating.
● A combination wire stripping and crimping tool for use with insulated electrical crimp fittings.
● A tool that is often referred to as a "grabber." Consisting of a flexible steel cable about twenty-four inches long, it has a plunger-type handle at the upper end and spring-activated wire jaws at the lower end. You open the jaws to grab something by pressing down on the

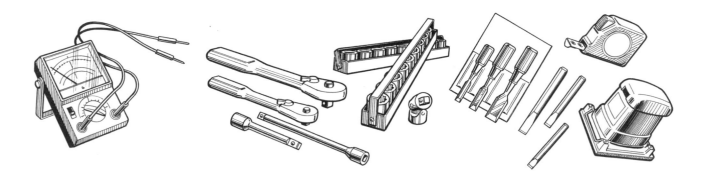

plunger, then release this to let the jaws close on the object you want to retrieve.

● A metal punch or small nailset. This comes in handy for setting small brads and nails when nailing wood moldings in place, as well as for use as a punch that can be used with a hammer to free up stubborn bolts and nuts.

● A couple of medium-size C-clamps for making repairs in wood when gluing is required, or for holding things together when soldering or epoxying small assemblies.

Where and How to Store Tools

Wherever possible it is best to store tools where they can be easily reached in a hurry and where you won't have to search through a whole pile of assorted odds and ends to find the tool you need. Select a convenient place in one of the lazarettes, in a deck box, under a settee, or in the bottom of one of the lockers where you can keep your tool box, rather than down in the engine room, where they will be hard to reach. It's best to keep all your tools in one place, but if you must split them up—say, to keep some tools in the engine room—keep the most frequently used ones above.

You may want to store tools loosely in a drawer or cabinet, perhaps under the ladder going down to the main cabin, but years of living and working on boats has taught me that keeping them in a portable tool box or carrier is preferable. If you have a lot of tools, one box might be too large and too heavy to carry around, so split up the tools into two or even three smaller boxes. Let one box hold the most frequently used tools—this is the one I always call my "90 percent kit." It holds the tools needed to do 90 percent of the work around the boat.

Stay away from metal tool boxes; even the best ones rust, and they are more likely to cause scratches, dents, and dings as you carry them around the boat. The new plastic tool boxes are lighter and much safer—and they won't rust. For my "90 percent kit" I have found that one of those plastic or canvas tool bags is handier than a tool box; it is lighter in weight, more compact, and it comes with a rope drawstring or handle that makes it easy to carry.

Regardless of where and how you store your tools, get in the habit of buying only top-quality tools. Avoid "bargains"—they will only lead to grief. Cheap tools rust more quickly, break easily, and can lead to unnecessary frustration and even accidents in some cases.

Taking good care of your tools is equally important. Spray regularly with a rust-preventive lubricant to protect against corrosion, and make sure blades on knives, chisels, and other sharp cutting tools are kept sharp.

Also, get in the habit of wiping tools clean to remove grease and oil after you have used them. Slippery handles can lead to accidents because you cannot get a good grip.

Small Tool Box

People often receive gift packages of wine that consist of several bottles housed in a neat and surprisingly sturdy wooden box—often with a hinged wooden lid and a rope handle on the side or the end. I have found that such a box can be used as a convenient tool box for small tools, or for small parts of various kinds.

Unlike the usual metal tool box, these boxes won't rust, and unlike plastic boxes they won't trap and hold damp-

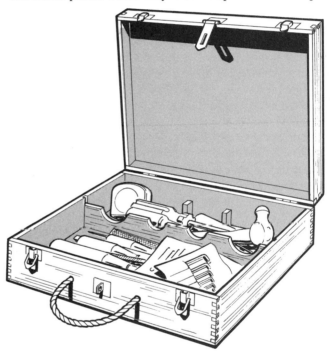

ness. The box can be either painted or varnished to help protect the wood, and I usually attach a small brass safety hasp to keep the lid from falling open at the wrong time. If necessary, the original hinges can also be replaced with stronger ones that are attached with small screws, or with very short bolts that go through the wood.

Screw Starter

There are many times when it would be handy to have a screwdriver that can hold a screw in place against the tip of the blade—times when you just can't reach in with a second hand to hold it in place, or when space is too tight for more than the screwdriver blade.

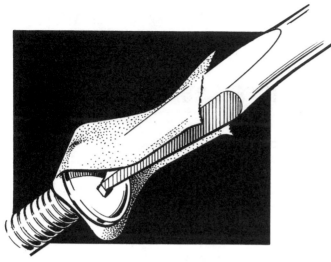

In all these cases a strip of masking tape or electrician's tape will solve the problem for you. Tear off a short piece (about two inches long), then punch a small hole in the center with an ice pick, knife point, or similar tool. A pointed screw will easily make its own hole.

Push the screw through the hole from the sticky side until the head is all the way up against the tape. Now push the tip of the screwdriver blade firmly into the screwhead's slot, then put the tape taut up against each side of the screwdriver blade as shown in the drawing. This will hold the screw firmly in place against the tip of the driver so you don't need a second hand to get the screw started. After it is firmly started you can pull the tape off (or twist the blade to tear it off) and then drive the screw the rest of the way in as usual.

Portable Power Tools for the Boatowner

Although most jobs around a boat can be completed with only hand tools, electric power tools can sure make chores a lot faster and easier to accomplish. For example, a crank-operated hand drill can be used for most small holes—but imagine trying to use it with a three-inch-diameter hole saw. And can you picture trying to drill stainless steel by hand? Onboard jobs like these are why an increasing number of boatowners are turning to power tools.

When buying any electric tool for use around a boat or dock, one of the first things you should shop for is a double-insulated model (often called shockproof). These have a two-wire cord and plug and need no third wire for grounding, so they are much safer to use around a boat.

Electric Drills

At one time everybody started out with a ¼-inch drill, but nowadays most people will buy a ⅜-inch drill instead (the size of a drill refers to the size of its chuck). A ⅜-inch drill costs only a little more (in some cases no more) than a ¼-inch drill and has a motor that develops more torque at lower speeds, which is better for larger bits. Also, ⅜-inch drills are more widely available (some dealers no longer carry ¼-inch drills).

Drills come in single-speed and variable-speed models, and my advice is to pay the difference and get a variable-speed drill. Variable-speed drills make it a lot easier to start a hole in fiberglass or metal where you don't want the bit to skitter around or slip and scratch the surface. You can start at a very slow speed for maximum control, then speed up after the point has started to "grab."

Variable-speed models can also be used as electric screwdrivers when equipped with the right bit. Most are also reversible, so they can be used for removing as well as driving screws—a welcome feature when you have to drive dozens of screws while installing trim or moldings.

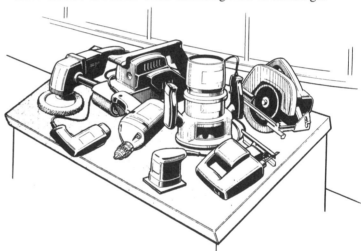

A cordless drill with rechargeable batteries can also be a great convenience—eliminates the need for running long extension cords every time you need a couple of pilot holes. However, a good ⅜-inch cordless drill will cost more than a comparable 110-volt model, especially if you want one with variable speed control. In addition, I have found that they are often not quite as powerful and cannot always handle heavy jobs, like boring with a hole saw.

Sanders

Another very popular power tool is the electric sander. Three types are available: disk sanders, finishing sanders (often called orbital sanders), and belt sanders.

Disk sanders are usually rubber-backed disks that are chucked into an electric drill. They are only good for rough work and have little use around a boat. They tend to

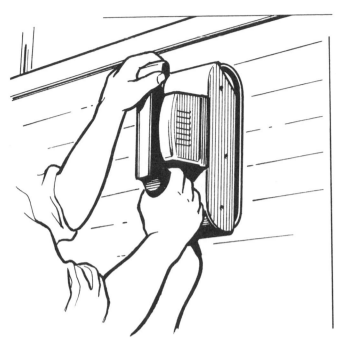

optional accessory or as standard equipment, is a vacuum bag attachment that catches most of the dust as you work. Not only does this make breathing a lot easier when you are working in an enclosed space, but it also can be a boon when there is wet paint or varnish nearby (like on your neighbor's boat). And it certainly cuts down on the amount of cleaning up required afterward.

Portable Saws

For cutting fiberglass, wood paneling, plastic laminates, aluminum, copper, brass, and other materials, the tool that is used most often around a boat is the electric saber saw (or jigsaw). Equipped with the right kind of blade, it can cut almost anything—and it can cut both straight lines and curves.

One big advantage offered by an electric saber saw is that it can make blind or pocket cuts—openings in the center of a panel—without any need to drill a starting hole for the blade. As shown in the accompanying drawing, you can tilt the tool forward onto the front of its shoe or base so that the projecting blade does not quite touch the panel. Then start the motor and slowly lower the base of the tool toward the surface. As the blade comes in contact with the face of the panel it will penetrate until it cuts all the way through. When the base of the tool is flat against the surface, cutting can proceed in the usual manner.

Saber saws come in single-speed, multispeed, or variable-speed models. Those with more than one speed are generally more versatile. The ability to run at a slower speed is advantageous in some cases—for example, a

gouge the surface if not carefully handled and will almost always leave whirl marks and scratches.

Finishing sanders are the most popular. They have a flat pad that uses regular sheets of abrasive paper that have been torn in half, in thirds, or in quarters, depending on the size of the machine. The very inexpensive ones are a waste of time, so stick to one of the good-quality models with a powerful motor. The easiest type to handle, and the one that seems to be preferred by many pros, is the palm-size model that can be held in one hand, such as the ones made by Black & Decker or Makita. These high-speed sanders do a great job of smoothing, and you can use them for hours at a time without becoming overly tired.

Belt sanders are mainly used for large, flat surfaces where you want to remove a lot of stock in a hurry or want to sand off many layers of paint or varnish. Because they work fast, you have to be careful how you handle them; if they're held in one place too long they will dig in and create dips or gouges in the surface. However, because they work so fast they are great for large, flat surfaces such as decks, cabin sides, bulkheads, and so forth. It just takes a little practice, preferably on scrap material, to learn how to do a fast job of smoothing or trimming or finish-removing with one of these machines.

Belt sanders use belts that are either 3 or 4 inches wide. Most are quite heavy to handle when working on vertical surfaces or overhead, but some companies (Skil is one that I know of) have introduced lightweight models that are much easier to handle. These accept 2½- or 3-inch belts and are light enough and compact enough to be controlled with one hand. Thus they are much more suitable for use around a boat.

One feature available on many belt sanders, either as an

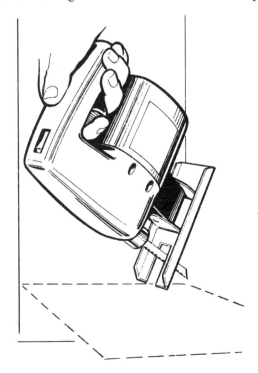

high-speed saw might partially melt acrylic plastic when cutting through it.

Another feature that comes in handy in a saber saw is "autoscrolling." This means there is a knob on top, at the front of the handle, that enables you to turn the blade as you are cutting without having to turn the whole body of the tool. This makes it much easier to maneuver the blade when cutting tight curves or intricate patterns. Ripping attachments are available for most models to permit straight cuts when trimming within a few inches of a straight edge. To make straight cuts that are not near an edge, you simply clamp a long straight edge to the surface of the work and use this as a guide for the tool.

If you do lots of straight cutting in plywood or similar materials, then a portable circular saw is a lot faster and more accurate than a saber saw. The most widely sold models are those that use 7¼-inch blades, but these are fairly heavy and often awkward to handle around a boat. However, the type often referred to as a panel saw is lighter and more compact and thus a lot easier to handle. It takes saw blades that are only 5½ inches in diameter, adequate for any plywood or lumber you are likely to encounter when working around a boat. These saws are not quite as powerful as their larger cousins, so they may cut just a bit slower in heavy stock, but they also cost less than standard-size models of comparable quality.

Routers

This is a tool that you probably won't need very often, but when you do need one it is the only tool that will do the job. It takes steel bits in a wide variety of sizes and shapes and spins them at a very high speed—something like 25,000 rpm—so that they do a clean job of trimming, shaping, and carving wood or plastic.

Cabinetmakers and professional carpenters usually use a router to carve or shape the edges on shelves, countertops, and cabinettops as well as to make woodworking joints such as dovetailed corner joints, dadoes, rabbets, and half-lap or full-lap joints. Around boats you'll find it handy for trimming off excess material on the edges of plastic laminates when covering countertops or adding built-ins, and for carving out fancy name boards, transom boards, and documentation boards. When remodeling or altering interiors, the router is often needed for finishing decorative wood railings, cabinet doors, and wood trim.

Routers come in various sizes and in new, electronically controlled models that are easier than ever to use. Sears makes one that automatically adjusts for the best and most efficient speed to prevent scorching while still ensuring a smooth cut. All you have to do is feed in the information about the hardness of the wood, the depth of the cut, etc. Another handy feature on some models is a small light that lets you see more clearly where the tool is going.

Lamb's-Wool Buffers

If you have a fiberglass boat and if you regularly do your own waxing and polishing, then a good buffer may be a worthwhile investment. Even renting one each spring can speed up commissioning chores.

Most buffers have disks or buffing wheels that vary from seven to nine inches in diameter. The best ones have an orbital motion while they rotate. In other words, while the disk is rotating, its center is also moving in a slightly orbital or oval pattern. The result is a smoother finish, with fewer rings or "burn" marks.

Equipped with a proper lamb's-wool or sheepskin bonnet, buffers do a great job of shining wax—and they do it a lot faster and easier than you could by hand. However, it does take a little practice to learn how to handle the high-speed disk properly, so try using it first on some scrap surfaces and start on some of the least conspicuous parts of the boat.

The idea is not to press the whole face of the buffing pad against the surface; hold it at a slight angle so that only about one fourth of the surface of the pad is in contact with the boat. Keep swinging the rotating pad back and forth in a series of gradual arcs as you are working, and make sure you don't hold it in one place too long. A separate cover can be used to apply the wax, but be sure you buy a wax made for use with a machine. Some soft waxes, and almost all of the liquid polishes, are designed to be applied and polished by hand.

Heat Guns

Although a portable electric heat gun is not strictly a power tool, the new ones made by Black & Decker, Sears, and others do need electric power. They put out a powerful blast of heat when the trigger is pressed and come in handy for many jobs around the boat.

Shaped like an electric drill, these tools are often referred to as strippers by dealers and manufacturers because they throw out enough heat to soften and blister paint or varnish so it can be easily scraped off without sanding or using a chemical paint remover. They are also handy for such jobs as speeding up the drying of fiberglass patches and resin-type patching compounds in cool weather or when you are in a hurry, as well as for drying wet or damp joints before filling or caulking. I have also used mine for softening the end of a plastic hose so it will be easier to install, for heating rigid plastic so it can be bent to shape, and even for drying out wet electrical connections that were accidentally flooded.

Just remember that these guns put out a lot of heat, so you can accidentally scorch or even burn materials if you are not careful; learn to use them with a reasonable amount of caution. If you want only mild heat, don't hold the gun on one place too long—keep waving it around—but don't hold it too close, either.

Choosing and Using Common Fasteners

One assortment of hardware that every boatowner soon accumulates is a collection of boxes, jars, and other containers full of screws, nails, and other fasteners. Most of the time it is not hard to pick out the type of fastener you want to use—if you are joining pieces of wood together, or if you are fastening something to wood, you use wood screws or nails; if you are fastening something to metal or fiberglass, you use self-tapping screws, blind rivets, or perhaps an expansion-type anchor.

However, there are times when the choice is not quite that simple—either because there is more than one type of fastener that could be used for a job, or because there is doubt about the size or style you should use.

To help you choose the best fastener for a particular job and to guide you in working with the various types of fasteners most commonly used around a boat, here are a number of time- and work-saving tips that should prove helpful to all *More Boatkeeper* readers:

Wood Screws

Wood screws are available in many different metals, but as a rule boatowners will be interested only in those made of brass (plain or chrome-plated), bronze, or stainless steel—for their rust-resistant qualities as well as for strength. Screws made of plain steel (plated or not) have no place on a boat, since they will begin to rust almost immediately.

When choosing a screw for a particular job, there are three factors to consider: length, diameter (specified by a gauge number), and type of head. Ideally, when joining two pieces of wood together, the length of the screw should be such that its shank (the unthreaded part under

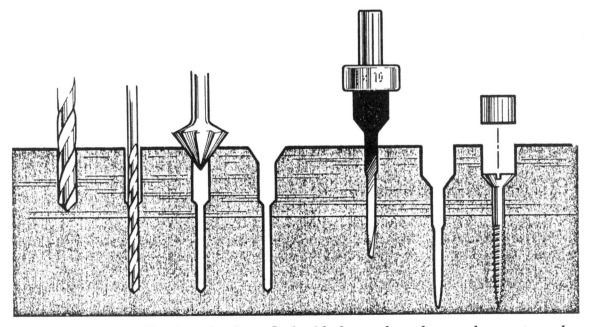

Flat-head screws can either have heads set flush with the wood, or they can be countersunk and plugged, as at right.

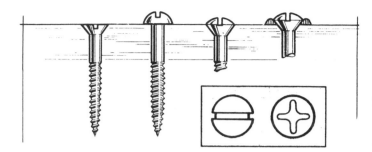

Screws come with flat, oval, and round heads, and with slotted or Phillips-type heads.

the head) goes through the first piece of wood, while the threaded part should be long enough so that about two thirds of its length will go into the second piece. If the second piece is not thick enough for this, then you'll have to settle for the longest screw possible.

The diameter or gauge of the screw should depend on the load it will support, but this may be limited by the thickness of the material or the size of the hole in a piece you are installing.

Just remember that the heavier the screw, the stronger it will be; so pick the heaviest one you can use without splitting the wood or marring the appearance.

Screw heads come in three basic styles: flat-, oval-, and round-head. The choice will depend on how and where the screw is to be used. Flat-head screws are designed so the head sits flush with the surface, but they should also be used when you plan to countersink the head below the surface, using a wood plug inserted in the hole to cover up the head.

Oval-head screws have heads that are only partially buried in the wood when they are driven home—the curved part will stick up slightly and gives a more finished appearance when left uncovered. Oval-head screws are used to mount fixtures that have countersunk holes bored in them, since the oval head gives a neater appearance when installed. They are also used when you don't intend to use wood plugs to cover the screw. Very often they are used with a finishing washer (also called a cup washer) under the head, one advantage being that this makes it easier to remove and replace screws without damaging the wood—for example, screws with washers are often used to hold panels that have to be removed periodically for servicing components behind them.

Round-head screws have heads that remain completely on top of the surface when installed. They generally do not make as neat an appearance as do oval-head screws and often are used when you want to use a flat washer under the screw head to spread the load, or when screwing plastic to wood. (When screws are used to secure sheets of rigid plastic, the heads should not be countersunk for flat-head or oval-head screws, as this builds up stresses that will result in cracking later on.)

Before driving screws in, pilot holes should be drilled in the wood to prevent splitting and make driving easier. A pilot hole should be slightly less than the core diameter of the screw's shank—the solid core of the threaded part—for normal wood and about equal to the core diameter for hard wood. A clearance hole should also be drilled in the top piece (the piece being fastened in place) to allow the shank of the screw to pass through easily.

If the screw hole is to be plugged, you will have to counterbore a hole for the head in addition to drilling a pilot hole in the base material and a clearance hole in the top piece. To eliminate the need for drilling three separate holes, you can buy special pilot hole bits that will drill all three holes at one time. These usually come in sets to fit all of the most popular sizes and lengths of wood screws.

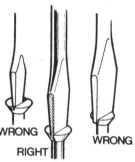

The right size screwdriver blade makes the job both easier and neater.

Make sure when driving screws that you pick a screwdriver with a blade of the proper size. It should almost fill the thickness and width of the screw slot, as shown in the drawing. Blades that are too narrow will tend to slip and won't allow you to apply all the torque needed; screwdriver blades that are too wide will gouge the wood around the screw and may tend to slip out of the slot.

Self-Tapping Screws

Self-tapping screws are available in stainless as well as in plain steel or aluminum. Only the stainless-steel screws should be used around boats. Plain steel will rust, and aluminum doesn't have the strength—when you try to drive one into hard aluminum or fiberglass it may snap off under the extra torque needed to drive the screw home.

Self-tapping screws differ from wood screws in that they are threaded all the way up to the head and don't taper much from point to head. Sometimes referred to as sheet metal screws (which are slightly different in that they don't have as much of a point), they cut their own threads

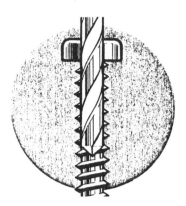

Check drill bits against self-tapping screws to determine correct size.

in soft metal and hard plastic and are also used in place of wood screws when fastening thin materials to wood. However, their biggest use on boats is for fastening to fiberglass and to aluminum spars.

Like wood screws, these, too, come with a choice of head styles: flat-, oval-, or pan-head. Flat-head and oval-head look just like their wood screw counterparts. The pan-head screw is used where you would use a round-head screw. It sits on top of the surface, but the top of the head is flat rather than half round.

Self-tapping screws also require that a pilot hole be drilled in the material first—but with self tapping screws the size of this pilot hole is much more critical. When driving any kind of screw into wood you can usually get by with a pilot hole that is a little too small or too big, or even by just punching a hole with an awl or ice pick. This won't work with a self-tapping screw when driving into fiberglass or metal. The size of the pilot hole needs to be almost exactly the size of the core diameter. If you have to err, make it just a tiny bit bigger than the core, rather than smaller.

The easiest way to check for the right size bit is to hold the screw up to the light, then hold the drill bit you are going to use for the pilot hole in front of it, as shown in the accompanying drawing. If the bit is the right size you should just see the threads protruding on each side; you should not see any of the solid core.

After you have drilled your first hole, try to drive the screw in. If it binds and starts to get exceptionally hard to turn when you are about one quarter in, stop and take the screw out. Then drill a slightly larger hole. Using excessive pressure to force the screw in when the pilot hole is too small is a sure way to break the screw off inside the hole, or cause splintering and flaking of the gel coat on the surface.

Nails

Although nails are not commonly used on fiberglass boats these days, owners of wood boats will still find plenty of use for nails. And even on a fiberglass boat there will be times when you may need them—when fastening wood cleats to the inside of a cabinet or wood locker, or when building some simple wooden racks in the engine room or bilge.

As with screws, only rust-proof nails of bronze, copper, or aluminum should be used. Unless you are building something temporary that you intend to take apart in the not too distant future, use annular threaded or "ringed" nails that will grip almost as well as wood screws. They are not as likely to pull out or work loose from vibration as ordinary nails are.

When driving nails in, try to drive them in at an angle, rather than straight in. If there is more than one nail going into the joint, slant them in opposite directions. This increases gripping strength, especially if you are driving

Nails should be driven in at a downward angle to hold heavy loads.

into end grain. And when driving several nails into the edge of the same board, try to avoid lining them up along the same grain lines; staggering them will greatly minimize the chances of splitting the wood. If you are nailing horizontal cleats in place—for example, to support a shelf—slant the nails downward rather than driving them straight in (as shown in the drawing at the left) because then the load will tend to make them dig deeper into the wood as it increases.

Blind Rivets

Blind rivets are useful for permanently joining sheet metal, leather, plastics, and other thin materials, as well as for riveting these materials to thin metal and plastic when you cannot reach the back side. Often called Pop Rivets, even though this is actually the brand name of one large manufacturer, blind rivets are very handy for such jobs as fastening a metal hook or bracket to a steel stanchion or

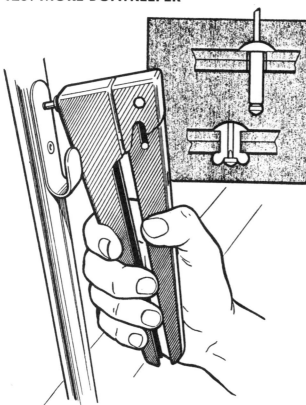

A "Pop-Rivet" gun is useful for fastening thin materials to surfaces where the back side is inaccessible.

railing, repairing leather and canvas straps, fastening small cleats or brackets to metal spars, or for fastening to sheet plastic and metal where only one side is accessible.

Although there are many different brands on the market, basically all of these "pop-type" rivets work in the same way and use a similar type of "gun" to clinch them in place. You insert the naillike mandrel from the rivet into an opening in the gun's jaw, then push the shank or body of the rivet through the hole in the materials to be joined. Then squeeze the scissorlike jaws of the tool together to pull up on the mandrel and compress the rivet body. When it is squeezed tight against both sides it snaps the mandrel off and leaves the rivet locked firmly in place. The mandrel is then slid out of the gun's jaws and thrown away.

The rivets come in steel or aluminum, so for outside use make sure you buy the aluminum ones. (Some companies supposedly also make them in stainless, but I have never been able to find these in any local stores.) They come in three diameters: ⅛ inch, ⁵⁄₃₂ inch, and ³⁄₁₆ inch. Naturally, the heavier ones are also the strongest ones and will take the most stress.

Rivets also come in three different lengths to accom-

modate materials of different thicknesses: short, medium, and long. Short is for materials up to ⅛ inch in thickness; medium is for materials up to ¼ inch; and long is for materials up to ½ inch in thickness. To keep the compressed rivet heads or flanges from pulling through when joining soft materials such as leather or canvas, there are special backup plates—like small washers—that can be slipped over the rivet body before you set it.

Expansion-Type Anchors

For those jobs where extra holding power is required in fiberglass, you can use expansion-type metal or plastic anchors instead of self-tapping screws. Very similar to "Mollys" and other expansion-type anchors that have long been used in homes and other buildings, these anchors provide much greater holding power and are generally easier than screws to install properly. Those made for marine use differ from those designed for home use in that they are made of rustproof brass, stainless steel, plastic, and similar corrosion-resistant materials.

At least one company, Marine Development & Research Corp. (116 Church Street, Freeport, N.Y. 11520), is currently marketing an assortment of such anchors through regular marine supply outlets. Called Fibergrip and specifically designed for use in solid fiberglass as well as in hollow-core construction of wood or fiberglass, these anchors come in various sizes to accept different-size screws and to fit different material.

When used in solid fiberglass where the fastener will not go all the way through, they are designed to make the plastic plug swell or expand as the screw is driven home through the center. This locks it firmly and permanently in

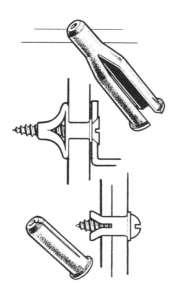

Expansion anchors hold screws securely in thin-wall materials.

place. When used in thin-wall materials with a hollow space behind them, the anchor mushrooms open behind the material as the screw in the center is tightened, thus locking it permanently in place so it cannot pull out.

Removing Broken Bolts

Like most people who work around boats or mechanical equipment, on several occasions I have broken off a bolt or screw that wouldn't come out and then tried to use various screw-extracting tools, but I have never had much success. Using them usually requires drilling a hole down through the center of the bolt or screw, and I find it difficult to do this accurately without also stripping or damaging the threads inside the hole. In addition, the extracting tool seems to strip and pull out before the screw is loose enough to be removed.

Now when I am faced with a broken-off screw or bolt I use a method that always works well. If the bolt broke off because it was badly rusted, I first file off the rusted stub that is sticking up till it is flush with the surrounding surface (this is not necessary if the metal of the bolt is sound). Then I use a hand-held motorized tool (such as the kind made by Dremel) equipped with a small abrasive wheel to cut a slot across the top of the bolt stub so that a large screwdriver blade can be inserted to turn the bolt or screw out.

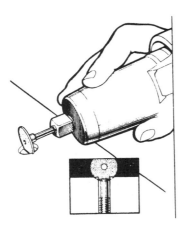

The abrasive wheel I use is about ⅟₁₆ inch thick and ¾ inch in diameter. It is held so that the abrasive wheel's edge cuts the slot. You must be careful to cut slowly by applying only moderate pressure, since the wheels are brittle and break easily. If the bolt was broken off flush, cutting a slot deep enough for a large screwdriver means also cutting a groove into the metal on each side of the screw hole, but this will generally not have much effect on the strength of the surrounding material.

When You Need a Larger Hose Clamp

Every boat needs to keep an emergency stock of stainless steel hose clamps on board—just in case. But at times you may find yourself stuck because you don't have a clamp large enough to do the job. When this happens, remember that you can usually join two or more smaller-size hose clamps to make one big one.

Simply open each of the smaller clamps all the way so you can take them apart and partially straighten the slotted band. Then insert the male end of one hose clamp into the female or worm-screw head of the other one. You'll end up with a longer strap—and thus a larger-diameter clamp that is just as dependable as a single large one.

Enlarging Existing Holes

Anyone who has ever been faced with the job of making an existing hole in wood or fiberglass bigger knows what a job it can be. For example, when changing a through-hull fitting or when installing a new instrument in a control panel, it often happens that the original hole of, say, two or three inches has to be an inch bigger to accept the new fitting or meter face. You can't use a regular hole saw because there is already a hole there, so there's nothing for the pilot drill in the center of the hole saw to grab or bite into.

One common method of accomplishing this is to do a lot of tedious work with files, rasps, and similar tools. Another is to cut out a round block or disk of plywood for a snug fit inside the existing hole, then ram this temporarily into place inside the hole to fill it, or fasten a block temporarily in place from behind to cover the hole. Then

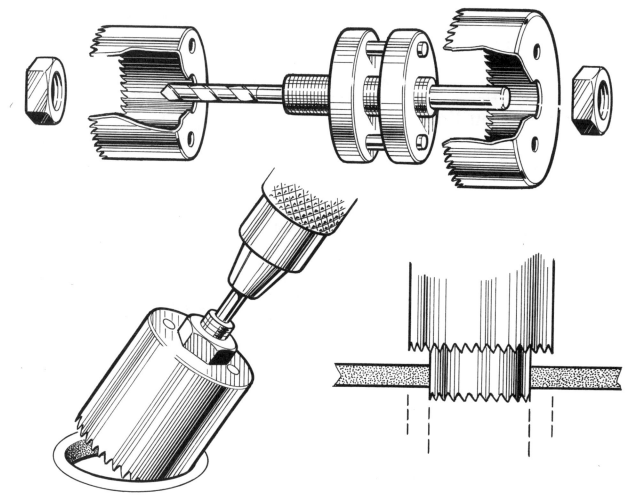

you locate the center of the existing hole as best you can on this block of wood, after which you can use this center point for the pilot bit on your hole saw so you can cut a new, larger hole that is centered over the original one.

Two New Tricks

As an electronics technician who has frequently been required to do this kind of job when changing instruments, I can recommend two methods that eliminate the need for a block to fill or cover the old hole and that also give better results in most cases:

1. This method is one that can be used when the diameter of the new hole is only slightly larger (less than a half inch) than that of the original hole. And this method requires a variable-speed drill.

Start by selecting a hole saw the same size as the old hole (or just a fraction of an inch larger). You then hold it at an angle inside the hole as shown in the drawing to literally scrape away or ''scallop out'' the edges of the old hole until it is the desired size. The technique is a bit

tricky and may take some practice on scrap material first, but once you get the knack, it works well. Here's what you do:

First draw around the existing hole a circle the size of the desired new hole, to serve as a guide. Push the hole saw partway into the hole but at an angle as shown, so it does not actually go through the hole—only about half its cutting edge fits through, while the rest of the saw's edge is aiming directly at the penciled outline (even though this circle is larger, holding the hole saw at an angle will make it seem to match the outline). Now cut two or more arcs in the surface, angling the saw from one side to another and using the penciled outline as a guide. You will soon wind up with a new hole of exactly the right diameter that may need a little touching up with a rasp or file.

2. This method works only if there is a sizable difference between the diameter of the old hole and the new one—at least a half inch. And it can be done only with some brands of hole saws—the kind where the individual saws thread onto an arbor that is chucked into the drill and that have a retainer and locknut that can be threaded on or off from the back end of the arbor (two such brands are Lenox Hole Saws and Blue-Mol Hole Saws). These permit you to screw two hole saws on a single arbor, one behind the other, as shown in the drawing.

First select a hole saw that is the exact size of the existing hole, then thread this onto the front end of the arbor. This one will serve as your pilot bit to center the arbor over the existing hole. Now thread the second hole saw—the one that matches the size you want your new hole to be—onto the back end of the arbor so it fits over (around the outside of) the first hole saw.

The retainer and locknut originally on the arbor won't hold both saws, but you will find that using the locknut alone will be enough to hold the second (outer) hole saw in place. The inner hole saw will screw on and will get tighter as you use it (if it gets too tight, you can ease it off with a wrench when the job is done). After both hole saws are assembled to the arbor as shown, the hybrid tool you have created will cut a new, larger hole that will be perfectly centered over the original hole. As a bonus, you can use this tool to cut doughnut-shaped rings out of wood or fiberglass for use as buttblocks or supporting pads.

Guide to Bedding, Patching, and Sealing Compounds

Although today's molded fiberglass boats do not have all the joints and seams that wooden boats have, they are assembled in sections and still have lots of seams and joints that need sealing. In addition, all boats, regardless of whether they are made of wood, fiberglass, or metal, have fittings and hardware installed around the outside where a bedding compound is needed to keep out water. Moreover, sooner or later every boat will develop nicks, scratches, dents, or other blemishes that will need patching (sometimes for purely aesthetic reasons, but other times to maintain watertight integrity).

That's why caulking, bedding, patching, and sealing compounds are essential products when it comes to maintaining any boat. But choosing the right one can be confusing—there are so many different types and brands available. Some are limited to specific jobs, while others are multipurpose compounds that can be satisfactorily used for several different purposes.

For example: Some sealants and patching compounds have definite limitations as to the temperatures at which they can be used, while others can be used at almost any temperature. Some work only on dry surfaces, while others will bond to damp surfaces; some will bond to metal and glass, while others will not; and some can be used over paint or varnish, while others cannot. In addition, some are suitable only for use on wood because they will not adhere satisfactorily to fiberglass or gel coat.

These are only some of the reasons why it is important to read the manufacturer's instructions and specifications before you use any of these products—or before you even buy them. Read all the fine print carefully and note any limitations listed. Also, see if special preparations are required. A knowledgeable marine supply dealer can be a big help in advising you, but remember that not all dealers are as well informed as they should be. And even those

who do know their stuff may have clerks working for them whose advice cannot always be relied on.

Broadly speaking, the compounds you will be using in the maintenance of your boat can be divided into two overall categories: those that remain at least partially flexible when cured, and those that harden into a rigid, nonflexible material when fully cured.

The rubbery, flexible compounds are the caulking, sealing, and bedding compounds designed to ensure watertight joints and seams around the outside of your boat. Some are also used as bedding compounds to keep water out when installing deck hardware and other fittings. The hard-drying rigid compounds are those used for patching and filling cracks, gouges, and other defects in wood, metal, or fiberglass, as well as for repairing broken pieces or building up sections where pieces are missing.

Caulking and Sealing Compounds

Although there are many brands and variations on the market, the three most widely used types of caulking and sealing compounds are the one-part, Thiokol-base polysulfide caulking materials (such as Boatlife's Life-Calk), the newer polyurethane sealers (such as 3M's 5200 Adhesive/Sealant and Sikaflex 241), and the silicone rubber compounds (such as those made by Dow and General Electric).

All three are completely waterproof and resistant to attack by oil and gas when fully cured. And when properly applied, all form a completely weatherproof seal that normally lasts for many years. So in many ways they are almost interchangeable—but there are differences you should know about.

Thiokol-base polysulfide caulking materials have been around the longest and generally sell for between six and eight dollars for a standard caulking cartridge (the size that will fit into a regular caulking gun). These are "self-vulcanizing" (self-curing) versions of the two-part Thiokol compounds used by boatbuilders for years to caulk teak decks, wood planking, and similar joints. They come in white, black, mahogany, and brown (teak) and are made in small, 4½-ounce squeeze tubes, as well as in regular-size caulking cartridges.

Although the one-part polysulfides are formulated to be just as durable as the original two-part compounds, the one-part material dries more slowly. It is also moisture-cured, but it gets its moisture from the air, so it takes up to two or three days to cure completely (drying to a rubbery consistency overnight in normal weather).

However, no mixing is required, and since it is moisture-cured, a one-part polysulfide will skin over even faster if the surface is dampened with water. In fact, it can be applied to damp surfaces. The rubbery bond formed allows it to flex and "give" as structural components of

the boat move, and it bonds well to wood, fiberglass, and most metals, but it does not adhere well to oily woods such as teak unless a special primer is applied first. It can be applied above or below the waterline.

The newer polyurethane caulking and sealing compounds come in standard-size caulking cartridges only. They cost about the same as the polysulfide types and also come in white, black, or mahogany. They can be used above or below the waterline and can be applied in temperatures as low as 40°F.

One thing about the polyurethanes is that they have considerably greater adhesive power than all other caulking materials—in fact, the joint formed is almost as permanent as one formed by a strong glue. So don't use one of these in a joint or seam that may have to be taken apart in the foreseeable future.

For example, some years ago I used one of these compounds to bed down some wood moldings around the outside of a cabin windshield on my previous boat. A few months later an accident caused that glass to break, so it had to be replaced. But when I tried to pry the moldings off I found them impossible to remove in one piece; the wood pieces actually split apart before the compound let go.

These polyurethane sealants do bond well to glass, metal, and wood—including oily woods like teak—without a primer. However, surfaces must be dry. Polyurethane sealant should not be used on teak decks or similar places where a strong teak cleaner will be used; the cleaner may tend to soften it permanently. They are slower-drying than the polysulfide caulking materials—two to three days to dry tack-free and up to seven days to cure completely—but the white doesn't tend to yellow as much as the Thiokol types when it ages.

Silicone rubber compounds are the newest addition, having first become popular for home use around bathtubs, sinks, and ceramic tile. They come in regular caulking cartridges as well as in smaller (three-ounce) squeeze tubes and are available in clear, white, or black. They cost more than the others (about seven to eight dollars for a caulking cartridge) and do not shrink at all when used in thick layers or in fairly wide joints. They adhere well to any clean, dry surface but do not have as much adhesive power as the polyurethanes. Most of the silicones cannot be painted (or varnished) over, so don't use them in wood joints that will have to be painted.

To ensure a neat job when using any caulking compound to fill long joints, it is a good idea to apply masking tape along each side of the joint, spacing the tape as far apart as you want the finished bead of caulking to be. Smooth the caulking down with your finger if necessary, then peel the tape off promptly. This will leave you with neat, straight edges along both sides of the seam.

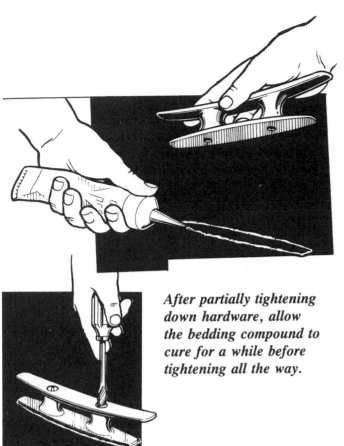

After partially tightening down hardware, allow the bedding compound to cure for a while before tightening all the way.

Bedding Compounds

All of the caulking and sealing compounds mentioned above are also suitable for use as bedding compounds—in addition to the old-fashioned type of oil-based bedding compound that is still preferred by some people.

Polysulfide caulking compounds probably are the most widely used. They form a rubbery, waterproof seal that weathers well and conforms easily to irregular surfaces, and they normally remain pliable for years. Yet it is not too difficult to pry them off or scrape them off if necessary—a desirable feature.

This is not true of the polyurethane sealants. They are very difficult to scrape off on fiberglass and can be almost impossible to remove on wood, so don't use them for bedding anything that may have to be removed.

Silicones make excellent bedding compounds because they remain rubbery and flexible almost indefinitely. They also form a good bond with all the materials used in boat-building if the surfaces to which they are applied are clean and perfectly dry; yet they peel off quite easily. Silicone can also be used to form a semipermanent "rubber gasket." Apply liberally, then press pieces together partway so the compound is squeezed between them and excess oozes out around all sides. Allow to cure, then slice off the excess around the outside. Now you can peel off a custom-formed gasket that can be used over and over. If you don't want it to stick to the hardware (or the base material) at all, insert a sheet of wax paper first.

The old-style oil-based bedding compounds do have some advantages—especially for use on wood boats or where hardware needs bedding against wood. For one thing, they are much less expensive than the others and in some ways are easier to use (they spread neatly with a putty knife without smearing and sticking to everything). They never dry hard, so the joint formed is easily taken apart when servicing makes that necessary. Residue that is left is simple to scrape off without leaving a stain, and they will create a watertight joint even if the surface is not quite as clean as it should be (though it must be dry).

Rigid Patching Compounds

For patching nicks, scratches, and dents in wood, use a one-part trowel cement or surfacing compound. Use trowel cement where there are larger or thicker areas to be filled, as well as to smooth surface irregularities left by rough grain and weathered wood. It dries hard in two to three hours and can be easily sanded to a smooth finish.

Surfacing compounds work better on smaller patches or for spot patching of screw holes and small, deep indentations. These compounds shrink less than trowel cement and they dry much more quickly (when applied in thin layers they can be sanded in twenty or thirty minutes). That's why you cannot spread them easily over large areas.

On fiberglass boats two different kinds of patching materials are most often used: polyester putty and epoxy putty. Each is a two-part compound that must be mixed before use.

Polyester compounds come in cans that contain a putty-like material with a small tube of catalyst that is packed separately. To use the material, you scoop out a blob of the putty and then mix in a few drops of the catalyst. The instructions will give the recommended amounts, but this is not always critical. In fact, the amount

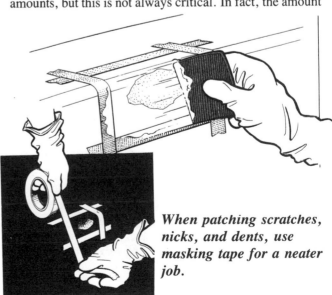

When patching scratches, nicks, and dents, use masking tape for a neater job.

of catalyst added can be deliberately varied to speed or retard drying time.

Epoxy putties also come in two parts. Some are sold as two equal-size packages of putty or mastic that are mixed in equal parts when you are ready to use it (the catalyst or hardener is in one of the compounds). Others come as a larger can of putty with a separate can or jar of liquid (the catalyst) that is mixed with the putty. Here proportions are fairly critical or the compound won't cure properly.

One big difference between these patching compounds is drying time. Polyesters may dry hard in twenty or thirty minutes at temperatures of 70°F or higher, depending on how much catalyst is added. Epoxies will take from a few hours to a whole day, depending on temperature. Another difference is cost: Epoxy is more expensive in almost every case.

Polyester putties are better for shallow, small nicks and depressions when only a thin layer is required (most epoxies are harder to spread smoothly). As a rule, the neatest job will be obtained in either case if you surround the area to be patched with masking tape so that compound only goes onto and into the damaged area.

Remember that most fiberglass boats are built with polyester resin, so it stands to reason that polyester putties (which contain similar resins) will be compatible. They can also be used on wood that is clean and dry, but they won't stick to wood that has been treated with a preservative.

Epoxies take longer to set up, but curing can be speeded

by applying mild heat from a heat lamp. Below temperature limits recommended by the manufacturer they won't cure at all, or will cure only partially. However, when properly cured they form a much stronger bond than polyester, and they will bond to wood, metal, and glass as well as to fiberglass.

Epoxy is also much stronger when used in heavy layers without fiberglass reinforcing—for example, to build up missing sections or pieces of metal that have chipped or cracked (polyester putty does not work on metal). Some types can even be applied underwater in an emergency.

All epoxies are more highly resistant to attack by strong solvents, oil, and grease, and most experts agree that they will last longer than polyester putties when used below the waterline or where they will be immersed in water or oil.

Caulking Saver

Marine caulking comes in handy cartridges that are easy to use with an ordinary caulking gun. However, when only part of that expensive cartridge is used at one time, chances are that what is left will soon harden and become completely useless before the next job rolls around. Many's the partly used tube that's been thrown out because air has ''frozen'' the material solidly in place, making whatever usable compound is left impossible to get at.

Here is an easy, inexpensive way to prevent this from happening. Go to your local variety store or toy store and buy some cheap party balloons of medium size.

The next time you use only part of a cartridge and you want to save the rest, take one of these balloons and stretch it open so you can slide the neck down over the end of the caulking cartridge. Roll the balloon down onto the outside of the cartridge a few inches and leave it there. It will stay in place and form an airtight seal that will keep your caulk from hardening.

Guide to Marine Fabrics

There was a time when marine protective fabrics meant cotton canvas . . . but not any longer. Today's synthetics offer a wide range of fabrics with varying properties designed to meet many different needs, but unless you are aware of the available choices, you may find that fabric is determined according to your canvas loft's inventory rather than your own specific needs. An understanding of the major fabric types currently in use will help you give an informed answer when your canvasmaker asks, ''Did you have any particular fabric in mind?''

Two-part epoxy putties must be mixed before applying.

Ubiquitous Blue

You know the blue stuff you see when you look down any dock full of sailboats? That's acrylic, one of today's most popular fabrics not only for sailcovers but also for almost any Bimini top, dodger, awning, or other cover. It comes in that royal blue, plus an amazing spectrum of solids, stripes, and tweeds, and some brands of acrylic are guaranteed colorfast for up to five years (don't trust the bright red no matter what they say). Its relatively soft finish and light weight make it easy to handle, and it is resistant to mildew and rot. With normal use it will not shrink, and like other woven fabrics it will breathe, preventing the buildup of moisture and mildew under the cover. The water-resistant finish applied to acrylic will eventually wear off, but you can spray silicone on the fabric to replace it.

There are disadvantages to this wonder fabric, however. Acrylic does not have as high a resistance to chafe and strain as many other synthetics and so must be reinforced along any areas where fastenings will be installed or where the cover is likely to rub and wear. Similarly, it is not a good choice for covers and curtains that will provide winter protection; acrylic will not stand up to ice and snow. And while many people like acrylic for cushion covers, some find the fiber causes itching or rashes against bare legs.

Dacron is the fiber that revolutionized sails, a strong synthetic that has exceptional resistance to ultraviolet rays that weaken many other fabrics. Dacron cover cloth, a different weave than sailcloth, brings the same properties to Biminis, dodgers, side curtains, and bridge covers. Since it holds its shape and withstands chafe so well, it is often used to reinforce other fabrics. Unfortunately for the color-conscious, Dacron cover cloth comes only in white.

For Outdoor Cushions

Vinyl laminates and vinyl-coated cottons or polyesters take up another good-sized chunk of the marine fabric market. Many manufacturers produce a variety of vinyl fabrics with different specific characteristics; many, though not all, of these varieties are treated to make them fire-retardant. The vinyl coating assures that these are easy fabrics to clean and are extremely waterproof (seams may have a tendency to leak more than on other fabrics—but most vinyls are made in wide widths for fewer seams). The chief disadvantages of vinyls become evident in cold weather: They tend to shrink somewhat and to become very brittle and hard to handle. If folded, the vinyl may crack, weakening the fabric and eventually tearing; again, this is a cold-climate problem. In hot, humid weather, mildew can run rampant, since vinyls don't breathe.

A newer fabric known as Destiny 2 + 2 seems to work well in almost any marine application, from full boat covers to interior cushions. It is a woven Fortrel polyester treated for mildew and water resistance, it wears well without reinforcement in most cases, and it is strong enough to be used for year-round coverage. Like vinyls, 2 + 2 comes in wide widths; the resulting fewer seams mean less leakage, less initial labor, and fewer seams to be restitched later on. In addition to these advantages, this fabric breathes. Before you decide it sounds perfect, be warned that the selection of colors is much more limited than acrylic; the fabric, especially white, can be hard to clean; and the use of harsh detergents and bleaches is discouraged by the manufacturer.

Nylons—the first synthetics to be widely used—have lost popularity now that other, newer fabrics are available. While nylon is extremely lightweight, it has very little ultraviolet resistance and is not strong enough to hold fastenings without heavy reinforcement.

Boat-shrunk canvas is still around, of course—a fabric heavy, durable, and water-repellent enough to have met the needs of boatmen for many years. Canvas colors are limited and are never as bright and true as they are in a synthetic. Synthetics also allow for easier care: A wet canvas cover must be allowed to dry thoroughly before it is removed from the boat and stored, or mildew and shrinkage are inevitable. Nothing else can replace the traditional look and feel of canvas, however, and it may well be worth the extra time to you.

Today's textile industry offers these and many other specialty products designed to withstand marine conditions. There are wax-coated winter storage ducks, vinyl-coated meshes, upholstery materials, and a bevy of natural cottons. The important thing to remember is that different choices are available, because the ''best fabric'' to use in any situation should be defined first and foremost by individual needs, expectations, and particular uses.

Scraping and Sanding— Tools and Techniques

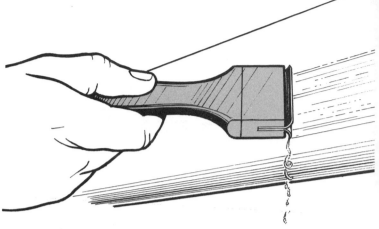

Although owners of fiberglass boats do not spend as much time scraping and sanding as do owners of wooden boats, anyone who has taken care of a boat for more than one year knows that these chores are virtually unavoidable. Regardless of whether it is preparing the bottom for painting each season, or preparing the brightwork for a fresh coat of varnish, before any paint or varnish is applied some sanding—and possibly some scraping—will be required.

Scrapers

Scrapers are primarily used for removing accumulations of paint or varnish after the finish is badly worn and in need of stripping. Scraping the finish off is usually faster than sanding it off, but it is not as fast as using a chemical remover—and it is certainly a lot more work.

There are two types of scrapers: the paint scraper, which has a flat blade and is similar to a putty knife (except that the blade is much stiffer); and the hook

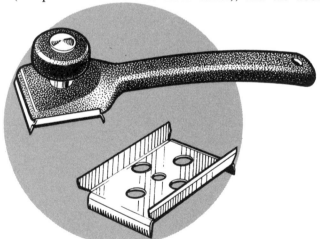

scraper, which you pull toward you with one hand while bearing down hard on the surface with the other.

Paint scrapers are most often used for scraping off paint or varnish that is loose and flaking, and for removing the softened goo that remains after using a chemical paint remover. They come in widths from about ½ inch to four inches, and often have a stiff, relatively thick, chisellike blade useful for all kinds of scraping.

Hook scrapers similar to the one shown in the accompanying diagram come in various sizes, with blades that range from about 1 inch to 2½ inches in width. One version has a two-sided blade with only a narrow strip sticking out from the handle. The other type of hook

scraper has a reversible blade with four edges, two straight (for fine scraping) and two with serrated edges (for rough scraping). The blades can be reversed (turned over) to expose either the fine or the coarse blades by loosening a screw in the center.

The smaller hook scrapers are designed for one-hand use, while the larger ones have a long handle for two-handed pressure. One hand is used to drag the scraper toward you, while the other hand is used to bear down hard on the cutting end. The blades can be sharpened with a file, but most people find it easier simply to replace them when they become dull.

One word of caution when using a scraper in a confined area or when working overhead: Wear safety goggles to protect your eyes against flying chips and flakes. When scraping bottom paints, wear a respirator to keep from inhaling potentially toxic dust or flying debris.

Choosing Sandpapers

Sanding is never a pleasant job, but it will be easier if you choose the right type of abrasive paper. Although most people refer to them as "sandpaper," none of the abrasive papers are actually made with sand. Flint paper, the oldest and still the least expensive type of abrasive paper, is coated with quartz crystals, a natural mineral that looks like sand (hence the name). The trouble with this abrasive is that flint dulls quickly and clogs easily. In addition, the paper backing tears easily, so it can't be used with an electric sander.

That is why—even though flint paper costs less than all of the others—it is actually not any cheaper in the long run. It's also much slower cutting and requires more effort to use, which is why it is now probably the least popular type of "sandpaper" (some dealers don't carry it anymore). About the only time it pays to use flint paper is when sanding off soft paint or other surfaces where the paper has to be thrown away every few minutes because it becomes clogged long before it wears out. On such jobs the lower cost of flint paper may result in some actual savings.

The most popular type of abrasive paper is the kind that is coated with aluminum oxide, a synthetic mineral that is much sharper, faster-cutting and longer-lasting than quartz. Aluminum oxide papers have a much stronger backing that is more resistant to tearing, and they are almost always used with electric sanders. Normally light brown in color, aluminum oxide paper is also excellent for hand sanding of wood, metal and fiberglass as well as for sanding between coats when varnishing or painting.

Like all other abrasive papers, aluminum oxide comes in a full range of grades, ranging from very fine to very coarse. Grades are indicated by a number that varies with the coarseness of the paper—the higher the number, the finer the grit or grade.

For most sanding when you are trying to smooth down raw wood prior to painting or varnishing, it's usually best to start with #80 or #100, unless the wood is already smooth. Coarser grades of paper are used only when you are trying to shape or remove some of the wood (and, of course, when you are trying to sand off an old finish). After the first sanding, finish with #120 or #150, then dust thoroughly and wipe the surface down with a tack rag or rag moistened with paint thinner before going ahead with the first coat of paint or varnish.

When you are sanding down paint or varnish to prepare it for a fresh coat, you should seldom use anything coarser than #120 for the first sanding. Then finish by sanding with #220 for the final smoothing before the fresh paint or varnish is applied. Sanding between coats usually is done with #220 after the first coat has hardened, and with #300 or #400 after the second coat has dried (if you are putting on three coats).

For an ultra-smooth finish before the last coat of varnish is applied, or for final polishing on a freshly applied gel coat patch, serious workers will use a "wet or dry" silicon carbide paper instead of an aluminum oxide paper.

Silicon carbide also is a synthetic mineral, but it is even sharper and harder than aluminum oxide. However, it tends to dull faster and wears down more quickly, and the paper clogs more easily. The abrasive is black and comes on a special water-resistant backing so it can be dipped into water and used either wet or dry. Around boats this abrasive paper is mostly used only in the finer grades (#220 to #600), and then it is almost always for wet sanding (dipping the paper into water as you use it) because this gives the smoothest finishes.

Dry or Wet?

Wet sanding with this material is the technique almost universally used for final smoothing and polishing on fiberglass and gel coat, or when you want to rub down the final coat of varnish for a mirror-smooth finish. Dry sanding does not give as smooth a finish as wet sanding,

so it is more likely to leave fine scratches on the surface.

Another abrasive paper that is occasionally used on metal is emery cloth. Emery is a natural mineral that usually comes on a cloth backing so that it is much more flexible for wrapping around the outside of tubing and curved surfaces. It is not as sharp as aluminum oxide, so it is less likely to leave scratch marks when used for polishing and cleaning metal surfaces. It is mostly used for removing light rust and fine scratches on metal, but is not of much use on wood, paint, or varnish.

When sanding by hand it is always best to fold the sheet and tear it in half, then fold each piece in half again with the abrasive face toward the outside. This will give a folded sheet one quarter the size of a full sheet that will fit neatly in the palm of one hand with two abrasive faces. When one side gets worn you simply turn the folded piece over and start sanding with the other side. Get in the habit of periodically slapping the abrasive paper against a hard surface to help keep it from clogging.

On flat surfaces it's best to use a sanding block of some kind—either a block of wood with the abrasive paper wrapped around the outside, or a sanding block that you can buy in most hardware stores. When using a simple wood block, staple a piece of carpet or foam rubber to the face of the block to act as a resilient backing for the paper to protect it against tearing and scratching the surface.

For sanding curved or rounded surfaces there are flexible "sanding sponges" or pliable "sanding blocks" (shown in the drawing) that you can buy in fine and medium grits. These are flexible enough to conform to curved, rounded, or contoured surfaces. When they become clogged, they can be rinsed under running water and reused. Sold under several brand names (3M Sanding Sponge and Glit Sanding Block are two), most of these abrasive-coated sponges come with fine abrasive on one side and medium on the other side.

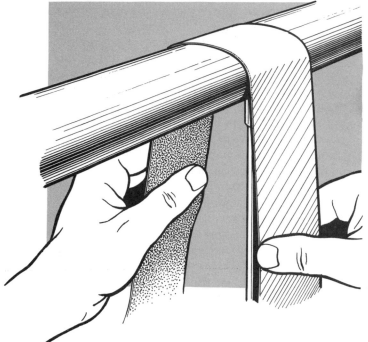

When you have to sand handrails, poles, small-diameter sailboat masts, and booms or other round objects, an even faster way to get the job done is to cut aluminum oxide or silicon carbide paper into strips and then use these "shoeshine" style by rubbing the flexible strips back and forth across the curved surface, as shown in the drawing. If you have trouble with the strips tearing, place several strips of masking tape along the back side to reinforce the paper backing.

There are three types of portable electric sanders you can use: disk sanders, belt sanders, and orbital sanders.

Ordinary disk sanders really have little or no use around a boat—they are suitable only for rough work and even then are likely to do more harm than good. Occasionally a disk sander will come in handy when used as a portable grinder for smoothing rough metal or fiberglass edges, but even then care is required to avoid gouging and scratching.

Belt sanders are heavy-duty, fast-cutting machines that use an endless abrasive belt that travels around two drums at the base of the machine, one at the front and one at the rear. Sizes vary, so make sure you buy the size abrasive belt that will fit your machine. Mainly useful on large, flat surfaces, these sanding machines must be carefully handled to avoid taking off too much material and to avoid gouging.

Always sand parallel to the grain, and keep the machine moving as long as the belt is turning. Start the motor before bringing the paper in contact with the surface, and don't release the trigger until you have "arced" the machine up and away from the surface. Stopping for even a moment while the belt is moving and in contact with the surface is likely to create a hollow or depression that will take a lot of extra sanding to remove.

Controlling Dust

Belt sanders throw off a lot of dust, so selecting a machine that has a dust-catching bag attached is always a good idea. There are also belt sanders that come with a vacuum attachment—you can hook any standard shop vacuum or household vacuum to an outlet at the back end of the sander so that most of the sanding dust will be sucked away.

Belt sanders are primarily useful on decks, cabintops, hulls, and other large, reasonably flat areas. They are

excellent for removing paint and varnish as well as for shaping and smoothing newly installed planking, wood trim, and joinerwork. But be careful when going past an edge not to allow the front end of the machine to dip; this may cause undesirable rounding of edges or ends. Since the machine tends to pull away as you work, always keep a firm grip as it is traveling forward.

Orbital sanders—also called finishing sanders—are by far the most popular of all portable sanding machines. They are light and easy to handle and have a flat pad that moves in an oval or orbital pattern. These sanders use cut sheets of standard aluminum oxide paper, which makes replacing the abrasive paper a lot cheaper than with a belt sander. Machines vary in size; some use a third of a standard sheet; others use a quarter of a sheet. The most versatile and easiest-to-handle models are the "palm sanders," which can be held in the palm of one hand. These are ideal around boats, where you often have to work with one hand or have to reach into awkward corners.

When using any sanding machine, avoid bearing down so hard that you start to slow down or overload the motor. Use only enough pressure to ensure firm contact with the surface. Pressing harder will slow the cutting action and may cause the motor or the abrasive to overheat.

Wherever possible, move your sander back and forth so it is traveling parallel to the grain. This rule can be violated without causing serious problems when using a high-speed orbital sander such as one of the "palm sanders" mentioned above, but you could leave lots of scratches that will be very hard to conceal if you don't follow this rule when using a belt sander or one of the larger orbital sanders. With any type of sander, it is a good idea to stop frequently and shut off the machine, then slap the abrasive paper (or abrasive belt) hard with a scrap block of wood to bang excess dust out of the abrasive paper.

Choosing and Using Bottom Paints

All antifouling paints are designed to do the same job—keep barnacles and other underwater organisms from adhering to the boat—but most boatowners are confused when it comes to deciding just which type to buy. Many major paint companies put out a wide range of bottom paints under different brand names, so that even if you have long favored one particular company's products you may still be confused.

For example: Are you better off with a finish that dries hard, semihard, or soft? Should you stick with bottom paints that use a copper-based toxic ingredient, or with those paints that depend on an organo-tin compound? And are you better off with one of the well-known vinyl-base bottom paints, or that same company's brand of epoxy-based bottom paint?

It is not hard to understand why even boat dealers often disagree about bottom paint. I have talked with technical representatives and chemists at several different paint companies and I've discovered that even these experts don't always agree on generic descriptions and on the advantages or disadvantages of different formulations. But there are some general guidelines and descriptions that boatowners should be aware of—points on which most experts *do* agree—that can help when trying to select and apply a bottom paint.

Depending on the type of finish they dry to, antifouling bottom paints can be roughly divided into three categories: those that dry to a very hard finish, those that dry to a semihard finish, and those that dry to a relatively soft finish.

Hard and Soft Finishes
Hard finishes are preferred by many racing sailboat owners who like to wet-sand their boat bottoms to get the smoothest possible finish prior to a race. Hard finishes are also popular with many owners of high-performance powerboats. However, they often require a lot more sanding and scraping when its time to repaint—they are harder to scrape off and sand smooth, especially after the bottom has been painted several times and the old paint has started to crack or flake off.

Semihard finishes are more popular for general use on

cruising boats—both power and sail. They are also preferred for most boats that are trailered because they are hard enough not to rub off every time the boat is launched and hauled, yet they don't become quite as brittle as the hard finishes and aren't as difficult to sand down. Also, when a semihard finish has to be removed, it will be easier to scrape off than a hard paint.

Soft finishes are still widely used on many wood boats and fishing boats. Their one big advantage is that they are much lower in price. But they do tend to wash away more rapidly.

Not all soft bottom paints are at the low end of the quality or price scale. For example, at least one brand—KL-990 Polycop—is a relatively high-grade soft finish that has extra antifouling ingredients and is specifically formulated for slow-displacement boats. In this case the soft finish helps the paint to leach off more easily even when the boat moves slowly through the water, and unlike most vinyls, it wears off smoothly so you don't end up with a pockmarked surface.

Many feel that even the least expensive soft copper paints still give them the most value, especially in areas where the boating season is quite short. Most soft bottom paints go on thicker than the hard paints, so you seldom need more than one coat.

Bottom paints in all three of these categories are made by most of the larger paint manufacturers, including International Paint (Interlux), Rule Industries (Gloucester and KL-990), Pettit Paint Company, Woolsey, and Baltimore.

Toxic Ingredients

In addition to film hardness, antifouling paints also vary in the toxic ingredients added to kill underwater organisms. Some have a higher percentage of toxins than others—a factor usually reflected in the price—and some are formulated to withstand better the heavier fouling encountered in warm waters.

Boatowners who really want the best often wonder why they shouldn't simply buy the brand that contains the highest percentage of toxic ingredients, even though it is mainly formulated for use in tropical waters and they do their boating only in the North. The answer is that they can, but they will probably be wasting money because some of the toxicity is unnecessary. Also, with most conventional antifouling paints a high percentage of the toxic ingredients leach out during the first few months, so that even if there is still a lot of paint left at season's end, it may have lost much of its toxicity.

Antifouling Compounds

The most widely used toxins are the copper compounds, usually cuprous oxide, However, some antifouling paints use organo-tin compounds, and some use a combination of both. As a rule, the copper compounds are more effective in a single coat. The organo-tin compounds are more sensitive to film thickness and thus will require at least two coats for maximum effectiveness. They also cost more, but they permit manufacturers to produce brighter, clearer colors, and they can be used safely on underwater metal, including aluminum hulls and outdrives (copper bottom paints should never be used on aluminum). In addition, the organo-tin paints are more resistant to weathering when out of the water, so if the boat is hauled during the season you won't have to repaint before it is launched again.

The tin compound often used in formulating antifouling bottom paints is tributylin (TBT), which is probably also the most effective biocide available. However, such paints are rapidly disappearing from the consumer market due to restrictive regulations recently passed by several states and soon to be passed by Congress (the EPA already recommends banning the use of paints containing TBT on all boats under 65 feet in length, although they favor an exemption for aluminum boats).

To get around these restrictions, all major paint companies are introducing new formulations that do not use TBT, including new copolymers that do not contain tin. These use a copper-based biocide instead.

Experts in the field, including chemists with the leading companies, don't all agree as to just how these copper-based formulations will compare with the long-established TBT paints. Many feel that the copper formulations are not quite as effective and generally won't last as long, but some feel that the new paints will prove to be just as effective in the long run. Almost all agree, however, that they won't last as long, so that painting will be required more often than was the case with the TBT paints.

Except for those who have been using the multi-season copolymers, recreational yachtsmen who haul their boats and store them on land each winter have repainted the bottom each year anyway. The new copolymers that don't contain tin still won't lose their potency when out of the water for several months, so you will still be able to skip painting some years, but chances are that the new coatings won't last quite as long as the original TBT formulations did.

Also affected will be fishermen and others who use their boats all year long. Many have been able to go anywhere from three to six years without having to repaint. Chances are that owners of those boats will now have to paint their bottoms more often.

Antifouling paints differ as to the type of vehicle used. Some have a modified epoxy base, some have a vinyl base. The cheapest ones, which are also the softest, usually have a rosin base.

Opinions differ as to whether vinyls or epoxies are better when talking about the longer-lasting finishes. Most experts seem to agree that an epoxy bottom paint can be formulated with a higher percentage of cuprous oxide, thus making the finish more toxic. The epoxies also do not seem to become as brittle when they age, so they may not crack or flake the way some hard vinyls do—but even this varies with the quality and quantity of binders used.

Scraping Required

Another factor to be considered when choosing between a vinyl and an epoxy is whether the paint can be applied without having to scrape off all the old coating first. Vinyls often contain solvents that can attack layers underneath. As a rule, most bottom paints can be used over a vinyl paint, but some vinyls cannot be applied unless you scrape the old paint off first. If in doubt, test first on a small section.

The newest development in bottom paints is the copolymer types that will last several seasons when initially applied in the proper film thicknesses (at least two or three coats are recommended). These differ from ordinary antifouling paints in that the toxic ingredients are "cooked" with the paint so that they become an integral part of the paint's chemical mix. In conventional bottom paints the toxic ingredients are merely mixed into or suspended in the paint film. These toxic ingredients leach out separately, leaving microscopic "holes" or "pockets." As the paint leaches away or washes off it continually exposes new particles of toxin, causing the surface to become rough and pockmarked.

Like a Bar of Soap

The new copolymer paints work differently. Because the toxic ingredient is chemically part of the paint, it does *not* leach out separately. As the paint washes off, the poison washes off with it so that as long as any paint remains it is still as toxic as when first applied. And as the paint wears the film gets smoother and smoother, much like a bar of soap that gets slicker as it wears down. Yet that last sliver of soap is just as effective as the full bar was.

Another advantage of copolymers is their effectiveness when out of the water. You can paint your boat's bottom when it is hauled in the fall (when things aren't as hectic) and launch it in the spring. Then when you haul it next fall, all you have to do is wash the bottom off and it will be ready to launch again the following spring—without repainting. You can do this two, three, or even four times, depending on the number of coats you apply and the amount of wear your boat gets.

User's Report on Copolymer Bottom Paints

The new copolymer bottom paints can eliminate the need for possibly the dirtiest and messiest job faced by every boatowner each year—the need to sand, scrape, and paint the bottom. This is true even if your boat is hauled and stored out of the water every year during the winter; unlike ordinary bottom paints, the new copolymer bottom paints do not lose any of their growth-fighting toxic qualities when left out of the water for months at a time.

After first hearing about these new paints, I was so impressed with what I had learned and with what I had heard from boatowners who had used them that I had the bottom of my new forty-seven-foot Atlantic painted with a copolymer made by the International Paint Company. The boat was given two coats when it was first launched by the builder in Florida in April 1983; then it was brought up to New Jersey on its own bottom. It was hauled by the dealer, who kept it out of the water for about two weeks in early June. During this time nothing was done to the bottom, since it was still perfectly clean.

The boat was launched again in June and then brought up to my home marina on Long Island Sound, where it remained in the water until it was hauled again about sixteen months after it had been painted. I had it hauled because I wanted to have the propellers changed. And much to my delight, there were absolutely no barnacles on the bottom and no long grass tentacles hanging down—nothing but easily removable slime.

Hardware Growth

There was, of course, considerable growth on the props and shafts and some on the struts, but that was all. The slime on the hull bottom easily washed off with a hose right after the boat was hauled, and the surface looked as though it had just been painted. If the boat had not been hauled for other reasons, the slime could have been washed off with long-handled brushes or sponges while standing on the dock, or by a diver while the boat was still in the water (thus saving the cost of a haul).

This meant I did not have to pay for another bottom paint job, and there was no need for sanding or scraping. I was pleased to get three more years out of this same bottom paint before it had to be redone—although I did hire a diver several times during this period to have the slime washed off and to install new zincs when necessary.

Not only does the paint job last, but also I found on close examination of the bottom after it was hauled that the paint was actually smoother than it had been right after it was painted—entirely unlike my previous experiences with bottom paint. Usually rough spots developed after a few months and many pockmarks could be seen where the paint had worn off unevenly. All this marred the finish enough to warrant sanding and/or scraping each time new bottom paint was applied.

Pettit's Horizons

A neighbor in my marina had his boat painted with another brand (Pettit's Horizons) a little over a year ago, and when it was hauled early this summer his experience was much the same as mine—except that he had applied only one coat and thus had to put another coat on because much of the original paint had worn off. Also, because his boat is a fast sportfisherman, the paint tends to wear a bit faster than it would on a slower boat.

Copolymer bottom paints differ from ordinary bottom paints in that the biocide—the toxic chemicals in the paint that actually kill marine life that comes in contact with it—is mixed in with and chemically bonded to the paint. In ordinary bottom paints the biocide is a separate additive; the chemical poisons are merely suspended in the paint film and gradually leach out as time goes on, leaving the paint behind and thus leaving tiny cavities or pockmarks in the surface of the paint.

With copolymers this doesn't happen. The paint itself washes away in microscopic layers as the boat passes through the water. Each microscopic layer of paint has some of the biocide in it and washes or wears away at a constant rate from the time the paint is first applied until it is all worn off. As a result, the paint is just as effective in killing marine growth at the end of the film's life as it is on the day the boat is launched. With regular bottom paints, the biocide leaches out much more rapidly in the first few months than it does as the coating ages, and in some cases more than half of a typical bottom paint's effectiveness is lost after the first three or four months.

In other words, with copolymer bottom paints you know you are getting full effectiveness as long as any paint remains on the surface. With conventional bottom paints you may see plenty of paint, but the biocide may all be gone.

Another way to explain how a copolymer bottom paint wears is to compare it with a bar of soap. It wears away gradually as it is used, but the last piece of soap is just as effective in washing and lathering as the original full-size bar was. The same thing happens as a copolymer bottom paint wears off. And—again just like a bar of soap—the gradual erosion of the surface causes the paint film to become smoother and slicker because the paint wears off in continuous smooth layers—there is no separate biocide leaching out to leave pockmarks or tiny cavities in the surface. This wear pattern means that you always have a

smooth surface on the bottom, so there is less drag underwater. Also, when the time eventually does arrive for a new coat of paint, chances are that little or no sanding will be required.

Like regular bottom paints, the copolymers can be applied by brush or roller (professionals can also spray them on), but as a rule a roller will prove faster and easier. At least two and preferably three coats are recommended to build up the desired film thickness and thus ensure the longevity of the final job (the life of the paint is almost directly proportional to how thick it is). Copolymers can be applied over old coats of hard-finish vinyl or epoxy bottom paints that are in reasonably good condition, but they cannot be applied over soft, copper-base bottom paints. These would have to be completely removed first. The old surface must be thoroughly sanded to remove all loose or flaking paint and to ensure a smooth and solid surface that will act as a base for the new paint.

Secrets of a Good Bottom Paint Job

Good bottom paints are not cheap. Even a medium-priced antifouling paint will cost around $100 a gallon, while the copolymers described above list for about $160 per gallon. Since putting them on is always tedious and time-consuming, it pays to use only a top-quality paint. A bargain-basement variety only wastes a lot of time and effort, and—if you are paying the yard to do the job—a lot of money for labor.

That is why it makes sense when applying bottom paint to do everything you can to get a good job that will stand up the way it should. Here are some pointers to keep in mind:

● Make sure you buy a good-quality paint that is formulated for use where you normally do your boating. If in doubt, ask local boatowners and boatyards, and don't hesitate to contact any of the larger paint manufacturers for their recommendations.

● Always clean the bottom off thoroughly before applying any new paint. Make sure you scrape off all loose or flaking material and sand liberally until the old surface is nice and smooth. If you are doing the work yourself, make sure you wear an approved face mask to avoid inhaling dust and fumes, and an old shirt with long sleeves to keep the powder off your skin.

● Fill in all dents, gouges, and scratch marks before you begin. On fiberglass use an epoxy filler or one recommended by the manufacturer of the bottom paint. Let this dry hard and sand it smooth before applying any paint.

● If there are bare spots where the surface under the paint is exposed, or if you have made any sizable patches as described above, make sure you touch these up before you start. Use the primer or undercoat recommended by the manufacturer of the bottom paint you will be using. If the bottom is fiberglass, wash it with a suitable solvent first to make sure there is no wax or other foreign material on the surface that will keep the paint from bonding properly.

● It is essential that you mix the paint thoroughly before you start, and then mix again at frequent intervals while you are working. This is the only way to keep the consistency and film thickness uniform and to keep the biocides (in conventional bottom paints) evenly dispersed throughout the paint during the whole job.

● Do not try to stretch the paint as you apply it. It is important to lay bottom paints on in the thickness recommended by the manufacturer so you build up a film that will last until the next time the boat is painted. Thin coats wear off fast.

● Where possible, always try to apply two medium coats rather than one thick coat. Two coats will always last longer, especially in tropical waters—in many cases, three times as long as one heavy coat.

● When putting the paint on with a roller, use a three-eighths-inch nap roller to ensure the proper thickness. When the roller cover starts to run dry and extra pressure is required to make the paint cover, stop and pick up more paint.

● Don't thin the paint if you can avoid it. If you must add thinner to keep the consistency workable, use only the kind recommended by the manufacturer and add no more than absolutely necessary. Pour in a little at a time and stir thoroughly before adding more.

● Don't forget to paint the bottom edge of the keel and the places that are temporarily covered by shoring blocks or by the sling from the travel lift. This may mean moving the sling or the shoring at one point, but it should not be neglected.

● After the boat has been in the water for a while, try to wash any slime off regularly by rubbing with a sponge or brush at the end of a long pole, or by using a brush while wearing a face mask and swimming along the waterline. This slime not only slows the boat down as it travels through the water but also interferes with the toxic action of the paint, since it may keep the biocides from leaching out as rapidly or as evenly as they should.

More Effective Use of Paint Removers

When you're using a paint-and-varnish remover, the strong solvents often evaporate before they get a chance to soak into and soften the old paint or varnish completely. Here is a simple trick I have learned to keep the solvents working longer and to prevent them from evaporating so quickly.

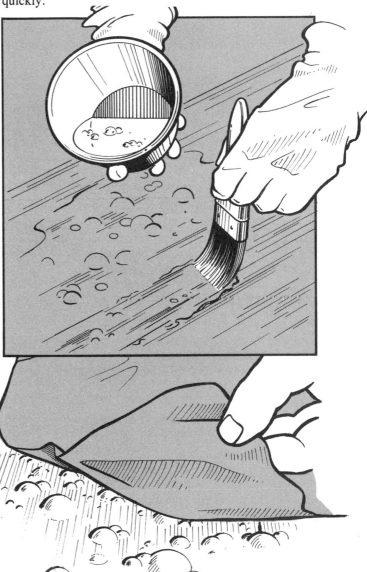

After brushing a thick layer of the remover over one section, cover it with a heavy cloth to keep the solvents wet. Wait a few minutes, then take the cloth off and spread on another layer of the remover. Cover it again with the same cloth. After doing this three times you will find it easy to scrape the varnish off neatly in large sheets—and with a minimum of effort.

Using waterline/bootstripe tape on a hull is quicker and easier than painting.

Choosing and Using Adhesive-Backed Tapes

Every knowledgeable boatowner is certain to have at least one roll of electrical tape in his tool kit, but many do not realize that there are several other types of adhesive-backed tape available that can be equally useful on board a boat—for fixing, holding, patching, wrapping, sealing, and protecting all kinds of objects as well as for finishing off or decorating many different surfaces around the inside and outside of the boat.

Some of these pressure-sensitive tapes are specifically designed for marine use and are widely available in marine supply outlets, but others that can be equally useful around the boat—even though they are primarily designed for use around the house—will not be found in most marine stores. You'll have to look for them in local hardware stores or home centers.

Let's start with a discussion of the marine tapes—the kind that are aboard boats designed for marine use and the kind you are likely to find in many marine supply shops.

Electrical Tape: In addition to the ever-popular black plastic type, which comes in rolls of various lengths, there is also the traditional cloth type, called friction tape, that can still be useful for some jobs—for instance, in those locations where the tape will be exposed to a lot of heat or to constant exposure to oil and grease. Friction tape won't soften as easily as plastic tape will under these circumstances, although the plastic tape is more resistant to moisture and to attack by acids and alkalies.

Bootstripe Tape: Also referred to as waterline tape, these are brightly colored plastic tapes that come in a choice of colors and are specially designed to be resistant to sun and salt water. They do not get brittle or fade with exposure, and they are also exceptionally resistant to abrasion—all qualities that make them well suited for use on hulls where you want to apply a waterline stripe or bootstripe for painting. Needless to say, putting one of these tapes on is a lot faster and easier than doing the job with a brush and masking tape. They are most widely available in solid colors and in rolls either one inch or two inches in width and 50 feet in length; some dealers also stock these tapes in tricolor stripes that create a multicolor effect with one strip of tape. These multistripe tapes come in two widths: 13/16 inch and 3 inches. Each roll is 22 feet long.

Gold Cove Tape: Packaged in 50-foot rolls and available in 1/2-inch and 1-inch widths, this is a tough, metallic gold plastic tape that is highly decorative and looks almost like real gold, although it costs only a fraction as much to put on. Ideal for gold cove stripes on the side of a hull, this tape eliminates the need for masking and painting, and it will not fade or discolor, the way most gold paints will. It is also highly weather-resistant and almost impervious to attack by salt water.

Fine Line Masking Tape: When you want painted edges to be really smooth so they will blend in smoothly, then using Fine Line Tape (made by 3M), or professional-quality striping tape is the answer.

Fine Line Tape is not only thinner than regular masking tape, it is also more easily flexed to follow a curved line, and it peels off cleanly without allowing paint or varnish to "creep" in under the edges. It comes in ¾-inch-wide rolls (1,080 inches long) and costs three to four times as much as regular masking tape, but where neatness and a crisp edge are essential it is well worth the price. Unfortunately, it is not easy to find in all marine supply outlets. If your local dealer doesn't carry it (and won't order it for you), try an auto supply store or a supplier that sells to auto body shops—they use this type of masking tape in most of their work.

Chafing Tape: These are tough, weather-resistant, vinyl-coated white cloth tapes designed to do just what the name implies—protect surfaces and materials against chafing and abrasion. Usually sold in 1-inch-wide rolls that are about 25 to 30 feet in length, this tape is ideal for

wrapping dock lines, mooring lines, and anchor lines at the point where they pass through a chock (as shown), or curve over a toerail, rubrail, or corner of a transom. The tape is also good for wrapping around turnbuckles, life-lines, spreader ends, and similar hardware where there are cotter pins or sharp edges and corners that can catch sails or cause cuts and abrasions when someone falls or scrapes against them.

Rigging Tape: This is a white vinyl plastic tape that usually comes in ¾-inch-wide rolls of various lengths. Its most common use is for wrapping turnbuckles, cotter pins, spreader ends, and similar sharp edges and surfaces that are likely to cause chafe or injury. It is not as resistant to abrasion as chafing tape is, but since it is all vinyl it stretches easier and is more flexible, so it will conform better when wrapped around odd-shaped surfaces or irregular objects.

Nonskid/No-Slip Tapes: Usually sold by the foot by dealers who stock large rolls, this is a tough, flexible material that has a sandy, nonskid texture and is made to be walked on or stepped on. Designed to provide a nonslip footing on boarding ladders, companionway steps, decks, engine hatch covers, docks, and diving boards, it can be purchased in ready-cut strips as well as by the foot. It is usually available in a choice of widths—1 inch, 2, 4, and 6 inches—and comes with a protective paper backing that you have to peel off before pressing the adhesive-backed strips into place. The material is very weather-resistant, but when it does start to wear you can simply peel it off and replace it.

Hatch Cover Tape: This is a closed-cell, adhesive-backed foam insulating tape used around hatches and doors for sealing out water, dust, and fumes. It comes with a pressure-sensitive adhesive coating protected with a paper backing that you peel off when you apply it. Basically similar to the various insulating foam tapes sold in hardware stores and home centers for sealing around doors and windows in the home, the marine versions are all closed-cell foams that create a more airtight and watertight seal than do open-cell foams, and they will not soak up water the way open-cell foam tapes will. The marine versions usually are ¾-inch wide and ¼-inch thick, but you can buy rolls that are thicker, thinner, wider, or narrower.

Nonslip Grip Tape or Handle Tape: Currently made for the marine trade by at least one company (Marine Development & Research Corp., which calls their product Grip Tape), this tape is specifically designed to create a nonslip grip on steering wheels, tiller handles, boat hooks, oar handles, and similar equipment—even when surfaces are wet. It comes in 1-inch wide, 10-foot rolls and provides a slipproof grip but does not have an abrasive surface. (Tapes similar to this are also sold in outdoor stores and sporting goods stores for use on tennis rackets, golf clubs, etc.)

Sail Repair Tape: Made of nylon cloth that has an adhesive backing, this tape is designed for making temporary repairs to sails when a tear occurs while under way. Made in a choice of three colors, rolls are usually 2 inches wide and 25 feet in length. Although this tape is supposed to hold well on all sails, I have tried it several times and find that it doesn't last long when exposed to wind, sun, and normal stress. In fact, I have found that almost any flexible cloth or plastic tape will do almost as well as sail repair tape, especially the superstrong strapping tape described later in this section.

In addition to these marine tapes, there are some other general-purpose tapes I have also found quite useful for various jobs around the inside or outside of a boat. Some of these may be available through regular marine outlets, but others will be found only in local hardware stores, lumberyards, and home centers.

Aluminum Tape: Actually made of a heavy grade of flexible aluminum foil, this all-metal tape has very high tensile strength and can withstand high temperatures.

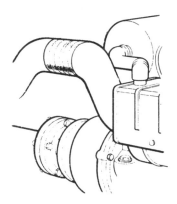

These qualities make it useful for temporary repairs to tanks, pipes, engine manifolds, and mufflers, and since it is nonflammable it is safer to use than cloth or plastic tapes (it is also much stronger). It comes in a two-inch-wide roll that is either five or ten yards in length and can be used to form a decorative covering on inside or outside corners where a metal cove molding or outside corner molding would otherwise be used.

Duct Tape: This high-tensile-strength silver-gray cloth tape is made for sealing heating ducts and air-conditioning ducts, but its strength and tackiness combined with its two-inch width also make it ideal for quickly sealing out air and water in an emergency when something breaks or cracks on a boat. It will stick stubbornly to almost any dry, reasonably clean surface, yet it peels off easily without leaving a lot of sticky residue when you want to remove it.

Like most full-time live-aboards I have often used this tape for sealing windows and other openings against winter storms and have also found it handy during the season for temporarily mending cracked hoses and water lines (the surface must be dry when you put the tape on, or it won't stick).

Strapping Tape: This is a translucent plastic tape reinforced with fiberglass filaments that run lengthwise through the tape. Widely available in stationery stores as well as in hardware stores, it comes in half-inch-wide rolls as well as in two-inch-wide rolls. The tape is incredibly strong and cannot be torn or ripped with your hands—that is why it always comes with a special dispenser that includes a serrated cutting blade for cutting the tape to length (you can also cut it with scissors or a knife).

One use I have found for it is as a replacement for sail mending tape—I used it for mending a tear in my dingy sail early last year, and it was still in place at the end of the season—which is more than I can say for the sail mending tape I have tried on several other occasions. I have also used strapping tape for bundling wires and tubing to keep them out of the way. When used for this you can also leave part of the strip sticking out to one side and then use a small screw and washer to fasten the wires or tubing to a bulkhead or stringer.

Colored Cloth and Plastic Tapes: These multipurpose tapes are useful for temporarily mending tears in cushions and upholstered seats as well as for mending foul-weather gear, boots, rain hats, books, and curtains. I have also found that keeping an assortment of colors on hand makes it easy for me to color-code wires, tubing, pipes, and hoses. For example, I use strips of red tape for all fuel lines, blue tape for fresh water lines, green tape for salt water lines, etc. Electric cables and wires are color-coded

in the same way—especially those that were added after the boat was built.

Double-Faced or Double-Stick Tapes: There are basically three types of doublestick tape available. The first is

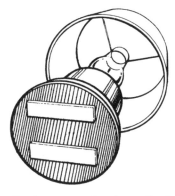

the clear cellophane tape that has adhesive on both sides instead of only one side. The second is a heavier-duty paper or plastic tape (usually white) that also has adhesive on both sides and is most often called carpet tape (because it is mainly used for holding down carpet). The third is a heavy-duty, double-sided foam tape that usually is called mounting tape (because it is mainly used for mounting pictures and various fixtures on vertical surfaces—in fact, the phone company has used it for permanent mounting of wall phones).

The cellophane tape may not be of much use around a boat, but the carpet tape is perfect for holding carpets and small area rugs in place inside the boat—or even in the cockpit and up on the bridge. All you need are a few strips of this tape in the corners and along the edges, and you can use it inside or outside. The tape allows you to pick up the carpet easily when necessary without taking out a lot of screws or removing extra moldings, and it is invisible when in place. After a few times the tape may have to be replaced, but this takes only a minute or two.

The heavier-duty foam mounting tapes are also quite useful around the boat. I wouldn't feel safe depending on the tape alone to support a heavy picture frame or clock, but I use small squares to keep pictures from swinging or shifting after hanging them on a single hook (which means fewer holes in the bulkhead). The tape is also more than enough to hold small pictures and decorative plaques in place when under way.

Another use I have found for this tape is holding table lamps and other decorative objects in place when under way. A couple of strips of this tape used under the base of a lamp will hold it securely. Then I don't have to bolt or screw the lamp down to avoid having to store it each time we leave the dock.

4 ENGINES AND PROPULSION EQUIPMENT

Commissioning Checklist for Gasoline Engines

After a long, cold winter marooned indoors, most boatmen are anxious to head for the nearest body of water and get up on plane. But first there's the little matter of spring commissioning. Here is a checklist aimed at helping you and your rig start the season well prepared.

● For safety's sake, the first step is to pull the cables from the spark plugs to prevent accidental starts and painful injuries.

● Next, review the storage preparations you made last fall. Obviously, you don't need to repeat maintenance already performed. Lay-up should have included draining and refilling both crankcase and gearcase; fogging the engine to prevent rusty cylinders; and storing the battery in a warm, dry place.

● Check all the fluid levels even if they were topped off during lay-up. If the lift pump is low on oil, top it off. Run the outdrive up and down several times. Recheck the level. If it is low again, check hydraulic lines and connections for leaks.

● Beneath the engine cover, inspect the alternator/water pump drive belt or belts. Is it frayed or cracked? If so, replace it. Correct tension allows for about ¼- to ⅜-inch play, measured midway between the pulleys.

● Squeeze the cooling hoses. If one feels lifeless, brittle, bulged, or is cracked, replace it. You can spot cooling system leaks by the telltale stain left at the scene of the crime. On the engine block, simply follow a rust streak upstream to find its source. Later on, when you run the engine, look for steam vapor—another clue that you're losing your cool.

● Remove the flame arrester. Soak it in a No. 10 can full of kerosene, then shoot it dry with compressed air. Blow from the inside out to eject lint and dirt. Hint: When compressed air isn't available, forget the kerosene. In-stead, spray the arrester clean with an aerosol can of carburetor cleaner.

● Work your way around the engine—first with a screwdriver and then with a handful of wrenches. Tighten the clamps on fuel lines and coolant hoses. Replace any that are obviously corroded or damaged. Next check the bolts—some may have vibrated loose. Lay a wrench on every nut and bolt in sight, including engine mounts and manifold bolts. Don't forget the steering linkage. Tighten, but do not overtighten, as necessary.

● Before lubricating the grease fittings, wipe them clean with a shop towel so the gun doesn't pump grit into the vital surfaces. It's important to squirt in enough to replace all the old grease with new, because clean grease will flush out the dirt and moisture. Pump the gun until you see clean grease squirt out alongside the old.

● Charge the battery. Clean and coat its terminal connections with grease. Next, examine the wiring and connections, making sure they are tight and free from corrosion. That green patina you're liable to see on the copper connections resists the flow of electricity. Clean and tighten as necessary. If you find a blown fuse, don't automatically reach for a fresh one. Find out *why* the fuse blew, and replace it after fixing whatever went wrong.

● Remove the spark plugs and wipe them dry of fogging oil. Then crank the engine for ten to fifteen seconds. This prelubes the engine bearings, fills the carburetor float bowl, and blows the fogging oil out of the combustion chamber. Finish up by gapping and replacing the spark plugs.

● Check each one of the propeller blades. File nicks and burrs smooth, but remove as little metal as possible to prevent unbalancing the wheel. Coat the prop shaft with antiseize compound. Considering taking a shortcut on this one? If you neglect to coat the shaft with at least a dab of salt water-resistant grease, you'll have a devil of a time removing it in the fall.

● Click on the bilge blower to make sure it works, and to ventilate the engine compartment. After the blower has cleared the air, start the engine. Monitor the oil pressure and temperature gauges as the engine warms up. The engine should stay in the green. If it overheats, shut it down immediately.

● Easy on the throttle for the first few minutes, while coolant circulates and the seals soften after too long a winter. Look around the engine for any sign of leaking hoses and drain petcocks. Once the engine is up to operating temperature, unscrew the coolant filler cap. It's bad news if the coolant bubbles; it means there's a good chance the head gasket is blown and leaking combustion chamber gas into the cooling system.

● Rough idling and stuttering on acceleration are often caused by carbon buildup on piston domes and cylinder heads. An easy way to clean it off is by squirting internal engine cleaner into the combustion chamber. Basically, the process entails flooding the engine with the aerosol spray until the engine conks out. Let the solutions work for half an hour. Restart the engine. Blipping the throttle a few times will blow the loosened crud out the exhaust.

● Our spring commissioning includes a test run. But before launching, inventory and inspect the safety gear. Does the fire extinguisher register a full load? When is it due for a recharge? How many life jackets are on board?

● Satisfied that all is in order? Okay, cast off the lines. Once you're past the no-wake zone, open the throttle. Given the usual load and at full throttle, the tachometer should read within the recommended operating range. If the wrong wheel is screwed onto your stern, the results will make themselves known by inadequate top speed, reduced power, and horrendous fuel consumption. Because of the wide variety of pitches available to match a myriad of load conditions, it's always a good idea to consult a knowledgeable marine mechanic.

How to Rebuild a Carburetor

Rebuilding a carburetor is easy—all you need are the right tools. First, remove the fuel and vacuum lines; if any are stubborn, ease them off with a screwdriver blade. Then disconnect the throttle linkage. Outboard motors may have

GOOD IDLE SCREW

BAD IDLE SCREW—GROOVE WORN ON NEEDLE

spark advance linkage and an electric starter to contend with.

Two to four nuts attach the carburetor to the intake manifold. Remove them carefully. Keep a firm grip, as they are mightily prone to fall down into the inaccessible recesses of the engine. If not retrieved, they can end up knocking about in the combustion chamber, punching holes in piston tops, and scoring cylinder walls.

Slide the carburetor off its mounting studs and remove the old gasket. If you hear any fuel swishing around in the float bowl, be careful not to spill it. Contact with skin or eyes can be a painful experience. Now unscrew the four or more screws that hold the airhorn to the float chamber. Separate the two halves.

Look inside the float chamber. Is there a great gob of sludge and gum? Examine the float. Has it sprung a leak and filled with gasoline?

The high-speed orifice, or jet, is screwed into the base of the fuel bowl. Removing it is essential in performing a solid repair job. Some outboards require a specially tipped screwdriver for removal. The cost is nominal; in fact, this special tool will pay for itself the first time you complete a rebuild. Have your parts man order one for you. If he seems hesitant, shop around.

On the airhorn side of the carb is the inlet needle and seat. Use an extra-wide-bladed screwdriver on the seat; otherwise trying to remove it can be frustrating. It's made of very soft brass and resists skinny screwdrivers.

On outboards, loosen the locking nut, then back out the idle mixture needle. You'll also find nylon or fiber washers. The nylon version is easy enough to remove, but be scrupulous when pulling out the fiber kind. They tend to break up upon disassembly, and tiny particles can enter the idle passages and plug them up.

With the carburetor completely taken apart, examine each one of the pieces. A bad idle mixture screw will have a ring worn around its tip. That's because gasoline cuts a groove in the brass or steel, much the way the grand canyon has been eroded by flowing water. When a needle valve wears, it becomes impossible to tune the engine. Inlet needles wear out the same way. Both let too much gas slip past.

When buying replacement parts or carburetor kits, parts men are usually a lot more helpful when the customer knows exactly what he wants. So bring the make, model, and serial numbers.

To rebuild a carburetor it's important to soak the disassembled housings in cleaning solvent overnight. Be prepared—it's expensive. Also, be careful—it burns. Wear rubber gloves while handling the solution. The morning after, rinse the parts with plenty of hot water to neutralize and dispel the solvent. Blow it dry with compressed air.

To reassemble, install the high-speed jet in the fuel bowl. Outboards get the low-speed needle along with its prescribed number of packing washers. Screw in the needle slowly until it just barely bottoms out. Back it off from ½ turn to 1½ turns, depending on the engine's specifications. Outboards then get the locking nut screwed in firmly, but not too tightly. You'll be setting the idle later and will need some slack to adjust the needle valve. Don't leave it too loose, or air will leak past the packing washers.

Install a new inlet seat and washer. Coat the inlet needle's rubber tip with a light coat of oil to prevent it from sticking. Install the float and hinge pin. Lay the gasket on the airhorn, top side down. Hold the assembly at eye level. Set the float so it's parallel to the carb base. Adjust the level with a pair of needle nose pliers, applying the jaws squarely on the flat between the float and its hinge.

Naturally, some kits have other techniques for adjusting the float, and in these cases the instructions usually are included.

Check the float drop by flipping the assembly upside down. The float should have enough drop to let the inlet needle open and let fuel into the bowl. If not, bend the little tab on the back side of the hinge until it allows enough clearance.

Replace the airhorn and bowl and install the assembled carburetor on the engine. Replace throttle and spark advance linkage and hook up fuel and vacuum lines.

Start the engine and run it until the temperature gauge shows it's at operating temperature. Slowly, in increments of ⅛ turn, screw the idle mixture needle clockwise until the engine backfires. Then back the needle off about ½ turn from where it just started to backfire. The leaner the setting, the slower the engine will run, and therefore the better for trolling, as long as it isn't backfiring. On outboards, once satisfied with the mixture, tighten the locking nut so the needle won't vibrate out of adjustment.

Multiple carburetors will need to be synchronized with each other. To do so, set the top carb's idle needle first, then do each of the others, one at a time. Go through the sequence a couple of times.

Another important adjustment is the linkage. In general, the key is to adjust each carburetor so its throttle plate is at its lowest rpm setting at the same time the other carburetors are at their lowest rpm setting.

With everything shipshape, top off the fuel tanks and make knots.

Caring for Your Gasoline Generator

Gensets are the big reason we can enjoy onboard creature comforts. You will be glad to hear that you can save money and keep electrical appliances humming by doing most of the work yourself when it comes to genset maintenance, without special tools and without having to spend much time at it.

Daily Checks
Work through your own checklist before cranking up the generator. Pull the dipstick and also inspect the coolant level. Top off as necessary. If your genset is air-cooled, check the air inlets and outlets for air flow obstructions. The wiring also rates a quick inspection—make sure none of the wires is loose or frayed.

Next, start the genset without a load and look for fuel leaks. Most occur around the base of the carburetor and at fuel line connections. The fuel lines shouldn't touch anything that can cut or rub through the rubber or metal hoses.

Oil Changes
One of the essentials for a long-lasting engine is to maintain the proper oil at the right level. For best results use oil rated SF/SE/CC. Expect the engine to consume more multigrade than single-viscosity oil. When in doubt about what type to buy, consult your owner's manual.

It's also essential to change the oil regularly so that corrosive and abrasive elements don't have a chance to attack the bearings and journals. Most manufacturers recommend that you first change a new generator's oil after twenty-five hours running time and every fifty hours thereafter.

Some engines are fitted with spin-on oil filters; others inexplicably aren't. If your genset does have a filter (check owner's manual) replace it with each oil change.

Air and Fuel Filters
A dirty air filter richens fuel mixture, causes carbon buildup, and dilutes crankcase oil with raw gasoline. The result is prematurely worn-out pistons, valves, and bearings. To prevent this, change the air filter at least every hundred hours.

Fuel filters require attention after every hundred hours' running. To complicate matters, gensets are equipped with a variety of fuel filter types, but the general rule is to replace the throwaway in-line filter after about a hundred hours. Bowl and screen fuel filters should also be cleaned and replaced at a hundred hours. And it's a good idea to carry spare air, oil, and fuel filters.

Spark Plugs and Brushes

Replace the spark plug or plugs during spring commissioning or after every hundred to 150 hours of operation. A misfiring spark plug wastes fuel, and a dead plug washes the oil from cylinder walls with the raw gasoline it never ignited.

If your genset has brushes, inspect them every five hundred hours. The specifics of the procedure vary, so consult your owner's manual for details, but in general the brush faces should be smooth, without deep grooves. Also inspect the commutator, or the rotating surface the brushes rub against. If the commutator is grooved, consult a marine mechanic. Replace the brushes if they're worn shorter than the owner's manual specifies. Break in the new brushes by running the generator with a light load for fifteen minutes.

Winterization

Just like your propulsion system, your genset needs proper mothballing to prevent rust and corrosion. The first step is to run it with a 50 percent load for about an hour, so that most of the sludge and corrosives will drain out along with the hot crankcase oil. Refill with whatever oil the manufacturer recommends, and then restart the engine.

Close the fuel lines and run the engine out of gasoline. However, if you treat the gasoline with fuel stabilizer it's not necessary to run the engine out of fuel. Next remove the spark plug or plugs, spray fogging oil into the cylinder or cylinders, and bump the starter, cranking the engine a couple of revolutions. Spray more fogging oil into the cylinder or cylinders, then replace the plug or plugs.

Remove the cranking battery. Clean, then coat the posts with grease or Vaseline. Charge and store the battery in a cool, dry place, and at least once during the winter charge the battery again.

Commissioning

Install the fully charged starting battery. Remove the spark plug or plugs, then crank the engine for about a minute to blow the fogging oil out of the cylinder or cylinders. Clean and gap the old spark plug or plugs, or, preferably, install new ones.

Before starting the genset make sure all the appliances, radios, lights, and other electrical loads are switched off.

Open the fuel lines. Expect several seconds of cranking before the fuel pump fills the carburetor with fuel and the engine catches. A judicious shot of ether down the throat of the carb can speed the process somewhat. However, be forewarned: *Ether in a closed compartment is both a health and a safety hazard.*

Once it has started, the engine will smoke and run rough until all the cylinders burn clean. Operate the smooth-running genset for one hour with a 50 percent load. Then it is ready for the season.

Proper genset care requires regular maintenance at specified engine hours. Those hours are logged by an hour meter, which measures an engine's running time; install one if you don't have it.

Preventive Maintenance for Diesel Generators

Diesel-powered generating sets have become commonplace on pleasure boats over thirty feet. Their durability and reliability make them virtually trouble-free engine room components—so much so that generators are often overlooked when it comes to preventive maintenance. But like everything else aboard a boat, they *do* need periodic attention to keep them purring along without a hitch. With this in mind, here are a few maintenance tips to help you keep your diesel-powered genset operating properly.

Due to the wide variety of gensets in use today and the diversity of installations, it is not possible to zero in on any one make or model; therefore this section will be general in nature, but it can be used as a checklist for servicing almost any small diesel-powered generator.

First, you should have adequate access to the genset area and adequate space around it to work. The compartment should be well ventilated, so that both the diesel and generator receive plenty of cool, dry air for efficient operation.

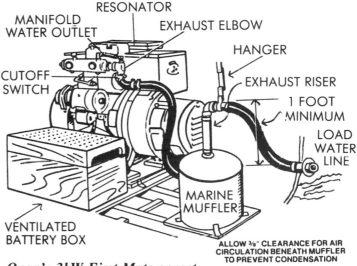

Onan's 3kW First Mate genset.

Your genset should be mounted on vibration isolators and the isolators mounted to a strong bed or base of sufficient size and strength to support its weight. A firm mounting not only secures the genset, it also helps to prevent the transmission of noise and vibration to other areas of your boat. Much can be done to minimize the noise nuisance with the installation of sound shields and other soundproofing equipment, along with good exhaust silencers. Remember: Do not terminate your exhaust pipe near an opening port or a bulkhead opening.

All electrical lines, exhaust and water cooling pipes, and fuel lines should be firmly strapped to the boat and connected to your genset with flexible lines and connections. Fuel shutoff valves should be present in the fuel lines.

Because of the danger of fire and explosion from possible fuel oil leaks and from sparks from the generator, the installation should be according to U.S. Coast Guard regulations, and the compartment should have exhaust and fresh air blowers.

Regardless of where your genset is located, it should never feed off the same fuel lines as your main engines, or you will be starving your generator when you run your engines.

Remember to change your fuel filters regularly according to the schedule in the service manual; and don't forget to eyeball the fuel/water separator before each startup. If you don't have a water separator, I strongly suggest you install one.

To ensure the cleanliness of your engine's lube oil system, always change filters when you change your lube oil. Check your manual for the number of hours between changes (usually fifty to seventy-five).

Whatever cooling system you have, it should be short, simple, efficient, and without any restrictions to the flow of water. Always use two- or three-ply silicone rubber hoses and two stainless steel worm gear clamps for connections.

At the beginning and end of each season, check the zink anodes and engine thermostat. Raw water pump impellers and sea strainers tend to be the most vulnerable parts of the cooling system, so learn to check these two areas regularly—before they are responsible for cutting off the electrical current to your beer cooler.

All starting batteries should be mounted in a cool, dry location and as close to your set as possible. Keeping the cables short will help keep "voltage drop" to a minimum. Your heavy-duty three-way electrical throw switch should be marked with ship-offshore labels.

If not abused, the main components of your generator will operate for long periods of time without requiring any replacements. They should, however, be checked each spring and, if necessary, be cleaned out with low-pressure dry air.

Make a habit of wiping the whole genset down when it is not in use. If you spot a leak, take immediate steps to fix it.

If your genset didn't come equipped with safety switches and alarms for low lube oil pressure and high water temperature, I definitely recommend that you have a set installed. They just might save you the price of a new diesel engine.

A diesel engine is a heat and work engine, so never run your diesel-powered genset at less than 75 percent of its capacity for long periods of time.

A final point to remember: Always run your genset compartment blower for several minutes prior to starting up your generating unit.

Transmission Tips for Diesel Engines

Today's hydraulically operated marine transmissions are dependable and built to function for many years with a minimum of attention. Here are a few operational and maintenance tips, however, to ensure that your transmission will remain trouble-free and in peak condition.

The movement of a single lever at the control head governs a marine transmission's forward/neutral/reverse operation. Control cables, pulleys, linkage, and other components must be lubricated regularly so they operate freely. They must also have sufficient "throw" to shift fully and freely into forward, neutral, and reverse.

Clutch life can be significantly prolonged by always shifting gears correctly. Remember: Rapid shifting at high engine speeds places a heavy strain on all marine gear parts, and unnecessary heat is created by clutch slippage. Unless an emergency requires a high-speed shift, don't do it.

Overheating

If your transmission suddenly starts to overheat, slowly pour several buckets of water over its housing (not on your engine) to help cool its parts and lube oil. And then quickly check the oil dipstick for correct level. Most overheating troubles can be traced to: (1) incorrect oil level; (2) dirty oil cooler or screen; (3) clutch slippage due to an improper adjustment or installation.

Water in Transmission

A leaky transmission oil cooler is the most common cause of oil contamination. The warning signs are cloudy or gray-colored oil spewing out of the transmission breather. If your transmission should ever fail and have to be worked on or replaced, make sure you completely clean the oil cooler and its plumbing of any dirt or metal particles.

Warner Gear sells a transmission alarm kit that when installed into your transmission housing will alert you to overheating. It's a simple installation and costs only a few dollars.

Free-Wheeling

Transmission companies are either vague on the question of "free-wheeling" (the spinning of a transmission in neutral when running on only one engine or when being towed, caused by water pressure on the dead prop) or will not comment on it at all. Warner Gear says yes, it's okay on their gears, but use caution and watch the lube oil.

Walt Ferguson, a Twin Disc engineer, says letting your hydraulic clutch spin is something that must be done "cautiously." The centrifugal effect of long-extended free-wheeling of a clutch will throw all the lube oil from the center out, thereby robbing the center portion of lubrication; so fill the transmission with as much lube oil as you can jam into it to help keep it well lubricated.

Certain Twin Disc models can be "back-driven" (propeller free-wheeling or windmilling with dead engine); check with your Twin Disc dealer to see if you can do it with yours.

Locking Propeller Shaft

If you have to shut down one of your engines and come home on the other, Dale Scoog, a Detroit Diesel engineer, recommends protecting the marine gear on the shut-down engine against overheating and lack of lubrication by preventing the rotation of the downed engine's propeller shaft. One method is to lock the shaft or coupling with a large pipe or crescent wrench securely tied against something solid, or by securing the shaft or coupling with rope.

Some Volvo hydraulic gearboxes come equipped with a mechanical safety "get you home" device, for use when the transmission itself malfunctions, which locks the input and output together, giving you only a solid forward speed. It makes a solid connection from the engine flange straight through to the shaft. Twin Disc and Allison transmissions can be rigged for emergency forward speed in case of breakdowns. Check with your dealer for the proper procedures.

Caution: Regardless of which "come-home" method you use, check your transmission's oil level regularly and replenish if necessary. Always keep a sharp eye on oil temperature as well.

Routine Checks

- Check oil level.

- Check for oil leaks at gasket sealings and at output shaft oil seal.
- After startup, give a quick listen for any unusual noises.
- Check cooler and oil connections for leakage.
- Check oil pressure and temperature when running.

Annual Checks

- Check shift linkage adjustment to ensure that the transmission shift lever is positioned so that the spring-loaded ball enters the chamfered hole in the side of the shift lever. The selector controls on the bridge must position the shift lever exactly in F, N, and R selector positions, with the ball poppet centered in the shift lever hole for each position.
- Check all bolts for tightness.
- Check water lines, oil lines, and connections for leakage. Make sure lines are securely fastened to prevent shifting.
- Change lube oil and clean oil screen.
- Check oil pressure and temperature.

What You Should Know About Marine Batteries

A marine battery by any other name is in essence the same thing as its automotive counterpart. The only differences are purely cosmetic. Instead of the conventional terminal posts, marine batteries have quick disconnect wing nuts to facilitate easy removal of the cables. To make lay-up and fitting out an easier task, there is a little rope-carrying handle. Actually, the big difference is the shorter warranty offered, and that's due to the greater neglect and adverse operating conditions that marine batteries usually suffer.

Component-wise there is precious little difference in starting batteries. They're capable of short, furious bursts of energy, and then it's time for a recharge. Throughout the first 25 percent discharge of their rated capacity, they perform like champions. But once past that point, they'll fade away into nothingness. That's what's happened when instead of the engine cranking over there's nothing but a low groan that slows down and finally stops. As a battery dissipates, its voltage drops. A twelve-volt starter runs slower at nine volts, and even slower at six.

It's very hard on a starting battery to be heavily discharged. When it happens, lead sulphate builds up on the plates and then flakes off. That's plate area and energy storage that're gone forever. Little by little, with each abuse, the storage battery loses its oomph. So if an engine won't start after a few turns of the key, troubleshoot the problem and don't drain the battery. Also, charge it during the lay-up procedure, and at a minimum, at least once during the off-season. Once a month would be even better, since starting batteries are intended to be maintained at a nearly full state of charge.

Warning: Don't clamp a trickle charger on a battery, and walk away for a few hours; since this kind of device is unregulated, it will keep charging a battery past its full charge, which will shorten its lifespan. Instead, use a regulated charger—the kind that automatically shuts off the current flow once the battery is fully charged. If you must use a trickle charger, use a hydrometer to monitor the charge.

Deep-cycle batteries are a different breed of workhorse. They release current more slowly, and unlike a starting battery, can discharge completely and be brought back to a full charge without damage. They thrive on powering trolling motors, depth finders, and other electronic gear. As they hold a charge for a longer period of time, once fully charged, most won't need any attention during lay-up. In fact, some boast such a miniscule self-discharge rate during storage that one charge per nine months is adequate.

It would be reasonable to expect one of these to outlast a starting battery by three to five lifetimes. Some skippers are forgoing dual battery and switch installations in favor of one deep cycle battery. That's okay as long as it's not heavily discharged. Deep cycle batteries can be used for starting marine engines, although the cranking speed will be somewhat slower. On the other hand, if you're having starting problems, the deep cycle battery will crank longer, albeit slower. Note, however, that the slower cranking speed is relative. A deep-cycle battery that's a bit bigger than a starting battery will crank just as fast.

Another category you've heard about is the maintenance-free battery. These units don't need water or electrolyte checks. All they do need is a good set of cables mated to clean posts and terminals. Assuming the batteries are kept at least reasonably charged, they will last longer than conventional starting batteries. However, they do claim a lower self-discharge rate than conventional starting batteries.

As you might expect, combination maintenance-free and deep-cycle batteries are available, offering the best features of both kinds of battery all in one package—namely, long life, minimal maintenance, and the ability to start an engine or power a trolling motor and still discharge and recharge time after time. For the sake of illustration, consider the Globe marine battery, which, according to its manufacturer, will last 250-plus full discharges. That's about five times what you could expect from a starting battery.

When buying a battery, how much is enough? One

measure of capacity is measured in cold cranking amps. Figure you'll need about one amp for every cubic inch (c.i.d.). Therefore, a 230 c.i.d. engine would need a 230-amp cold cranking battery, while a 350 c.i.d. would need 350 amps. If the engine in question is rated in liters and not cubic inches, then figure on needing sixty cold cranking amps per liter. Therefore, a three-liter engine needs a battery with a 180-amp cold crank rating. This guideline provides the absolute minimum battery. One should actually go with a little more battery—the idea being that what you want is not just a battery that will start the engine, but one that will last. Every year of its life, a battery loses some of its power. Start out with a little extra, and it will last that much longer. If bigger is better, how much is too much? Easy. Remember: The battery needs to be carried on board by somebody each spring, and then back off again each fall, and that somebody probably is you.

Don't be tempted by bargain batteries. Even though one may be the same size as the more expensive brand, the real measure is what's inside. Cheap batteries come with smaller plates, which means less cranking power. Compare both the weight and the cold cranking capacity.

Remember that the warranty period is less for a marine battery. Most marine starting batteries are replaced at about the twenty-four-month mark. But deep cycle batteries can last from four to ten years. Once a battery is installed in your rig, two crucial factors determine if it will live out its planned life-span. The first key is proper installation. Heat kills. While a battery needs to be installed as close to the starter motor as possible—to reduce voltage loss in the cables—it should still be protected from engine heat. A strap-down battery box affords thermal protection as well as helping to reduce banging around.

Maintenance also is important. Keep conventional cell batteries topped off with distilled water so that the plates don't sulphate. Maintenance-free batteries need care, too. Charge them before lay-up, at least once during lay-up, and again when fitting out. Always keep terminals and posts clean.

Refinishing Outdrives

Outboards and outdrives that are used in salt water are almost always troubled to some degree with surface pitting of the metal that is underwater all the time. The dissimilar metals that are used create a perfect environment for corrosion in sea water, especially when combined with stray electrical currents that are often present from boats that are not properly grounded. The mottled appearance this corrosion causes makes the unit look old and uncared for.

Normally, regular painting on top of a suitable primer should inhibit much of this electrolysis, but after a period of time when the pitting and peeling on my outboard's lower unit became too unsightly I decided to take a different approach.

First I wet-sanded the lower unit down to the bare metal using #80 grit wet-or-dry abrasive paper. I paid particular attention to cleaning out each pit mark, using a thin wire brush to remove salt and oxidized metal from those depressions that were too small for the sandpaper to reach into.

After the whole surface was clean and dry I wiped all the metal down with acetone, then used a two-part gray epoxy marine filler (such as Marine-Tex) to fill in and level off all the imperfections in the metal. The epoxy was allowed to harden overnight, then wet-sanded—first with #150 wet-or-dry paper and then with #220, using a sanding block each time on the flat surfaces.

When done, the surface was once again washed clean and then wiped down with acetone, after which I applied two coats of a zinc chromate primer, sanding the final coat gently with #320 paper. The job was finished by applying three coats of outboard lacquer. The end result was a like-new lower unit that resisted pitting for the whole summer.

Acetone-soaked rags should not be stored on board. Acetone fumes in a tight space can cause spontaneous combustion.

Eliminate the Oily Mess

Changing oil filters is almost always a messy job—oil inevitably drips all over hands and clothing and makes another mess in the bilge. An easy way to prevent all of

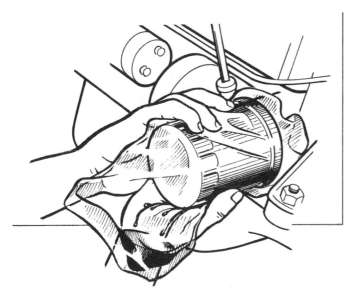

this is to use two heavy-duty sandwich bags that are large enough to slip easily over your oil filter cartridges. Use the filter wrench to loosen the filter enough so that you will be able to spin it off the rest of the way by hand, then slip one of the plastic bags inside the other (I like the doubled bags because if one should split or tear, the second one will still catch all the drippings).

Now slide the doubled bags over the filter cartridge and when the filter is completely enclosed (inside the bags) spin it the rest of the way off by hand. Turn slowly by pressing hard against the bags on the outside of the filter and keep a firm grip while doing this because once the filter comes completely free the weight of the cartridge and the oil it contains will make the bag suddenly quite heavy. Hold the bag in place under the filter fitting until all dripping stops, then carry the bag containing the used oil and the cartridge outside where you can dispose of it neatly. You shouldn't even get your hands dirty.

Installing a Dual Battery System

Ever been stranded because all the electronic goodies on board drained the battery so low it wouldn't crank the engine? That frustrating situation can be avoided by installing a second battery and a selector switch. With this set-up, storage batteries can be dialed up individually or together. Usually one battery will be selected to power ship-to-shore radio, trolling motors, and onboard electronics, while the other, fully charged, is held in reserve for engine starts. Once under way, the selector switch can route recharging voltage to either battery or to both batteries.

To make this installation, first decide on where to locate that extra battery. Just like the original battery, it should be a marine-grade, deep-cycle battery. An automotive battery will not do. A deep-cycle battery is built to withstand up to two hundred charges and discharges, while a no-maintenance car battery will last only from twenty to fifty. The no-maintenance, marine-grade, deep-cycle batteries are made with gelled electrolyte.

Since batteries are rather weighty, they should be located close to the keel and as low as possible. To keep voltage drop to a minimum, they should be located as close to the engine as possible. The shorter the battery cables, the less voltage loss. However, right next to the engine is no good—all that heat will kill the battery.

Fresh air is a necessity. A battery under charge gives off explosive hydrogen fumes. Never set a loose battery down in the bilge. Instead, locate it in a securely mounted, acid-tight box. Allow at least a foot of clearance around the box for air to circulate. The lids on these boxes are

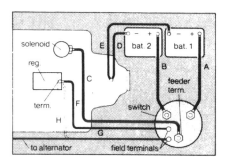

Typical dual battery installation.

vented, so even when strapped down, they breathe. Make sure that leaks and spray are not getting to your batteries. Salt water splashing on a battery creates toxic and explosive chlorine gas.

With the battery mounts secured, disconnect the existing battery. Route the cables from the main and auxiliary battery to the selector switch. Again, since cable length determines voltage drop, the distance from the batteries to the switch and back again, should be as short as possible. Naturally, a compromise must be established between length and convenient access to the switch. Most are mounted so they are easily accessible when raising the engine cover.

The cables should be stranded, insulated copper. Single wire cable is prone to fatigue and breakage. When routing wires through bulkheads, fit them with a grommet to prevent the sharp-edged fiberglass from cutting through the insulation. It's also helpful to color-code the wires—red for positive, black for negative. Wire size is also important: The higher the number, the smaller the wire.

Typically, the selector switch will have three large terminals and two smaller ones. One of the large ones will be marked BATTERY #1; another, BATTERY #2. Connect one cable to terminal #1 and route it to the main battery. Do not connect the battery. Connect the cable on terminal #2 to the auxiliary battery. The remaining large terminal is the common feed line. Its polarity is positive, and it connects to the starter solenoid. Use wire ties to band the new cables to the existing wire harness.

Those two small terminals provide a circuit that automatically disconnects the alternator when both batteries are switched off while the engine is running. This prevents voltage surge from burning out the alternator.

To connect the alternator cutoff circuit, locate the voltage regulator's field terminal. It's usually marked "F" or "FLD." Loosen the screw and remove the wire. Replace it with one of the two small wires running from the selector switch. Snip off the terminal lug from the disconnected field wire. Strip off half an inch of insulation. Likewise strip the second small wire from the selector switch. Splice the two together.

Now you are ready to mount the switch. Cut an oblong piece of three-quarter-inch marine plywood to fit. Use the switch as a template. Lay it on the piece of plywood and center-punch the mounting holes. Remove the switch and drill those holes. Wood screws are usually provided with battery switch kits. Fasten the switch to its backing plate and then lay the backing plate against the hull. Drill three or four more holes to attach the backing plate to the hull. A dab of fiberglass or epoxy glue on the threads will keep the screws from vibrating loose.

The last step is to turn the selector switch to "OFF" and connect the cables to the batteries. Naturally, the battery posts and terminals need to be squeaky clean and coated with corrosion-resistant protectant. To test the new electrical system, flick on the running lights. Rotate the switch through all its positions. The lights should stay lit on all three battery choices, but douse on OFF.

No-Spill Oil Changes

Changing the oil in my stern-drive engine has always been a messy job that involved lots of cleaning up afterward. There are only about five inches between the oil drain plug under the engine pan and the bottom of the bilge, leaving little room for funnels and the like.

However, last year I worked out a solution that makes draining the old oil simple. I use an empty one-gallon antifreeze jar, the flat kind, as shown. I cap it tightly, then cut a hole measuring about four by five inches on one of the flat sides. Next I line the bilge under the drain plug with a large plastic trash bag or garbage-can liner bag to catch anything that spills. On top of this I place the bottle with the cut-out opening facing up, centering it under the drain plug for the oil.

Now I can remove the plug (after warming up the

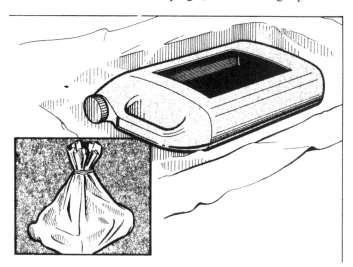

engine), then let the oil run out. The bottle will catch 99 percent of what comes out. When you've finished, gather the plastic bag up around the bottle and then slide the whole thing out of the bilge. You may have to tilt the bottle to get it out, spilling a little oil, but it will be caught inside the plastic bag.

Some may feel that a better method would be to pump the oil out through the dipstick tube using an electric drill-powered pump, but the above method is a lot faster and more efficient. It does a better job of getting the sludge out, since the oil comes out while it is still hot and much faster than by pumping it out through a thin hose inserted in the dipstick tube.

No-Mess Oil Change

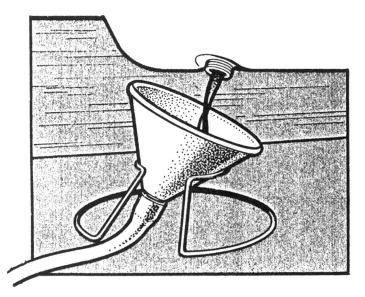

My boat has an inboard/outboard engine. I trailer it to the water when I want to use it and do most of my own maintenance on the boat. One job that I've always found quite messy is changing the oil—it involves working on hands and knees down in the bilge. But I have now discovered a simple solution that makes it neat and easy.

I use a length of small-diameter hose that will fit through the drain hole in the transom and is long enough to reach from the drain plug in the bottom of the oil pan to a pail or pan on the ground outside the boat (under the transom drain hole). I insert a small funnel into the inside end of the hose, then rig up a wire tripod (out of an old coat hanger) to support the funnel in a vertical position under the drain plug. Now all I have to do is remove the drain plug and watch the oil run out through the hose to the pan or pail on the outside.

How to Eliminate Vibration in Diesel Engines

Webster defines vibration as "a periodic accelerating motion of a rigid body resulting from a disturbance." Causes of vibration from diesel engines are varied and many. All parts, such as flywheels, vibration dampers, accessory drives or pulleys, pumps, alternators, and marine transmissions radiate some vibration. So remember to use flexible hoses and fixtures for all fuel, water, exhaust, and other connections between your diesel and your boat's hull to lessen the transmission of vibration. Besides, solid connections at these points would eventually fatigue and break.

The quickest and most effective way to help eliminate annoying vibration is to isolate the engine with new engine mounts or with a flexible coupling.

However, a boat may have vibration caused by components other than the engine. Here is a list of trouble spots to check:

- Engine mounts—are they worn or loose?
- Alignment between your engine and prop shaft.
- Bad or worn shaft bearings.
- Bent prop or shaft.
- Hull appendages, such as struts, sternpost, and rudders—are they properly faired into the flow stream?
- Are you overpowered for your boat's size and design?
- Are propellers properly pitched and dynamically balanced?
- Do you have a damaged blade, or is some line or sea debris wrapped around the blades or shaft?

Obviously, making sure your engine is well tuned and running smoothly is the first step in eliminating vibration. If it persists after your diesel is tuned and hitting on all cylinders, there are several areas you can check for vibration that occurs only when your diesel is running but not engaged in either forward or reverse.

Engine mounts usually are prime culprits in engine vibration noises. A worn, loose, or broken engine mount can cause excessive engine and hull vibration and damage and can also create angular misalignment between the engine and prop shaft. Some engine mounts can be adjusted to align your engine, transmission, and prop-shaft assembly properly. Mounts are inexpensive, are quickly and easily installed, and require no special tools. When flexible mounts and/or flexible couplings are used, all engine-to-hull connections must also be flexible.

Malleable metal leveling wedges sometimes are used for aligning an engine with its propeller-shaft assembly.

Inserted singly under each engine mount, they can compensate for the angle of installation.

If vibration persists after new engine mounts are installed, remove the accessory or component drive belts one at a time and operate your diesel after each one is removed to locate noise originating from these components, or from their pulley or brackets. Caution: Overtightening a belt or a crankshaft pulley can cause side tension, and the strain will eventually cause damage or failure of the pulley, shaft, or shaft bearing.

Next observe and listen to what happens to any vibration from idle to top rpm. Is the vibration even throughout the entire speed range, or only at one or two speed bands?

Critical Speed

Critical speed is simply an excess amount of vibration and noise that may suddenly appear and be amplified during a very short range (twenty-five to thirty rpm) of rpm speed and then just as suddenly disappear. Almost all diesel engines have it; mechanics know about it, and accept it and sales engineers don't care to discuss it. However, as critical speed vibration tends to fatigue and crack metal, it is best to avoid it and pass as quickly as you can through its short rpm range.

Make sure you have your engine adjusted to the correct idle rpm speed. Most diesel engines are not engineered to operate smoothly below their designed (four hundred to five hundred rpm) idle range.

Propeller vibrations may be caused by plastic, rope, wire, or sea debris wrapped around the prop or shaft, or by a bent blade. If after a quick underwater inspection you find none of these, I suggest you check with a propeller specialist, as your prop may be out of balance or have a bad wobble. Remember, the taper and keyway must be machined to fit perfectly.

Out of Synch

Twin-screw boats sometimes develop annoying vibrations because of the different beat of the two propellers caused by a variation in engine speed. This is not only annoying but also can loosen engine and prop-shaft mounts. The installation of an engine synchronizer probably is the best way to eliminate this type of vibration or noise.

Engine and propeller alignment should be checked periodically, as it is rather common for a hull to change its form under various loads or sea conditions and with age.

Disc drives constructed of molded thermoset polyurethane and other nonmetallic material inserted between the transmission flange and the prop-shaft flange can sometimes reduce vibration by providing a barrier between your engine and its propeller. They will control torsional and thrust vibration and also help block electrolysis from getting to your diesel engine.

Vibrations and noises that are caused by a condition within your diesel and that tend to remain the same through its entire speed range can best be located with a vibrometer (a vibration-detecting instrument) by your engine distributor.

Eliminating Smoke, Smell, and Noise with Diesel Engines

No . . . your diesel engine does not have to smoke, stink, and knock . . . at least not excessively. Some "diesel knock" is perfectly normal, and diesel engineers are working overtime trying to reduce this annoyance with new engine designs, improved fuel injection, and new combustion techniques.

Occasionally an engine will come off the assembly line that is a bit noisier than it should be. Why? In this day and age of electronically controlled perfection, nobody really knows. In these rare cases it is best to have an experienced mechanic check out the problem.

Improper fuel injection, preignition or delayed ignition due to timing, too-rapid burning, sluggish burning, or after-burning of the fuel all will affect the exhaust's temperature, density, odor, and noise. While a diesel's exhaust can become overly noisy, it need not be, as it is usually easiest to remedy.

Silencing the Exhaust

The object of the muffler or silencer in your diesel's exhaust system is to accept the large, explosively pulsing flow of exhaust gases from your engine's cylinders, break them up, and smooth them out into a peaceful flow with adequate sound reduction. It should do this without excessively impeding the bursts of exhaust gases from the cylinders. If this isn't accomplished efficiently, your engine will develop a power loss and eventually burn its exhaust valves.

Today most owners of pleasure boats prefer the hori-

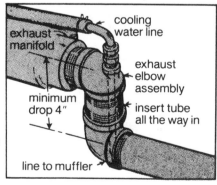

Wet-type exhaust system.

zontal wet-type exhaust system, where the raw (salt) water is sprayed directly into the exhaust system near the elbow. This system helps cool the exhaust gases, muffles the sound, and reduces the diesel's exhaust odor.

If you find your exhaust noise objectionable, check your entire exhaust system, including the muffler. Maybe you don't have the right size piping or correct model and size muffler for your particular engine.

Sometimes an engine's exhaust noise and odor can be lowered with better-controlled water injection into the exhaust system. But remember that the more cooling water you inject into the exhaust stream, the more back pressure you subject your engine to.

Turbocharging

Turbocharging engines usually are noticeably less noisy than comparable naturally aspirated models. A "T" engine's exhaust gases are broken up, and their pulsations smoothed out and cooled, while passing through the turbine under pressure, which contributes greatly to the arresting of a turbocharged engine's exhaust noise and odor. "T" engines usually tend to have a lighter exhaust.

The installation of a good exhaust system and silencer cannot be expected to solve all your engine's noise and aroma problems, but it can help considerably. Dale Skoog, a leading Detroit Diesel engineer, advises: "Learn to read your engine's exhaust signals: White smoke, blue smoke, black smoke, or no smoke—it all adds up to the fact that your engine is trying to tell you what is going on inside."

Air Intake Noise

Air intake noise is another engine-related noise that is often easy to reduce. On a naturally aspirated diesel it results from the pulsations caused in part by the opening and closing of the intake valves. Air cleaners with built-in silencing elements can effectively reduce this noise. Some intake silencers are constructed with an open-cell polyurethane cleaner pad that also acts as an air filter. But remember: Most air silencers are *not* constructed to filter inlet air. Shortages of intake air will also cause a smoky exhaust.

Fuel

A bad grade of fuel oil or an improper adjustment in your engine's fuel system are frequent sources of faulty combustion and heavy exhaust. Diesel fuels vary widely in quality depending on geographic area, suppliers, and climatic conditions. Using fuels other than those specified by your engine's manufacturer can only result in poor engine performance.

Try to use fuels containing less than 0.4 percent sulfur to help minimize the sulfur dioxide and its odor in your exhaust. Also remember to order a fuel that has a cetane number of at least forty to help provide good starting and reduce white smoke during engine warm-up periods.

Fuels with a cetane number of sixty or above tend to increase smoke density during full-speed operation.

Fuel Additives

Detroit Diesel and Cummins engineers say additives should only be put into the fuel by the fuel producers or a qualified chemical engineer.

Purging Air and Water

While returning from the Bahamas on his diesel sport-fisherman, a friend of mine noticed a steady drop in his engines' rpms, causing a loss of power and speed.

He started out from the islands with a cruising speed of twenty-one hundred rpm. But then the engines gradually dropped to nineteen hundred rpm, then to seventeen hundred rpm; they finally leveled out at fifteen hundred rpm and stayed at that speed for the remainder of the trip back to Miami.

The following day, his mechanic checked both diesel engines and found that the fuel he had purchased in the Bahamas was contaminated with dirt and water and had partly clogged his fuel filters. Fortunately, there was just enough fuel getting through to keep the engines going at a reduced speed and get him back across the Gulf Stream.

Needless to say, if he had had a pair of fuel/water separators in his fuel system, he could probably have corrected his trouble easily by draining the water and dirt from the separator's bowl.

An Attack of Asthma

When you have a loss in power or a decline in your engine's rpms, always check the easiest and most obvious things first. Did it sound like it had an attack of asthma before it started to lose power? Or did it have a sudden and complete shutdown?

The quickest way to find out if you have a clogged air filter is to pull the filter off and listen to the engine. If the rpms suddenly increase when you remove the filter, you've found your trouble. Then you can either replace it, clean it, or deep-six it and come home without one.

The next most obvious cause of power loss is a blocked fuel system. Most fuel problems fall into two categories: air being sucked into the fuel system, or dirt and water contamination.

As the causes and the remedies of these two problems usually overlap one another, I'll discuss them first in general, and then be more specific, outlining different procedures for various makes.

Air suction leaks usually can be fixed quickly by tightening all connections in the fuel lines—starting from the fuel tanks right up to the injectors. Check all gaskets on fuel strainers and filters. Most air bubbles will disappear once the suction leak is corrected, provided you have a strong enough battery or a hand priming pump on your engine. A lot of today's diesel engines are "self-bleeders," and the air will eventually travel back to the fuel tank via the fuel return line.

Water and other contaminants can also be eliminated in almost the same manner as air, except that it takes a lot longer, since all the strainers and filters have to be cleaned or replaced and the fuel pumps and injectors purged of the gook.

Bleeding or purging a fuel system is slightly different on each make of diesel, but a couple of general procedures apply to all of them. First, make sure there is sufficient fuel in the fuel tanks you are drawing from. A low fuel level may result in the fuel intake pipe being exposed and air being sucked into the fuel system. Next, make sure the fuel shutoff valve is wide open.

Then check to see that the fuel/water separators are clean. CAUTION: *As diesel engines have high-pressure fuel lines, always cover all bleed openings with a rag while purging. And always secure the hand priming pump before starting the engine.* Also, never tinker with your governor. It was set by the "pros," so leave it alone.

Now for some tips on purging individual engines:

Caterpillar

Caterpillar's 3208 fuel comes from the tank through a fuel/water separator to a filter mounted on the front of the engine. The hand-operated fuel priming pump located at the same position should be operated until the flow of fuel from the filter outlet is completely free of any air bubbles. From there, the fuel flows to a fuel shutoff solenoid, a high-pressure fuel pump, and a second bleed valve, all located together in the Cat's deep "V." From there the fuel travels to each of the injectors where (only if necessary) you can do the final purging by loosening each injector line nut a few turns and cranking the engine over for a few moments till the fuel oil flows clear of bubbles from the injector line.

Cummins

On Cummins' 555 and 902 series, after checking the fuel/water separators you crack the fuel line nut leading from the final fuel filter open a few turns, then crank the engine over several times until the fuel flows clear. Then tighten the nut and continue cranking the engine over for several minutes until the engine starts. The P.T. high-

pressure fuel pump will purge and correct itself through the return line to the fuel tanks. About 75 percent of the fuel that passes through the pump on its way to the injectors is returned to the tank. These Cummins engines have internal drilled fuel passages in the heads, and there is no way to purge air, etc., at the injectors.

Detroit Diesel

On Detroit's two-cycle engines, you open the air vent plug on the first filter after the transfer pump, then crank the engine over until the line is free of air bubbles. When it is, then tighten it. If necessary, open the fuel line nuts at each injector inlet one at a time, while cranking the engine over a few turns; then tighten each nut and go on to the next injector.

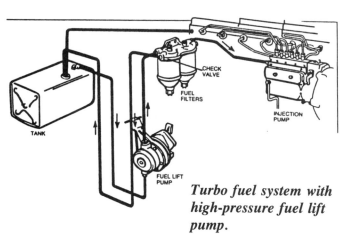

Turbo fuel system with high-pressure fuel lift pump.

Detroit's four-cycle 8.2 diesel has internal drilled fuel passages in the cylinder head. On this engine you should first check for any loose or faulty external connections to and from the junction box, the fuel pump, the fuel filters, and to each cylinder head. Some installations also include a fuel cooler, in which case check its connections, too.

I suggest you crack open the nut on the fuel pump discharge side, crank the engine until you get clear fuel, then tighten that connection. Repeat the same operation at the discharge side of the fuel filter and at each connection (if possible) till you reach the cylinder head's inlet and, finally, the fuel oil cooler.

Some 8.2 fuel systems include a primer pump. If yours does, this will help eliminate some of the engine cranking.

Lehman

First check the primary fuel/water separation bowl for cleanliness and tightness. Then loosen the bleed screw a few turns on top of the inlet side of the first fuel filter. Operate the priming lever located on the side of the fuel transfer pump until you get a clear flow of fuel coming out, free of any air bubbles and contamination. Then tighten the bleed screws and loosen the bleed screw on top of the filter's outlet side and repeat the operation.

Next, loosen the bleed screw nearest to the inlet side of the high-pressure pump and repeat the procedure. Then do the same on the second bleed screw on the outlet side of the pump. Continue pumping for a few more moments until you think you have purged all the air from the lines right up to the injectors and you feel a slight back pressure.

Perkins

On Perkins' TV8.540M, loosen the vent plug on top of the final filter a few turns and do the same on the bleed screws on top of the injection pump and at the rear of the injection pump. Then unscrew and operate the priming pump located at the fuel filter until the fuel flows free of any air bubbles, etc., at all three venting points; then tighten the plug and screws.

Next, screw back and secure the priming pump. Loosen the fuel line nuts at the injectors a few turns; then place the speed control in the fully open position and make sure the stop control is in the "Run" position. Now you can crank the engine over for a few moments until the fuel at the vents is free of bubbles. Finally, tighten all line nuts and purge pumps.

On Perkins' V8.540 NA diesel, the procedure differs in that the only vent plug is on the side and toward the front of the high-pressure injection pump. On Perkins' four-cylinder models, the bleed points generally are a hex plug on top of the final fuel filter and one on top of the fuel injection pump. There also is one on the side of the governor housing, plus the usual injector line nuts.

Volvo

On Volvo's popular D40s, you open the venting screw on top of the engine's fuel filter a few turns with a 10mm wrench; then, using the hand lever on the side of the fuel transfer pump, pump until clean fuel flows, then tighten the screw.

This should do the job. If it doesn't, crack open each injector's delivery line nut a few turns and crank the engine over until the fuel flows clear from each line. When it does, tighten each nut again and start the engine in the usual manner.

Learning to bleed air and to purge water contaminants from your engine's fuel system is almost a must for any boatowner with a diesel who ventures offshore. It's simple and rewarding (when you're successful), and someday it might just save your trip, or even your life.

Starters

"It won't turn over." How many times have you heard those words? Well, here are some tips to help keep you from saying them.

A quick and efficient engine start depends on several things, the foremost being enough starter power and rpm speed for your diesel to obtain ignition by its own "heat of compression" energy.

All starting motors are pretty much the same in design and operation. They differ mainly in the type of (Bendix) drive they use. Generally they come in six, twelve, or twenty-four volts, but you might run across a thirty-two volt job. (I once had a pair of them.)

Each diesel has its own starting characteristics and needs, determined by the engine's cubic-inch displacement, number of cylinders, required torque speed, and a few other factors. Because diesel engines have such a high compression ratio (eighteen to one), their cranking motors must be heavier and more powerful than gasoline-engine starters.

The cranking motors used on most of today's marine diesel engines usually are special overload-type motors capable of delivering a high horsepower output for a short period. Direct (d.c.) current is used because d.c. electrical energy can be conveniently stored in batteries and then tapped whenever it is needed. This energy can then quickly be restored by recharging the batteries with the diesel's alternator. The only components needed on an electrical system like this are the starter, batteries, alternator, and a few protective and control switches.

Most diesel engines will start at a cranking speed of about 250 to three hundred rpm. However, under adverse conditions like freezing temperatures or infrequent use, a diesel will defy all your efforts to start it. Then you need a starter and a set of batteries with a large amperage capacity and possibly a higher voltage.

Many starter problems result from improper practices, such as holding down the starter switch for a few seconds after the diesel has turned on. This invites an overspeeding condition in the starting motor that can result in damage to the pinion, clutch, and armature windings.

High electrical current can create considerable heat, and if your starter operation is continued for more than ten or fifteen seconds at a time, the accumulated heat will cause serious damage to the starter windings, so never crank your diesel over for more than a few seconds. Then pause for several moments to permit the windings to cool down again.

Most marine starting motors are designed to be maintenance-free for long periods of time. However, an eyeball check every so often to make sure there are no loose or corroded cable connections is a good habit.

Maintenance Tips

If the starter will not crank your diesel, first check your batteries' specific gravity and voltage and then make sure you have clean and tight cable connections, including the ground connection.

Check the engine starting switch on the instrument panel and, if necessary, bypass it with a jumper wire.

If you have a draw meter, use it on the cable as close to the starter as you can. It will help tell you if your diesel is locked up.

You can check your starter by removing its cover band and examining it for worn brushes or thrown solder. The latter can result from overheating caused by excessively long periods of cranking.

Most starters are easy to remove and check on a workbench. The brushes must be examined for wear. Be sure the brush screws, connections, and leads are tight and that the brush spring tensions are sufficient. Brushes should have free movement to seat on and follow the commutator. If these parts are worn or rusted, they should be replaced.

Next, take a good look at the copper commutator for any burned spots or bars. These may indicate an open-circuited armature coil, which would prevent proper cranking. If the commutator is just dirty, it can be cleaned with fine #00 sandpaper or a brush-seating stone while you crank it over on the bench with a spare battery. Then clean the whole area with a few shots of white carbon tetrachloride and a low-pressure air gun.

If the commutator is worn, rough, or has a high mica, the armature should be removed and the commutator turned down in a lathe.

While the starter is disassembled, check for worn bearings, a bent shaft, or loose pole shoe screws, which might cause the armature to drag or lock up.

When reassembling, make sure your cover band's gasket is in good condition and in place for protection against any sparking into the engine compartment.

Solenoids

The so-called piggy-back solenoid switch on a marine starting motor does two things: It engages the starter pinion (or Bendix, as it is most commonly called) with the ring gear on your engine's flywheel. It then activates an electric switch to energize the motor, which starts the engine rolling. Solenoids normally are energized directly from the battery through a push-button switch, or in conjunction with a solenoid relay.

Switches or solenoid plungers that tend to stick or bind after repeated use or through corrosion can cause total starting motor failure and should be cleaned or replaced. Starter parts do wear and burn out, and deciding whether to repair or replace them is often a problem.

Replacing or repairing parts can result in unnecessary cost and downtime. If the starter is an old one and you are in a hurry, I suggest that you check the cost of a rebuilt one with your marine engine dealer—it may pay you in the long run.

Preparing a Diesel for Cold Weather Operation

Basically, the problem of starting and operating a diesel during freezing weather stems from the very nature of the beast—it's a heat engine, and cold presents problems for heat engines. Low cranking speeds mean less compression pressure, and less compression pressure means less heat being generated on the compression stroke to help ignite the fuel being injected into the combustion chamber.

Detroit Diesel states that during winter operation, particular attention must be given to your diesel's electrical, cooling, lubricating, and fuel systems. Your battery must be of heavy-duty marine quality and be fully charged at all times.

If your cranking speed drops below 125 rpm, starting will become almost impossible. In cases like these, a booster or helper battery will be required.

Generators, alternators, and the entire battery, wiring, and charging system should be in top condition. Check your starting motor for broken or frayed insulation or wires, and replace if necessary. Also check all battery cables and connections to make sure they are of the right size, and are tight, clean, and properly routed.

Use your starter in short bursts (twenty seconds), because constant grinding in cold weather can overheat the starting motor and kill the battery. Always allow the starter to cool a few minutes before attempting to use it again.

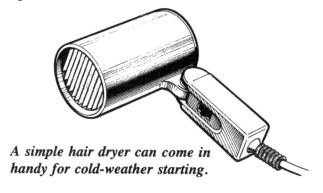

A simple hair dryer can come in handy for cold-weather starting.

Glow Plugs

If your diesel comes equipped with glow plugs, make sure to test all the plugs to see that they are working properly, and, if necessary, replace any faulty ones. If your diesel doesn't come equipped with glow plugs and you are going to be using your boat quite a lot this winter, I suggest you look into installing an ether starting aid system to assist in starting your diesel on those extremely cold days. Ether, if properly used, makes cold weather starting a much more tolerable chore. CAUTION: *Because of its volatile nature, misusing or using too much ether can result in serious damage to your diesel.*

Generally speaking, an engine preheater is safer and usually preferred over the ether starting system. It will also help in eliminating unburned fuel oil from washing down your engine's cylinder walls, will help shorten engine cranking time, and will help your engine's battery and starting systems last longer.

If you have shore current and the time, heat up the entire engine room compartment with an electric heater, or use your wife's hair dryer. Locate it near your engine's air intake while you are cranking your diesel over. But make sure you remove the paper or poly air filter first.

Cooling

Check both cooling systems. Your closed coolant system should have plenty of antifreeze in it. On the raw water system, make sure there isn't any ice to choke or clog intake strainers. Then watch these strainers during operation.

A good precaution to take when you shut down after a run is to close the raw water intake valve or seacock, and, if possible, drain as much of the sea water out as you can, especially in the circulating pump. But remember to reverse this procedure before you start up.

Perkins engineers say, "Sometimes a small amount of water remains lodged in the bottom of the water pump after draining. If this freezes, it could prevent the impeller from turning the next time the diesel is used. If the water pump cannot be turned by hand, the cooling system should be filled with lukewarm water before starting."

Lube Oil

During low temperatures, engine lube oil thickens and tends to drag moving engine parts, resulting in greater engine wear, so check your manual as to the correct winter oil to use in your engine.

If you have a turbo diesel, I strongly advise that you prelubricate its bearings with a few drops of lube oil before attempting to start your engine in extremely cold weather.

Fuel Oil

When the temperature hovers near or below freezing, water and wax can cause fuel problems, such as hard starting, uneven engine operation, stalling, and loss of power. Since water in diesel fuel is disastrous, especially in freezing weather, care must be taken during winter operation to see that your fuel is properly filtered through a fuel/water separator. Otherwise water droplets will freeze in fuel lines, pumps, and injectors.

Racor makes a fuel heater element for their filter separators. This solid-state heating element can be fitted into the base of their fuel/water separators.

Small amounts of isopropyl alcohol (one pint to 125 gallons of fuel) also can be used to preclude fuel line freeze-ups.

If obtainable, use #1 fuel oil or a mixture of #1 and #2 fuel for better starting and winter operation.

Winterizing Your Diesel's Electrical System

The cold, damp air of winter will quickly prey upon the slightest weakness in a boat's electrical system. Although a diesel engine's electrical parts usually do not require a lot of special winterizing, it is best to check and correct any weak links in the system before cold weather sets in. Here are a few tips that may save you some aggravation this winter.

One of the most important considerations for boatowners who operate in low ambient temperatures is the ability to crank their diesels fast enough to start them. You need a cranking speed of at least two hundred rpm even to begin building up enough cylinder compression and heat to achieve ignition. If you drop below the hundred-rpm mark forget it, because regardless of how many "starting aids" you use, the task will be impossible. However, once your diesel is started and warmed up, external ambient temperatures will have little effect on its operation.

Starters

The electrical starter on your engine is only one member of the electrical team. The other members—battery, cables, terminals, switches, and alternators—all play an equal part. To minimize starting problems, remove the starter's band and inspect the wiring for broken or frayed insulation; also check the commutator and brushes for wear. Replace the brushes if they are worn down halfway or more, then clean the commutator until it shines brightly.

Remove the cable connections from your battery and

starter and wire-brush any corrosive buildup from their ends. Then look the cables over for any cracks in the insulation. If cracks are found, reinsulate the whole cabin with weather-resistant plastic tape, making sure both the cables and the connections are the right size, properly supported, and have the shortest routing to lessen current-flow loss and resistance; then coat terminals with grease and tighten the connections.

Starter switches and solenoid plungers should be checked, cleaned, and tested, and if found to be faulty or sticking, they should be replaced. Then give them all a quick shot of WD40, CRC, or similar moisture-displacing lubricant.

Batteries

If possible use a twenty-four-volt or a twelve-volt high-output battery system to start your diesel, and also install slave jumper terminals at the battery to provide for extra amperage power if you find they're necessary. Remember: Batteries connected in parallel increase amperage; connected in series, they increase voltage.

If you're operating in extremely cold weather, better use blanket-type heaters to insulate and keep your batteries warm and up to par. The use of a starting aid such as ether will help keep your batteries fully charged by reducing the cranking time needed to start the engine. However, *exercise caution when using ether.*

Good housekeeping is critical. Keep your batteries free of any acid, corrosion, or dirt that might cause current leakage. Maintain correct electrolyte level, specific gravity, and voltage. Also periodically check your trickle charger if you have one to see if it is working correctly.

The higher the specific gravity, the less likely it is that your battery will freeze. You can gauge its condition by taking readings with a hydrometer: 1.260 to 1.280 indicates a full charge; 1.200 to 1.220 means it needs recharging; 1.160 or less means you need a new battery.

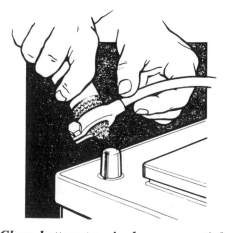

Clean battery terminals are essential.

An inexpensive, portable, hand-held voltmeter with easy-to-control probes is another handy diagnostic tool. A fully charged twelve-volt battery should read thirteen volts, or a hair over two volts per cell.

Remember, at $+15°F$ a fully charged battery is only 50 percent effective; at $-20°F$, only 30 percent effective.

Your Alternator

Any difficulty in turning the shaft or pulley by hand might indicate bad bearings or an accumulation of dirt in the air gap between the rotor and the starter. Check for loose mounting bolts and nuts and also examine the terminal nuts—they must be clean and tight or they may cause overheating and loss of current flow.

If necessary have the diodes tested, and buy new ones if defective. Replace brushes that are worn down to less than half their original length. Also check belts for correct tension, using a tension gauge. Any glazed or worn belts that might slip or squeal on sudden acceleration should be replaced. If you have any other alternator trouble I suggest you have a pro do the work, as he has the requisite knowledge and meters. Regulators can be tricky, and they are easily damaged.

Other Hints

Use the lube oil recommended by your engine manufacturer for the prevailing temperatures in your operating area. If possible install lube oil, coolant, and fuel oil heater in their respective systems.

An electric hair dryer sometimes comes in handy as a starting aid, but be sure you remove the paper or poly foam from the intake air filter first. And make sure you use an antifreeze liquid in your closed cooling systems.

Safe Starting with Ether

Many boatowners find that an aerosol can of ether is handy to have on board when problems arise with starting a diesel engine in cold weather. While it is often a big help, ether must be used very carefully to avoid fire or a dangerous explosion when spraying it directly into the air intake on the engine.

One way to minimize the threat is *not* to spray the ether directly into the intake. Instead, spray the starting liquid onto a loose wad of paper towels or onto a crumpled rag. Then hold this rag or towel slightly above the air intake and about six inches away from it before starting to turn over the engine. If done correctly the ether fumes will be drawn from the rag (ether is very volatile) along with air into the intake. It will therefore be less concentrated and more evenly dispersed and thus less likely to cause an explosion that could seriously damage the engine, or cause injury to anyone on board. CAUTION: Make sure you hold the rag or paper towel firmly with no loose ends sticking out. You don't want the rag or paper towel to get drawn into the engine with the fume-filled air. Foreign matter drawn in could cause real damage.

Easy Impeller Installation

Changing the rubber impellers in the raw water pumps on my diesel engines has always been a real hassle. You have to hold the impeller blades partially folded along one side to fit the impeller inside its housing, while at the same time trying to push the impeller onto the shaft—all the while trying to make certain the impellers are folded over in the proper direction so you don't accidentally damage the fins or blades as you push them in.

After about twenty years of swearing, sweating, and scraping knuckles on this task, my wife, Judy, discovered an easy way to speed up and simplify this job. All we do now is stretch a short length of shock cord around the forward end of the impeller (the end that goes into the housing first) to keep the fins or blades partially folded over as shown. Care must be taken to make certain all the fins are bent in the same direction.

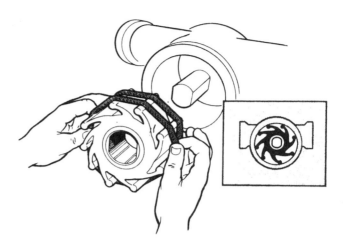

A second piece of shock cord is tied around the aft end of the impeller; then the whole thing is coated with liquid Ivory soap. All we have to do then is line it up properly on the shaft and push it in. As it slides forward into the housing you roll the forward shock cord aft out of the way, then keep shoving until all the fins are in and the shock cords have rolled off on the aft end. Using this method I installed the last water pump impeller in less than two minutes.

5 TIPS FOR TROUBLE-FREE CRUISING

A Guide to Hassle-Free Cruising

Most boatowners set off on a cruise with the highest of expectations—they look forward to a relaxing, pleasant time out on the water, even if it's only a few days. All too often, however, aggravation is the end result, simply because the boat was not properly prepared or because there was needless tension between skipper and crew. Yet this unpleasantness could have been avoided with some commonsense planning and a thorough discussion of the chores and duties each crew member is expected to handle.

Since equipment breakdown can quickly dampen spirits on any cruise, it makes sense to do what you can to avoid it. Obviously, no amount of preparation can guarantee that everything will function perfectly. But there are some simple precautions boatowners can take to keep problems from developing and to help resolve any difficulties that do crop up. Here is a checklist that describes some of them:

● Even if you did it in the spring, check all belts in the engine room before you leave. Replace any that look the least bit doubtful. In addition, make sure you have a spare on hand for each belt before you leave. Otherwise it can mean a delay of hours—or even days—if you can't find a replacement when you need one. The same goes for hoses in the engine's cooling system: Replace any that look doubtful before you leave, and make sure you have spares with you, just in case.

● One thing that can put a damper on any vacation cruise is a head that doesn't work. If the flapper valve or joker valve in your toilet hasn't been replaced during the

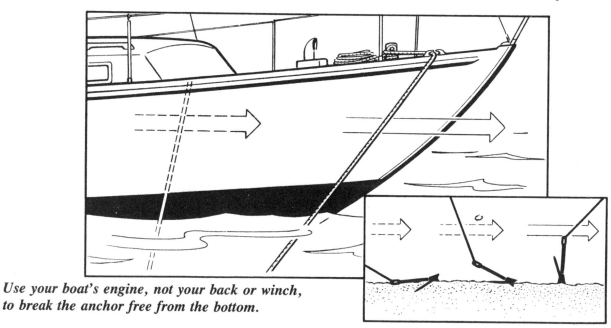

Use your boat's engine, not your back or winch, to break the anchor free from the bottom.

past year, do it now. Also, make sure you have a repair kit on hand that contains the parts most likely to wear out.

● The same goes for the water pump in your fresh water system, too. If it is more than two or three years old, overhaul it with one of the repair kits you can order from the manufacturer. If you feel this isn't necessary, at least make sure you have the repair kit on board before you cast off.

● As added insurance against possible engine problems due to bad fuel you may pick up along the way, make sure you also have spare fuel filters on board. If you haven't replaced the filters this season, put new ones in now.

● Fill your water tank at least half full before you leave. In that way you will have plenty of water in case you decide to anchor out or have to tie up at a dock where water is not readily available, or if you have doubts about the quality of the water at a particular dock.

● Buy all the charts you think you will need before you leave, or order them ahead of time if necessary. If you wait to buy them locally you may find that local marinas are out of the charts that cover their own area (they sell out of these first every summer).

● If your compass has not been compensated or checked for accuracy in the past few years, or if you have made changes on your boat that could affect the compass, have it checked for deviation before you leave. In that way you will know you can depend on it.

● Put enough quarts of extra engine oil on board to last for the whole cruise. You can buy oil as you go along, but sometimes you won't be able to get the same type or brand you have been using—and most experts agree that sticking with the same brand of oil is always best.

● If your boat is fiberglass, give the superstructure a good cleaning before you leave, then finish with a coat of liquid wax, or use a cleaner/wax. This will help seal the gel coat so it will be easier to hose salt and dirt off at the end of each day's run.

● Test each piece of navigational gear at least one week before you leave to allow time for repairs in case they are needed. For example, try out your radar, Loran, radio or radios, direction finder, searchlight, etc. Also, turn on all the navigational lights to see if new bulbs are needed, or if the lenses are dirty or cracked.

● To avoid accidents caused by slipping on a wet deck, apply self-adhesive, nonskid strips to toerails, coamings, and other potentially slippery places where you or your crew are likely to step in a hurry when docking or casting off. While you're at it, think about installing additional handholds where experience has shown they may be needed.

Perfecting Your Techniques

In addition to making sure the boat is properly prepared

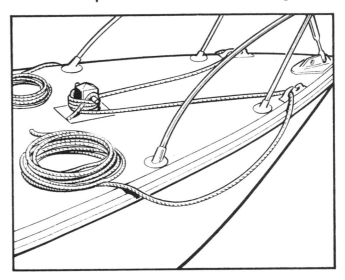

Bowlines should be made ready by securing and coiling them in the proper position before approaching a dock.

for your vacation cruise, it is equally important that you and your crew organize your docking and boat-handling procedures to minimize confusion—particularly on rough days or when things aren't going smoothly.

For example, when approaching the dock at a strange marina, make sure the necessary lines are coiled and ready to throw *well before* you get close to the dock. This will not only eliminate a lot of last-minute rushing around and order-shouting, it will also prevent countless arguments (probably the most frequent cause of friction between boating couples).

One trick that my wife, Olga, and I have learned during our years of cruising is to have lines rigged on each side of the boat as we approach a dock or marina. Before we are close enough to start docking maneuvers, Olga always secures one line to each side of the transom or stern, as well as one on each side of the bow. These lines are secured to the appropriate cleat or bit, then led out through the chock and pulled back inboard so they can either be draped over the rail, where they will be easily accessible, or coiled neatly on deck.

Having four lines at the ready in this manner means that, as I approach the dock, Olga can stand near the bow or stern (depending on whether we are going in stern or bow first) with a spring line in hand, ready to throw to someone on the dock. She never actually throws that line until I tell her I'm ready for it. In that way we avoid having someone on the dock yanking on the line before I want them to, and I can specify exactly where I want the line to go. Once the spring line is ashore, the bowlines and stern lines can quickly be picked up or handed ashore without a lot of frantic running around and looking for extra lines—and without having to move lines from one side to the other.

Another good habit is planning each day's run the night before, rather than waiting till the morning when you are ready to cast off. Get out the charts you will need and plot all your courses and distances so you will have a clear idea of how many hours each leg of the trip will take. In that way you can calmly discuss any changes either of you would like to make. Note alternate harbors you can use if problems develop along the way or if the weather turns unexpectedly nasty, and then plot a course to each of them, too.

During the day's run, your charts—with the plotted courses clearly marked on them—should always be near the helm where the skipper can refer to them at frequent intervals to check out navigation markers and landmarks as well as to update his position periodically.

Since charts tend to blow around and are hard to handle when piloting a boat from an open cockpit or exposed flying bridge, some type of transparent case or holder is an absolute necessity. You can buy clear plastic envelopes or similar chartholders, but years ago I made my own chartholder out of two sheets of clear acrylic plastic (Plexiglas or Lucite), and this homemade chart case still is the most useful one I've seen.

It is rigid, so the charts are always flat and easy to read, and it can hold two of them, one on each side facing outward. I sometimes put the large chart and the more detailed harbor chart back to back; then I can simply flip the case over to go from one to the other. I made my case eighteen by twenty-four inches and have found this is about right for most charts when you fold them to expose

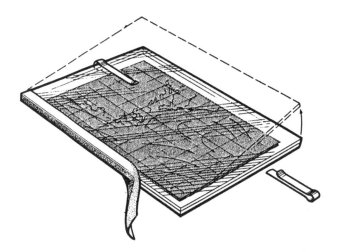

This double-sided, clear plastic chartholder is easy to make and keeps charts from blowing around.

only the area you are interested in for that day's cruising. The size, of course, can be varied. The rigid, clear plastic also allows me to make notes or course marks right on it with a marking pencil. These marks won't wash off if it rains, yet they can be easily wiped off with a dry cloth when you no longer need them.

I hinged the two sheets together with a wide strip of heavy-duty duct tape applied along one of the long edges. To hold the case closed with the charts on the inside I use two stainless steel chart clips (also called blueprint clips) similar to the ones shown above. These are sold in many art and stationery supply stores.

Raising the Hook

Another unpleasant hassle that can be avoided with proper planning is figuring out how to haul up the anchor. Many people try to use too much of their own muscle for the job, or expect too much from their anchor winch. The smart skipper remembers that the boat has a powerful engine that can do most of the work for him. Here is the system we have worked out to save our backs and eliminate short tempers.

After starting the engines, I tend the anchor and line while my wife takes over the helm. From my position at the bow I direct her (with hand signals) when to go ahead, when to turn to port or starboard, and when to shift into neutral or reverse.

First I signal for slow ahead while I point toward the anchor. Then we maintain just enough headway to come up over the anchor while I keep pulling in the slack line and dropping it on deck. When the anchor line is straight up and down, she stops headway while I temporarily secure the line by taking one or two wraps around the bow cleat. Then I again signal for slow ahead and allow the boat's engines to pull the line forward until it breaks the anchor free. She shifts into neutral and I wait for the boat to lose most of its headway (at the same time our forward movement is washing most of the mud off the anchor and chain). Then I take that line off the cleat and finish hauling the anchor up onto the deck.

Here are some other useful cruising pointers we have learned over the years:

● Carry one or two gallons of bottled water on board in case you don't like the taste of the water you pick up along the way (always taste the water in a strange marina before you fill your tank with it).

● Make sure your foul-weather gear is stored where it will be easily accessible.

● If possible, prepare sandwiches, snacks, and hot drinks before you cast off so there will be no need for someone to work in the galley while you are under way.

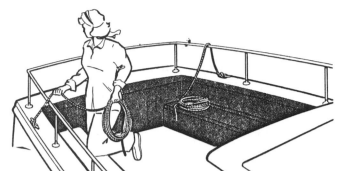

Be prepared with lines on both port and starboard sides.

Too many accidents can happen, even on a calm day, if an unexpected nasty wake rocks the boat while one of you is preparing something in the galley.

● Make sure your spouse knows how to run the boat—just in case the skipper has an accident or is temporarily disabled. She doesn't have to know the fine points of docking and navigation, but she should know how to get the boat into a harbor if necessary and how to operate the radio. The resulting peace of mind will help to relieve the tension if a sudden emergency should develop.

● When you need fuel for the next day's run, try to fill up on the way into the marina, rather than waiting until the next morning when you are ready to leave. Many marinas require that you stop at the gas dock to register anyway, so this will eliminate the need for an extra delay when you are ready to take off. While fueling up you can check the engine room for any minor problems that may need attention. In that way you can make sure they are taken care of well before you are ready to leave the following day.

More Cruising Tips

My wife and I have been cruising and living aboard for the past eleven years and we have found that there are a number of things that can be done when it comes to docking and tying up to make life a little easier for the cruising couple. Here are a few suggestions:

1. Like most boats, we carry docking lines in various lengths to meet various needs. The only trouble we found was that as I was docking the boat my mate would sometimes be frantically sorting through these lines trying to figure out which one was the length we needed at that moment. We have solved that problem once and for all by color-coding all our docking lines. Pieces of colored tape are wrapped around the splice on each line, and a piece of

the same color tape is wrapped around the other end to make quick identification even easier. You can work out your own color scheme, but we use red for our thirty-five-foot lines, green for the thirty-foot lines, and black for the short twenty-five foot lines. Now, whenever we need a line of a certain length, we just reach for the appropriate color.

2. When cruising you will often find that the eye in the end of your line is just not large enough to go over some of the pilings you encounter when docking, especially when the pilings are doubled or have utility pipes running alongside them. To solve this problem we made up all our docking lines with an eye splice in the end that is at least twenty-four inches in diameter. This not only handles most of the pilings normally encountered, it also makes "lassoing" pilings easier when you are backing in and have to connect on your first try.

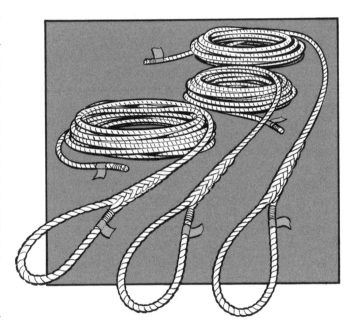

3. Trying to adjust lines to allow for tide changes in the middle of a rainy night or when gusty winds are blowing you off the dock can be a nasty business if you have to get off the boat to make the necessary adjustments. This happens when the free end of each line is neatly secured to a cleat, bollard, or piling on the dock while the eye of the line is secured to the boat. To avoid this kind of problem and to make sure you can always adjust lines *from on the boat* instead of from the dock, remember that old seaman's adage, "You always tie the boat to the dock, *never* tie the dock to the boat." In other words, make sure the free end of each line is secured to a cleat on board the vessel, not to something on the dock.

Anchor Chain Markers

There is a simple and inexpensive way to mark anchor chains which we have found is also surprisingly durable and a lot longer-lasting than most commercially available plastic markers. Use acrylic yarn as a marker (synthetic fibers are much more resistant to rotting and discoloring than natural fibers are). Cut off a thirty-inch length of yarn and bring the ends together to double it. Now fold this doubled length in half again, in effect creating four strands, each 7½ inches long. Feed one end of this "bundle" through a link of the chain where you want the

mark to be, then bring the ends together and tie them around the link with a square knot.

Don't trim the ends—leave them as is. Bright colors work best, different colors to mark different footages. You can also fix these markers on regular three-strand nylon rope. Just feed the "bundle" between the strands before tying the square knot.

We are cruising liveaboards who use our anchor almost every day and have been surprised at how long these markers last—easily two to three times longer than the paint we had been using previously. When the yarn does break, it goes one strand at a time, so there's plenty of warning when it's time to replace it.

To save the job of remeasuring—in the unlikely event that all strands go before you do replace the marker—it helps to twist a small piece of stainless steel wire tightly around the link where each marker is tied. This wire does not show up well as a marker, but it does save measuring again when the yarn is gone.

Take the Dents Out of Rafting Up

One thing most of its enthusiasts agree on is that much of the pleasure of boating comes from the social activities we all get involved in—like getting together with friends out on the water by rafting up on a lazy summer afternoon to go swimming, to paddle around in dinghies while the kids play together, and maybe even to swap stories over lunch and a cool drink.

Regardless of whether it is only for a few hours or for a long holiday weekend, owners of powerboats and sailboats alike often enjoy cruising to a favorite mooring area where one boat will anchor so that others can raft up alongside. Although this should be—and normally is—a pleasant experience that everyone enjoys, raft-ups can sometimes result in shortened tempers, lost friendships, scratched topsides, dented railings, fouled lines, and even painfully mashed fingers or other injuries.

This sort of unpleasantness is unnecessary and easily avoided, however, if everyone involved simply follows a few commonsense rules. It helps even more if all participants remember to observe traditional rules of nautical courtesy when one boat approaches, and then ties up with, another.

One of the first rules of courtesy is never to invite yourself into a raft-up. When you enter a harbor or mooring area and find a friend (or group of friends) already anchored there, don't assume that you should go ahead and tie up with them—unless they specifically invite you to do so or unless the raft-up was planned ahead of time. Instead, you can approach the other boat while moving *very slowly* and wave a friendly hello. Then wait and see if they invite you to tie up alongside before you make any preparations to do so.

Once the decision has been made to raft up with another boat (or group of boats), traditional etiquette demands that the newly arrived boat supply the necessary fenders and lines needed to tie up properly, so have everything ready before you make your final approach. Of course, since most rafting involves dealing with people you are friendly with, they are likely to hang out additional fenders and even supply some of the lines needed for tying up, but don't count on it. Always be prepared with your own.

You will need at least three fenders on the side you will be tying up on: one near the stern, one approximately amidships at the widest part of your boat, and one near where you estimate the widest part of the other boat will be when you are alongside. Try to estimate the height for each fender, as well as its location; but in most cases you

Once you've been invited to join a raft (never invite yourself), be sure your fenders are out at the proper height and your bowlines and stern lines are ready to throw before making your approach.

will have to make height adjustments after you have tied up.

After fenders are rigged, the crew should stand on or near the bow of the boat with a line coiled and ready to throw to someone standing on the bow of the host boat. Another line should be rigged near the stern, with a second crew member standing by that one. (If you have no second crew member, have the line rigged anyway so that after the bowline is passed to the other boat, one of you can get the stern line across without wasting time.) Unless there are physical problems that prevent your crew from doing it, have them pass the eye end to the other boat so the crew on your boat can make the necessary adjustments and can secure the line when you give the command.

Approach the other boat from behind and off to one side while coming in at about a thirty- to forty-degree angle to the anchored boat. Approach as slowly as possible, shifting in and out of gear if necessary to maintain just enough headway to make steering possible. Head into the wind or current if practical, giving preference to whichever of the two seems to be having a greater effect on how the boats lie at anchor. If in doubt, or if the wind or the current seems particularly strong, don't hesitate to come to a complete stop for a couple of minutes while still a safe distance away. Then study the way the wind or current—or both—are affecting both boats before you move closer.

If the other boat seems to be swinging quite a bit, try to approach it while it is swinging away from you. Or time your approach to reach the other boat just before it reaches

the far end of its swing. You don't want the boat swinging into you before you are tied up—too much chance of bending handrails or creating dings in the rubrail. If an

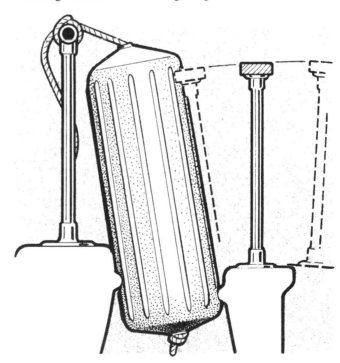

Handrails should be protected by fenders, as shown, in case the boats begin to rock when rafted together.

unexpected wake or roll makes it necessary to fend off suddenly, don't allow crew members to reach out with a leg or foot to push the other boat off. A bent rubrail or handrail is a lot easier to fix than a broken bone. And remember that the slower you are going at the time, the less chance of damaging your boat or the other person's.

By the time your bowline is passed over to the other vessel there should be no headway left on your boat. Depending on wind and current, you may find it necessary to give just a tiny amount of reverse gear to stop all forward motion and to help kick the stern closer to the other boat. When your crew ties the bowline down, make sure they do not pull the line tight at this point. It should allow for plenty of slack between boats until after the stern line is secured. If there is another crew member on board to handle the stern line, then the one handling the bowline should stand by it until after the stern line is secured. Otherwise the same person will have to move quickly aft to pass the stern line across.

The stern line should be pulled in tight enough to bring the stern of your boat up against the stern of the other one (with a fender between) before making it fast. After the stern line is tight you can take the excess slack out of the bowline, but only enough to bring the two boats approximately parallel to each other. Then move fenders as necessary to keep the widest part of each vessel from coming in contact with the other one.

Often you will find that after the boats are secured, their handrails or bridge rails will be only a few inches apart. This is no problem as long as the water is relatively calm, but if a careless skipper goes by and throws up a wake, or if the wind suddenly comes up, then the boats could rock and bring the railings in sharp contact with each other. To prevent this, always hang additional fenders between railings or other parts that are so close that they could bang into each other or cause damage if and when the boats do give an unexpected roll.

Since rafting boats are seldom the same size and shape, the general rule with powerboats is to bring the sterns in line and pull them reasonably tight, then let the bows swing out slightly as necessary. This not only makes for a more comfortable raft, it also makes it easier for people to climb back and forth between boats, or to pass over one on the way to another—which is really the essence of rafting up.

With sailboats there is an additional problem to contend with: the rigging. It is not always practical to bring the sterns in line with each other, or even to try to bring them close to each other, because doing so may result in spreaders, shrouds, or stays banging against each other or interlocking when the boats rock (as often happens when sitting in a raft-up). To prevent this, make certain that sailboats are tied so the rigging from one boat cannot get

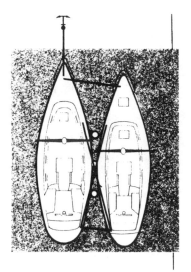

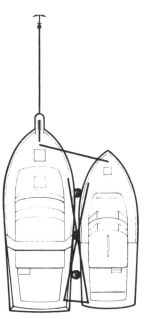

In addition to bowlines and stern lines, it's also a good idea to set crossed spring lines fore and aft.

tangled up with the rigging of the boat next to it, even if this means moving one slightly fore or aft of the other. This also applies to sportfishing boats with outriggers.

After bow and stern lines have been secured and fenders repositioned (if necessary), it is important to rig spring lines between boats as shown in the drawing. These are necessary to keep one vessel from riding backward or forward in relation to the other, a condition that could cause fenders to shift and allow parts of one boat to scrape or bang up against parts of the next boat.

Although some people claim that a single spring line, from the stern of the host boat to the forward quarter of the guest boat, is adequate, years of rafting up have taught me that two crisscrossed spring lines are a lot safer, as shown in the drawing. It's surprising how just a minor shift in position can upset the arrangement of fenders and lines you have tied and allow one boat to damage another. The extra protection of the additional line is well worth the effort.

Secure one spring line by going from the stern of the larger boat to the forward quarter of the smaller boat. Draw this up to bring the sterns into line (or to position the boats where you want them relative to each other), then secure the second spring line from the stern of the smaller boat to the forward quarter of the larger boat.

When planning a group raft-up where several boats of different sizes will be involved, it is generally best to have the largest or heaviest one put its anchor down first (it probably will have the largest anchor anyway). Wait till that anchor is firmly set with plenty of scope out, then have the other boats raft up one at a time on alternate sides so the boat with anchor down always remains in approximately the center of the raft.

In calm waters, with only a minimum amount of wind, it is not unusual to see as many as ten or twelve boats in one huge raft-up. However, unless it is very calm it's safer to limit the raft to no more than about five or six (no more than four if there is a wind blowing). If you have more than five or six vessels rafted, it is a good idea to have at least one additional anchor put down by another boat, preferably near the end of the raft. The best way is to have one of the boats drop an anchor forward of the raft before tying up, then pay out enough line to permit backing down to where it can tie up to the end boat.

However, in most cases things don't work out this way—the raft just grows like Topsy until someone finally says, ''Shouldn't we put out another anchor?''

The solution then is *not* just to drop another anchor off the bow of one of the boats in the raft (which I've seen happen). The extra anchor should be carried well forward of all the boats in a dinghy, or floated out by using several cushions or life preservers. Then the anchor is dropped so the rode can be pulled tight to get the anchor set properly. Make sure your second anchor has about the same scope as the first one does, or you will wind up with one anchor

taking all the strain. For day anchoring, both should have put out enough line to equal at least five or six times the water depth at its deepest.

As mentioned above, a sensible rule is to allow no more than four or five boats in any one raft-up, even on a relatively calm day. When a larger raft develops, however, it should promptly be broken up into smaller groups if it starts to get windy, or if there is much rocking due to wave action or wakes. Under no circumstances should there be more than two boats in a raft when staying at anchor overnight (having each on his own anchor is even better).

And finally, never leave the boats unattended while everyone goes ashore to have dinner or for some other land activity where the boats cannot be seen. Always make it a rule to leave someone on board to keep watch when several boats are rafted together—just in case an anchor should break loose or excessive rocking should cause problems.

Single-Handed Docking

We are senior citizens who don't like reaching across a wide gap from dock to boat when untying, or having to

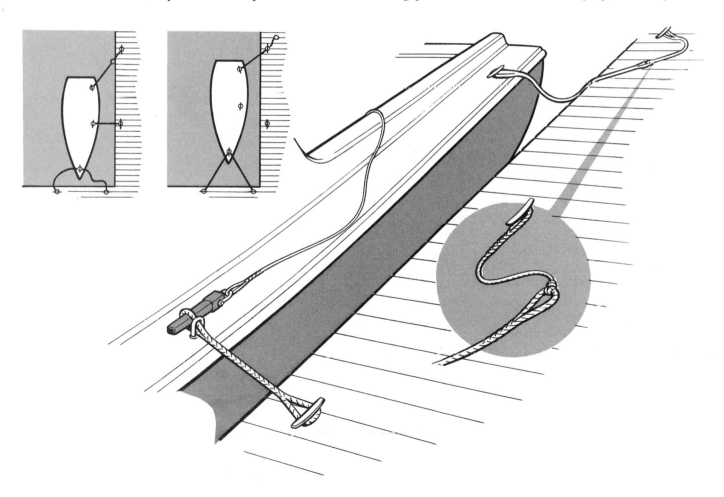

jump across open water when docking or undocking. There are also times when I like to go out alone. Being able to do all this easily is important to our boating enjoyment. Our small cruiser is tied to the dock with two bowlines and a stern line. These secure nicely and allow it to ride easily, but there is always some distance between it and the dock. Here is the system we use to solve these problems:

The regular stern line is fitted with an extension link that has a second eye splice at the dock end. This extension is long enough to allow the boat to move forward an extra eighteen inches when the extension eye is on the dock cleat instead of the original eye splice. To set up the docking system, hook this extension eye over the dock cleat where the stern line normally goes and pull the boat forward the extra eighteen inches; then mark a point on the dock that lies exactly opposite a midship pad eye installed on the boat (if there is no midship pad eye on deck you will have to install one). At that point on the dock mount another cleat directly opposite this pad eye.

Now make up a short docking line with an eye splice at one end. This eye should be small enough to fit through the pad eye on the boat. The line itself should be just long enough so that when secured to the boat and the dock (while the stern line extension is used and the boat is in its forward position) the boat will be held close against the dock for easy boarding or debarking. To secure the other end of the line to the new dock cleat you can make either another eye splice or a knot. On the boat the line is secured to the pad eye by means of a wood pin that is passed through the eye after it comes through the pad eye, as shown in the drawing. The wooden pin is attached to a light line leading to the cockpit.

Here is how the system works: When leaving the dock I first remove the bowlines and take the stern line's eye off the dock cleat so I can extend that line with its extension link (slip the extension eye onto the dock cleat). I then pull the boat forward and engage the short midship line with the wooden pin in place on the boat. The free end of the stern line is left on the dock, where it can be easily reached when we return. Now I can cast off by simply pulling the wood pin free from the cockpit.

Landing back at the dock is just as easy. As I come slowly alongside the dock I pick up the free end of the stern line and drop it on the stern cleat. The extension link stops the boat just before the bow can hit the dock, and it also swings the boat in close to the dock so that the bow cleats can be easily reached. Then I can reach over and hook up the short midship line if I want to hold the boat close to the dock.

Anchor Shackle Safety Tie

For years the method used by prudent mariners to make certain that the threaded pin on the anchor shackle would not loosen accidentally was to secure or "safetie" the pin with a short length of copper or galvanized wire. The wire is passed through the hole in the shackle pin's head, then wrapped around the body of the shackle itself. It is then crimped or twisted a few times to keep it from unwinding. Although this wire does do the job expected of it, in time the metal corrodes or turns brittle, or it gets attacked by galvanic corrosion. In addition, when handling the anchor and line, the wire ends sometimes can cause a nasty cut or scrape if you are not careful.

I have found that the safest and easiest way to get around these potential hazards and yet safely secure the shackle pin is to use a plastic electrical harness tie wrap instead of metal wire. Available at all stores that sell electrical or electronic supplies, these tie wraps cost only a few cents each and will never rot or corrode. After tightening the anchor shackle in the usual manner you

thread the tie wrap through the hole in the shackle pin, then draw it up tight, just as you would when wrapping wires. Excess length can be easily trimmed off with a rigger's knife.

Guide To Anchors and Anchoring

On most pleasure boats one type of cruising gear that is often largely ignored is the ground tackle—the anchor and

its rode. Yet selecting the proper ground tackle and maintaining it so that it's ready for instant use is essential to safe boating. Some boatowners *never* anchor out—they just cruise from dock to dock—but they still need a suitable anchor and an adequate length of anchor line. Boats can't just pull over and park if the engine suddenly conks out; an anchor is needed to hold a boat in one place while repairs are made, or until help arrives.

Every boat should have at least two anchors and anchor lines with at least one anchor secured to its line and ready to go at all times—not only in case one anchor line breaks or an anchor is lost, but also because there are many occasions when it is safer, or even necessary, to put out two anchors. One of these anchors should be stowed on deck, complete with line attached, where it will be instantly ready to lower in an emergency.

Most experts recommend that cruising boats also carry a third anchor—a large storm anchor that can be used if you are ever caught out in a real gale. Boats that do not have an anchor winch for hauling in the anchor may also find it convenient to carry a "lunch hook"—a light anchor that can be used for a quick swim or a brief stop.

There are four types of anchors in widespread use on today's pleasure boats: (1) the "old-fashioned" or kedge-type anchor (also called a fisherman anchor); (2) the lightweight or Danforth-type anchor; (3) the CQR or plow-type anchor; and (4) the Bruce anchor.

The size anchor required will depend on the size and configuration of your boat—this is what determines the horizontal load the anchor must withstand. Choosing the right size anchor for your boat is a matter of consulting manufacturer's published load ratings for each of their anchors, then matching this up with the load needed to anchor your boat properly. Most manufacturers publish tables that help select the best anchor for boats of different sizes and types (they tell you how to estimate the working loads required for your boat).

Lightweight or Danforth-type anchors generally provide the greatest amount of holding power in proportion to weight, and they are probably the most popular type of anchor in use on today's pleasure boats.

Danforth anchors come in two classifications—Standard and Hi-Tensile. The difference between the two is in the strength of the steel used and thus in the amount of holding power provided for anchors of the same weight. Typically a Hi-Tensile model will provide 30 to 35 percent more holding power than a Standard model of the same weight. Danforth also has introduced a new line of anchors called Deepset. These also come in Standard and Hi-Tensile versions and in both styles provide up to 50 percent more holding power.

All these anchors provide excellent holding power in mud or sand because the flukes are designed so the anchor

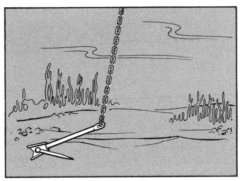

will bury itself in the bottom as the pull (load) increases. However, they are not as efficient in kelp or grassy bottoms.

Like most other lightweight anchors, Danforth anchors are resistant to line fouling, but they do tend to pull out when the boat swings close to 180 degrees. In most cases they will bury themselves again when the boat settles into its new direction, but the anchor line should be checked each time there is a change of current or wind direction.

The CQR or plow anchor (CQR is the original brand name, and it still is the best of its type) bites in quickly and also buries itself to provide excellent holding power in most bottoms. This type tends to grab better than the Danforth-type anchor when you are dealing with a grassy or kelp-covered bottom, or when there is coral on the bottom.

For a given amount of holding power, a plow has to be heavier than a Danforth anchor, and it is more awkward to stow on deck. That's why these anchors usually are stowed in a steam head roller or anchor davit that projects out over the bow. Because the shank is pivoted, the CQR can withstand moderate changes in the direction of pull without pulling out, and like the Danforth, this one is also easy to break out when leaving.

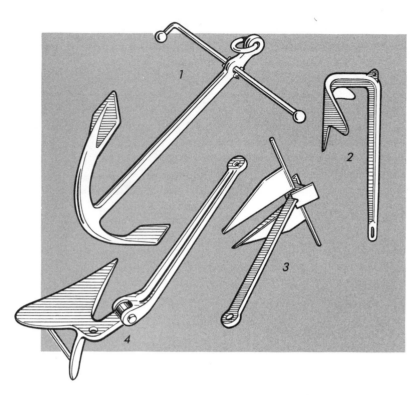

(1) kedge or fisherman; (2) Bruce; (3) Danforth-type; (4) CQR.

The Bruce anchor is a one-piece, burying-type anchor that was originally developed to hold offshore drilling rigs. Its holding power in various bottoms is similar to that of the plow, but for the same load the Bruce anchor must be heavier. It is good in most bottoms and once set is able to swing a full 360 degrees without pulling out, yet it can still be pulled out easily when weighing anchor. Like the CQR, it is impossible to stow on deck, so it is usually stowed in a stem head fitting.

The "old-fashioned" kedge or fisherman anchor is seldom used on pleasure boats anymore, except perhaps as a reserve anchor. It works well on bottoms that are covered with rocks, coral, or weeds, but pound for pound these anchors offer much less holding power than the others.

Anchor lines may be either rope or chain. Nylon, twisted or braided, is better than Dacron because of its elasticity—the way it stretches under load (Dacron won't stretch). This helps the line absorb shocks created by surges and wind or wave action, so it puts less strain on mooring bits, chocks, and other deck fittings. In addition, in a choppy or windy anchorage the boat doesn't leap around as much.

Although chain doesn't stretch, its weight causes it to form a deep curve when you are anchored. When there is a surge or strong pull, all that happens is that the boat pulls the chain straighter and picks up some of the extra weight, thus absorbing most of the shock without putting a strain on the boat or on the anchor line. The added weight of the chain also causes the portion closest to the anchor to hug the bottom more, creating a more horizontal pull that increases holding power.

All anchors hold better when the pull is horizontal, and the one way to ensure this is to put out an adequate amount of scope. "Scope" refers to the proportion between the length of line put out and the depth to the bottom. Depth to be considered should include the height of the deck above the water as well as the actual depth of the water. For example, if you are anchoring in ten feet of water and the freeboard at the bow is four feet, then the total depth to be considered when figuring scope is fourteen feet. For a scope of seven to one you would have to let out ninety-eight feet of line.

With a rope anchor line, a scope of seven to one is considered a minimum, but ten to one is safer. With chain, a scope of seven to one is usually adequate, but more is advisable when windy or choppy conditions are expected. Also remember that when anchoring in tidal waters the scope must be figured at high water. For example, if you anchor in six feet of water at low tide where the tidal range varies by seven feet, allow enough scope for thirteen feet of water—assuming you will be staying long enough to go through a change of tide.

On most pleasure boats nylon rope is more popular than chain because it is lighter and easier to handle—particularly on boats that do not have an anchor winch. Rope is subject to abrasion and is adversely affected by exposure to the sun's ultraviolet rays, which is why anchor lines should always be stored out of direct sunlight. A galvanized anchor chain will last for many years in normal use, but it can pose a problem with weight, not only because of the effort required to haul it in if you have to do this by hand, but also because of the weight it adds to the bow in some boats.

One advantage of chain over rope is that it can withstand rubbing against rocks, coral, or other abrasive material. When an anchor buries itself, the last few feet of the line are also buried in many cases, and this creates abrasion that can cause the rope to break. With chain you don't have to worry about this.

To get around this when using nylon for your anchor line always add at least six to eight feet of chain at the anchor end. The weight of the chain keeps the line closer to the bottom, creating a more horizontal pull that increases holding power.

When securing the line to the anchor, make sure a metal thimble is used to reinforce the eye splice where the nylon is secured to the anchor shackle or ring.

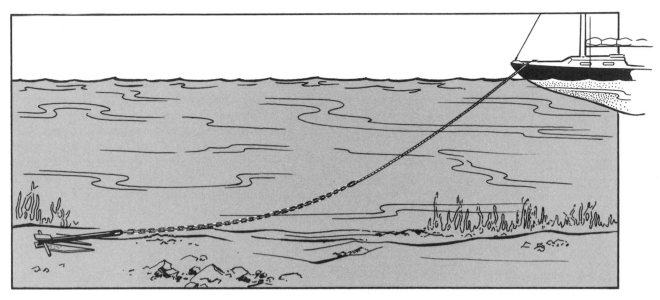

Scope—the ratio of amount of line let out to the depth—is crucial to safe anchoring.

One trick that will help lengthen the life of any anchor line is to turn the line end for end at the beginning of each season so all the wear doesn't occur at one end. When you buy a new anchor line it is a good idea to start out with a line that is at least 20 percent longer than you need. In that way you can cut off a few feet at the worn end, thus greatly adding to the number of years the line can be safely used.

Inexperienced boatmen often lower the anchor and then throw over all the line required in one toss. The trouble with that system is that the anchor may foul in the line, or will never bury itself properly—or it may drag a considerable distance before it does get properly set.

To avoid such problems, start out by feeding out only enough line to let the anchor settle on the bottom. Then pay out enough additional line to approximately equal the depth of the water. Give the boat a little reverse power and shift into neutral as soon as it is moving in reverse. Snub the line up temporarily and wait till you feel the anchor bite into the bottom, then pay out about the same amount of additional line. Now reverse the engine again, feed out the rest of the scope, and then secure the line. Wait till the line comes taut, then give a short burst of reverse power at idle speed. Make sure the anchor line pulls tight and the anchor shows no sign of further dragging before you shut off the engine and leave the bow.

When retrieving the anchor, always use the boat's engine to break out the anchor. With the bow pointed directly at the anchor, put the engine in gear and move forward slowly while someone takes in the line. Shift into neutral and let the boat drift forward until the bow is directly over the anchor. When the anchor line is straight up and down, snub the line on the mooring bit, then shift the engine into forward again and let the boat ride over the anchor. This should pull it straight up and out. As soon as the anchor breaks free, shift into neutral again while you haul in the anchor. If you have an anchor winch, this is when to use it—to haul the anchor up on deck *after* you break it free of the bottom.

When dropping the hook in a crowded anchorage, try to visualize how much the boat will swing. Putting out sixty feet of line, for example, means you may swing in a circle about 120 feet in diameter when wind or current changes, so make sure you allow plenty of room between yourself and any neighboring boats. Even then, you may still have to get up during the night to make certain the anchor resets itself properly each time the direction changes.

One anchoring technique that eliminates this problem is to put out two anchors in opposite directions—but both from the bow. One anchor goes forward; the other anchor goes aft in a direction that is 180 degrees from the first—in other words, directly astern of the boat. This can be done by first anchoring in the usual manner with one anchor from the bow and a normal amount of scope. Get the second anchor and line ready, then pay out enough additional line on the first anchor to allow the boat to drift backward (or give it a slight amount of reverse way).

Wait until it has moved back by a distance equal to the original length of the first anchor line, then drop the second anchor and get it set properly. Now power forward to your original position between the two anchors and secure both anchor lines to the boat (separate bits are preferable) so that your boat is midway between the two anchors. One anchor line will now be running forward and the other aft. No matter which way the bow of the boat swings, the location of the boat will remain the same and both anchors will remain in place—first one holding it and then the other. The worst that can happen is that the two lines may get wound around each other—but that won't be difficult to correct when you are ready to pull the lines in.

Anchor Line Protector

Many boatowners prefer nylon rope to chain for anchoring because nylon is so much lighter and easier to handle. It is strong and has more "give" or spring to it than chain does. Another advantage of line over chain is that line will not scratch the finish of the boat. However, anchor lines of nylon can sometimes chafe against underwater coral, rocks, abandoned fish traps—or even old engine blocks that were once dropped overboard to act as mooring anchors.

Even with ten to fifteen feet of chain at the end of the anchor line, when the line goes slack and dips down near the bottom it can rub against abrasive materials and chafe badly enough to snap the next time the boat moves suddenly. I had this happen to me not too many years ago when my line chafed through while at anchor because it had snagged on something sharp on the bottom, even though I had twenty feet of anchor chain at the end of my anchor line.

Now I've discovered a way to keep that from happening again. Each time I anchor I tie an underwater float to my anchor line to keep it from lying along the bottom. As shown here, I attach the float from six to ten feet from where the chain ends. I have found that an empty plastic sixteen-ounce shampoo bottle that is tightly capped has just about enough buoyancy to lift the chain and hold my three-quarter-inch anchor line safely off the bottom and away from jagged or abrasive materials. Try to arrange things so the float will remain suspended about six feet below the surface.

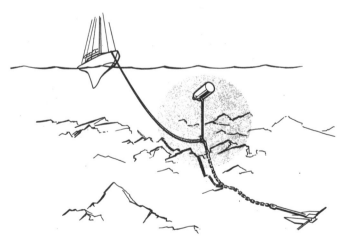

Intercom for Anchoring

When anchoring, many boatowners find they have a definite problem trying to communicate with the person on the bow who is tending the anchor line. Hand signals are effective, but take a fair amount of practice and teamwork—and of course seldom work with a helper who is unfamiliar with your usual signals. Voice communications are also undependable, requiring lots of shouting, and are difficult to hear when the wind is blowing or when the person on the bow forgets to turn around when talking.

After playing with various ideas I finally decided to use

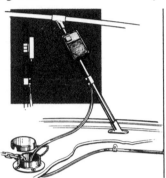

an intercom, the kind that is powered by its own nine-volt battery in the master unit. I purchased a two-station system with sixty feet of connecting cable, then mounted the master unit up on the bridge and ran the cable down through the boat to where I could bring it up onto the bow. I didn't want to drill a new hole through the deck for the cable, nor did I want the intercom permanently up on the bow (the intercom is not weatherproof), so I brought the cable up onto the bow deck through the anchor line deck pipe opening. The cable used is very thin and needs protection when exposed, so I ran it through some five-eighths-inch clear plastic hose from the chain locker to where it was attached to the intercom up on the bow. The intercom is attached to the bow rail with a snap-on rail clamp that makes it easy to remove or replace. This clip is attached to the plastic hose with two plastic tie wraps. I punched four holes through the hose with a hot ice pick, then pushed the tie wraps through these to secure the clamp.

Increasing Ice Box Efficiency

Keeping the ice box adequately supplied with ice is really a problem in hot weather—especially in older boats where insulation may not be as efficient as it is in many of the newer boats.

One way to make the ice last longer is to make sure the box is as full as possible; another is to do what you can to improve the insulation in the top of the box and in the lift-up lid. I accomplish both these objectives by using a number of large Zip-Loc plastic kitchen bags (sold in supermarkets for storing food).

Each bag is filled with wads of Styrofoam balls or pieces of foam rubber, then sealed. As you close each bag, allow some air to remain trapped inside to maximize the insulation each of these ''pillows'' will provide. Now place as many of the bags as will fit on top of the food inside the ice box. Cover the entire area from side to side and from back to front and as high as space permits, but make sure the ice box cover will still fit snugly and properly.

These foam-filled bags will not only fill the empty space at the top of the ice box so there is less air inside, they will also create an effective thermal barrier that will help keep food colder and make the ice last longer. The ''pillows'' can be easily moved around and then repositioned when you want to reach some of the items inside the ice box, or removed when you want to add items.

The contents of an ice box will also last longer if you freeze as many items as possible before placing them inside the ice box. Bring drinking water from home after freezing it in plastic jugs—then store these jugs in the ice

box until you need them. Also, many home cooked foods can be frozen before bringing them to the boat, and even many brands of beer (in cans) can be frozen without spoiling their flavor after they have thawed. Freeze them at home, then put them in the boat's ice box while still frozen to help extend the life of the ice inside the insulated box.

Examine the Fuel First

The old maxim that ''oil and water do not mix'' was never as true as when applied to the fuel used by diesel engines. While a gasoline engine might tolerate a small amount of water in the fuel, a diesel engine cannot tolerate any.

Although water can find its way into the fuel in a number of different ways, one of the most common is from taking on fuel from a storage tank that also contains a sizable amount of water mixed with the fuel. Bad fuel of this type is sometimes dispensed when the storage tank at the dock is very low, or when fuel is purchased in some foreign marinas or from a place that does not sell very much and is not careful about the quality of what they do sell.

The simplest way to prevent taking on a load of fuel that has water in it is to check the fuel first. One way to do this is to carry an empty half-gallon juice bottle with a wide neck on board. Label the jar clearly with the word *diesel* so it won't get used for anything else. Each time you stop for fuel, unscrew the cap on this jar and start pumping fuel into the jar first until it is a little more than half full. Wait till the bubbles dissipate, then hold the jar up to the light to see if there are any bubbles of water in the fuel, or a layer of water near the bottom of the jar. Also check for signs of dirt floating around in the fuel. If you see any, don't take on fuel at that dock. If the liquid in the bottle looks clear, pour it into your tank, then stick the fuel nozzle in and fill up with confidence.

6 FITTING OUT AND LAYING UP

Thirty Tips for Spring Commissionings

1. Removing Cover. Make sure your winter cover is dry when you take it off. If you have to remove it while it is wet, spread it out on the ground to dry before folding and storing it—otherwise it will wind up with rot or mildew. Before folding it, however, look for tears and worn sections that need repairing, as well as for broken zippers, torn-out grommets, and badly frayed tie-downs or lacing lines. Have all these repairs attended to before storing the cover, so you can be sure the cover will be ready next fall, when there usually is too much of a rush to get this kind of work done in time.

2. Check Vital Fluids. Without vital fluids to cool and lubricate, a marine engine is like a blue water sailor marooned on a desert island. It's only a matter of time before the buzzards start circling. Check the drive's gear oil. The owner's manual shows and tells which drain plug to open and how to peer in. If you don't have a manual, order one. In the meantime, look for one slot-edge screw about the size of a nickel near the skeg and another one about one foot straight up the leg of the lower unit. Caution: Never loosen the Phillips head screws in the lower unit. They're usually attached to the shift linkage— pull that screw and you have a mess inside.

Some stern drives have two oil reservoirs. Follow the gold miner's adage: Never fail to look. Only in this case, instead of finding a bonanza, we're preventing a dry hole. Not all motors require the same hypoid ninety weight. Again, check the manufacturer's specs.

On four-cycle inboards or I/Os, check the engine oil level. Likewise, check coolant level. Top off as necessary. Antifreeze's pH factor is slightly alkaline. If it's more than a couple of years old it should be replaced so it doesn't turn acidic. Don't overlook the trim/tilt unit's hydraulic level. Top off as necessary.

3. Tighten Belts. Examine all belts for cracks, wear, and lack of tension, then clean and brighten the pulley grooves; also check for wear and any looseness of the "hold in" cap screws and tighten if necessary. Then check for any pulleys out of line. All frayed, cracked, or worn belts should be replaced immediately.

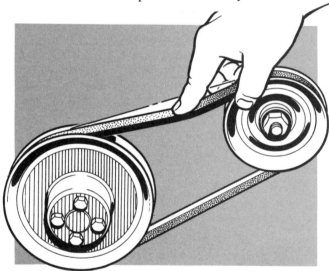

Adjust each belt to proper tension, about one-eighth- to one-half-inch play when depressed firmly between pulleys. Never pry or roll a belt into a pulley groove. Carry a few spares on board in a clean, cool, dry place.

4. Test-Run Electronics. As soon as all electronic equipment has been installed, turn each item on and let it run for several hours—just to make sure everything is working and will keep on working. Spray plugs and connections with WD-40, CRC, or other moisture-displacing lubricant to keep out moisture and prevent corrosion. Now is the time to discover if repairs or adjustments are needed on your electronic equipment— not when you are ready to take off on your first cruise of the season.

5. Inspect the Prop. A propeller's blades should be free of nicks. So file small ones smooth, keeping the prop's leading edge sharp, but not honed to a razor's edge,

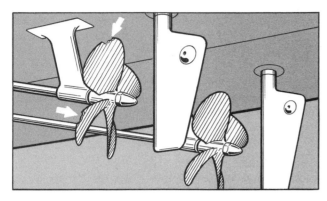

like a machete blade. Also important, too much metal knocked off a blade by rock-bashing leaves a wheel running out of true. The imbalance vibrates the prop and drive shafts, wearing out bearings and gear faces well before their time. New props cost hundreds of dollars less than a set of matched gears; they'll also make you smile at the improved performance and fuel economy. Hint: Don't deep-six the damaged prop. Instead, stow it in the spare-parts locker for an emergency. If you don't know whether the prop is dinged up enough to wreak havoc on the drive train, have a mechanic check it.

Remove the propeller and check the prop shaft for a wad of monofilament fishline. Coiled up on the propshaft, between the prop and the gearcase, fishing line worms its way into the seal, cutting the rubber lip. Centrifugal force, generated by the whirling gears, squirts lube out through the leak. The lost oil creates a vacuum. When the engine stops, the vacuum sucks in water. Since water does a poor job lubricating gears and bearings, you can guess what happens next.

If you do find line, then crack the bottom drain plug a couple of turns until gearcase lube trickles out one drop at a time (ten or twenty drops are sufficient). If only lube issues forth, breathe a big sigh of relief, tighten the drain screw, remove the fishline, coat the shaft with antiseize compound, and replace the prop.

Should half an ounce or more of water drip out, make an appointment with a mechanic to have the gearcase pressure checked for a cut propshaft seal.

Or, if you found fishline but only a scant amount of water came out, keep a close eye on the gearcase during the season.

6. Cooling System. Drain your enclosed fresh water cooling system, including oil coolers and heat exchangers. Your service manual will show you where the drain plugs are. Then flush with soft, clean, fresh water and refill the system with the correct amount of fresh water and rust inhibitor. Then replace the filter.

Remember, properly operating thermostats are essential for a running engine.

If you think the raw water pump needs checking, close

the seacocks or intake valve, remove the end plate, and check the impeller, shaft, and seal. If any is worn, replace it along with a new thin gasket. It's always a good idea to carry a spare impeller on board. And many boatowners make a practice of always carrying a spare water pump aboard in case an impeller change does not do the trick.

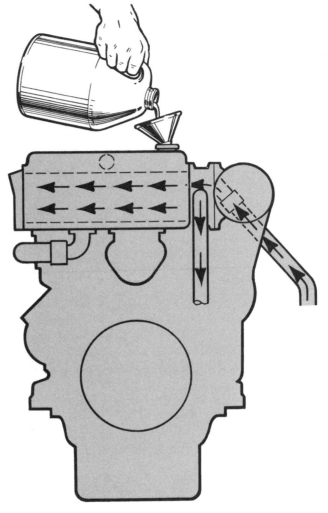

7. Inspect Lines. Rope is indispensable on every boat—for docking, for mooring, for rigging, and for sundry other uses. Most yachtsmen tend to take their lines for granted, until one breaks or parts when it is least expected. A parted anchor line can result in going to bed in one location and waking up in an entirely new one. To avoid such unexpected surprises, it's best to inspect all lines at the beginning of each season. Replace those that are frayed or worn in several places, and make new splices in those that look like only the eye splice end is worn. If all the wear seems to be at one end, you can sometimes turn those lines end-for-end to get additional life out of them.

The same holds true for anchor lines—especially if you frequently anchor in places where the water depth is about the same. All the wear will occur in the same place, usually where the line goes through the chock.

Turning the anchor line end-for-end and splicing in a new anchor shackle at the unused end will give you twice as much use from that line. If your mooring and docking lines are dirty you may find it worthwhile to soak them in a bucket of detergent and water (if the lines are stiff it sometimes helps to add a water softener to the solution).

Cleaner lines not only look better, they are also often easier to handle. After soaking the lines, stretch them out on the dock and hose them off with lots of water. Then leave them on the dock and allow them to dry in the sun before coiling and storing them.

8. Squeeze Hoses. Carefully check and squeeze all hoses before and while your engine is under normal operating pressure. Caution: Watch your hands around moving parts.

Any leaks on the suction side increase the chances of air and corrosion in your cooling system. External leaks are usually easy to spot since antifreeze and rust inhibitors tend to leave stains.

If you do uncover any hoses that appear old, spongy, or cracked, replace them with good silicone rubber hoses. Purchase good marine-type hoses and stainless steel

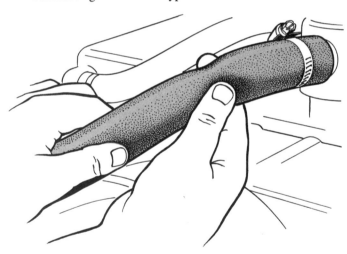

clamps. Double-clamp each connection; remember, they are easier to replace at your dock than out at sea.

Make sure all hoses are not resting on or touching shafts, couplings, sharp edges, or heated surfaces.

Rubber fuel lines anywhere in the boat should be supple, not squishy or hard. Methanol-laced fuel kills rubber fuel lines, resulting in leaks.

If a hose failure sneaks up on you under way, let the engine cool, then loosen the filler cap so the cooling system operates at atmospheric pressure. Then tape the riddled hose with electrical tape, or tie a rag over the hole. Without pressurized coolant, the system will leak much less.

9. Stuffing Boxes. Stuffing boxes are designed to create a waterproof seal where a shaft goes through the hull and into the water. With most stuffing boxes some water seepage is desirable for lubrication and cooling, so when the shaft is turning it's common to have a slight amount of leakage, usually no more than a few drops per minute. When a stuffing box leaks much more than this, usually it can be corrected by simply loosening the locknut, then tightening up on the packing nut slightly. Don't overtighten, as this can cause the bearing to overheat and could cause permanent damage to the shaft.

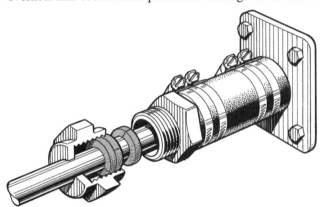

The best time to do this is when the boat is under way; then you can check the amount of leakage if any, and also feel the stuffing box to see if it's getting too hot (which means it's too tight). After the packing nut is right, the locking nut is then firmly tightened against it, but make sure while doing this that you hold the packing nut in position with another wrench.

If tightening the packing nut is not enough to stop a sizable leak, then chances are that new packing is needed (it's a good idea to replace this every two or three years anyway). The new packing is cut into short pieces and formed into rings that just fit around the circumference of the shaft, under or inside the packing nut. Three rings are required, without end overlapping and with each positioned so its joint does not coincide with the one next to it.

One thing many boatowners forget is that there are also stuffing boxes around each of the rudder shafts in most powerboats and in some sailboats. Don't neglect to check these at the same time.

10. Turbos and Air Filters. If you have a diesel engine equipped with a turbocharger, prelube its center bearing by removing the turbo oil line fitting and squirting several drops of clean lube oil into the bearing housing.

Turn the rotating blade a few times by hand to prelube the bearing, and reconnect the line and nut. Then check the blades and the turbine area for any cracks, nicks, or dirt. Finally, clean the whole turbocharger system area, including the blades.

Next, remove and check your engine's air intake

silencer/filter. Clogged-up air filters can choke off your engine's breathing air and reduce engine power. And don't forget to clean the crankcase ventilation filter, too.

After startup, check the air tube and its connections for leaks. Whistling or hissing sounds are signs of leakage.

11. Diesel Tips. Clean and/or replace all fuel filters, strainers, and water separators. Fill all of them with clean fuel before replacing them. Be sure their sealing surfaces are clean and free of any grit, and remember to use new gaskets. Next, check all lines and connections for tightness and any evidence of chafing. This is a must—don't live dangerously; then purge air if necessary and possible.

If you have a diesel, your first attempt at starting probably will result in coughing, spitting, and uneven running for a few moments, but as the air is purged from each line and injector, your engine will even itself out and eventually purr like a kitten.

Never change your lube oil when your diesel is cold; always bring it up to operating temperature, then drain it when it is warm and while the sludge, acids, and dirt are still suspended in the oil. Change all filters and strainers at the same time, and if possible fill them up before you install them back on the engine with new gaskets. Use the type of lube oil recommended by your engine manufacturer.

If you have an electric fuel shutoff solenoid, clean and tighten the connections, then try it a few times. Listen for the sound of a "click" when you push the engine shutdown button. If you have a "Jimmy," make sure the emergency intake flapper on the blower intake is working; then lubricate the bearing points.

Engine mounts are used to help isolate engine noise and vibration from the rest of your boat. Bad mounts can give

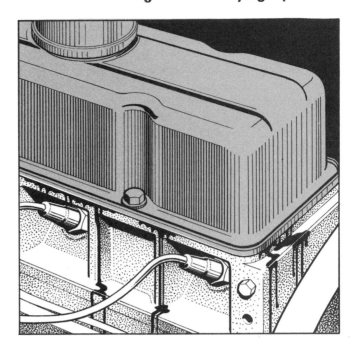

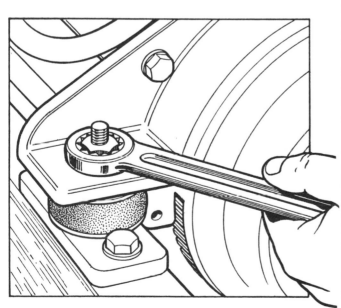

your diesel the "shakes" and may cause it to go out of alignment.

Give them a good looking-over: Check for any loose, broken, or worn rubbers, cracked steel bolts, or loose nuts, and replace any if necessary.

If you have glow plugs on your diesel, check and replace any faulty ones. Your owner's manual will tell you where they are and the easiest way to check them and remove them. A word of advice: Always carry a few spares on board in a dry place.

12. Lifelines and Railings. Most boats have lifelines or rigid rails to keep you from falling overboard if you lose your balance. Although lifelines are most often used only as handrails when walking along the deck, they can literally save your life when you have to go forward on deck in a pitching sea. That's why it's important that all stanchions are securely bolted to the deck and all lifelines are in good condition. Lifelines should not be taut—there should be some slack in them—but stanchions should be rigid.

Since all fasteners tend to work loose under the movement of a hull while under way, take time out now to use a wrench and/or large screwdriver for checking each nut, bolt, and screw on all the deck hardware. Tighten those that are loose, and replace those that seem badly oxidized or corroded. When replacing them, be sure you squirt a little silicone into the hole before retightening—just to make sure that water cannot enter.

13. Inspect Seacocks. Seacocks, as well as all other types of underwater through-hull fittings, seldom receive any attention until they are really needed; then all too often you find they are literally "frozen" in the open position and cannot be closed in an emergency—when a hose suddenly lets go while you are under way, for instance. To prevent such potentially dangerous situations, open and close each seacock once or twice before the boat is launched to make certain they're all working properly.

Give each valve a shot of grease or oil to ensure that it will continue to work easily, and if any are stuck, make the necessary repairs or replacements now—before the boat is launched.

14. Batteries. Charge the battery (or batteries), and clean the battery posts thoroughly with a wire brush. Do the same with the terminal ends on the cables that hook up to the batteries. Then replace them and tighten the clamps firmly. To prevent future corrosion and buildup of salts, coat each connection and battery post with a light film of grease or Vaseline, or use one of the sprays sold for this purpose.

While checking the battery connections, also be sure to check the connection where the heavy grounding wire from the negative terminal on the battery connects up to the main bus bar, and where this is grounded to the engine. The slightest loosening at either of these terminal points will cause a drop in voltage that could interfere with engine starting or with the operation of electronic equipment. Try the nuts with a wrench to make sure they are very tight, and be sure there is no paint or grease getting in the way of a solid electrical connection. If in doubt, take the connection apart, clean all the metal thoroughly, and then retighten.

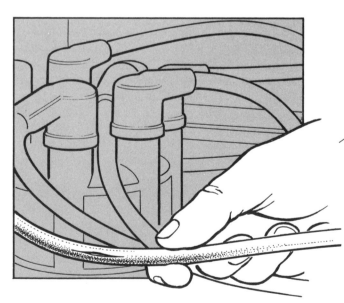

Also pay attention to the spark plug cables. If they are cracked and hard, they won't deliver full ignition spark. A weak spark affects both starting and running.

15. Vinyl Curtains. Roll-up vinyl curtains are not cheap and at best need replacing every few years, so it pays to take good care of them from the beginning. If possible, take them off the boat and lay them out on grass for a good washing. If you have to lay them on the dock, put down some old towels or pieces of canvas to prevent scratching. Wash with a sponge and mild detergent, then dry with old towels. You can help them to shed dirt and can minimize their tendency to cloud up and turn white by wiping lightly with one of the various vinyl coatings sold for this purpose. Apply the polish to both sides of the clear vinyl, but use only a small amount and spread it around uniformly. Then buff with a clean, soft cloth.

16. Check the Head. A frequent cause of problems with marine toilets is inadequate water flow on the intake side due to partial clogging of lines, valves, or passages.

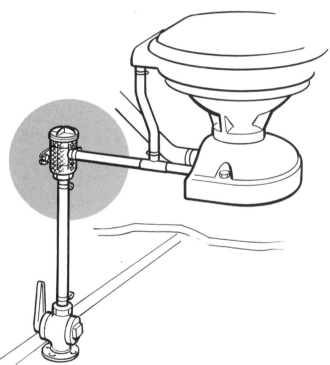

Grass, seaweed, and other debris get drawn in with the seawater when the head is flushed. Not only does this tend to clog the lines and interfere with proper flushing, it can also cause foul odors.

Most boatowners rely on externally mounted bottom strainers to prevent this, but there's a better way to keep out grass and small pieces of seaweed. An internally mounted water strainer, similar to the kind used on engines and auxiliary generators (but a lot smaller), can prevent this potential problem. Available in various sizes, these filters can be purchased in marine stores or ordered from marine catalogs and are simple to install. All you have to do is cut the intake water line and insert the strainer with a couple of hose clamps at each end. Just be sure you pick a convenient location so you can get at it to clean it out.

17. Say Good-bye to Regular. If yours is one of the two million rigs designed to burn regular gasoline, you may have a problem. Regular's TEL (tetraethyl lead), the additive that boosts octane and lubricates exhaust valves, is no longer available. (Since outboard motors don't have exhaust valves and seats, they are relatively unaffected by the lubrication deficit.) The short-term solution: Dump a bottle of lubrication supplement down the fill hole. Cost: about a nickel a gallon.

The long-term solution calls for rebuilding the cylinder head or heads. Depending on whether you remove the heads yourself or not, expect to pay from two hundred to five hundred dollars. But we advise holding off on the rebuild unless compression is low.

Another complication: Since lead, or more precisely the lack of it, affects gasoline's octane rating, fuel quality isn't what it used to be. As a result, you may be running an engine on a diet of junk-food gasoline, causing detonation. Dosing the fuel with octane enhancer solves the problem. Retarding the ignition can quiet the engine, with only slight horsepower loss.

When shopping for fuel additives, be advised that some canned cures solve just one problem: either octane or lubrication deficiency. Other brands benefit both. A wise skipper reads the labels. A welcome side effect only boatmen can appreciate: Most additives also stabilize fuel as well as curing octane or valve lubrication woes, thereby preventing the gasoline from turning into gum inside the carburetor. A final tip: Buy the highest octane fuel available and take care of the lubrication with additives.

18. Fresh Water System. If you added antifreeze to your fresh water system for the winter, then you must fill the tank and flush it out a few times to get all the taste and color out of the water. This process involves running your electric pump quite a bit (if you have pressurized water) or doing a lot of hand pumping. Even then you probably won't get the taste out of all the lines.

A better and faster way to flush out the lines is to disconnect the water hose at the bottom of the tank, then temporarily connect the hose that came off the tank to a hose leading to the dockside water hose. Now you can use dockside water to flush out all the lines inside the boat by opening one faucet at a time inside the boat. Just be careful not to turn the dockside water pressure too high or you may blow some lines. You can use dockside water to flush out the tank. As the water comes out at the bottom, you can turn on the bilge pumps to carry it overboard, or you can attach a hose to the tank and dump the water directly overboard.

19. Testing Out the Pumps. Bilge pumps are seldom thought of until they are really needed. In some large fiberglass boats that are exceptionally dry there may be some out-of-the-way bilge pumps that you haven't even seen, or used, in years, but they should all be tested before the season begins. Make sure all connections are tight.

Start by cleaning all debris out of the bilge to minimize chances of clogging any of the pumps; clean the strainers, then try each float valve to make sure that when it is raised, the pump kicks on. You don't have to fill the bilge with water to try this; merely raise the float switch by hand. If you want to test the floating action of the switch, you can temporarily remove it from its mounting and then lower the switch into a bucket of water to see if this starts the pump running.

20. Tip for Teak Caulking. Trying to do a neat job of replacing the black Thiokol or polysulfide caulking compound on teak decks is never easy. The quickest way to get the job done is to use a caulking gun, but you have to be careful about smearing the black compound all over the teak. The best way to avoid such a mess is to use masking tape, as shown in the drawing.

After digging out the old compound and applying a

primer if necessary (read the directions on the package), put down two strips of masking tape, one on each side of the joint. The edge of the tape should just line up with the edge of the seam, leaving only the open joint exposed. Force the compound into the joint and then use a narrow putty knife to smooth off the excess. Peel off the tape within an hour or two, or as soon as the compound starts to set up slightly. You will be left with a neat joint that has compound only in the seam, not on the face of the wood.

21. Replace Zincs. Now is the time to check your engine's zinc—rods, plugs, collars, etc. Salt water is highly corrosive and will cause electrolysis deterioration in an engine. Depending on your engine's make and model (check your manual), zincs are usually located near the inlet side of the raw water pump, the coolers and heat exchangers. To remove the plugs, close your salt water inlet valve first, then give the plugs a few shots of a good marine penetrating oil to free their threads, which usually are corroded.

Unscrew the zinc plugs and brush or scrape off any powdery deposits. Then tap the rods lightly with a small hammer. If a rod has deteriorated 50 percent or more,

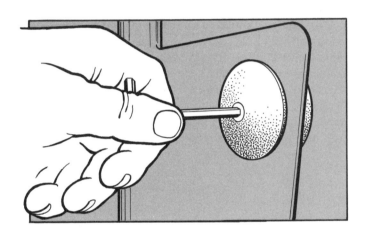

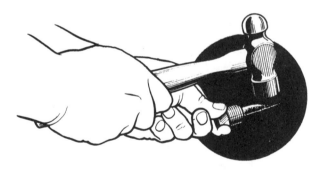

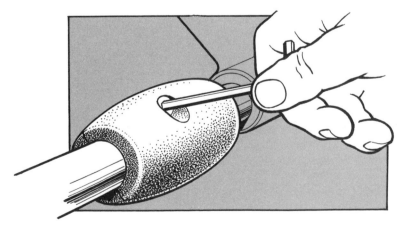

deep-six it. Then clean the plug hole threads and install a new zinc, making sure it has a good clean, tight, metal-to-metal contact. Engine zincs often are overlooked, but when they're gone, the engine block is next.

Normal spring maintenance also calls for checking the zinc buttons, plates, or collars that combat electrolysis. Don't make the mistake of not replacing those that look only partially eroded. Unless you plan to have a diver check them underwater on a monthly basis, it's a good idea to replace any of your zincs that are worn down by about one third or more.

22. Cushions. When cleaning and washing the inside of the boat, take all bunk cushions, mattresses, and other movable upholstered items outside and spread them out in the sun. Use a vacuum cleaner and a soft brush on each piece, making certain you clean all sides. By doing this outside you will be eliminating the likelihood of scattering any mildew spores around the interior of the boat, and airing everything in the sun is one of the best ways to get rid of any musty or dank odors that may have developed over the winter.

23. The Right Fuel. Double-check the owner's manual. What kind of fuel does the manufacturer recommend: regular or unleaded? If regular is specified, treat the fuel supply with supplemental lubrication to protect the valves from premature wear (see "Say Good-bye to Regular" earlier in this chapter). Ignore this caveat, and the exhaust valves could burn up just at about midseason. If your mechanic says the EPA phaseout isn't a problem, you need a new mechanic who is up to date.

Also check the owner's manual for recommended octane. Even if you match a pump's supposed rating to the engine's requirements, fuel quality has been dropping low enough that you may need to douse the fuel with octane enhancer. Your first clue will come right after a fill-up, when the engine develops a rattle on acceleration or at full power. You may also experience a loss of power. Should you run an engine on low-octane fuel and it needs hi-test, that rattling, or detonation, could punch a hole through the top of the pistons. In fact, keeping a can of octane booster in the emergency repair kit is a good idea.

24. Try Lights. Turn on all navigation lights and running lights to see if any bulbs are burned out. To ensure a trouble-free season, spray the base of each bulb, as well as the socket in which it fits, with a moisture-displacing lubricant such as WD-40, LPS-1, or CRC. Also make sure you have at least one spare bulb on hand for each of these lights, as well as spare fuses for each circuit (if your boat still uses fuses).

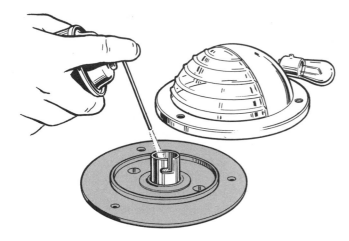

25. Don't Forget the Dinghy. If you have a dinghy, don't overlook it in the chaos of spring chores. All too often it is completely forgotten until the day you finally decide to use it. Then the motor won't start, or the oars are missing, or it is in such sad shape that you are ashamed of it. A few hours spent tuning the engine and washing and waxing will take care of all that and will make your tender an attractive addition to the boat.

26. Fire Extinguishers. Fire extinguishers are a must on all boats, but they should be maintained at full charge so they will always be ready if needed. Most have a gauge or indicator to show if pressure has been lost or if the unit needs recharging.

Check all your hand extinguishers for weight and availability; most discharge mechanisms deteriorate when

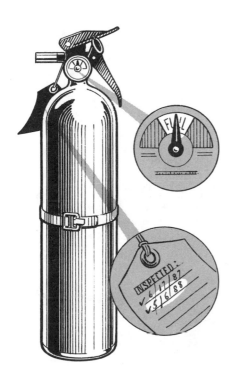

exposed to salt water dampness, and their contents will lose their effectiveness through temperature evaporation, age, or chemical change.

Tag each one with date tested or recharged. Locate them close by but not in an area where a fire might originate. Hand extinguishers aren't much help in an engine room inferno. A built-in automatic system is the most effective engine compartment fire fighter.

If you don't have an automatic system and you do have an engine room fire, unlock a couple of your hand extinguishers and throw them into the compartment and then close the hatches. They could effectively flood the engine compartment with enough CO_2 or Halon gas to put out the fire.

After checking your fire extinguishers, look at the life preservers aboard and make sure they're not moldy or torn. Flare guns should also be checked to see if they have become outdated.

27. Electrical System. Go over your electrical system. Look for any broken, cracked, frayed or corroded wires. If you find any, replace them one at a time with the right size wire. Then remove all wire and cable connections, clean, brighten, and tighten them back down again.

Clean your alternator by blowing out any dust that might have accumulated over the past year with a low-pressure air gun. If possible, remove the starter bands, and once again use a low-pressure air gun to blow out dirt and dust. Take a good look at the brushes and commutator for any wear. Then give the same area a short shot of *white* carbon tetrachloride and blow it out softly again. Use caution—don't breathe in—the carbon tet fumes.

Fill any oil cups and saturate any oil wicks with a couple of drops of #10 lube oil. Clean and tighten all wire and cable connections.

28. Portable Tank. An outboard motor's six-gallon can should be rinsed with fresh fuel if gasoline hibernated within it during the winter. It's more trouble with installed tanks. But a few quarts of alcohol also work well. Even better than spring-cleaning a gas tank, dump fuel stabilizer in the fuel at lay-up. Incidentally, nearly all the gasoline octane enhancers and supplemental lubes also stabilize the fuel.

29. Steering System. Check engine throttle, governor, and transmission control linkage and pins for freedom from sticking and wear and for proper adjustment. Then lubricate all linkage points.

Check all steering cables by sight and feel for free play and pulleys and pins for wear, then adjust or replace as necessary and lubricate with Marine Guard cable lubricant.

If you have a hydraulic system, examine the fluid for any contamination and replenish the fluid in the reservoir; replace the filter; inspect lines, hoses, and fittings; then lubricate the cylinder rods. Bleed the system if necessary to ensure total expulsion of air and positive control of rudder and wheel.

30. Look for Loose Bolts. Lay a wrench on all the bolts and nuts you can reach. Intake manifolds, ignition coils, alternator brackets, or valve covers might have vibrated loose. Tighten as necessary, but do not tighten already secure bolts. Your best bet is a torque wrench. On intake and exhaust manifolds/ housings, tighten the bolts in sequence. If your manual doesn't show that sequence, check a book covering this out of the library. As a last resort, tighten the inside bolts first and work your way outward, tightening the bolts only a little the first time through the sequence, and a little more each time until tight.

Finally, test run the engine with the engine cover up. Before leaving the dock, look in the bilge for signs of gasoline, oil, or coolant leaks. Sniff, look, and probe. On the engine, check around mating surfaces like valve covers, oil pans, timing covers, and oil filters, where fresh drips of lube may show up.

Look for coolant leaks at hose connections and alongside the engine block where freeze plugs have been known to spring a leak. Listen for strange clunks, rattles, and wheezes emanating from the engine compartment. Run the trim tilt up and down. Check the hydraulic lines and lift rams for leaks. Secure the engine cover, slip your moorings, and head for the open water. You can take it from here.

Spring Cleaning

April is not too early to begin giving your boat its annual spring cleaning—especially if you don't want to waste those beautiful spring weekends that are sure to turn up before you know it.

Regardless of the size of your boat, you should first formulate a plan of attack—a list of the chores that will need doing; then separate these chores into logical categories and make a list of the materials that will be needed for each job. Nothing is more frustrating than discovering that you forgot to pack some needed item just when you're ready to start work—and, since it's Sunday, all the stores near the marina are closed.

Chores around the outside of the boat will obviously require reasonably fair weather, but many interior jobs can be tackled in almost any weather, so plan accordingly. It's always surprising to me how many boatowners eagerly start by washing down the exterior when it is still barely above freezing, then find themselves cleaning and sprucing up the inside of the boat on some of the sunniest and warmest days of spring.

Although you can begin cleaning the interior while the boat is still fully covered, as a rule you are better off removing the canvas or plastic winter cover as soon as you're reasonably certain the likelihood of snow has

passed. Getting the frame and cover off will make it easier to climb in and out of the boat with a vacuum cleaner and other supplies and will provide more light and air while you are working.

To help you organize your annual spring cleaning, here is a list of some of the most troublesome tasks that boatowners are commonly faced with, along with some pointers on how to tackle them.

Hanging Lockers, Cabinets, and Drawers: Use clean

cloths or old towels to wipe down the inside of all cabinets and lockers, even if they look clean to you. Mildew thrives on dusty, damp, and dirty surfaces, so wiping them clean to remove a very light surface film of dirt or dampness will help eliminate or minimize this problem. Shine a bright light into the corners of cabinets and lockers to look for signs of mildew, since they are not easily seen in dim light.

Mildew is a living fungus growth—so merely washing or wiping it off is not enough. The spores must be killed if you don't want them to come back. Spray surfaces with an antimildew spray (sold in marine stores and supermarkets), as shown in the accompanying drawing, or wipe

them down with a rag dipped into a solution of one part Clorox and four parts water (wear rubber gloves). Wait about fifteen or twenty minutes, then wipe down with a wet sponge and dry with clean paper towels.

Upholstery and Mattresses: A vacuum cleaner with the appropriate attachment should be used on both sides of each mattress and removable cushions. Sleeper couches or folding bunks should also be opened and vacuumed to remove dust and dirt that could provide food for mildew. Then clean each piece with a commercial upholstery shampoo and wipe down with a damp sponge, but don't wet the cushions any more than necessary. Lay them outside in the sun to dry. Spots that are left can usually be removed with a dry cleaning fluid or commercial spot remover such as K2R.

Vinyl furniture is best cleaned with a soft brush or sponge dipped in a mild detergent solution; then wipe down with a damp cloth and dry with old toweling or clean paper towels. For stubborn dirt stains, try using rubbing alcohol or a commercial vinyl cleaner (sold in auto accessory stores).

Carpets: Besides regular vacuuming, carpets should be shampooed or cleaned by machine at least once a year. You can rent a carpet-cleaning machine at most supermarkets and home centers, where you can also buy the shampoo to go with it. If the carpets are easily removed, take them out on the dock to shampoo them; then leave the carpets outside until they dry. Clean the exposed decking under the carpet, and vacuum the back of the carpet before replacing it.

If the carpet cannot be removed, you will have to clean it in place. Vacuum thoroughly first, then shampoo according to the directions supplied with the machine. Try to do this on a dry day when you can leave portholes, hatches, and doors open to help circulate air and speed drying.

Wood Paneling: Use a vacuum to remove dust, then wipe with a damp cloth. Soiled areas can be cleaned by wiping down with paint thinner, but remember that this is highly flammable, so take proper precautions and make sure there is plenty of ventilation.

If the finish on the wood seems dull and lacks luster, you can wipe the wood with a rag dipped into a penetrating wood sealer. This works better than lemon oil or polish to brighten the wood and bring up the finish. Some people prefer to use a product containing tung oil, but I find this is slow-drying and takes lots of rubbing. One sealer that works particularly well, even where the finish is almost gone, is Minwax's Antique Oil finish. Just rub it on or apply with a brush, wait about five minutes, then rub off the excess and buff with a clean cloth.

Small nicks and scratches usually will become almost invisible when wiped down with oil in this manner, but if the scratch still shows up as a light mark, you can touch it up in one of two ways:

1. By applying a little wood stain, using a cotton swab or artist's small brush. Wipe excess off immediately with a clean swab or a rag wrapped around your finger, then let this dry and touch up with a little satin varnish. Allow to dry, then oil as described above.

2. Use a touch-up stick (sold in paint and hardware stores) for cabinets and wood paneling. These come in various wood tones and are something like crayons—you rub them on over the scratch to fill it in and color it.

Plastic-Topped Counters and Panels: Plastic laminates such as Formica are widely used in today's boats on countertops in galleys and heads as well as for bulkhead paneling. Normally, wiping these down with a damp rag occasionally is all that's needed to keep them clean and bright. However, when dirt or grease accumulates, mildew can form on the surface, so clean counters and paneling in the spring with a household cleaner such as Spray Nine, Formula 409, or Fantastic. Rinse off with a damp sponge, then wipe dry.

Stubborn stains that won't come off easily can often be removed by rubbing with a damp sponge that has been dipped into baking soda. If the stain still remains, try rubbing with a cloth dampened with Clorox or similar bleach (wear rubber gloves if your skin is sensitive). If mildew is evident, wipe down the whole surface with a solution of one part Clorox and five parts water. In either case, test first in an inconspicuous corner to make certain it will not affect the color.

Mirrors and Window Glass: Any spray cleaner made for use on glass will work well, but don't use soap—it streaks. I prefer a solution of one tablespoon ammonia and one tablespoon vinegar mixed into one quart of warm water. Wash with this, rinse with plain water, then dry the glass with a chamois or commercial window wipe. Avoid washing windows in direct sunlight (they tend to streak), and don't let the cleaning solution drip down onto finished paneling or painted surfaces (it could kill the gloss).

Heads and Galley Areas: If there are odors coming from a sink, shower, or toilet, scrub with a damp cloth dipped into baking soda, but don't rinse it off right away. Let it dry for a couple of hours, then rinse thoroughly. If odors persist, pour extra baking soda down the drain or into the toilet bowl and let it sit there for a day or two, then rinse.

Stains on appliances can be scrubbed off with a detergent, but if they are stubborn, try rubbing with a damp sponge and baking soda. A trick that often works with really caked-on, stubborn stains is to cover them with a rag soaked in liquid detergent. Leave it on for about thirty minutes, then scrub again.

In the head, bad stains or dirt rings in the toilet bowl can usually be removed by soaking with half vinegar and half water, then flushing with plain water. If this fails, use a dilute solution of muriatic acid and water (one part acid mixed with three parts water). Wear rubber gloves, and rinse the acid off the surface with lots of water (or flush the toilet) after about fifteen minutes. Stubborn stains in fiberglass shower stalls or washbasins can normally be removed by using a foam-type bathroom cleaner—Dow Bathroom Cleaner is one. If this fails, try a slightly abrasive product such as Soft Scrub (both can be found in supermarkets).

Topsides and Superstructure: Before trying to remove streaks and heavy dirt stains, give the boat a general washing with a good boat soap, using no stronger a mix than normal. Even though it doesn't look that way, heavy streaks and stains will often come off without strong scrubbing or using extra-strong detergents that will only wash off any remaining wax.

More stubborn stains and streaks can be removed with a spray cleaner such as Simoniz Boat Cleaner or Spray Nine, but I find the easiest way is to use a liquid wax/cleaner such as Boat Armor's Cleaner Wax, Seapower's Cleaner, and Wax or Simoniz Marine Polish. All work the same way: You rub them on, allow them to dry, then wipe off with a clean cloth. They are not only effective in removing stains, they also leave a light coat of wax on the surface and thus do not further dull the gel coat. Just be sure you keep changing the application rags as soon as they get dirty.

Canvas and Plastic Curtains: The best way to clean these is to take them off and lay them out on a dock or boat deck. Mop on plenty of detergent solution and let this soak for a couple of minutes. Before the canvas has a chance to dry, dip a soft brush into the same detergent, then scrub the whole surface. But don't scrub the clear plastic windows; use a sponge instead to avoid scratching them,

and make sure you spread a large beach towel under the plastic, as shown in the drawing, to keep it from getting scratched by a rough surface underneath.

After washing, hose off with lots of water, then drape each piece over a railing or lifeline so it can drip dry. Put the canvas back on the boat, then coat the clear plastic windows or curtains with Pledge, a liquid furniture spray wax that you can buy in any supermarket. Spray this on lightly, then wipe off with a clean rag. The wax helps to keep the plastic flexible and also helps it to shed dirt more effectively.

Windshields: When salt and chemicals that are caked onto the outside of a windshield (or window) won't come off with water or detergent, usually they can be removed by washing with a mixture of half white vinegar and half water. If this fails, try using a chemical toilet bowl cleaner such as Vanish, but be sure you don't get any on the gel coat or on painted or varnished surfaces.

Nonskid or Textured Decks: Ordinary scrubbing doesn't always work on nonskid because the dirt gets embedded in the crevices. Here's a trick that's often effective: Mop on a strong detergent and allow it to soak for a few minutes, then dip a scrub brush into the same detergent and scrub vigorously. If this doesn't get all the dirt out, you'll have to use a stronger cleaner. One that I like for this kind of work is E-Z Klean Soft-Rub (a marine cleaner made by Chemical-World, Holtsville, N.Y. 11742). Before that I used Soft Scrub. In each case, scrub with a brush or a coarse 3M Deck Cleaning abrasive pad.

Vinyl-Covered Cushions: Unless cushions were taken home over the winter, unzip the covers and take out the foam to make sure it stays dry. Lay the covers flat on the dock and scrub the outside. I find Spray Nine particularly good for this, although for really dirty cushions a vinyl shampoo (such as Star Brite) seems to work even better. When the covers are dry, turn them inside out to look for mildew. If you find any, spray with a mildew-killer such as X-19. Rinse thoroughly, then leave covers inside out till they dry. If the vinyl is several years old and seems a bit dull on the outside, apply a vinyl dressing after the covers are dry and the cushions are back inside.

Stanchions, Winches, and Other Hardware: Unless stanchions and other hardware are severely corroded, the easiest way to clean and brighten chrome and stainless steel is to wipe the metal down with Never Dull—a specially treated fleece that you wipe on over the metal to remove tarnish and oxidation. If the metal doesn't come up bright after this, then I use one of the cream-type metal polishes such as the ones made by BoatLife, Boat Armor, or Seapower. After the metal is bright and clean, wipe down with a liquid automobile wax, then buff with a dry cloth.

Fenders and Shore Cords: Nothing makes a boat look more weatherbeaten than dirty white fenders and dirt-streaked yellow 110-volt power cords. Ordinary cleaning agents seldom do a really good job of brightening these, so for years I used a kitchen steel wool pad (Brillo or S.O.S)—effective, but lots of work.

Now I get even better results on my fenders—and with a lot less work—by using either Seapower's Inflatable Boat Cleaner and Preservative or MDR's Fender Cleaner. For the yellow shore cords I had been using nonflammable dry cleaning fluid, but now I find that MDR also makes Cable Cleaner, which works better and is easier to use.

Twenty Tips for Fall Lay-Up

Fall lay-up invariably involves dozens of small chores that are easy to forget if you're not systematic in your lay-up procedures. Here's a list of lay-up tips to help you put your boat to bed for the winter, and to help ensure that your boat will weather the lay-up in good condition—and will be that much easier to get back into commission the following spring.

1. Clean Your Bottom Promptly. Your first chore after hauling the boat out of the water is to clean all grass and barnacles off the bottom—either by scraping or power washing. The job will be a lot easier when the bottom is still wet than after it dries. While cleaning the bottom, don't forget the struts, props, shafts, and other underwater metal parts, including all through-hull fittings and outside strainers. Remember that barnacles can grow inside the through-hull openings where you can't see them, so try poking a long screwdriver in from the outside to check for

Use putty knife, brush, and scraper on barnacles.

this. To clean growth off a transducer, scrub gently with an abrasive nylon pad or wet and dry sandpaper.

Use a wide putty knife and a stiff scrub brush to remove most of the grass and barnacles, and use a long-handled scraper (the kind used to chop ice off sidewalks or to do edging in the garden) to scrape off hard-to-reach places down near the keel. If the bottom-cleaning job will take more than an hour or so, use a hose to keep the uncleaned areas wet while you're working on the rest of the bottom.

2. Inspect Hoses and Strainers. This is the best time to inspect and clean out strainers, as well as hoses that lead to through-hull fittings on the inside. In addition to engine water-cooling hoses and strainers, don't forget the ones on the auxiliary generator and on the toilet. Take each strainer apart and clean it out, and replace any hoses that feel soft or are starting to show signs of cracking. Also replace hose clamps that are starting to rust, and tighten those that may have loosened during the season. Be sure all hoses that connect to through-hull fittings below the waterline are secured with double stainless steel hose clamps with stainless steel screws.

3. Clean and Grease Seacocks. Most spring commissioning lists mention greasing and testing all seacocks before the boat is launched, but experienced boatowners and maintenance men know that during fall lay-up is a better time to inspect and service these all-important valves. Why? Because they are easier to take apart and service now, and you have months to replace or repair them if necessary.

4. Don't Forget Deck Hardware. Wash off all cleats, chocks, stanchions, winches, and other chrome or stainless steel deck fittings with soap and water. Rinse with fresh water, then wipe dry with a towel. Apply a liberal coat of metal polish—*but don't buff or polish it.* Wait until next spring, then apply another light coat of the same polish and buff this with a clean, dry cloth.

5. Lubricate Locks and Hinges. Hinges, sliding-door tracks, hatches, and similar hardware should be sprayed with a moisture-displacing lubricant such as WD-40, LPS, or one of the newer versions that contain Teflon. After spraying, slide the hatch cover or swing the door back and forth a few times to spread the lubricant around. Also spray this same lubricant into the keyhole of all locks and padlocks to protect against freezing and corrosion.

6. Prevent Mold and Mildew. Be sure to give the inside of the cabin, head, galley, etc., a thorough cleaning before laying up the boat—if you don't want to be faced with mold, mildew, and musty odors next spring. Don't leave blankets, sheets, or clothing—including sneakers, foul-weather gear, and boots—on board. Take everything home and have it washed or cleaned before bringing it back next spring. Remove all food from galley cabinets and drawers, including canned goods; then scrub down the

Wipe all surfaces clean to prevent mold and mildew.

countertops and sinks as well as the interior of all cabinets, drawers, and lockers. Mildew, the biggest nuisance during lay-up, thrives on dirt and soil, so it has much less chance of getting started on clean surfaces. Pay particular attention to countertops in the galley and head, and to corners where food or liquid may have been spilled inside cabinets, sinks, and showers.

7. Scrub Icebox and Freezer. After scrubbing the inside of your icebox, wipe the plastic surfaces down with a solution of Clorox and water (one to five). Allow this to dry on the surface, then rinse off with plain water (don't get any of this on varnish or paint around the outside). Clean freezers, fish boxes, and ice chests in the same way. Leave all these uncovered after you are finished. As further protection against the development of odors, leave an open dish full of baking soda inside the icebox, freezer chest, and bait box. (Spreading baking soda around in the head and toilet area, and even in the bilges, will also help greatly to minimize the chances of obnoxious odors developing while the boat is covered for the winter.)

8. Wash Topsides Before Covering. Leaving your boat dirty over the winter may allow stains to become so deeply embedded they will be almost impossible to remove in the spring, so give it a good scrubbing before covering it. If you have teak decks or trim, oil the wood after it has dried thoroughly, then put a coat of wax on all the fiberglass, *but don't buff it*. Let the buffing go until next spring. At that time you can apply another light coat of wax, and then buff.

9. Winterize All the Water Lines. If you are draining your fresh water system, don't forget also to drain the lines leading to your icemakers, to the washing machine, to the cockpit washdown, and to other appliances. Drain the system by opening connections at the lowest point in the bilge. Be sure to leave all faucets and valves open during the lay-up period. If you are adding a potable antifreeze to the system instead of draining it, make sure the solution comes flowing out of all faucets and appliances before you turn off the pump.

10. Open All Doors and Drawers. Go through the entire inside of the boat and open all doors on lockers and cabinets as well as all drawers. Leave these open over the winter so air can circulate freely to help discourage mildew and musty odors. For the same reason, prop up all mattresses, cushions, and upholstered chair cushions before closing up the boat for the season.

Before doing this, however, vacuum all the upholstery thoroughly and use an upholstery cleaner or shampoo to remove dirt and food stains that may have accumulated over the summer (remember, *mildew is less likely to form on clean surfaces*). Don't cover the upholstery or the cushions with sheet plastic. If you want to keep dust off, use old bed sheets or other fabric that won't trap moisture.

11. Take Off Electronics. Remove radios, lorans, radarscopes, and other electronic equipment from the boat—both for security reasons and to keep them stored in a dry place over the winter. The same applies to compasses. They are not only a temptation for thieves, they also sometimes will develop air bubbles in very cold weather (even though they are not supposed to). Also take home your TV set, binoculars, navigation instruments, etc., to protect against rust and to prevent their ''disappearing'' over the winter.

12. Protect Switches and Cables. After removing electronics, spray the exposed plugs and cable ends with a moisture-displacing spray, then wrap with one or two turns of electrical tape to keep out dirt and moisture. Also spray all switches, terminal blocks, fuse blocks and holders, and the back of all instrument panels (including the wires) with the same kind of protective spray. When you're spraying, don't forget ignition switches and the ignition switch key holes.

13. Winterize the Head. All toilets should be drained of water; then use the special lubricant or conditioner recommended by the manufacturer to keep rubber valves and gaskets from drying out (check your manual for this).

If you have a holding tank, flush it out with clean water, then pour in a chemical deodorizer and disinfectant. If you have an approved flow-through treatment device, be sure you clean it and follow the manual as to lay-up procedures.

14. . . . And the Air Conditioner. As a rule, marine air conditioners need very little attention when you're laying up the boat—except for the raw water part of the system. Make sure these water lines are drained (or filled with antifreeze) from the compressor down to the through-hull fittings. Also make certain that there is no water left inside the pump.

15. Check Fire Extinguishers. Inspect all the fire extinguishers to determine if any of them needs recharging. If recharging is needed, have it done now, but make sure all extinguishers are put back on the boat during lay-up. A fire extinguisher won't do you much good at home or in the shop if a fire should break out while you are working on the boat during the winter.

16. Remove and Store Batteries. If the boat will be stored out of the water, storage batteries should be removed and stored in a warm, dry place and kept on a trickle charger. If the boat will be left in the water, the battery will be needed to operate the bilge pumps, so make sure the battery is inspected regularly and then charged when necessary. Better yet, install a marine-type charger to keep it constantly charged at all times.

Of course, this means you will have to keep the shore cord plugged into dockside electricity at all times, and you must be aware of periods when the marina shuts off power to the docks for any length of time. In addition, you must check on the boat after an extended power outage has occurred, or after you suspect that a storm may have knocked out power.

17. Don't Forget the Dinghy. Inflatable tenders should be thoroughly cleaned and dried before storing. If possible they should be laid out flat where the sun won't get at them, but if you have to roll one up for storage, make sure it is clean and dry. Fiberglass dinghies should be washed inside and out and all growth cleaned off the bottom while still wet. Store the dinghy upside down to eliminate the need for a cover, but block it up off the ground. If the dinghy has an outboard motor, be sure you follow the owner's manual on ways to lay up the motor for winter.

18. Remove or Unroll Canvas. Ideally, Bimini tops, dodgers, and covers of all kinds should be taken off the boat and stored in a dry place. If you cannot remove the curtains, make sure they are not rolled up or folded. Also, clean them thoroughly before the boat is covered. The same holds true for sails; either take them home for washing and storage, or send them to a professional for the winter. If your boat has a dodger or Bimini top, don't let

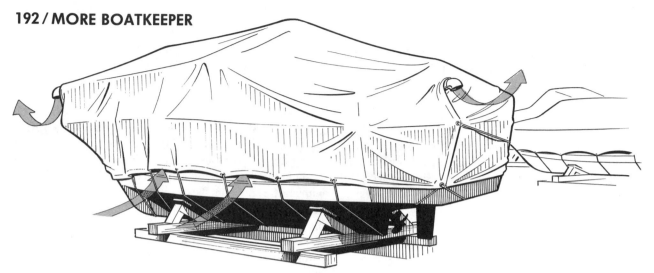

If you cover your boat for the winter, remember to provide for both top and bottom ventilation.

the winter cover rest on top of this. Erect a frame for the cover to allow air to circulate between it and the canvas.

19. Make Sure the Cover Is Ventilated. All winter covers should allow for plenty of air circulation underneath the canvas, so make certain there are at least two vents near the top, one at each end. There should also be room for air to enter at the bottom. In most cases you can wedge some type of padding or cushioned blocking between the hull and the canvas cover to allow air to flow up between the two. (Foam fenders or dock bumpers, squeezed between the boat and the canvas, work well for this.)

20. Visit Regularly. Although most responsible yards keep an eye on boats in winter storage, the frequency and actual amount of attention paid often leave a lot to be desired. During the fifteen winters I spent living aboard I saw many instances where covers became torn and tie-down lines were broken—yet yard personnel did little or nothing about it until I called it to their attention. So whenever possible, visit your boat at least once or twice a month to check the condition of the cover and the tie-downs—or make arrangements with someone who can be depended on to do the job for you.

Basically there are four possible options. First there is the question of whether to lay the boat up on land or leave it in the water—whether to have it hauled and then stored in a cradle or in chocks, or whether to opt for wet storage in a protected marina that has a suitable bubbler system or deicing system. Within each category you also have an additional decision to make: whether to cover the boat (with a full-length canvas or plastic cover) or not to cover it.

There are also some further choices to be made, depending on which of the above alternatives you opt for. You can, for example, have an expensive custom-fitted cover made, or you can simply use one of the large canvas or plastic tarps available in all marine supply outlets. Faced with all these decisions, how can you know what's best for your boat? Although not everyone will agree with my opinions, here are some of the pros and cons that I feel should be taken into consideration before you decide how to store your boat for the coming winter season.

Winter Storage: To Cover or Not to Cover? On Land or in the Water?

Every year boatowners north of the Sunbelt must make plans for winter lay-up, and one of the first decisions that most of them will have to make is where and how to store the boat during the coming months.

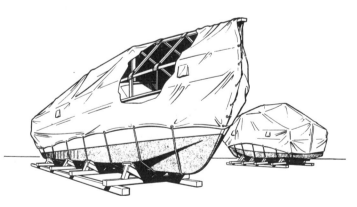

Owners build elaborate covers to protect their boats. But is it really necessary?

Laying Up on Land

This is by far the most popular method, and probably the safest procedure in terms of minimizing possible damage from the elements—especially if you are going to be away much of the time. Storing on land means you don't have to worry about checking on bilge pumps or battery chargers and batteries periodically, and generally will give most boatowners the greatest peace of mind.

However, unless you still have the original cradle for your boat, you have to make certain that the yard that does the blocking knows its job. Improper blocking can cause warping and distortion in the hull and can set up stresses that may lead to problems with engine alignment after the boat is launched. This is even more serious with wood hulls—poor blocking can cause buckling of planks and a loss of caulking that will result in serious leaks when the boat is in the water. In extreme cases it can mean you will have to replace some of the planks.

For those boatowners who like to come down and work on their boats during the winter or early spring, blocking the boat up on land means they will have to do a lot more climbing and hauling of materials. Also, getting electric current and water to the boat while it is up in the air may be more of a problem, depending on how convenient the facilities are at your particular yard. In the spring, varnishing and painting may also be harder to manage because you are often very close to the boat next to you, so less room to work, dust, and general activity in the yard may make your work more difficult.

Lay-up in the Water

This should be considered only if your marina or boatyard has a good bubbler system or a system of properly installed deicers—underwater agitators used for ice melting. You can buy your own deicers and install these around and under your boat yourself, but you will have to tend them by turning them on whenever it looks like a freeze is on the way.

Bubblers and water-circulating deicers work by bringing water up from several feet down. This water is warmer than the water at the surface, so bringing it up and agitating it keeps ice from forming. In tidal areas where there are pilings and floating docks to be protected, it is just as important to protect these against ice as it is to protect the boat itself.

For boats with wood hulls, wet storage is definitely the choice. Leaving the boat in the water keeps it properly supported in its natural environment so there is no chance of warping or buckling, and planks can't dry out or shrink and cause leaky seams.

However, wet storage is advisable only for boats whose owners will come down regularly to check on them during the lay-up period. If you are not going to visit your boat periodically, it's best to have it stored on land. Don't rely just on yard personnel to check on it; some may be very diligent and will do as they say, but there are too many others who really cannot be depended on.

So why opt for wet storage at all with a fiberglass boat? For one thing, it is often cheaper than hauling and blocking. For another, you can run your boat as late as you want into the fall and you won't be held up waiting for other boats to be launched in the spring—you can start your spring commissioning whenever you are ready and take your boat out when you want to. And, of course, working on your boat in the early spring or during the winter will be much less of a hassle if there is no climbing involved and if electric power is readily available.

Many people who lay their boat up in the water regularly come down on winter weekends to spend pleasant days working on it—getting jobs done or making improvements they never have time for during the regular boating season. In some yards and clubs, winter weekends may involve as much socializing with other boatowners as the spring weekends do.

Another side benefit, I have found, is that most people who use wet storage agree that boats tend to stay cleaner in the water than they do when stored up on land. Perhaps this is because there is not as much dust and there is less likelihood of tracking mud and dirt aboard.

If you do store your boat in the water you should make certain that the batteries are charged regularly, or use a built-in charger that cuts off completely when the batteries are fully charged. Keeping batteries fully charged not only protects them against freezing, it also ensures that there will be power for the bilge pumps if they are needed.

To Cover or Not to Cover

Any discussion of this subject is almost certain to lead to an argument, with most marina and boatyard operators insisting that a good canvas or plastic cover is essential to protect a boat over the winter months. Many boatowners obviously agree, since the vast majority of boats do get fully covered with a canvas or plastic tarpaulin, or a custom-fitted cover of some kind.

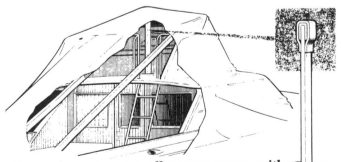

Remember to support all canvas covers with poles to keep water and snow from accumulating.

However, I'm one boatowner who does not agree. Even before I started living aboard, I was never fully convinced that all the expense involved was warranted. I feel that in many cases covering a boat is not really necessary—or even advisable. I know that many people feel this is almost akin to heresy, but how many times have you seen new or used boats for sale completely uncovered in a dealer's yard during the winter? It is obviously a lot easier to show a boat that is not under canvas, but those boats never seem to suffer much damage from the elements and are easily cleaned up when they are finally sold.

Remember that the worst enemy of varnish and paint is the sun, and there is much less sunlight in winter than during the rest of the year. Also, even when the sun is shining it is much weaker in the winter months than during the summer. Besides, all your varnish has to be recoated at least two or three times a year anyway—regardless of whether you cover it.

Here's another point to consider when you are trying to decide whether to cover your boat: It sits outside and is uncovered for from seven to nine months of the year, so why is it so important—and worth all that money—to cover it for the remaining few months? Remember that after the boat is laid up it usually takes at least a month until the yard actually gets around to covering it. Then in the spring it is uncovered a month or two before it is commissioned.

And how about your house? It is exposed to the weather all year 'round and still needs painting only at four- to six-year intervals. It's true that a cover will help protect seat cushions and chrome-plated deck hardware, but in many cases removing the cushions and coating the hardware with a protective film of wax or grease will be a lot easier (and a lot less expensive).

There are other drawbacks to covering your boat. One is that unless the cover is securely tied down, winter storms will cause the canvas to flap around a great deal, and this flapping and slapping can often do more damage to the painted, varnished, and gel-coated surfaces on the boat than the weather will. This is particularly true for loose-fitting tarpaulins with lots of folds in them. The metal grommets can start banging and scraping against the sides of the hull or cabin as the wind causes it to flap around.

On the other hand, if you tie your canvas down too tightly and pull it snugly up against the hull or cabin sides, chances are you may be inviting different sorts of trouble—chafing due to friction between the canvas and the boat, as well as mildew problems caused by lack of adequate ventilation.

In fact, lack of ventilation is probably the most serious problem that develops inside boats that are fully covered for several months. Insufficient air circulation under the cover can lead to the accumulation of large amounts of condensation inside the boat, creating severe problems with mildew and musty odors. I've been under the canvas inside a stored and covered boat on a cold but sunny day in mid-January and felt as though I were in a Turkish bath. The sun beating down on the canvas, even though it was cold outside, created a hot, steamy atmosphere under the fabric. After the sun goes down this humidity condenses all over the inside of the boat, leading to mold and mildew.

To avoid this it is essential to make certain that any cover you use has several good-sized vents installed in the canvas to allow air to circulate freely. Short pieces of stovepipe or hoodlike plastic vents can be installed to make sure the vents stay open all the time. Also, try to use fenders or other padding at intervals along the bottom of the cover to keep the canvas slightly away from the hull and superstructure—again to allow air to circulate freely.

If a full winter cover is used, it should be securely tied down with lines that go all the way under the hull from the bottom of the cover on one side of the boat to the bottom of the cover on the other side. If the boat is in wet storage, a dinghy or workboat will be needed to pull lines around under the hull.

Partial Covers

Although I'm convinced that usually it is not necessary to cover a boat completely, some boats should have a partial cover. One such case would be an open-cockpit boat such as a sportfisherman or sedan, or a center-cockpit sailboat. These need a partial cover that will keep wet snow from accumulating in the cockpit, unless you are prepared to go down and shovel it out each time. Otherwise the wet snow lying against a companionway or cabin door can allow water to build up and seep in under the door, thus wetting the carpet and other parts of the interior.

In most cases a sloping tarp or cockpit cover going from the top of the cabin down to the coaming or caprail on the stern will be enough to shed snow and water freely. Just be sure you put a "ridge pole" or vertical pole in the center to support the canvas and keep it from sagging under a load of wet snow or ice.

In the same way, boats with flying bridges or exposed helm stations should have these parts covered to keep snow and ice away from the instruments, control panels, and electrical systems. On the typical flying bridge with a one-piece cover that has only a slight pitch to it, you should install one or two vertical poles under the canvas to support it and keep it from sagging under accumulations of water, snow, or ice. Each pole is merely a short length of two-by-four that is long enough to be wedged between the deck and the canvas above it (tying with string may be advisable to keep the pole from slipping sideways). Scrap pieces of carpet should be nailed or stapled over the top and bottom end of each pole to serve as padding that will protect the canvas against tearing and keep the deck from getting scratched.

Reminders for Winter Lay-Up

Whether you do all the work yourself or hire the yard to do it, chances are there are definite instructions spelled out in your engine manual and in the various other equipment manuals that came with your boat that tell you most of what you need to know about the procedures for proper winter lay-up.

However, in addition to the steps described in all this literature—and spelled out by most boatyards when you give them the winter work orders—here are a number of additional pointers that often are overlooked during the lay-up process:

● Take a few hours to check all the hose clamps in the boat—not only those on the engines, but also those in the fresh water system, the bilge pump discharge hoses, the toilets, and the various drains throughout the boat. Make sure each clamp is good and tight, and replace those that look badly rusted or that cannot be tightened properly.

● While crawling around the boat and checking hose clamps, inspect all the hoses to see if any are getting soft or show signs of splitting or cracking. Many advise automatically replacing hoses that are more than three years old.

● As you tend to these and other chores, be on constant lookout for screws and other fasteners that may have vibrated loose or that are missing entirely.

● Open and close each seacock and other valves connected to through-hull fittings, just to make sure they work freely. Lubricate each one with waterproof grease, and tighten loose handles or knobs.

● If the boat is stored on land, crawl under the hull and inspect each through-hull opening. Shine a flashlight up into the hole to see if it is partially blocked with barnacles or other growth. Use a long screwdriver or stiff wire to clean it out if necessary. At the same time, check underwater strainers for clogging and make sure the screws or bolts that hold them in place are still tight.

● Take the cover off all water pumps that have rubber impellers so you can inspect the impellers and replace them if necessary. In addition to pumps on engines, don't forget pumps in electric toilets, water systems, and so on. Generally it's a good idea to replace all such impellers every two to three years as a preventive measure.

● If your toilet discharge hose is more than two or three years old, take it off and check the inside. Sometimes accumulations of sediment, salt, and chemicals will build up around the inside walls so much that they reduce the inside diameter by half. If you cannot clean all this out, replace the hoses entirely.

● Give the bilge a good cleaning to get rid of oil, grease, and water and to help prevent sour odors. If odors are noticeable, spread baking soda around liberally and leave it there over the winter.

● Coat all deck hardware with chrome-plated fittings with a liberal coat of paste wax, but don't buff it. Leave the wax in place till next spring, then buff and polish.

● Spray all electrical terminals, panel boards, and terminal strips with a moisture-displacing spray such as WD-40, LPS-1, or CRC to protect against corrosion and to keep out dampness.

● Remove as much electronic gear from the boat as you can, and store it at home or in some other safe place— to prevent theft, as well as to keep the items dry.

● Inside the boat leave all drawers and doors slightly open to allow air to circulate freely. Prop the door or cover to your refrigerator or icebox open, and leave oven doors open as well.

● If you are not taking cushions and mattresses off the boat, stand them up so air can circulate around and under them. Cover upholstery with light dust covers of cloth rather than plastic (old bed sheets are good).

● Don't leave any kind of food on board. Besides spoiling and creating odors, it will encourage the infestation of rats and other vermin.

Winter Inspection

During a boat's winter lay-up, or when you are starting to get it ready for spring commissioning, it's a good idea to check the outside of the boat for loose fastenings or other small defects before they can develop into real problems.

For example, when I am getting the bottom ready for painting, or when I am waxing the outside of the boat, I always carry a small assortment of different-size screwdrivers and wrenches in my tool belt. As I work I check each nut, bolt, screw, and cotter pin to see if that fastener is still tight or if it is badly corroded and perhaps needs replacing. At the same time I also inspect all cleats, chocks, and other deck hardware set in bedding compound to see if these items are still tight or if they need rebedding.

It's surprising how many fasteners and other pieces of hardware will work loose after a full season of boating. Having the tools with you as you work on other chores means it will only take a minute or so to tighten a loose fastener. In that way you are not as likely to forget to come back and do the job later on, and there will be fewer chances of breakdowns during the season.

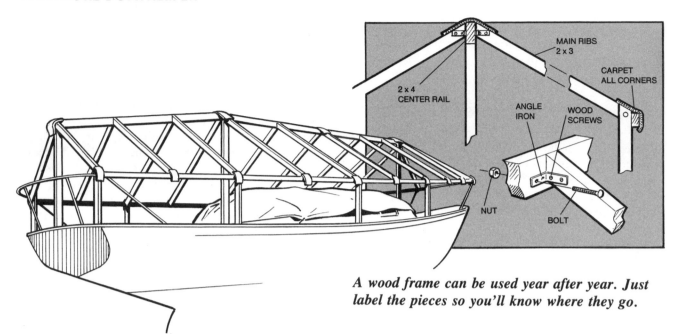

A wood frame can be used year after year. Just label the pieces so you'll know where they go.

Building a Frame for Your Winter Cover

Although some people don't think it is really necessary, most boatowners still prefer to cover their boats when storing them outdoors for the winter. Because it would be foolhardy simply to drape a large canvas or vinyl cover directly over the boat (the mildew problems would be horrendous), most people build some kind of frame to support the cover and hold it up and away from the boat so air can circulate freely beneath it.

The frame must not only be strong enough to support the canvas, it also must be designed to shed snow and water—otherwise heavy accumulations will build up and cause the whole thing to collapse. In addition, the frame should be designed to hold the canvas high enough to allow adequate clearance underneath if you want to be able to walk around on the boat after it is covered.

Over the years boatowners and boatyards have used many different techniques for building winter frame covers out of various materials. Most are "one shot" wooden assemblies that are knocked together (or tied together) out of inexpensive wooden strips, then thrown away at the end of the season. This means that the next season you have to go through the whole building process again.

Others prefer to build semi-permanent, more sophisticated frames that can be taken down, stored, and reused the following year. Obviously, these are a lot more work to put together when first built, but after that they can be quickly reassembled year after year at no expense and with

considerable savings in time and effort. In the long run most such "knockdown" frames will actually cost less than the "throw-away" kind.

When frames are built for one-time use only they are usually built of wood furring strips (one-by-two), plus one or two long lengths of two-by-four that are used as ridge poles down the length of the boat. The ridge pole, or "backbone," should be high enough to create a peak down the center to which all of the crosswise framing strips are fastened. These strips are tied to the ridge pole or poles at one end with string, or they are simply nailed to it. The other end of each strip of wood is then fastened to the handrails, lifelines, or stanchions around the entire outside of the deck.

When building a wooden frame, regardless of whether it is a temporary one or a permanent (reusable) one, it is important to make certain that all corner joints and places where two pieces of wood meet are padded to prevent chafing through the canvas before the winter is over. The type of padding most often used is scrap pieces of carpet, but heavy scraps of folded cloth or canvas can also be used (foam padding usually won't stand up under the chafing action of the canvas). The padding should be fastened in place with either nails or staples, or by tying with string, to keep it from slipping when the canvas starts flapping around in the wind.

Building a Reusable Wood Frame

Although building a semipermanent or reusable wood frame involves basically the same procedure as building a temporary one, you will want to take a little more care in cutting and assembling pieces if you know you will be reusing it next year. Also, for a "one time" frame you will probably try to buy the cheapest lumber available, but for one you will be using over and over you are better off buying a slightly better grade of lumber. Look for pieces that have fewer knots in them and avoid those that are warped or full of ragged edges and splinters.

To assemble a permanent frame you will use bolts and nuts rather than nails or string. This means drilling each member where a joint occurs, then inserting bolts and tightening nuts onto the other end. For most joints you will want to use washers as well. If you want to spend extra for wing nuts, you can do most tightening without tools, or with just a screwdriver.

As a rule, it is best to drill the holes for the bolts while the pieces are in position, rather than trying to drill them ahead of time. Tie pieces together temporarily with string, then drill the holes and finish by inserting the bolts that will hold them together.

Start out by rigging a two-by-four "backbone" or ridge pole down the center of the boat, propping up the ridge pole high enough to clear cabintops and all other projections. Don't rest this ridge pole directly on the cabintop or other part of the boat; instead have it supported by vertical two-by-fours set up on the cabintop or the deck. Use a twelve-inch square of plywood under the bottom of each vertical two-by-four to spread the load, and under this place a piece of carpet to keep from scratching the deck or cabintop on which it rests.

The ridge pole will probably have to be in sections, starting with one length down near the transom or over the cockpit. This will join another two-by-four that goes along almost horizontally over the cabin, and then a third piece (or perhaps even a fourth piece) that continues on down to the bow rail. The poles are joined end to end by using plywood or metal gussets on each side of the pole ends, with bolts going through them and through the ridge poles.

The framing strips usually consist of one-by-twos that are beveled to come up against the sides of the ridge pole. However, depending on the size of the boat and on its configuration, you probably will want to build one or two frames of heavier two-by-fours to add strength and rigidity to the whole structure.

Each one-by-two framing piece is joined to the ridge pole with bolts. To get a smooth fit this usually means that the end of each framing piece will have to be notched or beveled where it meets the ridge pole. This not only ensures a strong joint but also helps avoid sharp projecting edges that could chafe through the canvas.

If the boat has metal handrails, then the other end of each framing strip can be secured to this railing—either by tying them in place or by notching the ends of each strip so they fit over the rail and then putting padding inside the notch. However, if the boat has wooden handrails or only lifelines, you should tie additional framing strips vertically

against each of the stanchions. You can then bolt the end of each horizontal (or sloping) framing strip to this. Use padding on the outside of each of the joints formed, and if your handrails are varnished wood make sure the joints come up high enough to keep the canvas from chafing on the varnish.

After the entire frame is assembled, examine all joints for rough edges or corners that jut out and could puncture the canvas. Wherever possible, round them off with a rasp or a tool like a Surform; otherwise add padding, as has been described above.

When finished, use a waterproof marker or crayon to mark each piece of wood and indicate its place in the completed assembly. In that way, when you take the whole thing apart in the spring you will have no trouble reassembling it the following autumn. Some kind of code will be required to tell you where pieces go.

One simple code is to precede each ridge pole section with an "R" and a number, starting with "1" for the bow piece and then continuing through the numbers needed until you reach the stern. Framing pieces can be marked with a "P" or an "S" (port or starboard), again starting with "1" at the bow. Stanchion supports can be marked "SP" or "SB" (stanchion port or stanchion starboard) and again numbered from bow to stern. To further expedite setting the frame up next year, wrap all similar pieces (stanchion supports or framing pieces) together when you store them.

A Simple Wood-and-Rope Frame

For small to medium-size sailboats and cruisers, a simpler and much less expensive frame for a winter cover can be built by using rope for the "ribs" or framing strips. You start by setting up the two-by-four backbone or ridge pole as described above, supporting it with vertical posts spaced no more than about three to four feet apart. Then tie lengths of quarter-inch rope between this backbone and the side rails to act as "ribs" or framing strips (you can use inexpensive sisal if you want to throw the rope away each year).

Each piece of rope runs from the ridge pole across the decks and is tied to a long length of one-by-two furring strip that is tied to the lifelines about even with the tops of the stanchions. The rope continues on down to the deck and is tied to cleats or sail tracks along the toerail. If there are no cleats or tracks where you need them, either extra cleats can be installed, or another length of one-by-two can be laid along the toerail. This strip can be tied to the cleats that are already there, or to the stanchion bases, so the ropes that form the "ribs" can be brought down and tied to it.

You'll find that the best method for lashing these ropes in place is to start at the rail on one side of the boat, then bring the rope up and tie it firmly around the ridge pole before continuing on down to the rail on the other side of the boat. This will result in a very stable frame that has no sharp corners to create chafing problems. Just be sure the ridge pole is high enough to create a steep slope in the canvas so snow and ice will slide off without accumulating in heavy piles.

At the end of each winter the ropes can be cut off and discarded in minutes. The two-by-four "backbone" with its supporting posts can be taken apart and saved for reuse the following year, as can the various furring strips that were tied to the stanchions, lifelines, or toerail. Just be sure you label each piece carefully to indicate where it goes.

A Frame of Electrical Conduit

An increasingly popular method for building a take-apart frame for winter covers is to build the frame of thin-wall metal electrical conduit. This tubing is widely available in all electrical supply houses and is inexpensive and light in weight, which makes it easy to work with and install—and much simpler to store.

It is easily cut with a hacksaw or tubing cutter, and all kinds of couplings, tees, elbows and other fittings are available for assembling it. In addition, using a special tool called a "hickey," you can easily bend the tubing to almost any curve and shape. Frames can be assembled with curved pieces that eliminate the need for sharp corners and a multitude of joints and pieces.

Most boatowners make separate frames or "rafters" that straddle the boat. Each starts with a vertical length that comes up alongside each stanchion and is secured to the stanchion by tying or by using stainless steel hose clamps. The top end projects above the handrail or lifelines and then is curved over to meet a ridge pole that goes down the center of the boat at the peak of the frame. In this case the ridge pole is merely another straight length of the same conduit that runs fore and aft. It is attached to the crossframes either with a tee fitting, or by simply lashing with tape or rope. Rubber crutch tips on the bottom end of each frame leg protect the deck.

In addition to the three types of frames described above, another technique that has been used by a reader is described in the following section. It makes use of flexible plastic pipe instead of metal pipe, and it forms a strong but lightweight reusable winter frame that is easy to build.

Frame of Rigid Plastic Pipe

Another technique that is becoming increasingly popular is using plastic pipe rather than metal tubing. Rigid PVC pipe, which is widely available in all plumbing supply outlets, is ideal for this. You can use either 1¼-inch or 1½-inch pipe that is assembled with standard tee fittings and forty-five-degree elbows—plus lashing with string or

Thin-wall metal conduit frames are light and inexpensive.

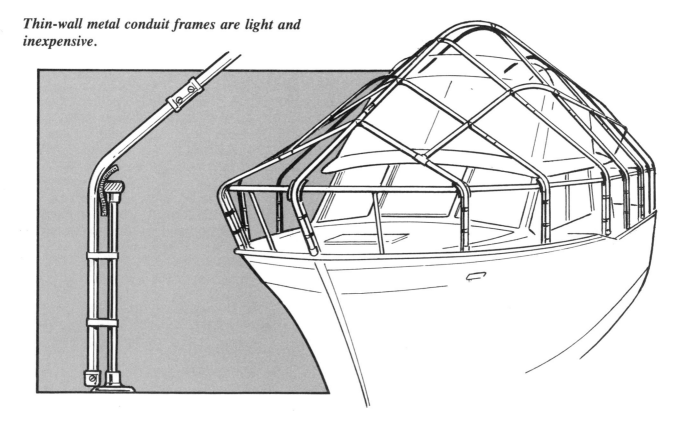

tape in those places where a joint cannot be easily made with standard fittings. The pipe can be cut to length with an electric saber saw or a hacksaw, but a tubing cutter will be even faster.

Start by first lashing short lengths of the pipe along the lifelines, between the tops of the stanchions as shown in the drawing. These lengths are joined together with standard tee fittings as illustrated. Try to locate the tee next to each stanchion, and position it so that the open end is facing up and is canted or tilted so it points up toward where the ridge pole will be.

The frames are formed by running lengths of pipe upward from these tees so they slope up at an angle toward where the ridge pole will be. A forty-five-degree elbow is fitted to the top end of each so that a short, straight length of pipe can be used to join the two forty-five-degree fittings together. This forms a finished frame or rib that goes from one side of the boat to the other.

The ridge pole or "backbone" that goes down the centerline of the boat then rests on top of these frames, or can run directly under the top horizontal piece. Either way, the ridge pole is fastened in place along the tops of the frames by lashing with ¼-inch line, or by wrapping with duct tape. To make a single length of pipe that will be

long enough to run the full length of the pole you will have to use couplings to join the individual lengths.

Although PVC pipe is normally joined to its fittings and to couplings with cement, you don't want to use cement when assembling a frame of this kind, since you obviously

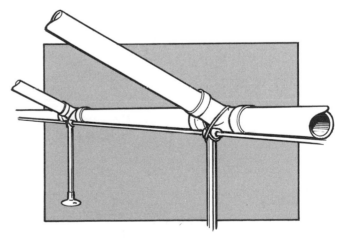

A rigid PVC plastic pipe frame is assembled with standard tee fittings and lashed to the stanchions with line.

won't be able to take it apart for reuse in the future. However, in many cases you may find it easier to cement a coupling or elbow onto one length of the pipe so it won't get lost when you take the frame apart, and so there will be less chance of pieces slipping out of alignment when assembling. Before you use any cement it's best to assemble everything dry first—then mark the exact angle at which the fitting must be located by drawing a line across the fitting and onto the pipe. After the cement is applied you can quickly twist the fitting until the lines coincide so that you are sure the angle is correct.

When cement is not used and there is a problem with fittings slipping or coming apart, a quick wrap with a single turn of duct tape around the outside of the joint will be enough to hold the pieces in place. (Have the tape overlap the end of the fitting and go partway onto the pipe so it sticks to both surfaces.) Needless to say, after the frame is complete and before you take it apart, make sure each piece is marked to indicate where it goes. For this you can use dabs of colored paint in various combinations to indicate where pieces meet, or you can label them with a waterproof marking pen (but try first to make certain it won't rub off when handled).

Frame of Flexible Plastic Pipe

Another easy way to build a frame for a winter cover is to use 1½-inch black polyethylene tubing. The tubing is light in weight, inexpensive, and—most important of all—flexible. This means it can be easily bent to make the curved "frames" needed to cover the boat, as shown in the drawing.

The first step in building such a frame is to set up a two-by-four ridge pole that runs down the center of the boat. This pole is supported by vertical posts set up wherever necessary. The bottom of each post rests on the deck, and the top end is either bolted or screwed to the ridge pole.

The lengths of polyethylene pipe needed to form the ribs are then bent over the top of this ridge pole and fastened to it by wrapping with duct tape. The ends of each rib are bent down to reach the cradle under the boat and secured to it by boring ¼-inch holes through the plastic pipe and then threading line through these holes to secure it. After the winter is over, the frame is easily taken apart and stored for reuse the following year.

INDEX